历史顾问 洪卜仁　Historical Consultant: Hong Puren

特别顾问 林聪明　Special Consultant: Lin Congming

中英对照

魅力鼓浪屿

Discover Gulangyu

潘维廉 著

厦门日报双语周刊 译

厦门大学出版社
XIAMEN UNIVERSITY PRESS

Gulangyu—The Garden Isle

Isle of Music and Arts

Enjoy Traditional Hand Puppet Shows
...and take some puppets home!

Enjoy the Song of the Surf in
Bright Moon Park's Seaside Cabins!

Home of Zheng Xiaoying
"World's Best Female Conductor"

Enjoy Open Air Traditional Music

Visit Asia's Largest Piano Museum

Feast Eyes and Ears on the World's Best Organ Museum

Zhonghua Rd.

Li Qingquan Villa(Flag-Hill Rd.)

#4 Anhai Rd.

#55 Anhai Rd.

#36 Anhai Rd.

#71 Anhai Rd.

#28 Fujian Rd.

#83 Fujian Rd.

Former Hope Hospital,Chapel,and Dr. John Otte Memorial

#6 Bishan Rd.

#17 Bishan Rd.

#24 Guxin Rd.

Former U.S. Consulate

#16 Jishan Rd.(Yin Chenzong's Home)

An Anxi Rd.Villa

#18 Jishan Rd.

#56 Anhai Rd.

#14 Yongchun Rd.

#85 Lujiao Rd.

#71 Yongchun Rd.

#99 Lujiao Rd.

Elegant Old Fujian Rd.

#28 Fujian Rd.

#44 Fujian Rd.

#36 Fujian Rd.

#32 Fujian Rd.

#38 Fujian Rd.

#30 Fujian Rd.

#40 Fujian Rd.

#15 Lujiao Rd.

East, West, and ?

#40 Huangyan Rd.

#97-99 Zhonghua Rd.

Haitan Rd.

#8 Gongping Rd.

#14 Gongping Rd.

Take Gulangyu Home!

Postcards Sets by Gulangyu-native Mr. Bai Hua

Catholic Church

Huang Xiulang's Villa

Shuzhuang Garden

Eight Diagram's Bldg.

See and Sky Mansion

Yang Villa(Bai Hua's hom

Golden Melon Bldg.

Fan Po Villa

Li Qingquan Villa

Huang Rongyuan Villa

Huang Yizhu Villa

Trinity Church

Magic by Moonlight

Bo'ai Hospital

Anxian Hall

Discover Gulangyu! ©2005

魅力鼓浪屿

Comments, suggestions, questions, corrections, or requests for additional copies of Discover Gulangyu!

E-mail: **amoybill@amoymagic.com**

Websites:

www.amoymagic.mts.cn (in China)

www.amoymagic.com (outside China)

Snail Mail: Dr. Bill Brown, Box 1288
Xiamen University
Xiamen, Fujian, PRC 361005

Complaints? Write my wife!

More information on Gulangyu, Xiamen and Fujian? Try Dr. Bill's:

"Amoy Magic—Guide to Xiamen" (English or Chinese versions)
《魅力厦门—厦门指南》

"Mystic Quanzhou—City of Light" (English version)
《魅力泉州》

"Magic Fujian" (Bilingual Chinese/English with MP3 CD)
《老外看福建》

If local bookstores are sold out, all titles are **always in stock** (and signed) at Nissi Bookstore 尼西书店, #384 S. Siming Rd (just over the hill from Xiamen University). Nissi's Phone: (0592)219-1219

Discover Gulangyu!

Dr. Bill 潘维廉博士
Xiamen University MBA Center

Contents

Part One	**Historical Tours**	**Page**
Chapter 1	Exotic Gulangyu Islet	2
Chapter 2	Koxinga, Last Defender of the Ming Dynasty	22
Chapter 3	Sunlight Rock	38
Chapter 4	Pioneering Modern Education	48
Chapter 5	Gulangyu's Medical Pioneers	68
Chapter 6	Pioneering Music, Arts, & Literature	90
Chapter 7	Gulangyu Churches	118
Chapter 8	Gulangyu Festivals & Folklore	130
Part Two	**Entertainment**	
Chapter 9	Gulangyu Gardens	144
Chapter 10	Dining, Shopping, Entertainment, Hotels	164
Part Three	**Museum of World Architecture**	
Chapter 11	Architectural Overview	176
Chapter 12	Longtou Rd Gulangyu's Mainstreet	198
Chapter 13	Lujiao Rd	214
Chapter 14	Fujian Rd Gulangyu's Best Architecture	230
Chapter 15	Zhangzhou Rd—the Most "Garden-like" Road	242
Chapter 16	Tianwei Rd—High Ground & High Society	250
Chapter 17	Fuxing Rd & Flag Hill Rd	262
Chapter 18	Guxin & Sanming Rds	270
Chapter 19	Anhai Rd	284
Chapter 20	Quanzhou & Jishan Rds	294
Chapter 21	Huangyan & Haitan Rds	304
Chapter 22	Zhonghua Rd	316
Chapter 23	Bishan Rd	326
Chapter 24	Yongchun Rd	336
Chapter 25	Gusheng Rd	348
Bibliography		353

"A good traveler is one who does not know where he is going to, and a perfect traveler does not know where he came from."

Lin Yutang

目 录

第一部分 历史巡游

第一章 异域风光鼓浪屿 3
第二章 郑成功——最后一位明朝的保卫者 23
第三章 日光岩 39
第四章 鼓浪屿——中国现代教育的摇篮 49
第五章 鼓浪屿医疗事业先驱 69
第六章 音乐、艺术和文学的先驱 91
第七章 鼓浪屿教堂 119
第八章 鼓浪屿的节日与传说 131

第二部分 娱乐

第九章 鼓浪屿——海上花园 145
第十章 饮食，购物，娱乐和宾馆 165

第三部分 国际建筑

第十一章 建筑概览 177
第十二章 龙头路——鼓浪屿的主干道 199
第十三章 鹿礁路 215
第十四章 福建路——鼓浪屿最棒的建筑群 231
第十五章 漳州路——花园式马路 243
第十六章 田尾路——富庶之地与上流社会 251
第十七章 复兴路和升旗山路 263
第十八章 鼓新路和三明路 271
第十九章 安海路 285
第二十章 泉州路和鸡山路 295
第二十一章 晃岩路和海坛路 305
第二十二章 中华路 317
第二十三章 笔山路 327
第二十四章 永春路 337
第二十五章 鼓声路 349

参考书目（英文） 353

“一个好的旅行家决不知道他往那里去，更好的甚至不知道从何处而来。”

——林语堂

Warm Thanks to

Susan Marie, my wife and best friend. Visit her Amoy Magic Websites (mirrored sites allow fast access both inside and outside of China):

http://www.amoymagic.mts.cn (in China)

http://www.amoymagic.com (outside China).

Susan Marie

Team Common Talk—my translators & editors.

Professor Hong Buren: Xiamen's Gulangyu-born historian, who helped weed out many historical (sometimes hysterical) inaccuracies.

Xiao Shi, my Xiamen University Press editor.

Mr. Lin Congming, Deputy Director, Publicity Dept's Xiamen Municipal Party Committee, Special Consultant.

Cheng jianming, Director, Gulangyu Administrative Office.

Mr. Lin Wende, Director, Gulangyu Tourist Center.

Mr. Bai Hua, Gulangyu-born photographer (formerly with Hong Kong's South China Morning Post), who led me about Gulangyu many times.

Lily Wang, a Xiamen University grad student and amateur photographer, for traipsing about Gulangyu in search of Kodak moments.

Professor Gong Jie, curator of Xiamen Museum, for his invaluable books, "Gulangyu Architecture" 《鼓浪屿建筑杂谈》 and "A Look at Gulangyu's Villas《到鼓浪屿看老别墅》.

Xiamen Int'l School http://www.xischina.com

Pastor Timothy Hao (Hao Zhiqiang, 蒿志强) of Gulangyu's Trinity Church, who shed many insights on Trinity, and helped open many doors.

Eight Xiamen University MBA students, who helped immensely with research: Yin Haiyi (殷海铁), Maggie Chen (陈丽园), Li Jingyu (李菁羽), Xin Chenggang (辛承刚), Catherine (朱莹), Huang Long (黄隆), Wen Chen (翁琛), and Wang Jia'an (王加安).

Rose Tang, journalist, and her father Tang Shaoyun, famous Xiamen University professor and artist, for introducing Gulangyu-born artist Teng Hiok Chiu.

Dr. Kaz Poznanski, for photos and information on chiu.

Mr. Ashley Brewin, of Hong Kong, for insights on Amoy Freemasonry.

Christopher "Kit" Haffner, author of "*Amoy, The Port and The Lodge*".

Paul Carr, an organist from England, for photos and information.

Mrs. Eucaris M. Galicia, Research Assistant, Seventh Day Adventist Archives and Statistic Office, for her invaluable assistance.

Royal Society for Tropical Medicine & Hygiene, London (for use of photos)

Frank Wei, founder and chairman of Master Translation Services (MTS), for sponsoring the **Amoy Magic Website**. Visit MTS at: www.xmmaster.com.

衷心感谢

苏珊·玛丽：我妻子和最好的朋友。可到她的网页查询最新信息：www.amoymagic.mts.cn（国内） amoymagic.com （国外）

双语周刊团队：我的译者、编辑和朋友（见下页）。

洪卜仁教授：在厦门鼓浪屿生活工作十多年的历史学家，（有时是极度兴奋地）帮助清除了很多史实谬误。

Xiamen's Walking History Book

小施：厦门大学出版社我的编辑。

林聪明：厦门市委宣传部副部长，百忙之中认真审阅本书，指正多处错误。

程建明：鼓浪屿管委会主任。

林文德：鼓浪屿游客中心主任，为本书的完成提供大量帮助。

白桦先生：鼓浪屿出生的摄影家（曾供职于香港南华早报），好几次耐心地带我在他的家园游览。

王莉莉：厦门大学研究生和业余摄影爱好者，曾为柯达瞬间寻找了许多鼓浪屿的照片。

龚洁教授：厦门博物馆原馆长，以及他那些见地深刻和极为有用的书——《鼓浪屿建筑杂谈》、《到鼓浪屿看老别墅》。

蒿志强：三一堂牧师，提供很多教堂的照片，还帮我开了很多回门。

八位厦门大学 MBA 学生：挑灯夜战帮我查阅资料：殷海轶、李菁羽、辛承刚、朱莹、黄隆、翁琛、王加安和 Maggie。

ROSE 唐：记者，她的父亲唐绍云，厦门大学著名教授、艺术家，介绍我认识鼓浪屿出生的艺术家周廷旭和 Kaz Poznanski 博士，他重新发现了这位被遗忘的天才。

Ashley Brewin 先生：在香港，他的关于麻笋教的见识和有关材料，以及使用他收藏的明信片。

Christopher "Kit" Haffner：《厦门，港口和游览地》的作者。

Paul Carr：英国的管风琴家，提供一整张 CD，内有新风琴博物馆的照片及具吸引力的信息介绍。

Eucaris M. Galicia 夫人：助理研究员，安息日会档案和统计办公室，为本书提供无价的协助。

韦中和：魅力厦门网站的合作者，厦门精艺达翻译公司（MTS）的创始人和董事长。欲了解 MTS 请访问：www.xmmaster.com。

Special Thanks to
Team Common Talk (双语周刊)

Common Talk (CT), Xiamen Daily's Wednesday English supplement, was the first of its kind in China, and is ***the*** source for the most up-to-date information on Xiamen. I even referred to CT as I wrote "Discover Gulangyu" to keep abreast of changes and new attractions (such as the Organ Museum, which will be the largest of its kind in the world). But my debt to CT goes much further.

Chief Editor Yayu and her CT colleagues not only translated Discover Gulangyu into Chinese but also pointed out literally dozens of errors in my English manuscript, ranging from miniscule punctuation problems to major historical inaccuracies. (Alas, not even Common Talk could catch all of my errors; I hope future editions are better).

Thanks, Team Common Talk, for helping Chinese and Foreigners alike better appreciate our beautiful little island home.

Visit: **http://www.common-talk.com** And visit the **Amoy Magic websites** (mirrored sites for fast access both inside and outside of China).

Discover Gulangyu!

Dr. Bill Brown, 潘维廉博士
Xiamen University MBA Center

特别鸣谢双语周刊！

《厦门日报》双语周刊（CT），逢周三出版，是全国党报首份双语周刊，也是厦门英语新闻的最大稿源。 我甚至在写作此书时还依赖于 CT 以保证更新资料、吸引眼球（就像鼓浪屿风琴博物馆将成为世界上最大的风琴博物馆这部分），但我欠 CT 的远比这更多。

主编亚宇和她的同事们不仅把《魅力鼓浪屿》一书译成中文，还指正了许多我英文部分的错误，从最小的拼写错误到较大的史实问题（唉，即使是双语周刊也不能确保歼灭所有错误，所以敬请原谅书中的一些错误，在新版本中我将竭尽全力提高质量）。

感谢你，双语周刊团队，因你的存在使得各色中外人士在这座被称为家园的美丽小岛上，生活得更加温馨和谐。

关注厦门最新信息请浏览双语周刊网站：http://www.common-talk.com 和我夫人苏珊的网站（海内外最快捷了解厦门的通道）。

现在请

走进鼓浪屿！

潘维廉博士
厦门大学 MBA 中心

Translator's Note

By Yayu Wu

Pleasure in Company

There is an old Chinese saying: taking pleasure alone or taking pleasure in company – which is the true pleasure?

If you discover a real gem, you shouldn't slip it into your pocket and save it for your own personal enjoyment. The good things of this world are to be shared, so that everyone can take pleasure in them. Dr. Bill Brown had this in mind when he took up his pen to write *Discover Gulangyu*; and it is in the same spirit that we present this Chinese translation of his book, to give even more readers the opportunity to appreciate this shining example of the fusion of western and eastern cultures.

Translating *Discover Gulangyu* was not easy. Too literal a translation would be disjointed and difficult for Chinese readers to follow. The difficulty was increased by the quotes in the text, many of them from international residents of Gulangyu over a century ago. The style of these quotes comes across as rather academic, not at all in keeping with the author's light touch. Readers of "Amoy Magic" or Dr Brown's other local histories will be familiar with his comic tone and tongue-in-cheek asides. However, for this book he has changed his approach somewhat, and swapped his light, observational tone for more rigorous and more academic investigation. This added to the difficulty of the translation, as it demanded careful research into the texts and sources used in the book.

Any translation will have its own individual style, and no translation can be regarded as final, or completely authoritative. What is important is that the message of the original text is shared with and appreciated by the readers.

In this translation we have made every effort to preserve Dr. Brown's concise style and pointed observations. Should anything in our translation detract from the loveliness and wonder of Gulangyu, then we sincerely apologize. We hope our readers will accept that our reason for attempting such a task was not born of any ambition to overreach ourselves, but a simple desire that the pleasures of this study should be shared by as many of our fellow countrymen as possible.

译者的话

让我们快乐同行

如果有人发现一颗夺目的夜明珠的话，他没有权利放进自己的口袋，独享光辉，而必须公诸于世，使每个人都能分享这份光辉。基于这个理由，作者为了向全世界介绍鼓浪屿不遗余力摇笔撼书；也是基于这个理由，我们很高兴有机会将《Discover Gulangyu》一书译成中文，因为如此一来，有更多人也能得到这颗融合中西文化的珍珠发散出来的光芒。

这正验证了中国的古话“独乐乐，众乐乐，孰乐？”。

翻译《Discover Gulangyu》，并非易事。如果照句直译，恐怕会显得生涩难懂、准确度不高；还有一种情况是，引文多出自一个世纪前居住在鼓浪屿的国际居民，因为笔调的关系使译文学术意味太浓，不符合潘威廉的本人风格。作者幽默诙谐、妙趣横生的文风在其《魅力厦门》等书中多有体现。然而，与过往大不相同，作者在此书中突破了以往轻松写实的风格，沉入了更多严谨学者型思考，所以，不得不增加了后期翻译的难度，使得过程充满了艰辛的引经据典和考证工作。

在译文中，我们尽量以不同的方式求得折中。希望能既不失却潘先生原来简明的展示风格，又能无损他见解的精辟入微。假如由于我们的转译，间接减损了鼓浪屿的原有光芒，我们在此表示深深的歉意。而之所以不自量力地试译，只是因为实在不忍这份回味的快乐，只属于少数人，却不能遍撒人间。

We just have room for one more thing: a heartfelt thank you to all Common Talk members, full and part time, who have devoted themselves to CT's development in the past three years. Any product requires painstaking attention to detail if it is to be perfected, and it is only through the tireless efforts and exhaustive research of our members that we have been able to pick out accurate translations for each part of the original text. What is perhaps even more impressive is that even through all the hard work we have still found time to laugh and enjoy the process. In the words of the first prize winner of Common Talk's Third Bilingual Writing Contest in July this year: choosing Common Talk is choosing to move with the times, to embrace the hope and splendor of our modern age; it's choosing youth, choosing happiness, choosing the very finest people.

I am sure that with the publication of this book we will bring ourselves closer not only to the brilliance and energy author Dr. Brown, but also to a greater number of readers than ever before. We hope that all those readers will be as delighted as we are to accompany the author around this magical island, and that together we can fully immerse ourselves in the beauty of the Garden on the Sea.

Common Talk Chief Editor Yayu Wu
Translators: Yayu Wu, Vivian Zhang, Jean Chen, Enid Chen, Beverly Cai, George Shen, Happy Hong, Lily Li

任何人的翻译，永远没有所谓最好或最后的翻译，有的只是风格不同，原书真正的含义能被译出而且与读者分享，才是最重要的。

言有未尽之处，则是由衷地激赏三年来为双语成长投入周身心血的每位团员，及兼职翻译。是她们不厌其烦的“众里寻他千百度”，才得以在浩瀚史海中捕捉与原文对应的点滴。因为所有成熟和精致的产品，必定包含每一分子日臻完美的努力，有一点点瑕疵都会一览无疑。而更难得的是，一路走来我们汗流浃背亦能欢歌笑语！正如今年 7 月第三届双语征文英文组一等奖获得者对我们的评语：选择与 Common Talk 同行，就是选择与这个日新月异精彩不断的时代同行，与一种总是向上的充满希望的时代同行！就是选择与这群优秀的人同行，与青春与快乐同行！

我知道，这本书出来，既是跟勤奋刻苦的天才——本书作者同行，也是选择与更多读者同行，且让我们快快乐乐地同行下去，不辜负这座海上花园的良辰美景。

主编:吴亚宇

译者：吴亚宇、张薇薇、陈少英、陈玉清、
蔡露虹、沈　洋、洪建福、李　利

Intro to Xiamen

Gulangyu Visitor Center

Your first stop on Gulangyu, our Visitor Center is an integrated service organization set up by Gulangyu Scenic Area Administration Office. The center is responsible for tourist consulting, scenic spot ticket booking, tour guides, handling tourist complaints, luggage services, and so on. There are no cars or bicycles on Gulangyu Island, so enjoy strolling the many small roads and lanes leading to our island's scenic spots.

Sometimes tourists may lose their way, so the Gulangyu Visitor Center has set up a tourist center in the Sanyou Holiday Tour City a couple minutes walk straight ahead of the Gulangyu Ferry Terminal. The hall provides visitors consulting, a topographical 3-D model of the island, description of major tour routes, scenic area photos and written materials, electronic touch-sensitive displays, audio-visual aids, electronic tour guidance, and all kinds of tourist promotion material.

Most Visitor Center services are free of charge, including guided tours every 30 minutes, as well as a chance to participate in one of Xiamen's most unique folk customs—the traditional mooncake gambling game.

厦门鼓浪屿游客中心简介

鼓浪屿游客中心，是鼓浪屿风景名胜区管理部门设立的国有多功能服务性机构，负责为游客提供景区咨询、景区票务、景区讲解、旅游投诉、行李寄存等相关服务。鼓浪屿没有公共交通，城在景中，景在城中，道路纵横交错，游客容易迷路。鼓浪屿游客中心在上岛 100 米处“三友假日旅游城”一楼设有功能齐全的旅游集散大厅，通过鼓浪屿模型、旅游线路指南、景点简介、人工咨询、电子视听、电子导游、电子屏幕等媒介，全方位向游客介绍鼓浪屿，让游客在上岛伊始，就能够充分了解鼓浪屿的概貌。

鼓浪屿游客中心提供的服务大多数是免费的，其中最主要的有两项：一是向游客免费提供景区导游讲解服务，每 30 分钟从集散大厅发一个团；二是游客可以免费参与堪称世界唯一的博饼活动，体验厦门独特的民俗乐趣。

鼓浪屿游客中心服务项目指南
SERVICES OF GULANGYU VISITOR CENTER

服务项目 SERVICES	项目内容 TEXT	服务时间 TIME	联系电话 TELEPHONE
景区展示 Scenic Spots Display	全岛模型、旅游线路指南、景点图文、电子视听、电子触摸屏 3D Topographical Model of Entire Island, Tourist Route Points, Photos and Text of Scenic Spots, Audio-visual Aids, Electronic Touch Screens	8:00-18:00	0592-2061777
景区咨询 Information	鼓浪屿的食、住、行、游、购、娱 Board and Lodging, Sightseeing, on-Island Shopping and Recreation	8:00-18:00	0592-2060777
景区票务 Tickets	景点门票 Ticket Sales for Scenic Spots	8:00-17:00	0592-2061777
景区讲解 Tour Guides	按规定线路免费为游客导游讲解，每 30 分钟发一个团 Free guided tours every 30 minutes of regular tourist routes	8:00-16:30	0592-2061777
旅游投诉 Handle Tourist Complaints	接受游客投诉，转交相关执法部门处理 Accept visitor complaints, and forward to related departments	8:00-18:00	0592-2060444
行李寄存 Luggage Service	行李寄存柜 2~3 元/ 柜，大件行李寄存 5 元/ 件 Luggage storing 2-3 yuan/one case; large luggage 5 yuan/one case	8:00-18:00	0592-2060444
急 救 First Aids	向游客提供紧急和简单的医疗服务 First Aid and simple medical care for visitors	8:00-18:00	0592-2060777
传真 Fax: 0592-2060777 0592-2570112	地址:厦门市鼓浪屿龙头路 8 号 Add: #8 Longtou Road, Gulangyu, Xiamen	邮政编码 Zip Code: 361002	

Welcome from Gulangyu Government!

Dear friends,

Welcome to Gulangyu Islet, the "Garden on the Sea"! During your sightseeing and visit, please take notice of the following:

1. For your own safety, please refuse illegal tour guides.
2. To insure safety, combustibles and explosive material are not allowed to be carried on to the islet. Please don't climb dangerous buildings or enter dangerous area.
3. Our home is your home—so please conscientiously protect the scenic area environment and communal facilities. Throw refuse into the classifiable bins. Finally, please don't smoke in public places.
4. If you need assistance, please phone 0592-2060777 or 0592-2061777.

"We wish you a pleasant visit on our Islet!"

游 客 须 知

尊敬的游客朋友：您好！

海上花园鼓浪屿欢迎您的光临，游览中请您注意：

一、为了维护您的权益，请拒绝无证导游；

二、注意旅途安全，请勿携带易燃、易爆等危险物品进入景区，请勿攀爬危险建筑或靠近危险地带；

三、自觉保护景区环境，爱护公共设施，在公共场所请勿吸烟，请将垃圾丢入分类收集的垃圾筒内；

四、您在游览过程中如需帮助，请致电：0592—2060777，2061777

祝您旅行愉快！

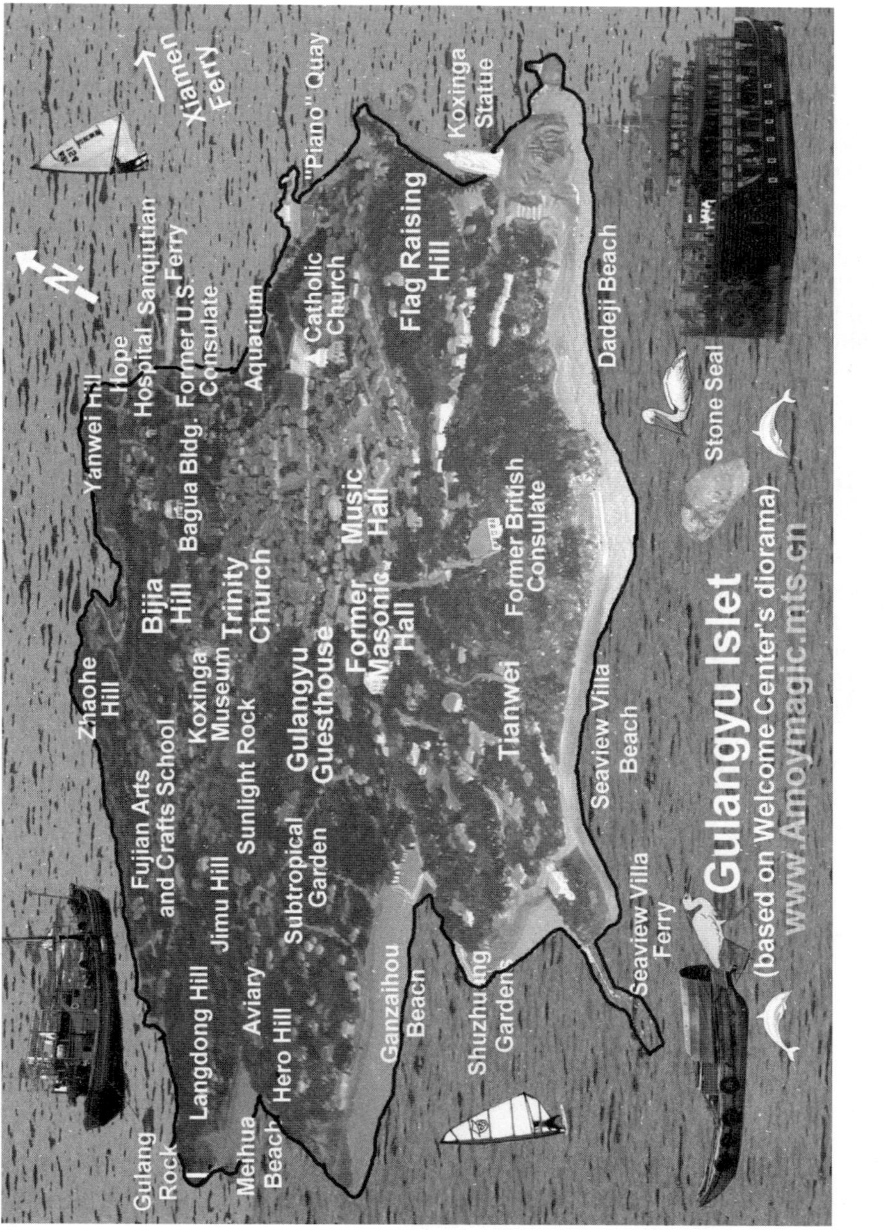

Xiamen Ferry
"Piano" Quay
Koxinga Statue
N.
Sanqiutian Ferry
Former U.S. Consulate
Aquarium
Catholic Church
Flag Raising Hill
Hope Hospital
Yanwei Hill
Bagua Bldg.
Music Hall
Dadeji Beach
Stone Seal
Former British Consulate
Bijia Hill
Trinity Church
Former Masonic Hall
Zhaohe Hill
Koxinga Museum
Gulangyu Guesthouse
Tianwei
Seaview Villa Beach
Fujian Arts and Crafts School
Sunlight Rock
Subtropical Garden
Jimu Hill
Langdong Hill
Aviary
Hero Hill
Ganzaihou Beach
Shuzhuang Garden
Seaview Villa Ferry
Gulang Rock
Meihua Beach

Gulangyu Islet
(based on Welcome Center's diorama)
www.Amoymagic.mts.cn

Gulangyu Tourist Center Suggested Tour Routes

Free Guided Tour Routes

Route A (About 1.5-hours): Ferry Terminal, Visitor Center, Former British Consulate, Former Japanese Consulate, Catholic Church, No.44 Villa, Huang Rongyuan Villa, Haitian Tangguo (Sea & Sky Mansion), Music School, Ma Yuehan Statue, Main Gate of Sunlight Rock

Route B (About 3-hours; visitor admission tickets required): Ferry Terminal, Visitor Center, Former British Consulate, Former Japanese Consulate, Catholic Church, No.44 Villa, Huang Rongyuan Villa, Haitian Tangguo (Sea & Sky Mansion), Music School, Ma Yuehan Statue, Main Gate of Sunlight Rock, Gulang Dongtian, Sunlight Rock Temple, "Coolness in Summer," Ancient Fort Gate, Ancient Summer Resort Cave, Ancient Command Platform, Zheng Chenggong Memorial Hall, Summit of Sunlight Rock, Hero Hill (Tingtao Bluff, Hero Garden, Gulangyu Aviary), Koxinga's Well, Shuzhuang Garden (Calligraphic Carving Museum, Twelve Rockery Caves, 44-turn Bridge, Piano Museum, Restored Ancient Relics Museum), Dagong Well, Longtou Road Shopping Street, Ferry Terminal

Route C (About 4-hours; visitors' admission tickets required): Ferry Terminal, Visitor Center, Former British Consulate, Former Japanese Consulate, Catholic Church, No.44 Villa, Huang Rongyuan Villa, Haitian Tangguo (Sea & Sky Mansion), Music School, Ma Yuehan Statue, Main Gate of Sunlight Rock (Gulang Dong Tian, Sunlight Rock Temple, "Coolness in Summer," Ancient Fort Gate, Ancient Summer Resort Cave, Ancient Command Platform, Zheng Chenggong Memorial Hall, Summit of Sunlight Rock), Hero Hill (Tingtao Bluff, Hero Garden, Gulangyu Aviary), Koxinga's Well, Shuzhuang Garden (Calligraphic Carving Museum, Twelve Rockery Caves, 44-turn Bridge, Piano Museum, Restored Ancient Relics Museum

景区免费导游讲解线路

A 线（行程约 1.5 小时）轮渡码头——游客中心——英国领事馆旧址——日本领事馆旧址——天主教堂——四十四号别墅——黄荣远堂——海天堂构——音乐学校——马约翰塑像——日光岩大门

B 线（游客需要购买景点门票，行程约 3 小时）轮渡码头——游客中心——英国领事馆旧址——日本领事馆旧址——天主教堂——四十四号别墅——黄荣远堂——海天堂构——音乐学校——马约翰塑像——日光岩（鼓浪洞天、日光岩寺、九夏生寒、古寨门、古避暑洞、古水操台遗址、郑成功纪念馆、顶峰）——英雄山（听海崖、英雄园、百鸟园）——国姓井——菽庄花园（刻字博物馆、十二洞天、四十四桥、钢琴博物馆、观复古博物馆）——大宫井——龙头路商业街——轮渡码头

C 线（游客需要购买景点门票，行程约 4 小时）轮渡码头——游客中心——英国领事馆旧址——日本领事馆旧址——天主教堂——四十四号别墅——黄荣远堂——海天堂构——音乐学校——马约翰塑像——日光岩（鼓浪洞天、日光岩寺、九夏生寒、古寨门、古避暑洞、古水操台遗址、郑成功纪念馆、顶峰）——英雄山（听海崖、英雄园、百鸟园）——国姓井——菽庄花园（刻字博物馆、十二洞天、四十四桥、钢琴博物馆、观复古博物馆）——观海园——印斗石——皓月园（郑成功巨型石雕、郑成功碑廊、皇帝殿、郑成功青铜群雕）——龙头路商业街——宿鼓浪屿——轮渡码头

Amoy town in 1873, from Kulangsu, with H.M.S. Hornet in foreground.
Used with permission of "Royal Society of Tropical Medicine and Hygiene" (London)

Suggested Self-guided Tour Routes

Route A Special Historical Tour (about 4-hours): Ferry Terminal, Visitor Center, Quanzhou Road, Hero Hill, Gulang Rock, Kangtai'an, Zhugonghe, Jiu'anhe, Zhongdegong, Bishan Cave, Former Joint Court, Former Municipal Council, Trinity Church, Yongchun Road, Sports Ground, Longtou Road Shopping Street, Ferry Terminal

Route B Special Geological Exploration Tour: including Springs and Ancient Wells: (about 6-hours): Ferry Terminal, Visitor Center, Fuding Ancient Well, Fuding Rock, Sword Rock, Yindou Rock, Shuzhuang Garden, Koxinga's Well, Ancient Summer Resort Cave, Sunlight Rock, Jimu Hill, Quanzhou Road, Zhonghua Road, Dagong Well, Longtou Road Shopping Street, Ferry Terminal

Route C Special Stone Inscription Tour (about 5.5-hours): Ferry Terminal, Visitor Center, Haoyue Park, Shuzhuang Garden, Sunlight Rock, Longtou Road Shopping Street, Ferry Terminal

Route D Special Historic Architecture Tour (about 4.5-hours): Ferry Terminal, Visitor Center, Catholic Church, Former British Consulate, Former Japanese Consulate, Octagonal Building, Huang Rongyuan Villa, No.44 Villa, Haitian Tangguo (Sea & Sky Mansion), Longtou Road, Quanzhou Road, Jingua Building, Trinity Church, Former Municipal Council, Former Joint Court, Yizu Villa, Guancai Building, Chunchao House, Fanpo (Foreign Woman) Villa, Yang Family Villa, Octagonal Dome Building, Former HSBC Mansion, Former U.S. Consulate, Sanqiutian Ferry, Electric Sightseeing Car Tour to Gangzihou Beach, Longtou Road Shopping Street, Ferry Terminal

Route E Special Music Culture Tour (about 4.5-hours): Ferry Terminal, Visitor Center, Music School, Concert Hall, Piano Museum, Gangzihou Beach, Electric Sightseeing Car Tour to Sanqiutian Ferry, Pipe Organ Museum (Octagonal Dome Building). Longtou Road Shopping Street, Ferry Terminal

Route F Historical Sites Tour (about 4 hours): Ferry Terminal, Visitor Center, Former Japanese Consulate (including the prison in which Chinese patriots were incarcerated during the war of Resistance Against Japan), Sunlight Rock (Zheng Chenggong Memorial Hall),, Hero Hill, Carefree Villa (Former CPC Underground Party Organization's Secret Meeting Place), Koxinga's Well, Shuzhuang Garden (Patriotic Overseas Chinese Lin Er-jia), Yu Garden (Dr. Lin Qiaozhi Memorial Hall), Haoyue Park (Zheng Chenggong Memorial Garden), Hu Xiang (Former CPC Organization of Fujian Province), Longtou Road Shopping Street, Overnight stay on Gulangyu, Ferry Terminal

景区自助专项游推荐线路

A 线（历史文脉，行程约 4 小时）轮渡码头——游客中心——泉州路——英雄山——鼓浪石——康泰垵——祖公河——旧庵河——种德宫——笔山洞顶——会审公堂旧址——工部局旧址——三一堂——永春路——体育场——龙头路商业街——轮渡码头

B 线（泉井与地质，行程约 6 小时）轮渡码头——游客中心——覆鼎古井——覆鼎岩海蚀崖——剑石海蚀柱——印斗石海蚀台——菽庄花园海阔天空滚石地貌——国姓井——日光岩古避暑洞滚石地貌——日光岩仙脚桶海蚀地貌——鸡母山海蚀崖——泉州路——中华路——大宫井——龙头路商业街——轮渡码头

C 线（摩崖石刻，行程约 5.5 小时）轮渡码头——游客中心——皓月园——菽庄花园——日光岩——龙头路商业街——轮渡码头

D 线（历史风貌建筑，行程约 4.5 小时）轮渡码头——游客中心——天主教堂——英国领事馆旧址——日本领事馆旧址——八角楼——黄荣远堂——四十四号别墅——海天堂构——龙头路——泉州路——金瓜楼——三一堂——工部局旧址——会审公堂旧址——亦足山庄——观彩楼——春草堂——番婆楼——杨家园——八卦楼——汇丰银行公馆旧址——美国领事馆旧址——三丘田码头——乘观光车到港仔后沙滩——龙头路商业街——轮渡码头

E 线（音乐文化，行程约 4.5 小时）轮渡码头——游客中心——音乐学校——钢琴博物馆——港仔后沙滩——乘观光车到三丘田码头——管风琴博物馆（八卦楼）——龙头路商业街——轮渡码头

F 线（红色之旅，行程约 4 小时）轮渡码头——游客中心——日本领事馆（关押抗日志士监狱）——日光岩（郑成功纪念馆）——英雄山——了闲别墅（婢女自拔会、中共地下党秘密据点）——国姓井——菽庄花园（爱国人士林尔嘉）——毓园（林巧稚纪念馆）——皓月园（郑成功纪念园）——虎巷（中共福建省委机关旧址）——龙头路商业街——宿鼓浪屿——轮渡码头

Mooncake Exhibit

Chapter 1
Exotic Gulangyu Islet

Something for Everyone!

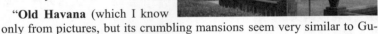

"To the rare foreign visitor, Gulangyu is astonishingly reminiscent of an amalgam of other places far away:

"**Old Havana** (which I know only from pictures, but its crumbling mansions seem very similar to Gulangyu's).

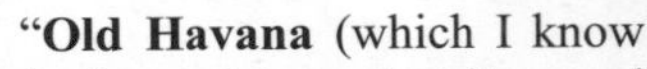

"**A Mexican hill town**, such as Taxco or San Miguel, even down to the tiled streets in some cases.

"**The Cinque Terre of Italy**--beautiful, balmy, quiet.

"**Hawaii**, with its wild poinsettias, bougainvillea, pleasant beaches.

"**An Austrian village**, with piano and violin music wafting from open windows.

"**A little bit of Las Vegas**, with gaudy lights every evening on every imaginable landmark on both sides of the channel.

"Put this all in a Chinese setting, and you have Gulangyu."

Brian Dearle[1]

Xiamen is China's "Garden Island" but her Crown Jewel is Gulangyu ("Drum Wave Islet"), the elegant 1.78 square kilometer haven just 700 meters across Xiamen Island. Settled during the Yuan Dynasty (1206-1368), Gulangyu was named Yuan Shazhou ("round sandy island") during the Ming Dynasty (1368-1644), but a geological mystery gave rise to its present name…

Ancient settlers were unsettled by eerie drum beats emanating from the clearly uninhabited island, but eventually discovered the ghostly drumming was caused by tides surging through a hollow rock on the island's southwest corner. Relieved that "Round Sandy Island" wasn't haunted, or a lair for cannibal tribes from across the Strait, they renamed their new home "Drum Wave Islet" (Gulangyu, 鼓浪屿).

While Stone Drum is silent nowadays, the islet drums up plenty of tourism because of its lush tropical gardens, rich musical and cultural heritage, and its unparalleled panoply of international colonial-era architecture.

---

[1] *China's Carfree Town*, used by permission of www.newcolonist.com

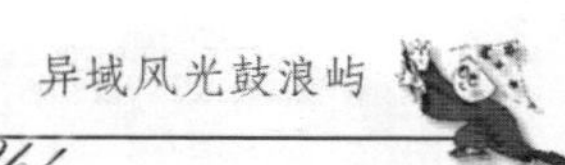

第一章

异域风光鼓浪屿

“对罕至的外国游客，鼓浪屿之奇在于，仿佛完美组合了其他遥远地方：

“老哈瓦那（我只看到图片，但其摇摇欲坠的楼舍与鼓浪屿的非常相似）。

“一个墨西哥山镇，如塔斯科或圣米格尔，有些地方甚至铺砖的街道都很像。

“意大利的五台堡——美丽、温和，宁静。

“夏威夷，野圣诞花、叶子花和迷人的海滩。

“一个奥地利乡村，从敞开的窗户悠扬飘出钢琴和小提琴声。

“拉斯维加斯的一小块，每当夜晚峡江两边处处梦幻地标华光闪烁。

“把所有这一切置于中国境内，你就有了鼓浪屿。”

——摘自布莱恩·戴尔《中国无车岛：鼓浪屿》[1]

厦门是中国的花园城市，但王冠明珠是“鼓浪屿”，一个优美的 1.78 平方公里岛屿，距厦门岛仅 700 米。鼓浪屿设立于元代（1206-1368），在明朝（1368-1644）被称为“圆沙洲”，但一个地质之谜赋予了它现在的名字……

古时居民被岛上发出的奇异鼓声所困扰，尽管岛上显然无人居住。穿越灌木丛林，循声而去，他们发现鼓声原是由浪潮冲过岛西南角一块空洞岩石引起的。确信“圆沙岛”并未闹鬼，也不是对岸游来的食人部落巢穴，他们把自己的新家园重新命名为“鼓浪屿”。

石鼓如今寂默无声，但该岛却鼓动招揽无数游客，因为它盛开的热带花园，丰富的音乐和文化遗产，以及举世无双千姿百态的殖民时代的国际建筑。

[1] 经 www.newcolonist.com 许可使用《中国无车岛》

Gulangyu's serpentine lanes wind past high-walled gardens on lushly shaded hills, and hundreds of aged but elegant mansions built during the heyday of the early 20th century. As you savor the scenery and sleepy silence, you can almost imagine the opulence of yesteryear, when this drowsy islet teemed with the International Settlement's turbaned Gurkha policemen, dignitaries of a dozen nations, and wealthy Chinese and Western businessmen borne upon ornate sedan chairs by attendants in uniforms emblazoned with pampered employers' monograms.

In 1920, Hutchinson wrote that Gulangyu had more wealthy people than anywhere on earth except Pasadena, California![1] The wealth is gone, but the rich international heritage remains.

Gulangyu at a Glance

1. **Area**: 1.78 km^2
2. **Population**: 15,000 (minus 2; Bill & Kitty Job moved off-island)
3. **Language**: Mandarin, Minnan (S. Fujian) Dialect
4. **Location**: 118 degrees East, 24 degrees North, and just S.E. of Xiamen
5. **Climate**: sub-tropic maritime monsoon, warm year-round with 20.9 ℃ average temperature, high of 35 C, low of 5 C.
6. **Nicknames**: Garden on the Sea, Piano Island, Isle of Music, Museum of International Architecture
7. **Unique customs**: Dragon Boat Festival duck catching, Mooncake Game, family music recitals, weekend philharmonic symphonies
8. **Culinary Treats**: Mooncakes (China's best!), prepared meats (from a shop opened in 1842!), Minnan cuisine, seafood, light soups, crispy friend dishes, fish balls, zongzis, green bean pie, coconut pie, etc.
9. **Main Attractions**:
   Sunlight Rock (Koxinga Memorial, Ancient Fort, Cable Car)
   Historic International Architecture (hundreds of elegant buildings)
   Shuzhuang Garden (and Piano Museum)
   Hero Hill: Tingtao Bluff, Hero Garden, Gulangyu Aviary
   Gulangyu Music Hall (frequent concerts), Xiamen Music Academy
   Bright Moon Garden (Koxinga Statue)
   Xiamen Museum (and Organ Museum)
   Gangzihou Beach, Drum-Wave Rock, Yindou Rock
   Xiamen Sea World (behind the giant octopus sculpture by the ferry)
10. **Shopping**—stock up on local specialties like Gulangyu pearls, prepared foods and mooncakes, as well as Anxi tea, Zhangzhou hand puppets, Hui'an stone carvings, Fuzhou's Shoushan stone—and Mr. Bai Hua's inimitable Gulangyu postcards.

[1] Hutchinson, 1920, p.160

鼓浪屿的曲折街巷蜿蜒起伏于郁郁葱葱的山间，两旁是高墙围护的花园和成百座建于 20 世纪全盛早期虽然古旧但却精致的楼舍。沉浸于此处风景和致睡宁静之际，你几乎可以想见它昨日的富裕。这座沉静小岛当年充满了万国公地包着头巾的廓尔喀警察、各国的达官显贵、坐在华丽轿子里的中外富商，仆从抬着轿子，身着饰有主人交织花字的制服。

1920 年，哈钦森写到，不算加利福尼亚的帕萨迪纳，鼓浪屿的富人比地球上任何地方都多！[1]如今财富已去，但丰饶的国际遗产仍存。

鼓浪屿一瞥

1. **面积**：1.78 平方公里
2. **人口**：1.5 万（减 2；Bill & Kitty Job 离岛了）
3. **语言**：普通话、闽南方言
4. **位置**：东经 118 度，北纬 24 度，厦门东南方
5. **气候**：亚热带海洋性季候，长年温暖，平均气温 20.9℃，最高 35℃，最低 5℃。
6. **昵称**：海上花园、钢琴岛、音乐岛、万国建筑博物馆
7. **独特风俗**：端午抓鸭，中秋博饼，家庭音乐演奏会，周末爱乐交响音乐会
8. **美食**：鼓浪屿馅饼（中国最好的！）、肉松（店家开办于 1842 年！）、闽南菜、海鲜、靓汤、薄饼、鱼丸、粽子、绿豆饼、椰子饼等等。
9. **主要景点**：
   日光岩（郑成功纪念馆，古寨，缆车）
   国际建筑群（上百座精致建筑）
   菽庄花园（有钢琴博物馆）
   英雄山（听涛崖，英雄园，鼓浪屿百鸟园）
   鼓浪屿音乐厅（不断上演音乐会）：厦门音乐学校
   皓月园（郑成功塑像）
   厦门博物馆（风琴博物馆）
   港仔后海滩、鼓浪岩、印斗石
   厦门海底世界（在渡口旁巨大的章鱼雕塑后面）
10. **购物**：选购当地特产如鼓浪屿珍珠、熟食和月饼，还有安溪茶、漳州布袋木偶、惠安石雕、福州寿山石——欲留存记忆可购一套白桦先生的鼓浪屿明信片。

[1] 哈钦森，1920 年版，第 160 页

Gulangyu Tour Themes

Historical Tour Koxinga made China's last stand for the Ming Dynasty, here on Gulangyu, and from here sailed off to rescue Taiwan from the Dutch. And a century ago this tiny islet's an international settlement was host to the planet's most powerful trading firms and consulates of 13 countries. Gulangyu and Xiamen were also the "Birthplace of Chinese Protestantism" with China's oldest Protestant churches.

Pioneering Medicine and Education Tour Known as "The Cradle of Tropical Medicine", Gulangyu was pivotal in developing both Chinese and Western modern medicine. The islet was also home to many pioneer educators (especially in women's education), and boasted over 20 institutes of learning.

Music & Arts Tour The "Isle of Music" , or "Piano Island" , has more pianos per capita than any other city in China, Asia's largest piano museum, and has produced dozens of famous musicians, including world-renowned pianist Yin Chengzong, and acclaimed conductor Madame Zheng Xiaoying. The islet was also home to the famous writer Lin Yutang and artist Teng Hiok Chiu.

Architectural Tour In 2001 alone, Gulangyu spent 7.5 million USD protecting hundreds of historic buildings in this "World Museum of Architecture" .

Garden Tour China's 1st ISO-authenticated administrative district, Gulangyu spent 120 million USD relocating enterprises off-island to preserve this botanical paradise. Key parks include:

Shuzhuang Garden (Shuzhuang Huayuan, 菽庄花园), Gulangyu's largest garden includes the Piano Museum (Gangqin Bowuguan, 钢琴博物馆).
Gulangyu Aviary (Bainiao Yuan, 百鸟园)
Bright Moon Garden (Haoyue Yuan, 皓月园) & Koxinga Statue.
Yanping Park (Yanping Gongyuan, 延平公园): miraculous Koxinga Well.
Subtropical Botanical Garden
Private Gardens—many historic private villas have delightful gardens.

Shopping & Entertainment Tour Gulangyu is a shoppers' and diners' paradise, with value-priced Fujian handicrafts, specialties, antiques, fine foods and teas, etc. You'll shop till you drop—or until your wallet is empty. (The best shopping is straight ahead of the ferry on Longtou Rd.) Enjoy the Minnan Tea Ceremony, the famous Mid-Autumn Mooncake game, and attractions like Xiamen Underwater World, the Cable Cars, and the beaches.

Peace & Quiet Savor the silence—Gulangyu has no cars or bikes (though you may see the cute little red fire trucks).

鼓浪屿旅游主题

历史之旅 从鼓浪屿，郑成功坚守了中国明朝最后一片立足之地，从这里扬帆赶走荷兰人，收复台湾。一个世纪前这座小岛是地球上最强贸易公司的基地，及驻有 13 个国家领事馆的国际居地。鼓浪屿和厦门还是“中国新教诞生地”，拥有中国最古老的新教教堂。

医学和教育先驱之旅 以“热带医学摇篮”著称，鼓浪屿是开启中西现代医学发展的钥匙，还帮助开启了现代教育，特别是妇女教育，同时还有 20 多所学校。

音乐和艺术之旅 “音乐岛”，或“钢琴岛”，人均钢琴拥有量超过中国其他任何城市，有亚洲最大的钢琴博物馆，培养了几十名著名的音乐家，包括享誉世界的钢琴家殷承宗，著名指挥家郑小瑛女士。该岛还是著名作家林语堂和著名画家周廷旭的故乡。

建筑之旅 仅在 2001 年，鼓浪屿投入 750 万美元保护成百座历史建筑，以保持该岛“万国建筑博物馆”的美誉。

花园之旅 中国第一个 ISO 认证的行政区，鼓浪屿花了 1.2 亿美元，将企业迁出岛外，以保持这座植物王国。主要公园包括：

菽庄花园　鼓浪屿最大的花园，包括钢琴博物馆
百鸟园
皓月园和郑成功塑像
延平公园——神奇的国姓井
亚热带植物园
私人花园——许多历史私墅都有宜人的花园

购物和娱乐之旅 鼓浪屿是购物者和美食者的天堂，具有超值的福建工艺品、特产、古玩、美食和茶等。你会一直购下去，直到拿不了或等到钱包空空！（最好的购物场所在渡口正前方龙头路）享受闽南茶艺、著名的中秋博饼，厦门海底世界等景点、缆车和海滩。

平和宁静之旅 享受宁静，因为鼓浪屿没有汽车和自行车！（也许你会看到可爱的红色救火车。）

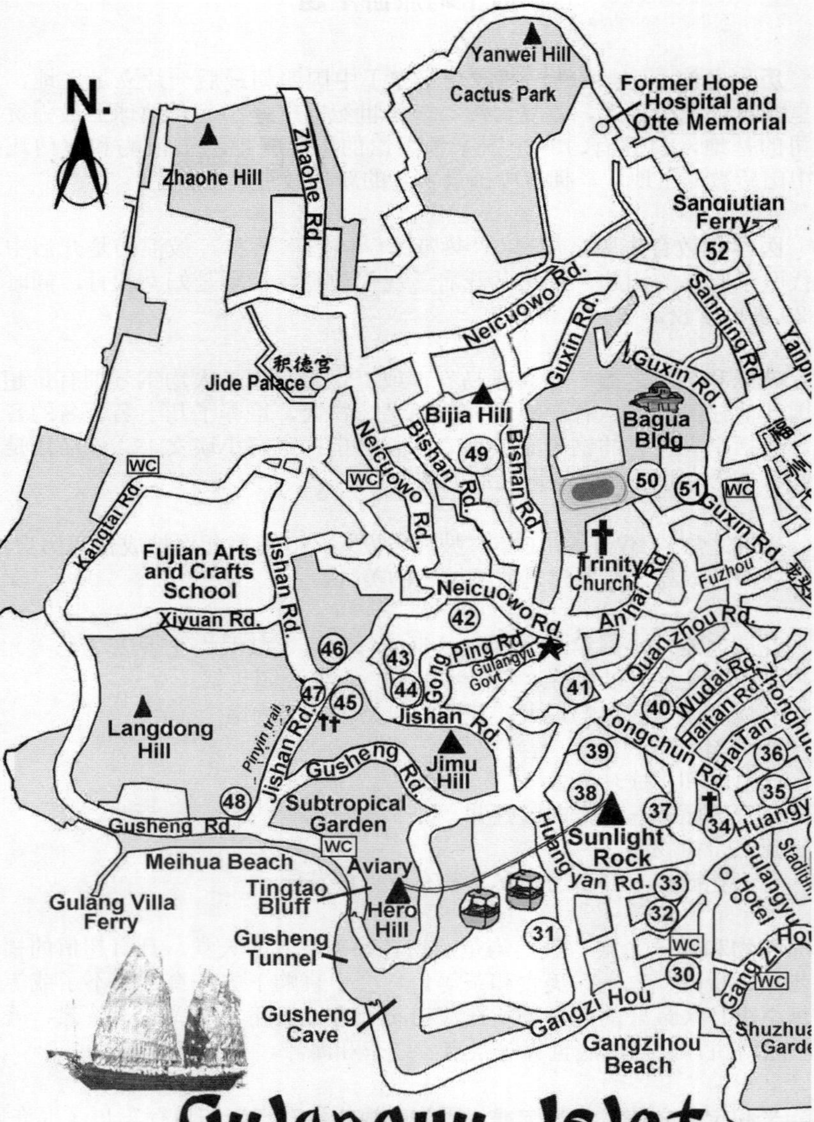

Gulangyu Islet

N.

Yanwei Hill
Cactus Park
Former Hope Hospital and Otte Memorial
Zhaohe Hill
Zhaohe Rd.
Sanqiutian Ferry
52
Neicuowo Rd.
Guxin Rd.
Sanming Rd.
Yanp...
积德宫
Jide Palace
Bijia Hill
Bagua Bldg
Bishan Rd.
Bishan Rd.
49
WC
Kangtai Rd.
WC
Neicuowo Rd.
50
51
WC
Guxin Rd.
Trinity Church
Fujian Arts and Crafts School
Jishan Rd.
Anhai Rd.
Fuzhou
Neicuowo Rd.
42
Xiyuan Rd.
Quanzhou Rd.
46
43
Gong Ping Rd
Gulangyu Govt.
44
47
45
41
Wudai Rd.
Zhonghua
Langdong Hill
Pinyin trail
Jishan Rd.
40
Haitan Rd.
Jishan Rd.
Yongchun Rd.
HaiTan
Gusheng Rd.
Jimu Hill
39
36
38
35
48
Subtropical Garden
37
34
Huangy...
Gusheng Rd.
Sunlight Rock
Huangyan Rd.
WC
Meihua Beach
Aviary
Gulangyu Hotel
Stadium
Gulang Villa Ferry
Tingtao Bluff
Hero Hill
33
32
31
Gusheng Tunnel
WC
30
Gang Zi Hou
WC
Gusheng Cave
Gangzi Hou
Gangzihou Beach
Shuzhua... Garde...

1. Gulangyu Welcome Ctr.
2. Former British Consulate
3. Post Office
4. Xinhua Book Store
5. Pearl World
6. Ye Qingchi Villa
7. Former Japanese Consul.
8. Catholic Church
9. Sea 'n Sky Mansion
10. Yi Yuan (Happiness Villa)
11. Huang Rongyuan Mansion
12. Xu's Mansion
13. Lin's Octagon Buildings
14. Fuxing Church
15. Li Qingquan Villa
16. Piano Island Hotel
17. Seashore Inn
18. Bright Moon Park
19. Koxinga Statue
20. Lodge Cabins- a favorite!
21. Lin Qiaozhi Memorial
22. Former Yude Girls' School
23. Lin Yu Tang's former hm.
24. Ma Yuehan's former hm.
25. Ma Yuehan Memorial
26. Library
27. Former Masonic Lodge
28. Cadre's Sanatorium
29. Former Denmark Teleg. Ofc.
30. Yanping Park
31. Army Sanatorium
32. Koxinga Miraculous Well
33. Dr. Lin Qiaozhi former hm.
34. Gospel Hall
35. Ms. Shu Ting's hm.
36. Daifudi (200-yr-old)
37. Sunlight Rock Temple
38. Koxinga's Fort
39. Koxinga Memorial
40. The "Castle"
41. People's Primary Sch.
42. Bishan Cave; Qín Statuary Exhibit
43. Yin Chengzong's former residence
44. Chen Shijing's Tomb
45. Christian Cemetery
46. Anxian Hall (7th Dav Adventist)
47. "Pinvin Memorial Walk"
48. Memorial to Lu Zhuangzhang
49. Xu Feiping's former residence
50. Xiamen #2 Middle School (Former Yinghua School)
51. Former U.S. Consulate

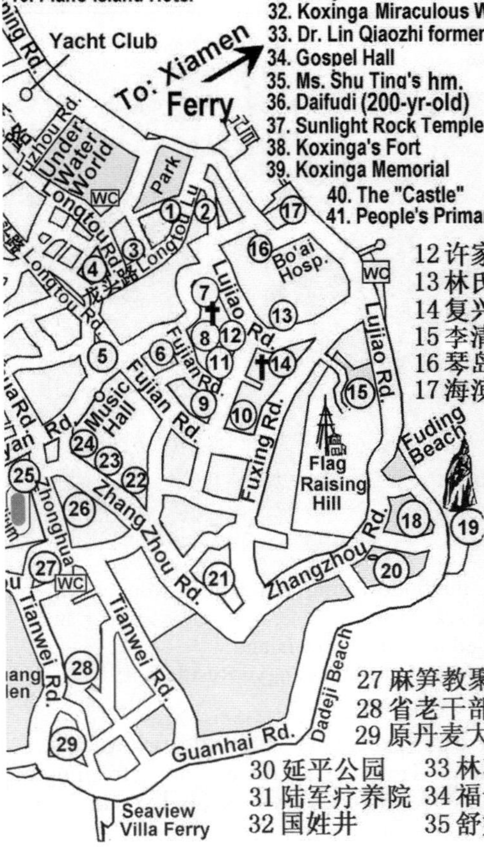

1 鼓浪屿游客中心
2 原英国领事馆
3 邮政局
4 新华书店
5 珍珠世界
6 叶清池别墅
7 原日本总领事馆
8 天主教堂
9 海天别墅
10 怡园
11 黄荣远堂
12 许家园
13 林氏府八角楼
14 复兴堂
15 李清泉别墅
16 琴岛酒店
17 海滨旅社
18 皓月园
19 郑成功雕像
20 休闲小屋
21 林巧稚纪念堂
22 原毓德女学
23 林语堂故居
24 马约翰故居
25 马约翰铜像
26 图书馆
27 麻笋教聚会所
28 省老干部休养所
29 原丹麦大北电报公司
30 延平公园
31 陆军疗养院
32 国姓井
33 林巧稚故居
34 福音堂
35 舒婷女士私邸
36 大夫第(200年历史)
37 日光岩寺
38 郑成功屯兵营寨
39 郑成功纪念馆
40 古堡
41 人民小学
42 笔山洞、秦俑馆
43 殷宅
44 陈士京墓
45 基督教徒墓地
46 安献堂（安息日会）
47 拼音纪念路
48 卢戆章塑像
49 许斐平故居
50 厦门二中（原英华书院）
51 原美国领事馆

Getting to Gulangyu Ferry Terminal (Xiagu Lundu, 厦鼓 轮渡)

Buses: 2, 3, 4, 8, 10, 12, 19, 23, 25, 27, 28, 30, 31, 32, 36, 44, 60, 51, 66, 67, 85

Ferries make the 10 minute crossing several times an hour. Specialty tour ferries include cruises around nearby Taiwan-controlled Jinmen Island.

Maps and Guides English and Chinese maps are available in local bookstores and hotels or from vendors at the Gulangyu Ferry Terminal.

Xiamen Tour Guides. Hire ***only*** official guides (I learned this the hard way). They wear light purple "China Xiamen Tourism" badges depicting a running horse (China's symbol of tourism) and a flying swallow (because some tour guides' tales are hard to swallow).

Getting About on Gulangyu

"There was no wheeled traffic on Kulangsu; no horses, no bicycles, no rickshaws. Man provided power for sedan chairs, wheel-barrows and carrying poles. The roads, in consequence, were quiet and narrow, running steeply up and down between high-walled gardens. The noises, except in the streets stretching out from the slipways facing Amoy harbour, were the quick, flat slap of weight-carrying bare feet, the hollow drag and clop of wooden sandals, and always the sound of the sea. The Chinese, with their respect and care for the appropriate name, called it Drum Wave Island."

Averil Mackenzie-Grieve (British Gulangyu Resident, 1920s)

Gulangyu has neither bikes nor cars (except for cute little fire trucks), so you either walk or take an electric tram. Trams save time and are refreshing on hot, muggy days, but to really experience Gulangyu you should spend 2 or 3 days traipsing the islet on foot—with frequent stops for Minnan tea!

去鼓浪屿轮渡

公共汽车：2、3、4、8、10、12、19、23、25、27、28、30、31、32、36、44、60、51、66、67、85

轮渡一趟 10 分钟，每小时数班。一些特别游轮还包括游台湾当局管辖的金门。

地图和向导：英文和中文地图在当地书店和旅馆或鼓浪屿轮渡附近货摊都有售。

厦门导游：只聘正规导游（我吃尽苦头才认识到）。他们佩带淡紫色"中国厦门旅游"徽章，形绘奔马（中国旅游标记）和飞燕[因为有些野导的故事难以"下燕(咽)"]。

游览鼓浪屿

> "鼓浪屿上没有带轮车辆，没有马车，没有自行车，没有黄包车。人工出力抬轿子、手推车和挑扁担。结果，路都宁静而狭窄，在高墙围护的花园之间陡然上上下下。除了从厦门港对面船台辐射出去的街道上，声音都是负重赤脚急促、单调的啪嗒声，木屐的空空拖拉声和得得声，以及常绕耳畔的海之声。中国人，考虑到它最贴切命名，称之鼓浪屿……"
>
> Averil Mackenzie-Grieve（鼓浪屿英国居民，1920 年代）

既然鼓浪屿禁行自行车和汽车（除了一些小巧红色消防车），你可以走路或坐电瓶车。电瓶车能节省时间，在炎热闷湿天气很是爽快，但要真正体验鼓浪屿，你得用脚在岛上漫步两三天，并且时常停下来喝杯闽南功夫茶才行！

Wheelbarrow Journey (Fullerton, 1910)

Supplement

Gulangyu—a Popular International Port of Call

Gulangyu was a popular destination for commercial and military ships from all over the world. On October 30th, 1908, Gulangyu hosted over 7,000 sailors from 8 American battleships: the Louisiana, Virginia, Missouri, Ohio, Wisconsin, Kentucky, Illinois, and Kearsage. Rev. Pitcher (1912) wrote:

> "They put in about 9:00 am, for coal and provisions, and were feted by dignitaries ranging from Imperial Prince Yu Lang and his Honorable translator all the way down to the local judge.
>
> Some folks, particularly the gentrified Europeans, doubted that tiny Amoy could survive 7,000 American sailors on shore leave at one time, but they spent their time buying presents, or at the YMCA tent writing letters to family and sweethearts."

Today, cliff inscriptions behind Xiamen's Nanputuo Temple commemorate that grand occasion and China and America's eternal friendship—which 30 years later saved tens of thousands of lives on Amoy.

In May, 1938, the U.S.S. Asheville commandeered a rice and water barge in Amoy and saved the lives of about 60,000 Chinese whom the Japanese interned on Gulangyu with neither food nor water. (Japanese occupied Gulangyu after the Dec. 1941 attack on Pearl Harbor, and surrendered on Gulangyu in the Seashore Inn on Lujiao Rd.).

Japanese Battleship off Gulangyu

附录

鼓浪屿——最受欢迎的国际停泊港口

鼓浪屿和厦门是全世界最受欢迎的商船和军舰停泊港口。1908 年 10 月 30 日，鼓浪屿驻扎了 8 艘美国战舰的 7000 多名水兵：路易斯安娜号、弗吉尼亚号、密苏里号、俄亥俄号、威斯康辛号、肯塔基号、依利诺伊号和奇尔沙治号。毕腓力牧师在 1912 年写道：

“他们约早上 9：00 进港，加煤和补养，广受达官贵人款待，上自于琅（？）及其尊敬的翻译，下至地方法官的欢迎。

一些人，尤其是中产欧洲人，很是怀疑小小厦门能否承受 7000 名美国水兵同时上岸度假，但他们或花时间购买礼物，或在青年会帐篷里给家人和甜心写信。

今天，在厦门南普陀寺（厦门大学旁）后面的岩石上，镌刻着纪念这一重要事件和中美永恒友谊的碑铭——这友谊 30 年后在厦门挽救了数万名中国人的生命。

1938 年 5 月，美国潜艇阿什维尔号在厦门征调了一条米水驳船，挽救了约 6 万名中国人的生命，他们当时被日本人断水断粮扣押在鼓浪屿上。（日本人在 1941 年 12 月偷袭珍珠港后占领了鼓浪屿，后来在鹿礁路上的鼓浪屿海滨旅社投降。）

Prince Yulang　Pitcher, 1912

An American Sailor's Letter from Gulangyu[1]

Amoy, China July 8, 1939

Hello Tuck,

Am writing this in answer to your letter that I received the day before my birthday, the fourth of July, and what a lousy day it was too, but I will tell you about it later on in the letter…

We have been to Shanghai, Swatow, and Hong Kong since then and now we are in Amoy or rather Kulangsu, which is an island just across the way from Amoy. It is more or less of an international settlement and the Japanese decided they wanted it, until Yarnell and Sir Percy Nobel of the Limey fleet intervened. The Tulsa was in here at the time so they sent an armed landing force over to stay at the American Consulate. We relieved them two weeks ago, yesterday and now I am one of the forty two guys over here.

The consulate is a big place so we are living in tents and having the time of our lives. Nothing to do all day long except lay around taking it easy and playing tennis or making liberty. I don't even have to stand watches for I am in charge of the issue room and the armory. The ship is real close, so we get our chow from there for each meal. I am in the armory now writing this. I stood one of the fellow's watches in here just so I could knock off a couple of letters… We have one more week of this and then I am kissing good bye to China for the last time!...We sail for Manila on the 17th and I catch the Henderson bound for the States on the 29th…They have an excess of seamen out here now and that is why I am going back earlier than was expected…

…Am sending this by Chinese mail as you wanted. Write soon and cut me in on the dope.

As ever,
Bunny

[1] Used by permission of Salty's Stamps http://rhodeisland-philatelic.com

一位美国水兵写自鼓浪屿的信[1]

塔克：你好。

现提笔答复你信，收到前信是在我生日前一天，7 月 4 日，也是多么糟糕的一天，但在本信下面我会告诉你有关之事……

我们从那时起到过上海、汕头、香港，现在厦门，或应说在鼓浪屿，厦门正对面的一岛上。它或多或少算是个国际居地，日本人决定想要它，直到英国舰队的亚内尔和珀西·诺贝尔先生出面干涉。当时塔尔萨部在此，所以他们派来一支武装登陆部队，驻扎在美国领事馆。我们两星期前接防，昨天和现在我是来此的四十二名弟兄之一。

领事馆是个很大的地方，我们住在帐篷里，自己过活。整天无所事事，就是东躺西卧优哉游哉，打打网球或找乐。我甚至不必站岗，因为我负责收发室和军械库。船离得很近，所以每餐我们都从那里领饭。我现在军械库写这信。我正赶上在这里值班，因此可以匆匆写几封信……

……我们在此要再待一周，然后我将最后一次吻别中国！……我们 17 号驶往马尼拉，29 日我赶乘亨德森号驶往美国。他们在这儿有太多的水手，此即为何我将比预期的早些回家……

……如你所愿用中国邮政寄发此信。盼早写信，慰我渴望。

永远的，
邦尼
中国厦门
1939 年 7 月 8 日

[1] 经 Salty's Stamps http://rhodeisland-philatelic.com 许可

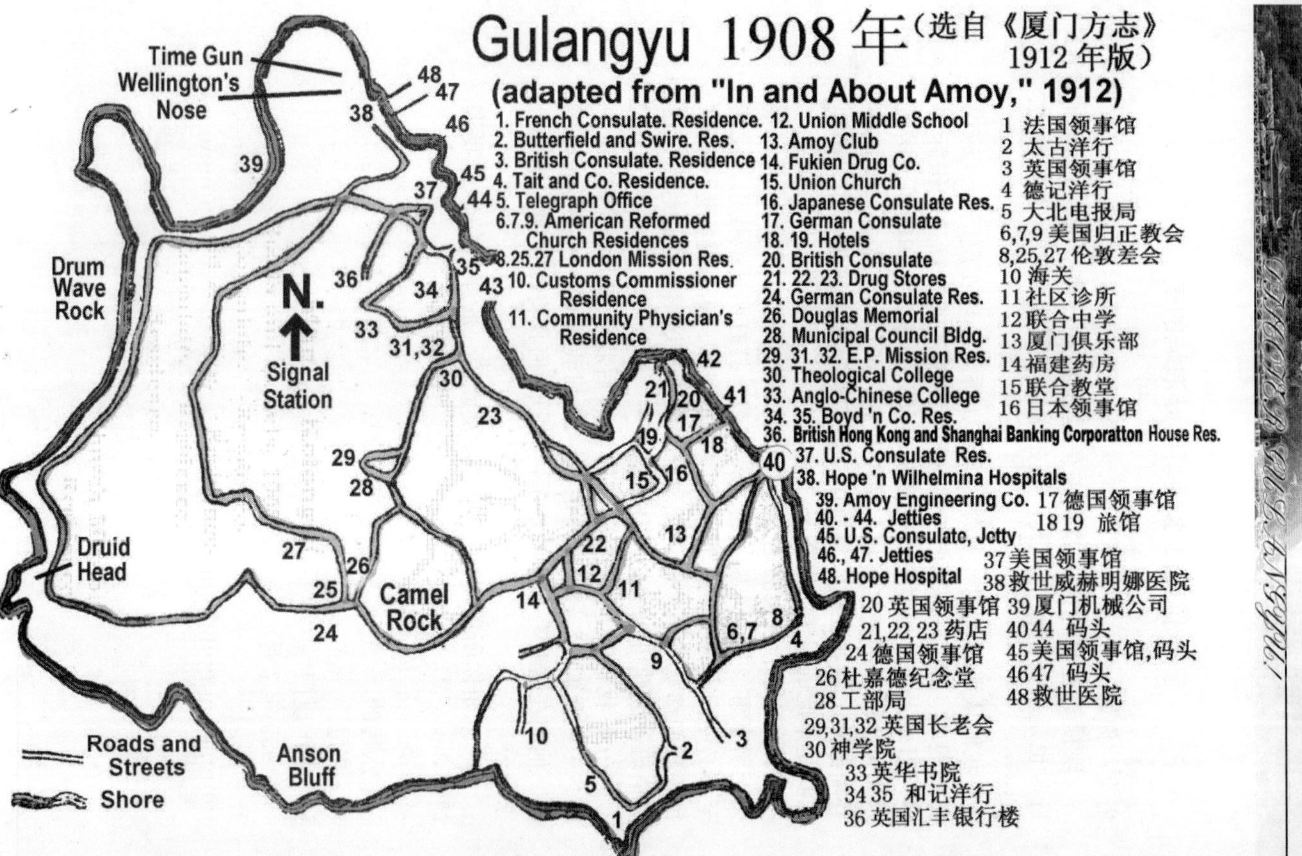
Gulangyu 1908 年（选自《厦门方志》1912 年版）
(adapted from "In and About Amoy," 1912)
1. French Consulate. Residence.
2. Butterfield and Swire. Res.
3. British Consulate. Residence
4. Tait and Co. Residence.
5. Telegraph Office
6.7.9. American Reformed Church Residences
8.25.27 London Mission Res.
10. Customs Commissioner Residence
11. Community Physician's Residence
12. Union Middle School
13. Amoy Club
14. Fukien Drug Co.
15. Union Church
16. Japanese Consulate Res.
17. German Consulate
18. 19. Hotels
20. British Consulate
21. 22. 23. Drug Stores
24. German Consulate Res.
26. Douglas Memorial
28. Municipal Council Bldg.
29. 31. 32. E.P. Mission Res.
30. Theological College
33. Anglo-Chinese College
34. 35. Boyd 'n Co. Res.
36. British Hong Kong and Shanghai Banking Corporatton House Res.
37. U.S. Consulate Res.
38. Hope 'n Wilhelmina Hospitals
39. Amoy Engineering Co.
40. - 44. Jetties
45. U.S. Consulatc, Jctty
46., 47. Jetties
48. Hope Hospital
1 法国领事馆
2 太古洋行
3 英国领事馆
4 德记洋行
5 大北电报局
6,7,9 美国归正教会
8,25,27 伦敦差会
10 海关
11 社区诊所
12 联合中学
13 厦门俱乐部
14 福建药房
15 联合教堂
16 日本领事馆
17 德国领事馆
18 19 旅馆
20 英国领事馆
21,22,23 药店
24 德国领事馆
26 杜嘉德纪念堂
28 工部局
29,31,32 英国长老会
30 神学院
33 英华书院
34 35 和记洋行
36 英国汇丰银行楼
37 美国领事馆
38 救世威赫明娜医院
39 厦门机械公司
40 44 码头
45 美国领事馆,码头
46 47 码头
48 救世医院
Time Gun
Wellington's Nose
Drum Wave Rock
Druid Head
N.
Signal Station
Camel Rock
Anson Bluff
Roads and Streets
Shore

Olde Gulangyu

(From "In and about Amoy," 1912)

Gulangyu in Foreground, Amoy in Background

Anglo-Chinese College

Gulangyu Beach and Famous

Talmage Memorial

Drum Wave Rock

American Consulate
Japanese Consulate

German Consulate
British Consulate

Gulangyu Mansions

Pioneering Women's Education

(From Johnston, 1907)

"Pigtails"

Schoolgirls Marching

Amoy Women's School

Amoy Women's Worker Conference, 1898

(From MacGowan, 1914)

Fishing Boats

Fortune Teller

Chinese Lady at Home

Schoolgirls

Selling Pears

View of Amoy from Gulangyu

(From MacGowan, 1912)

"Collaring" Criminals

Bridal Procession

Chinese Actors

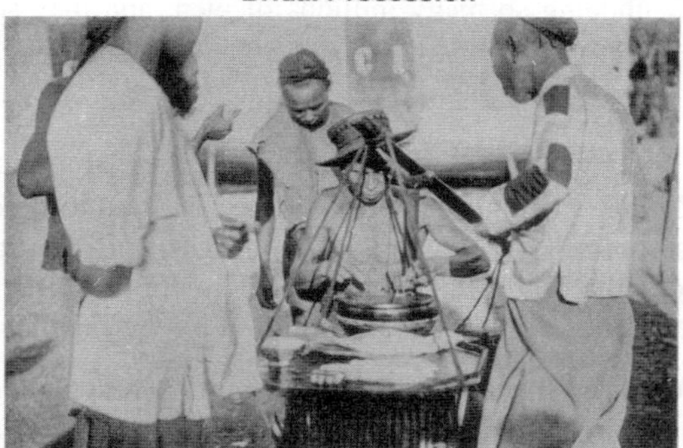

Streetside Chef

A Sea of Sanpans

Chapter 2
Koxinga, Last Defender of the Ming Dynasty

"Koxinga, nourishing the same implacable hatred against the Tartars, proclaimed himself chief of the dispersed Chinese and gathered large forces around him, with which, as well on land as on sea, he greatly harassed the enemy and conquered towns and villages; he performed such gallant deeds of warfare that the Tartars, who had conquered the whole of China, had more work in trying to exterminate the sole Koxinga than they had experienced in subduing so many millions of men, and they soon had to acknowledge that they were unable to consolidate their position." (Neglected Formosa, p.1,2)

The massive granite statue greeting ships in Xiamen harbor is of Koxinga (Zheng Chenggong, 郑成功), the last hero to defend the Ming from the Manchu usurpers. From Gulangyu's Sunlight Rock he trained troops to liberate Taiwan from the Dutch, and has been worshipped ever since not only by Chinese on both sides of the Taiwan Strait but by the Japanese as well.

"Made in Japan" Chinese Legend Koxinga (1624-1662) was born in Japan, the son of Chinese pirate Zheng Zhilong and a Japanese maiden of the Tagawa clan. Koxinga's exploits were so great that 18th century plays about Koxinga were as popular in Japan as Shakespearean plays were in Europe. Even today, Japanese legends claim that on the night of Koxinga's birth, the skies were ablaze with shooting stars, auguring an auspicious future for this product of an early Sino-Japanese joint venture.

Like all good fathers, Zheng Zhilong wanted his son to have what he himself had lacked as a youth—namely, lots of homework. He sent 7-year-old Koxinga to study in their ancestral home of Nan'an (an hour's drive north of Xiamen). While Koxinga excelled as a scholar, he learned too soon that the pen is not always mightier than the sword.

After a peasant army overthrew the Ming dynasty, the Manchus waltzed into the power vacuum and created the Qing Dynasty. The Han put up a futile fight, and after a defeat in Fuzhou in 1646, Koxinga's mother committed suicide and his opportunistic father capitulated. Confucian filial piety demanded Koxinga follow his father's lead, but he remained loyal to the Ming.

第二章

郑成功
——最后一位明朝的保卫者

“郑成功，自称是养着一批被驱逐的痛恨鞑靼人的中国人的首领。在他周围聚集着强大的军事力量，他带着军队，无论海陆、光复城乡，令敌人头痛不已。他领导了如此英勇的斗争，使得占领整个中国的鞑靼人不得不承认，消灭一个郑成功比征服上百万人还要难，也使得他们承认无法牢固其统治地位。”（《被忽略的福摩萨》第 1，2 页）

船驶进厦门港，迎面就是最后一个反清复明的英雄——郑成功的巨大的花岗岩雕像。在鼓浪屿最高处日光岩训练完部队后，他从荷兰人手中光复台湾，被海峡两岸的中国人乃至日本人所敬仰……

郑成功夫妇坐像 Koxinga and Wife

“日本出生”中国神话

郑成功（1624-1662）出生于日本，父亲是中国人郑芝龙，母亲来自日本的田川家族。郑成功从小受到相当好的栽培。在 18 世纪的日本，上演关于他人生故事的戏剧受欢迎程度堪与西方上演莎士比亚剧媲美。甚至在当今日本还流传着这样的神话，在郑成功诞生的夜里，天空被流星照得雪亮，预示着这场早期中日婚姻的后代将拥有灿烂的将来。

像所有的好父亲一样，郑芝龙想让儿子弥补自己年少时的缺陷——书读得太少了。他把七岁的郑成功送回家乡南安（离厦门一小时的车程），读书时郑成功就已出类拔萃 [illegible] 认识到有时候笔不比剑轻。

在农民军推翻明朝后 [illegible] 补权力真空，建立了清朝。汉族历经一系列徒劳抵抗后，[illegible] 役战败。郑成功的母亲自杀，他那机会主义的父亲投降 [illegible] 统孝道要求郑服从父亲的领导，但他却继续保持对明朝 [illegible]

Koxinga burned his scholarly Confucian robes, donned armor, and took up the cry "Remember the Ming!" (Siming! 思明!)

Retaking Taiwan On April 21, 1661, Koxinga crossed the Taiwan Strait with 25,000 men and hundreds of war junks to wrest Taiwan from the Dutch. The shrewd strategist had waited until the end of the north monsoon so that Dutch sailing ships could not send warning to colonial authorities in Batavia (now Jakarta).

The Dutch awoke on the misty morning of April 30th to find a "forest of masts upon the sea". They were surprised but not overly alarmed, because they assumed that all Chinese were cowards and would flee like farmers at the first whiff of gunpowder. They paid for this mistake with their lives.

In his fascinating book *Neglected Taiwan*, Frederic Coyett, the last Dutch governor of Taiwan, recounted the fate of the brave but brainless Captain Pedel, who waltzed into the midst of several thousand Chinese warriors with only a couple hundred men:

> "Pedel divided his troops into two companies, positioned them, and called upon them to be brave and to fear not the Chinese enemy, for victory was certain. Captain Pedel was unwaveringly confident, and his bright, hopeful attitude inspired the men, who believed that Chinese had no liking for the smell of powder, or the noise of muskets, and that after the first charge, in which only a few of them might be shot, they would immediately take flight and become completely disorganized.
>
> "Such an event actually happened in the year 1652, when two or three hundred of our soldiers quite overwhelmed and put to flight seven or eight thousand armed Chinese. Since then, the Hollanders regarded the Chinese in Formosa as insignificant and effeminate men, and cowardly in warfare. It was reckoned that twenty-five Chinese were not the equal of one Dutch soldier, and that all Chinese were the same, with no difference between peasants and soldiers; if he was but a native of China, he was a coward with no backbone. This had come to be quite a fixed conclusion with our soldiers, and although they had often heard the tales of Koxinga's brave exploits against the Tartars, proving his soldiers to be anything but cowardly, this did not alter the general opinion. Koxinga had so far only fought the poor, miserable Tartars, but had not yet had opportunity to fight the Netherlanders, who would quickly deal with them and make them laugh on the wrong side of their faces.

他烧掉了传统长袍，套上盔甲，高喊“思明”，继续战斗。

收复台湾

Dutch Ship (Koxinga Memorial)

1661 年 4 月 21 日，郑成功带领 25000 名士兵和上百艘舢板穿越台湾海峡，从荷兰人那里夺回台湾。这位精明的战略家一直待到北风结束，以致荷兰战船无法向殖民总督府巴达维亚（今雅加达）发出警报。

在 4 月 30 日薄雾蒙蒙的早晨，荷兰人醒来发现“海面上森林般密密麻麻的桅杆”，尽管惊讶万分但并没有完全清醒，因为他们一直认为中国人都是懦夫，会在火炮开始后一轰而散，他们为这一谬见付出了生命的代价。

在这本令人沉思的《被忽略的福摩萨》一书中，弗里德里克·揆一，最后一任台湾的荷兰总督，描述了一位有勇无谋的贝德尔上尉的命运，这个上尉只带领几百个人就卷入了与几千中国勇士的战争中。

“贝德尔把他的队伍分成两队，并号召他们表现勇敢不要惧怕中国敌人，因为胜利是理所当然的。贝德尔上尉非常笃定这点，他坚定和自信的态度也激励了他的士兵。他们确信中国人不能闻火药味或是听枪声，只要首次冲锋后，除击中的一些人，其余的将作鸟兽散。

“类似上述的战争的确在 1652 年发生过，当荷兰二三百名战士战胜七八千武装的中国士兵后。从那时起，我们就认为在福摩萨的中国人是无足轻重且娇气的人，在战争中的表现是懦弱胆小的。当时普遍认为二十五个中国人抵不上一个荷兰兵，而且所有中国人都一个样，不管是农民还是士兵，如果他是地道中国人，那他就一定是个没脊梁骨的懦夫。这个偏见是这样根深蒂固，尽管我们也耳闻郑是如何英勇地打败鞑靼人，足见他的士兵绝非懦夫，但这并没有改变成见：郑成功不过就是战胜了那些穷兮兮可怜巴巴的鞑靼人，他根本没机会战胜荷兰人，我们荷兰人会很快对付他们，给以厉害颜色。

"Preoccupied with such thoughts, Captain Pedel said a short prayer and then marched his men in formation straight towards the enemy, which sent 4,000 fully armored men to meet him. When the Chinese saw Pedel had only a couple hundred men, they detached seven or eight hundred soldiers around behind the hill to attack this little Dutch force from the rear.

"Pedel's troops courageously marched in rows of twelve towards the enemy, and when they came near enough, they charged by firing three volleys uniformly. The enemy, not less brave, discharged so great a storm of arrows that they seemed to darken the sky. From both sides a few fell injured, but contrary to expectations, the Chinese did not run away.

"When the Dutch saw that not only did those in front refuse to flee but that they were being attacked from behind as well, they realized they had underestimated their enemy. Fear now replaced the great courage they'd felt before battle, and many threw down their weapons without firing a shot at the enemy. Indeed, they took to their heels, with shameful haste, leaving their brave comrades and valiant Captain in the lurch. Pedel saw the folly in trying to stand against such overwhelming numbers and wanted his troops to retreat in good order, but his soldiers would not listen. Fear had the upper-hand, and life was dear to them; each therefore sought to save himself. The Chinese saw the disorder and attacked still more vigorously, cutting down all before them. They gave no quarter, but went on until the Captain with one hundred and eighteen of his army were slain on the field of battle, as a penalty for making light of the enemy."

Outstretched Necks It was a sore lesson, and as the siege dragged on, Koxinga rubbed salt in the wound by reminding Governor Coyett:

> "On land you saw how the pride of Captain Pedel was so much humbled that he with his men, who are as foolish as himself, could not even bear the look of my men; and how, on the mere sight of my warriors, they threw down their arms and willingly awaited their well-deserved punishment with outstretched necks. Are these not sufficient proofs of your incompetency and inability to resist my forces?"

Koxinga again urged the Dutch to accept their fate:

> "You Hollanders are conceited and senseless people; you will make yourselves unworthy of the mercy which I now offer; you will subject yourselves to the highest punishment by proudly opposing the great force I have brought with the mere handful of men which I am told you have in your Castle; you will obstinately persevere in this.
>
> "Do you not wish to be wiser? Let your losses at least teach you, that your power here cannot be compared to a thousandth part of mine.
>
> "…if you still persist in refusing to listen to reason and decline to do my bidding, and if you wish deliberately to rush to your ruin, then I will shortly, in your presence, order your Castle to be stormed. (Here he pointed with one hand towards Fort Provintia.)

"带着如此偏见，贝德尔上尉做了一个简短的祈祷，就命令他的士兵们朝着敌人勇往直前，那里有 4000 名全副武装的中国士兵。当中国人看到贝德尔只有几百人时，他们从主干部队分出七八百号人，从山的背后包抄并从后袭击了这撮荷兰人。

"贝德尔的部队站成 12 人一列向敌人挺进，当他们走得足够近时，他们一次就开了三炮。但是敌人，不但是勇敢的，还发射了那么多箭，黑压压地铺满了天空。虽说两翼都有士兵受伤倒下，出乎意料，他们并没有逃走。

"当看到不仅正面的敌军不能击溃，背后也遭到敌军袭击时，荷兰人这才意识到他们低估了对手。此时，荷兰人战前英勇的气概已消失了，取而代之的是内心的恐惧。许多士兵一枪未发就落荒而逃。实际上，他们已顾不上体面、接二连三地逃离勇敢的战友，背叛了英勇的上尉。贝德尔曾试图阻止这种大范围溃败，让军队能有秩序地撤退。他的努力被证明是愚蠢的，没有士兵遵从命令，因为恐惧已占了上风，生命对每个人都珍贵，每个士兵都想活命。中国人看到敌方溃不成军，战斗得愈发英勇，他们对敌人杀无赦，直到上尉和他的 118 名士兵全部战死。这就是荷兰人轻敌的下场。"

任人宰割　这是一个惨痛的教训。随着对敌围困的持续，郑成功步步紧逼，提醒总督揆一：

"你看，在陆地上骄傲的贝德尔上尉是多么的卑微。他和他的军队一样的蠢，我们不屑一顾。至少在我的勇士们看来，他们是放下武器，伸出脖子，等待罪有应得的惩罚。这些难道还不足以证明你们无能又无法与我抗衡吗？"

郑成功再次要求荷兰人投降

"你们荷兰人既自负又迟钝，你们不配同情。如果你们以仅有的少数人（我被告知你们的城堡里人数已经不多）愚顽抵抗我大军，你们将会遭到最严厉的惩罚。还要顽固抵抗吗，不想放聪明点吗？至少让失败教训你们，你们所有的力量加起来还不及我千分之一。

"如果你们仍然不听我们的劝说、拒绝我的命令，如果要自取灭亡，那么，我将很快当你们的面下令进攻（说到这儿，他手指要塞赤嵌城）。

"My smart boys will attack it, conquer it, and demolish it in such a way, that not one stone will remain standing. If I wish to set my forces to work, then I am able to move Heaven and Earth; wherever I go, I am destined to win. Therefore take warning, and think the matter well over."

Surrender On January 27, 1662, the Dutch surrendered their prize of 38 years. Chinese on both sides of the strait rejoiced, and Koxinga's men kicked back and played the "Mooncake Gambling Game", which Koxinga's associate invented to keep his homesick troops occupied, and which is played even today during Mid-Autumn Festival (read more under "Festivals"). But patriotism had taken a toll on Koxinga's health, for as one Chinese historian put it, he died five months later on June 23 of "overwork". May it be a lesson to us all.

In 1683, the Qing government merged Taiwan and Xiamen into one prefecture, "Tai Xia Dao", and though later they were again divided into two administrative areas, Xiamen and Taiwan have ever since enjoyed very close ties, since 80% of Taiwanese come from Fujian, and both sides are linked by reverence for Koxinga, China's great Made in Japan Hero.

The Koxinga Statue (郑成功塑像) towers 41.2 meters above the sea from its lofty perch upon Fuding (覆鼎岩) Rock, in Gulangyu's Bright Moon Garden (Haoyue Yuan, 皓月园). The garden was named after a poem by Koxinga inscribed upon a Gulangyu rock. "I miss you so much I can't sleep, while moonlight seeps through the curtains." (Sounds like MTV lyrics, or a Cantonese pop song).

Professor Shi Yi (时宜), from Beijing's Central Fine Arts College, spent 3 ½ years researching and building her 15.7 meter, 1,617 ton masterpiece, which consists of 625 blocks of granite. Locals claim the statue protects Xiamen from typhoons but after the disastrous storm of October, 1999 wreaked havoc on our beautiful island, I asked a friend, "Where was Koxinga when we needed him?"

"Koxinga was on a trip to Taiwan" he replied.

“我锐兵将攻破城堡，占领粉碎你们。如果我的军队进攻，他们将无坚不摧；不管进攻哪里，一定大胜而归。因此，听听我的忠告，仔细掂量一下吧！”

投降　1662 年 1 月 27 日，荷兰人投降了，交出了他们占领 38 年的殖民地。海峡两岸的中国人沸腾了，郑成功率领军队凯旋而归。但爱国也使郑成功付出了健康的代价，5 个月后的 6 月 23 日，他去世了。中国的一位历史学家指出郑成功是卒于过劳死，或许我们也该吸取教训。

1683 年，清政府把台湾和厦门合为一个行政区，称“台厦道”。尽管后来它们又被分为两个行政区，从那以后厦门和台湾的关系一直非常密切，因为 80%的台湾人来自福建，而且两地居民因共同尊奉中国民族英雄郑成功而紧密相连。

郑成功石雕像　雕像位于皓月园内，坐落在高耸的覆鼎岩之上，高出海平面 41.2 米。皓月园这个名字源自郑成功刻在鼓浪屿岩石上的一首诗，诗文如下：“思君寝不寐，皓月透素帷。”（听起来像是 MTV 里的抒情诗，或是广东的流行歌曲）

这座高达 16.2 米，重达 1617 吨的花岗岩雕像由 625 块花岗岩组成，是来自北京中央美术学院的时宜教授经过长达三年半的时间进行调研并建造而成的杰作。当地的居民感激地说它可以保护厦门风平浪静。在 1999 年 10 月台风肆虐我们美丽的厦门岛之后，我问一个朋友，“当我们需要他的时候，郑成功哪里去了？”

“郑成功去台湾出差了”他诙谐地说。

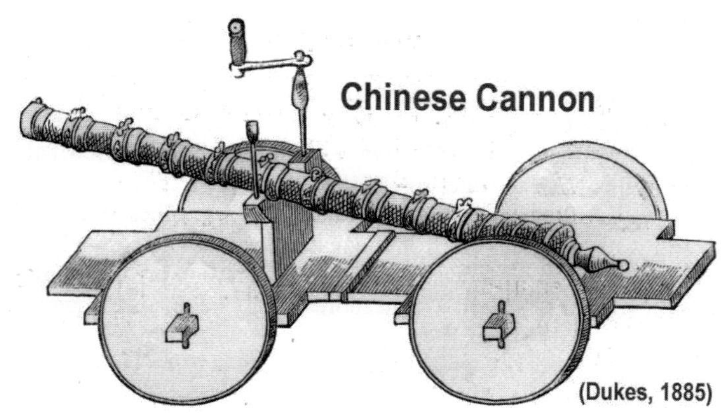

Koxinga Legends on Taiwan and Gulangyu

Xiamen has long been cozy with Taiwan, which for centuries was our "granary" because our island lacked enough arable land for its burgeoning population of merchants and traders. Both sides of the Strait are also united in their devotion to the "Sage King." Taiwan has 63 temples to Koxinga, and countless Koxinga legends and customs, most concerning food (not surprising, since Chinese are adept at both cooking and eating).

The Fairy Cave in Keelung City (基隆市) gushed endless rice to feed Koxinga's army. Alas, the lazy soldiers must have gone against the grain when they dug deeper into the cave because the flow of rice ceased.

Koxinga Fish Koxinga allegedly enjoyed certain kinds of fish and snails, which Taiwanese now call "Koxinga-Fish" (Guoxing Yu, 国姓鱼) and Koxinga-Snails" (Guoxing Wo, 国姓蜗).

Miraculous Sword Well on Anvil Hill (铁砧山剑井) When Koxinga's thirsty army passed through Taizhong's Dajia Town （台中，大甲), the Sage King pierced the earth with his sword tip and sweet water gushed forth. But Gulangyu also has its own miraculous "Koxinga Well"…

Gulangyu's Koxinga Well, in Yanping Park (Yanping Gongyuan, 延平公园) has supposedly produced sweet water for over three centuries, even though it lies so close to Gulangyu's Gangzihou Beach and the sea.

It is said that Koxinga's soldiers were digging the well when they encountered a stone at 3 meters, and plopped down on the ground, discouraged and exhausted.

Koxinga dropped by to see how the well was coming along. When he heard the hard news, he crawled into the hole to examine the well closely, and discovered the sandy soil was moist. "You're discouraged because of the stone," he said, "but in fact there is water just beneath it!"

As soon as Koxinga shook the sand from his robes, he heard a trickling sound, and water bubbled out from beneath the stone. Koxinga leaped out of the well, which brimmed with sweet water, and from that day until now people have marveled at Koxinga's Well. (Read more in the "Festivals & Legends" chapter)

台湾和鼓浪屿的郑成功传说

厦门一直以来和台湾关系密切，因为我们岛上没有足够的耕地承载大量涌入的商人，台湾几百年来一直是我们的谷仓。海峡两岸也因供奉同一“贤王”而紧紧联系在一起。台湾有 63 座供奉郑成功的庙宇和数不清的关于郑成功的传说及习俗，其中大部分和食品有关。这也不奇怪，因为中国人既擅烹煮又擅美食。

基隆市仙人洞 涌出了无数粮食使郑成功军队的粮草得到保证。唉，懒惰的士兵在向洞内深处挖的时候一定触犯了仙灵，因为现在仙人洞已经不涌粮食出来了。

国姓鱼　据说郑成功曾经喜欢好几种鱼和蜗牛，现在台湾人把那些鱼和蜗牛叫做国姓鱼和国姓蜗。

铁砧山剑井　当郑成功饥渴的军队经过台中大甲镇时，郑成功用剑尖戳地，顿时甘泉从地下喷涌而出。而鼓浪屿也有神奇的“国姓井”……

鼓浪屿国姓井，位于延平公园。虽然非常接近港仔后海滨浴场和大海，按照推测它已经不间断地喷涌甘泉 300 多年了。

据说，郑成功的士兵挖井时，挖到 3 米深遇到巨石。士兵们垂头丧气，筋疲力尽倒在地上。

郑成功正好过来视察水井的挖掘情况。当他得知遇到巨石，亲自爬进坑里仔细查看井壁，结果发现沙土有点潮湿。“你们因为巨石而气馁”，他说，“但是实际上水就在石头下！”

郑成功刚抖落衣服上的尘土，就听到一声清脆的响声，随后水潺潺地从石头底下涌出。郑成功从井里跳出来，水跟着就溢出来。直到今天，人们还对国姓井啧啧称奇。

在节假日和传说那一章，你将可以了解更多。

Koxinga's Well

Supplement
Frederic Coyett, Last Dutch Governor of Taiwan

Bill (left) as Governor Frederic Coyett

When I acted as Dutch Governor Frederic Coyett in a TV mini-series, and surrendered on bended knee to Koxinga, I wondered how the real Coyett would have felt—and now I know! After a long search I bought from a bookseller in Holland a rare English translation of Coyett's book *Neglected Formosa.*

Holland sentenced Coyett to death (transmuted to life imprisonment) for losing Taiwan to Koxinga, but Coyett put the blame where it was due by writing the "true story describing how, through neglect of the Dutch authorities in the East Indies, the Island of Formosa has been invaded, subdued, and conquered Koxinga."[1]

Governor Coyett, the son of a noble Swedish family in Stockholm, wrote *Neglected Formosa* to prove that Dutch officials had ignored warnings about a Chinese invasion since as early as 1646. He cited, for example, this letter from the Batavia Council to Governor Verburg on 25 July, 1652:

> "…numerous rumours are now current in China concerning the son of I-quan called Koxin, who, pressed hard by the Tartars, can no longer hold out in China, nor find himself safe there. He has therefore gone to sea with a great force, and adopted a course of piracy, intending to keep an eye on Formosa, with the view of ultimately settling down in that territory… we think it best to acquaint Your Honour with these reports, so that you may continue your preparations for defence and be constantly on your guard."

In March 10, 1654, Formosan governor Cornelis Caesar confessed that the threat of an invasion by Koxinga made "his hairs stand on end." Coyett wrote,

> "But, if in 1653 this man's hair already stood on end on account of the threats of a handful of harmless peasants, how would he have behaved had he been a governor of Formosa in 1661, when Koxinga, with all these and many more peasants, besides 25,000 well armed and intrepid soldiers hardened in warfare, invaded Formosa. Most probably his hair would not only have turned white overnight, but his heart would have sunk into his boots…"

---

1 "Neglected Formosa," by Inez de Beachair; translation from the Dutch of Coyett's *'t Verwaerloosde Formosa* (Amsterdam, 1675), Chinese Materials Center, Inc. S.F., 1975

附录

弗里德里克·揆一 ——台湾末任荷兰总督

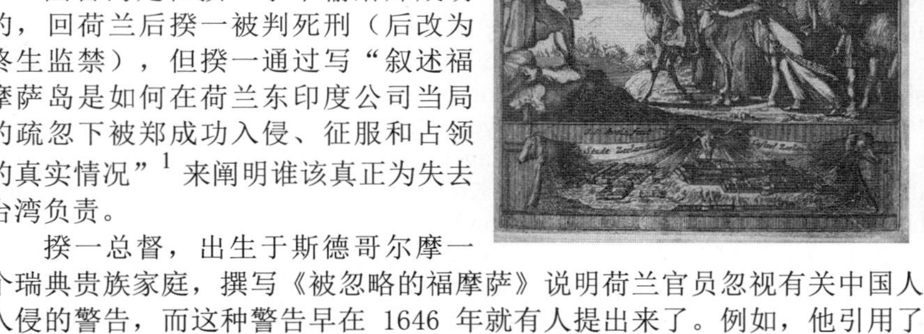

当年我曾在一部电视系列短剧中扮演揆一，屈膝向郑成功投降，我当时就想揆一当初究竟在想什么。现在我明白了！经过长时间的搜寻，我终于从一个荷兰书商手中买到一本十分珍贵的书，是揆一撰写的《被忽略的福摩萨》的英文译本。

因台湾是在揆一手中输给郑成功的，回荷兰后揆一被判死刑（后改为终生监禁），但揆一通过写“叙述福摩萨岛是如何在荷兰东印度公司当局的疏忽下被郑成功入侵、征服和占领的真实情况”[1] 来阐明谁该真正为失去台湾负责。

揆一总督，出生于斯德哥尔摩一个瑞典贵族家庭，撰写《被忽略的福摩萨》说明荷兰官员忽视有关中国人入侵的警告，而这种警告早在 1646 年就有人提出来了。例如，他引用了一封 1652 年 7 月 25 日由巴达维亚参议会写给总督费尔博格的信。信的原文如下：

“现在中国有很多关于田川氏的儿子郑成功的传言，说他在鞑靼人的高压下很难在中国立住脚，也觉得不安全。因而他率领一支军队到海上当海盗，还开始关注福摩萨岛，以图最终在这片土地上落脚……我们认为最好还是把这事通告尊敬的总督，这样您可以继续积极准备防御并随时保持警惕。”

1654 年 3 月 10 日，台湾总督凯塞尔承认郑成功入侵可能带来的威胁使他毛发竖立。揆一写道：

“但是如果这家伙在 1653 年因为一小撮没有威胁的暴民叛乱就吓得毛发直竖，那么要是在 1661 年郑成功带着更多农民，再加上 25000 多装备精良、英勇善战的士兵降临台湾，他还是台湾总督，他会有什么样的反应呢？恐怕他不仅一夜白头，而且要吓得心脏迸出了……”

---

1 《被忽略的福摩萨》，Inez de Beachair 著，由荷兰揆一的版本（阿姆斯特丹，1675 年版）转译，中国信息中心公司，1975

Coyett repeatedly asked for reinforcements but the Dutch government, fixated with wresting Macao from the Portuguese, accused Coyett of worrying over nothing. When a reinforcement of 12 ships did show up in October, 1660, the Dutch admiral scoffed at the so-called threat. After a bitter argument with Coyett he sailed to Batavia with nine of the twelve ships, badmouthed Coyett, and helped persuade the Dutch to replace Coyett with Clenk as governor.

Even as Clenk was en route to Formosa, the Dutch learned of Koxinga's invasion and sent a ship to return Clenk and inform Coyett that he was now Governor again. But Clenk never got the message, and when he saw the state of affairs in Formosa, he fled for Japan, leaving Coyett to fend for himself.

Koxinga demanded that Coyett surrender within 24 hours, but Coyett refused, even though he was hopelessly outnumbered and had no hope of reinforcement. Koxinga found he could not easily breach the castle's defenses, so he settled in for a long siege, figuring to eventually starve them out.

Months later, a pitifully small relief force of ten ships and 700 Dutch soldiers showed up, and the Manchu governor-general of Fujian and Zhejiang also offered to help fight Koxinga—but Coyett's hopes were dashed yet again. Coyett entrusted a Dutch admiral with messages and gifts for the Fujian governor, but the cowardly admiral panicked after Koxinga destroyed a few of his ships, and he fled home. Coyett was now truly on his own, against impossible odds.

In January, 1662, after months of bravely holding out against Koxinga's siege, the Dutch surrendered. Koxinga, perhaps in recognition of Coyett's futile but brave stand, allowed his enemies to leave on their own ships, sailing under their Dutch flag. But Coyett's own countrymen were not as merciful as his adversary. Although Coyett was the only Dutch leader to show foresight, integrity and courage, Holland sentenced Coyett to death for his "failure."

Fortunately, Coyett's meticulous records, and his collection of journals and letters, proved the truth of the matter. After 9 years of exile he returned home with honor to write "Neglected Formosa", which gives fascinating and often humorous insights into two great adversaries—Koxinga and Coyett.

Excerpts from Coyett's "Neglected Formosa"

Coyett describes Koxinga's troops: "He [Koxinga] had constructed no trenches nor erected any batteries, although he was well acquainted with the modes of warfare, and amply provided with heavy guns, as was proved during a later stage of the war. He evidently thought the Fort could be captured without any such trouble.

"The enemy's soldiers used various kinds of weapons. Some were armed with bows and arrows hanging down their backs; others had nothing save a shield on the left arm, and a good sword in the right hand; while many wielded with both hands a formidable battle-sword fixed to a stick half the length of a man. Every one was protected over the upper part of the body with a coat of iron scales, fitting below one another like the slates of a roof, the arms and legs being left bare.

揆一再三要求增援，但是荷兰政府正忙着从葡萄牙手中抢夺澳门，指责揆一杞人忧天。而 1660 年 10 月，当增援的 12 艘战舰真的来了，而荷兰舰队司令又蔑视所谓的威胁。在和揆一进行艰难谈判后，他率领其中 9 艘战舰到巴达维亚，他还说揆一坏话，并说服荷兰政府用克朗克取代揆一任台湾总督。

正当克朗克前往台湾就任时，荷兰政府得到郑成功入侵台湾的消息，当即派船前往召回克朗克并再次让揆一担任总督。但是克朗克没有接到通知，而当看到台湾战势时，他就逃到日本，让揆一自生自灭。

郑成功命令揆一在 24 小时内投降，但是尽管郑的人数远远超过他，而且增援无望，揆一仍然拒绝投降。当郑成功发现突破城堡的防守比较困难时，他采用长时间围困的战略，他知道最终他们会因为断粮而屈服。

数月后，少得可怜的救援兵力前来解救揆一，只有 10 艘战舰，700 名荷兰士兵。与此同时满清政府闽浙总督也愿意为打败郑成功提供援助。但揆一的希望又一次破灭了，他委托荷兰舰队司令带信和礼品给福建总督。但在郑成功摧毁他几艘战舰后，怕死的司令自己逃回荷兰。揆一这一次真的只有靠自己，毫无胜算。

1662 年 1 月，在英勇地抵抗郑成功包围数月后，荷兰人决定投降。或许，郑成功尊重揆一英勇但无用的抵抗，他允许敌人坐自己的船，悬挂荷兰国旗离开。但是揆一的同胞却不像他的对手那样仁慈。尽管揆一是唯一具有远见、正直和英勇的荷兰领导人，荷兰政府却因为他失败而判他死刑。

幸运的是，揆一小心翼翼收藏的档案，以及日记和信件证明了事情的真相。在被流放 9 年后，他带着荣耀回到家乡，并着手写《被忽略的福摩萨》。这本书引人入胜并不乏幽默地剖析了揆一和郑成功这对伟大的对手。

揆一《被忽略的福摩萨》节选

揆一眼中的郑成功军队

“他(郑成功)没有构筑战壕，也没有架设任何大炮，尽管他非常了解战争模式,而且拥有充足的重型武器装备，这一点在后来的战斗中得到证实。很显然，他认为将不费任何周折而夺取城堡。

“敌人的士兵使用各种各样的武器。一些士兵背上挎着弓和箭；另外一些除了左臂一块盾牌、右手一把利剑外什么都没有；而许多士兵双手都挥动着令人生畏的战剑，剑足足有半人长。每个士兵的上身都穿一件铁甲来护身，就像屋顶的瓦片环环相扣。他们的手臂和大腿是裸露的。

"This afforded complete protection from rifle bullets and yet left ample freedom to move, as those coats only reached down to the knees, and were very flexible at all the joints.

"The archers formed Koxinga's best troops, and much depended on them, for even at a distance they contrived to handle their weapons with so great skill, that they very nearly eclipsed the riflemen.

"Every tenth man of them is a leader, who takes charge of and presses his men on to force themselves into the ranks of the enemy. With bent heads and their bodies hidden behind the shields, they try to break through the opposing ranks with such fury and dauntless courage, **as if each one had still a spare body left at home.** They continually press onwards, notwithstanding many are shot down; not stopping to consider, but ever rushing forward like mad dogs, not even looking round to see whether they are followed by their comrades or not."

Koxinga's Response to Dutch protestations of friendship: "[Holland's friendship] held towards him was of the same nature as that held towards other Indian Potentates and Princes: namely, that from their side, it lasted just so long as there was any advantage to be gained by it; for if they saw it to be to their advantage, no such friendship was observed, but they would not scruple in the least to throw a net over any one's head when it suited them to do so."

Koxinga's view on Taiwan's relation to mainland China: "Hitherto this island [Taiwan] had always belonged to China, and the Dutch had doubtless been permitted to live there, seeing that the Chinese did not require it for themselves; but requiring it now, it was only fair that Dutch strangers, who came from far regions, should give way to the masters of the island....He came not with a view to wage war against the Company (although his men had on several occasions been very unkindly treated by them), but only to take possession of his belongings; and to prove that he had no intention to enrich himself with the Company's means, he would allow them to embark their goods and effects in his own junks, and to break down the Castles and remove the cannon with other materials to Batavia; provided all this were done immediately. In that case, the friendship between him and the Company would remain undisturbed..."

Gulangyu's Koxinga-related tourist sites: Sunlight Rock: Koxinga Memorial Fort Gate, Ancient Fort; Koxinga Granite Statue (Bright Moon Park); Yindou Rock (Folklore chapter); Koxinga's Well (Yanping Park).

“这为防止步枪攻击提供全面的保护，而且能够活动自如。因为那些铠甲只是延伸到膝盖位置，而且每个交接处都非常灵活。

“弓箭手是郑成功最精良的军队，而且是他的主要依靠力量。因为即使在很远的距离，他们也能以娴熟的技术操使武器，这使得我们的步枪手黯然失色。

“每 10 个人中，就有一个队长，队长掌管队伍并促使他的队伍向前，迫使他们向敌人的队伍进逼。他们弯着头，把身体藏在盾牌里，以激烈和不屈的勇气，向对方进攻，像是家里还有一副多余的躯体似的。他们不断地向前进逼，尽管很多人被击毙，他们想都不想，仍然像疯狗一样向前冲，也不向四周看看有没有同伴跟上。”

郑成功对荷兰人所谓友好声明的回应

“[荷兰人的友谊]就像他们对待其他印度当权者和王公贵族一样，即只从他们自身利益出发，只要有利可图，友谊就能维持。如果他们占优势，就不会表现出友谊。但是，如果他们认为合适，会毫不犹豫向任何一个人下手。”

郑成功关于台湾和大陆关系的论述

“然台湾者，早为中国人所经营，中国之土地也……今余既来索，则地当归我。荷兰人毫无疑问只是被允许居住而已，荷兰人，来自遥远地区的外国人，只有把她交还给她的主人，才是公平合理的。他并不是发动与荷兰东印度公司的战争（尽管他的手下曾经多次被他们不友善地对待），而只是想要回属于他的东西。为表明他没打算要用荷兰东印度公司的财产发家致富，他同意他们把自己的东西和财产装到船上，把城堡推倒，把大炮以及其他物资搬运到巴达维亚，如果他们立即搬走的话。那样，他和荷兰东印度公司的友谊将丝毫未损……”

岛上与郑成功相关的景点

日光岩（郑成功纪念馆、龙头山寨、水操台）、郑成功石雕像（皓月园）、印斗石（见民间传说那一章）、国姓井（延平公园内）

Sunlight Rock Sculpture

Chapter 3
Ṣunlight Rock

> "For situation and natural attractions, with its beautiful harbor and grand hills around it, it [Gulangyu] is unsurpassed anywhere along this entire coast. From two hundred to two hundred and fifty foreigners reside here in very comfortable homes... Nature has made it grand and rugged. Almost in its very center is a gigantic pile of rocks grouped in most marvelous shapes and raising their heads three hundred feet in the air. From certain points of observation, the outlines of a camel reclining can be easily seen in this mass of rocks. It is called Camel Rock."
>
> Rev. Pitcher, "In and About Amoy," 1912

Chinese say the 92.7m high Sunlight Rock, known as Dragon Head Hill (Longtou Shan, 龙头山) by Chinese and Camel Rock (Luotuo Shan, 骆驼山) by foreigners, faces Tiger Head Hill across the bay on Xiamen Island, and that the dragon and tiger team up to guard Xiamen Harbor's entrance.

In America, "rolling stones gather no mos," in China, they gather no inscriptions. But Sunlight Rock, like any Chinese rock that sits still long enough, is covered with calligraphic inscriptions—over 80, in fact, the most famous being "Heroic Spirit of South Fujian Sea," a eulogy to Koxinga, Another inscription claims that in 1609 a Ming Dynasty official named Chi Zhifu (池直夫) built a flower and bamboo garden at the foot of Sunlight Rock, and researchers have unearthed Ming Dynasty relics in the area.

Sunlight Rock's oldest carving was inscribed about 400 years ago on a rock near the main gate and reads, "Gulang Dongtian" (鼓浪洞天): "Gulangyu—a Fairyland." The 100-year-old characters to the left read, "Lujiang Diyi" （鹭江第一): "#1 Scenery of the Lujiang River." The horizontal characters, "Tianfeng Haitao" (天风海涛), carved in 1915, suggest that you can hear both roaring wind and raging sea as you climb Sunlight Rock, though all I could hear was my exhausted friend's protests that we should have taken the cable car.

第三章

日光岩

“美丽的港湾与周围环绕的群山，使鼓浪屿在整条海岸线上的地理位置和自然风光无与伦比。大约两百到两百五十名老外在此安居，大自然成就了其大气与粗犷。岛的中心位置是个巨大的岩石堆，各具形态，有的高达 300 英尺，巍然挺立。从某个角度观察，清晰可见诸石构成的形似骆驼斜倚的轮廓线，故称‘骆驼山’。”

选自毕腓力 1912 年著《厦门方志》

中国人说他们把高 92.7 米的日光岩叫做龙头山，而老外称之为骆驼山。它与厦门岛上的虎头山隔岸相对，据说龙虎二山相配，把守着厦门港的入口。

美国人说“滚石不聚苔”，但在中国却是滚石不聚墨。正如中国许多林立的峭石，日光岩上刻有 80 多处碑文。其中最有名的是郑成功的颂文“闽海雄风”。另一处碑文记载着，明朝官员池直夫于 1609 年在日光岩下建造了一个花园，研究人员在此处确也发现了明代遗迹。

日光岩上最古老的一块碑文镌刻于大门边的一块岩石上，距今已有 400 年，上刻“鼓浪洞天”：鼓浪仙境。左边是历经百年的四个大字“鹭江第一”：鹭江第一景。上面是刻于 1915 年的“天风海涛”，意思是说，极目日光岩顶，可以凭风听涛。然而每次我听到的却是筋疲力尽的朋友们抱怨说真该坐缆车上去。

Camel Rock (Pitcher, 1912)

Camel Rock in the 1940s

"The same old baggage carriers were hired and as we ambled along the narrow lanes, a picture of Kulangsu in summer became planted in my mind; an island of contrasts, barely two miles in circumference…after traversing a narrow winding path for a few minutes a new scene unfolded, through green foliage and pink blossoms, of the sea breaking on to stretches of yellow sand with a murmuring leisurely rhythm; birds darting and twittering across the paths of butterflies, veined and striped with bright yellow markings, and watched by the nervous piercing eyes of scampering lizards. A few more minutes and all was obscured by the towering obstacle of a steep hill rising in the centre of the island, and capped with grey black boulders loosely knit and tied together into the shape of a camel's hump and head.

"My new abode was snuggling between Camel Rock and the sea. From the back room, the rock loomed up with frightening and precipitous sheerness. One of the boulders from the camel's hump was perched unsecurely on its side, a standing menace to those opposite should it ever be rocked from its precarious hold. From my front room, the view opened out on to the wide expanse of sea studded with islands, with Quemoy in the distance…."

Neill, 1956, p.58-9

The Fort Gate, one of the islet's most prized sites, is all that remains of Koxinga's fortress. The gate is 74 cm wide by 174 cm high. The largest stones had holes that supported the houses' roof beams.

The Fort Gate of course has its share of classic chiseled inscriptions, such as this poem about Koxinga written by educator Mr. Cai Yuanpei (蔡元培):

Master of wind and waves,
Amidst the cloud of battle calmly commands,
Though he sacrificed his steadfast spirit,
He was upright to the last.

四十年代的骆驼山

“我们雇的还是这位老挑夫，漫步于巷弄之间，夏日的鼓浪屿宛如一幅画卷，深深印入脑海；方圆两英里的小岛充满了强烈的反差……在弯弯曲曲的石板路上徜徉片刻后，一片新的景象便展现在你面前：绿叶红花掩映着一片金黄的海滩，海水一路拍打、浅吟低和着，身上布满明黄条纹的鸟儿在蝴蝶飞舞的小道上唧唧喳喳地穿行，吓得蜥蜴紧张地瞪着眼睛张望。再往前走几分钟所有的景物就被岛中央耸立的一块峭石挡住了。峭石顶部散布着灰黑色的圆石块，看上去很像驼峰和驼首。

“我的新房子依傍在骆驼山和大海间，从后屋看，骆驼山的形状险峻得让人望而生畏，驼峰上的一块圆石摇摇欲坠，好像如果晃动一下不稳的一边，其他各面都很危险。从前屋望过去，大海在小岛的点缀下宽广无垠，远处是金门……”

——Neill 1956 年版 第 58～59 页

龙头山寨 小岛上最具价值的景点之一，即郑成功所建要塞的旧址。门高 1.74 米，宽 0.74 米，带孔的巨石原是兵营顶梁的支撑。

寨门上同样刻有碑文，其中有教育家蔡元培先生为纪念郑成功而写的一首诗：

叱咤天风镇海涛，
指挥若定降云高。
虫沙猿鹤有时尽，
正气觥觥不可淘。

Fort Gate

Koxinga's Command Platform, Through the Fort Gate and to the right is "Wanzai Pavilion" (宛在亭). "Wanzai" infers "heroic spirit yet remains", and from this 15 meter high by 6 meter wide granite outcropping, the great man commanded his troops.

The large engraved characters, "Minghai Xiongfeng," eulogize Koxinga's heroism and determination. The sea is now a good distance from the command platform but in Koxinga's day junks could sail closer to Sunlight Rock.

The Ancient Summer Resort Cave A century ago, the famous Taiwanese poet Shi Shijie (施士洁) painted on the cave's roof "Gu Bi Shu Dong" (古避暑洞): "Ancient Summer Resort Cave." But it isn't really a "resort", per se (if it were, it would be my last resort).

It's not really a cave either, but Chinese apply that appellation loosely to just about any natural configuration that casts a hint of a shadow. This so-called "resort cave" is but a 10 meter enclosure formed by one massive rock leaning against another. But this happy consanguinity afforded centuries of pleasure to Chinese who, lacking television, watched rocks instead (an eminently patient people!), and delighted in naming these rocks after whatever they resembled. The "resort cave's" two stones supposedly resemble "ren" (人), for "people"—though I would not award Mother Nature an "A" in calligraphy.

Mad About Mooncakes My favorite Sunlight Rock sculpture is of Koxinga's soldiers playing the Mooncake Game, which Koxinga's army used to keep homesick troops occupied, and which is played today in South Fujian and Taiwan during the mid-autumn festival.

Our sons Shannon and Matthew used to enjoy the game so much that they played year round for paper "mooncakes".

If you are in Xiamen during Mid-Autumn festival, your Chinese friends will invite you to play, so learn about the game's background and rules in the "Festivals & Legends" chapter (p. 122). For more on Koxinga, read Chapter One, or visit his birthplace and Memorial Hall in Nan'an, an hour north of Xiamen.

郑成功水操台 从要塞正门向右，是郑成功的练兵台，又叫“宛在亭”。“宛在”意指英雄气概长存，在这块距地面 15 米、宽 6 米的断岩上，郑成功操练着他的将士。巨幅雕刻“闽海雄风”颂扬了郑成功的英雄主义和收复台湾的决心。现在海平面距离练兵台相当远，但在郑成功时代，乘平底舢板船便可靠近日光岩。

古避暑洞 一个世纪前，台湾著名诗人施士洁在洞顶刻写了“古避暑洞”几个字。实际上它还算不上是个真正的避暑胜地，如果真算得上，我也不会去。

它也算不上是个洞穴，但中国人习惯于把任何天然的外形似遮蔽之处都称为洞穴，所以这个“避暑洞”只不过是长 10 米、由一块巨石斜倚另一块巨石而形成的一片圈地。几百年来，这片乐土为中国人带来了无尽的欢乐，那时他们没有电视看，只好看石头（中华民族是一个超有耐心的民族！）

中国人还喜欢根据石头的形状命名。“避暑洞”里的两块石头据说形似“人”字，（我可不会用字母“A ”来表示大自然母亲。）

让人痴迷的月饼 日光岩壁刻中我最欣赏的是郑成功将士中秋博饼图，博饼是解战士思乡愁绪的一种游戏，至今闽南和台湾中秋节时仍流传甚广。

我儿子神能和马太特别喜欢博饼游戏，一年到头都为“纸月饼”博得不亦乐乎。

如果在厦门过中秋，中国朋友一定会邀请你去博饼，参阅“节日和传说”一章可以了解一些背景知识和游戏规则。要更多的了解郑成功，还可参阅第一章，或北上距厦门一小时车程的南安参观他的故乡和郑成功纪念馆。

A Sunlight Rock Temple sign says in English, "Clergymen Free". I'm not sure if it refers to Buddhist monks or *Free* Methodists!

Sunlight Rock Temple (Riguangyan Si, 日光岩寺), one of Xiamen's four most important temples during the Ming and Qing Dynasties, was built between 1506 and 1521 and called Lotus Temple (Lianhua 'An, 莲花庵). It was rebuilt in 1596 and renamed Sunlight Rock Temple, and is now dedicated to worship of Guanyin (观音), goddess of mercy (a formerly male deity whom Chinese women changed to female over 1,000 years ago because they felt male deities were unsympathetic to their needs).

Sunlight Rock Temple, which is partially within a cave, is often called "One Tile Roof" (Yipian Wa, 一片瓦) because a large rock forms part of the roof. It is also called a "Pocket Temple" because it encompasses only 2,856m. But though its location, scrunched up within a rock, prevents it from sprawling like other temples, it makes up for size by its exquisite setting, with uniquely Chinese eaves, arches, columns, and glazed colored tiles. The neighboring European architecture only reinforces the essential Chineseness of this pocket-temple. And I am told that this is China's only temple in which the Buddha Hall (大雄宝殿) and Maitreya (Milefuo) Hall are face to face. There was also a Xu Booth (旭亭) built between 1723 and 1735, but all that remains is a cliff inscription.

Abbot Liuzhan （六湛法师） administered Sunlight temple from 1851 to 1872, and built Yuanmin Palace (圆明殿). Yuanmin Palace was replaced in 1854 with the 'Study Buddha Hall' (Nianfo Tang, 念佛堂). After a fire damaged the hall in 1960, Abbott Zhengguo （正果法师） asked for donations from his master Shanqi (善契法师) in the Philippines. The Biguang building, Gongde Hall（功德堂), Zu Hall (祖堂) were removed and the dorms were rebuilt. Gulangyu Electric Works took over the temple during the Cultural Revolution but returned it in 1983, and the temple got a two million Yuan facelift after Xiamen became a Special Economic Zone.

日光岩寺有块“神职人员免费”的英文示牌，不知道它指的是佛教徒还是指卫理教徒。

日光岩寺 始建于 1506—1521 年间的日光岩寺（时称莲花庵），是厦门明清时四大名寺之一，1596 年重修后更名为日光岩寺，现用于祭拜观音菩萨。观音最初是男神，1000 年前女信徒们把他改为女神（因为他们觉得男观音对于女性心愿缺乏真正怜悯之情。）

日光岩寺俗称“一片瓦”，因为寺庙部分掩身于洞穴中，寺顶覆盖着一大块巨岩。由于方圆只有 2856 平方米，日光岩寺又叫“口袋寺”。尽管蜿蜒的碎石小道使日光岩寺不能像其他寺庙一样宽阔延伸，但精美的装饰，传统的雕梁画栋仍然异彩流光，周围的西式建筑，更加突出了口袋寺的中国味。据说，这是中国唯一一座大雄宝殿和弥勒佛面对面的寺庙。以前这里还有一座旭亭，建于 1723-1735 年间的旭亭，现在只残留了一处崖刻。

1851-1872 年主持日光岩寺的六湛法师修建了圆明殿。1854 年圆明殿改为念佛堂，1960 年毁于一场大火。为此正果法师向他旅居菲律宾的师父善契法师求助。闭关楼、功德堂、祖堂被迁走，建起了佛舍。“文革”时鼓浪屿电容器厂接管了寺庙，但于 1983 年归还。厦门成为经济特区后政府拨款 200 万元，用于寺庙的修缮。

Hongyi—Master of the Law

Abbott Qingzhi (清智法师) arrived in 1912, rebuilt Sanbao Palace（三宝殿，now called, 大雄宝殿）, and in early 1936 welcomed the famous monk and "Master of the Law", Hongyi (弘一法师）by building the 30 m^2 apartment Sunlight Villa （日光别墅). Hongyi lived and worked for about 8 months in what was then called Biguang Building (闭关楼). There is now a modest memorial hall to the Buddhist holy man.

Master Hongyi (originally named Li Zhutong) was born in 1880 to a wealthy Tianjin family. When he was 19 he enrolled in Shanghai's Nan yang Public School and while there he started the Shanghai Painting and Calligraphy Society.

In 1905 Hongyi went to study music and the arts in Tokyo, where he formed the Chun Liu Drama Society, which was the first Chinese drama group to perform Western works such as Camille.

After graduating in 1910 Li returned to China and worked for two years as a newspaper and magazine editor before he taught painting and music in Zhangzhou and Nanjing, where he was the first Chinese to teach Western music (most first generation modern Chinese musicians were his students). He also created a stir by being the first Chinese artist to use nude models.

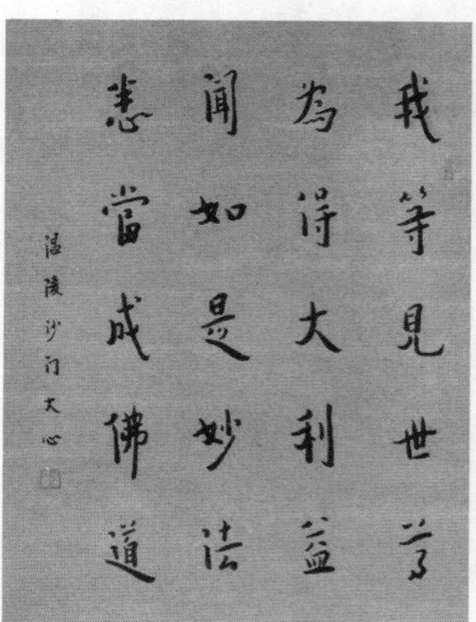

In 1916, Li experienced a spiritual transformation after a 17-day fast in Zhangzhou, and in 1918, the 39-year-old artist became a Buddhist monk in the Zhangzhou Hua Temple under the master Liao. Hongyi gave up the arts that had fascinated him since childhood—except for calligraphy and the painting of Buddhist works of art.

Fortunately, these did not require nude models, for otherwise how could he have painted Guanyin, who started out as a man?)

One of Master Honey's most unusual works was an 11-meter calligraphic scroll on which he teaches about "entering" and "leaving" the world.

弘一法师

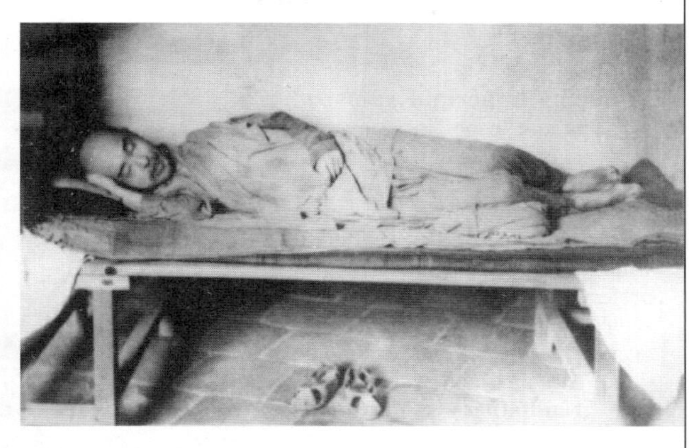

清智法师1912年重修了三宝殿（现在的大雄宝殿），1936年初为迎接高僧弘一法师，建了一座30平方米的日光别墅。弘一法师在这座当时叫闭关楼的别墅居住修行了约8个月。至今还有一方纪念这位佛教高僧的简朴厅堂。

弘一大师原名李叔同，1880年生于天津一富贵人家。19岁时考入上海南洋公学并始创上海书画社。

1905年弘一远赴东京学习音乐艺术，他组织了春柳剧社，成为第一个上演《茶花女》等西方剧作的中国社团。

1910年毕业回国后，李叔同做了两年的报刊编辑，之后在杭州、南京教授绘画、音乐，成为教授西方音乐的第一人（中国第一代现代音乐家中有许多是他的学生）。他还是用尼姑作模特的第一人并引起轰动。

1916年经过在杭州17天的斋戒，李叔同经历了一次大的精神转变。1918年，这位39岁的艺术家在杭州虎跑寺出家为僧，师从了无大师。弘一放弃了自幼热爱的艺术，但仍然练习书法和佛教画作（幸好佛教画作不需要尼姑模特，不然他怎么画观音像，观音开始可是男神啊？）

弘一大师最有名的杰作之一是一幅长达11米的书法作品，他在书卷中传授了“出世、入世”的道理。

Chapter 4
Pioneering Modern Education

Lifelong Imperial Exams

(Dukes, 1885)

"Failure to obtain a coveted prize never baffles or discourages the indefatigable competitor. In some cases the contest continues a lifetime with the prize never won. For example, at a single prefecture 10,000 candidates presented themselves, under the old regime, at the regular examination. **Among them were found the grandfathers, sons, and grandsons, all competing for the same prize**, i.e., the same degree. In 1889 the Governor General of Fukien reported that at the autumnal examination in Foochow there were nine candidates over eighty, and one over ninety years old. At still another, thirty five competitors were over eighty and eighteen over ninety. Such indomitable perseverance along educational lines...has been seldom witnessed outside of China. If ever her educational methods conform to Western ideas...Chinese scholarship is destined to take first rank.

Rev. Philip Wilson Pitcher, "In and about Amoy," 1912, p.84

For 1,500 years, Chinese scholars prepared for government office by memorizing Confucian classics and composing literary treatises and couplets. But eventually Chinese realized that survival on our shrinking planet required revamping the 1500-year-old Confucian system that churned out what Chairman Mao called "scholar bureaucrats". And few places had greater impact on modern Chinese education than the tiny islet of Gulangyu.

Confucius (Werner, 1922)

第四章

鼓 浪 屿

——中国现代教育的摇篮

科考一生

“对于不屈不挠的应试者，科考的落榜不会令他垂头丧气或心灰意冷，有时连续拼搏了一辈子却还不能及第。**举个例子，在参加定期会考的 10000 名贡生中，就可以找到祖父、儿子和孙子同为考取同一官衔或同一阶位而来。**1889 年，福建总督报告说，在福州的秋季考试中，有九名考生年过八十，还有一位年逾九旬。还有一次，三十五名应试者年过八十，十八名年逾九旬。如此面对逆境百折不挠、坚持不懈作鲤鱼跃龙门式的冲击……除中国以外是难得一见的。假如中国的教育方法顺应西方的理念……中国的学识水平定然是一流的。” 毕腓力 1912, p. 84

整整 1500 年，中国的学者为了功名而背诵儒家经典文篇、创作策论和对联。然而，随着世界各国趋于融合，中国领导人最终看到，滋生出被毛主席称之为“士大夫”而沿袭了 1500 年的儒家教育体系必须革新了。小小的鼓浪屿对中国现代教育的影响是其他地方难以相比的。

Students' Cells **Dukes (1885)**

Anglo-Chinese College, Kolongsu

Gulangyu has produced not only dozens of famous musicians but also internationally famous folks like the writer "Lin Yutang" (林语堂), the artist Teng Hiok Chiu (Zhou Tingxu, 周廷旭), the astronomer Yu Qingsong (余青松, 1897-1978), and China's first modern sports coach and athletics pioneer John Ma (马约翰). Gulangyu's trailblazing in women's education helped birth talents like pioneering obstetrician Madame Lin Qiaozhi.

Educational reform began with 19th century Protestant missionaries on Gulangyu, who opened about 20 different schools—everything from China's first kindergartens to vocational schools and colleges. Gulangyu hosted one of China's first day-schools, started in 1845 by Rev. Lyman Burt Peet (弼来满). William Young (养为霖) opened Fujian's 1st school for girls about the same time.

The London Missionary Society (伦敦差会) established Fujian's first seminary, "Holy College" (圣道学院), and Gulangyu's first primary and middle school, "Fumin Primary School"[1] (福民小学) and "Chengbi Middle School" (澄碧中学). While Chinese schools' materials were edited and published by the Chinese Educational Bureau, Christian schools wrote their own materials. The American Reformed Mission's (美国归正教) popular "3 Character Christian Primer" suggested their primary goal was evangelism, not education, but even Chinese officials admitted these programs helped revitalize Chinese education.

Gulangyu Huaide Kindergarten (鼓浪屿怀德幼儿园), the first in China, was built in early 1898 at the site of present-day Sunlight Kindergarten (Riguang You'er Yuan, 日光幼儿园). Two middle schools opened on Gulangyu in 1881 were joined in 1907 to form the Yinghua School of the three Missions.[2]

[1] John Ma (马约翰), China's pioneer in modern sports, was a Fuming alumnus

[2] Gulangyu's Christian missions were virtually unique in China in their close cooperation in evangelism, church building, and education—often in the face of stiff opposition by denominational leaders in their home countries. Their example set the stage for indigenous Chinese churches' rejection of denominational molds.

鼓浪屿不仅培养出了几十位知名的音乐家，也造就了其他蜚声海外的人才，如作家林语堂、艺术家周廷旭、天文学家余青松（1897-1978）以及中国的第一位现代运动教练和体育先驱马约翰。鼓浪屿首创女子教育，培育出了诸如妇产科先驱林巧稚女士这样的天才。

鼓浪屿的教育改革始于 19 世纪的新教传教士之手。他们开办了 20 所各级学校——从中国的第一所幼儿园到职业学校直至学院。中国最早的全日制学校之一是 1845 年由弼来满在鼓浪屿设立的。差不多在同一时间，养为霖开办了福建的第一所女校。

伦敦差会设立了福建第一所神学院——“圣道学院”，以及鼓浪屿的最早的小学之一 “福民小学”[1] 和第一所中学“澄碧中学”。中国学校的教材由中国教育部门编撰印刷，而基督学校则自己编写教材。美国归正教普及《基督教三字经》，提出他们的首要目标是传播福音而非教育，但即便是中国官员也承认，这些教学大纲有助于振兴中国的教育。

作为中国最早的幼儿园， “鼓浪屿怀德幼儿园”建于 1898 年初，就是如今的日光幼儿园的前身，和两所 1881 年建于鼓浪屿的中学于 1907 年合并为“英华书院”。[2]

(Dukes, 1885)

[1] 马约翰，中国现代运动的先驱者，福民小学校友。

[2] 鼓浪屿的各基督教会之间在福音传道、教堂建筑和教育方面协作之密切在中国堪称一绝——他们经常面对本国教派领导的严厉反对。他们的事例促成了中国的本土教堂与教派模式之间的分庭对抗。

Gulangyu Yangyuan Primary School（鼓浪屿养元小学) was founded in 1889 in Xiamen and moved to Gulangyu in 1929. Famous alumni included writer Lin Yutang and astronomer Yu Qingsong.

The Tung-Wen Institute was started on Gulangyu in 1898 by Mr. A. Burlingame Johnson, then U.S. Consul at Amoy, and relocated to larger facilities on Amoy Island in 1902. Wealthy Chinese funded the school and formed the Board of Trustees, the president of which was the resident U.S. Consul.

The Weizheng (维正) Elementary School, near the Catholic Church, was established by Ma Shouren (马守仁) in 1912, and after Liberation renamed Longtou (龙头) School and merged into Lujiao（鹿礁）School.

The Fumin Vocational School (福民职业学校), founded in 1921 by Ye Guxu (叶谷虚) and others within Fumin Primary School (福民小学), is now Gulangyu's Bishan Primary School (笔山小学). It was expanded in 1925 and renamed "South Fujian Vocational School" (闽南职业学校), but closed after the Japanese invaded Xiamen in 1938.

U.S. and British church affiliated schools were suspended from 1942 until the Japanese' defeat. English and Christian lessons were forbidden, and students were forced to learn Japanese and Mahayana Buddhism. After 1949, the government took over church-run schools. In 1952, Tianwei Women's College became the "Adjunct Primary School of Xiamen Normal School" (厦师附小). In 1960 it was renamed "No.1 Central Primary School" (第一中心小学), and today it is the "People's Primary School" (人民小学). The school buildings at #18 Tianwei Road are the Xiamen Gulangyu Officer's Rest Home's dining room.

Pioneering Women's Education China had few female students and only 3 women's colleges when the American Reformed Mission opened its first primary school in Xiamen's Liaozihou (寮仔后) in 1845 and "Amoy Women's College" in 1847; this class of 12 girls debuted Fujian women's education. The first president, Maria Talmage (打马字·马利亚), was the younger daughter of missionary John Van Nest Talmage (牧师打马字), who served in Xiamen for over 40 years.

Amoy Girls' Middle School (Hong Buren)

(Johnston, 1907)
Girls in Amoy School Doing Math

“鼓浪屿养元小学”1889年成立于厦门，1929年搬到鼓浪屿，校友中不乏有诸如作家林语堂和天文学家余青松这样的名人。

“同文书院”由当时的美国驻厦领事韦荼斋先生始创于1898年，1902年搬到厦门岛一处更大的地方。中国富豪资助该校并成立了董事会，由美国领事担任董事长。

天主教堂附近的“维正小学”由马守仁设立于1912年，解放后改名为“龙头小学”，后归并到“鹿礁小学”。

“福民职业学校”于1921年由叶谷虚等人设立于“福民小学”校内，即现在的“鼓浪屿笔山小学”。该校扩建于1925年并更名为“闽南职业学校”，但1938年日本侵占厦门以后被关闭了。

从1942年到日本战败期间，美国和英国教堂的附属学校遭受停课。英语和基督课程遭禁，学生被迫学习日文和大乘佛教。1949年以后，政府接管了教堂办的学校。1952年，早年的“田尾女学堂”被改为“厦师附小”，又于1960年被命名为“第一中心小学”，也就是今天的“人民小学”，其校舍就在田尾路18号福建省政府疗养院的食堂所在的位置。

首创女子教育

美国归正教于1845年在厦门寮仔后开办了它的第一所小学，并于1847年设立“厦门女学堂”。当时中国只有三所女子学堂，女学生更是寥寥无几。“厦门女学堂”最早一期的十二名女生开创了福建女子教育的先河。

女学堂的第一任校长打马字·马利亚是在厦工作了四十多年的牧师打马字的二女儿。

The women's college burned down in 1880 and was relocated to Tianwei and named "Tianwei Women's College," or "Huaqi Women's School" (花旗女学). Soon afterwards, the Tianwei Women's college established the school which in 1921 became "Yude Middle School (毓德中学)." When Xunyuan Middle School (寻源中学) relocated to Zhangzhou in 1925, Yude took over their premises on Dongshanziding (东山仔顶). By 1934, Yude had 299 female primary and 254 middle school students. While Yude is no more, its legacy continues in overseas Chinese communities in such countries as the Philippines.

Yude's Legacy in Philippine Education

Gulangyu residents also pioneered education overseas. For example, in 1984, Madam Siokiau L. Holaysan (林叔娇), a Yude alumnus, founded Bethany Christian School in Xiamen's sister city of Cebu, Philippines. From the 70s, about 70 Yude alumni met annually in Cebu, but by the 90s the years were catching up, so in 1994 they passed on the torch to a new generation by holding a combined meeting of Yude Alumni and Bethany's first graduates.

The "Ciqin (慈勤) Women's School" established by Huang Yizhu (黄奕住) in 1921 is now Xiamen Municipal Trade Development Bureau's "cadre school".

Johnston (1907)

SIXTY-FIVE PUPILS IN AMOY SCHOOL WHO ALL BECAME TEACHERS.

这所女学堂于 1880 年毁于火灾，后来重建于鼓浪屿田尾并命名为“田尾女学堂”或称“花旗女学”。不久以后，“田尾女学堂”又成立了一所学校，于 1921 年成为 “毓德中学”。1925 年，寻源中学迁往漳州，毓德就接管了他们在东山仔顶的房产。到了 1934 年，毓德的小学部有女生 299 名，中学部则有 254 名。后来，毓德一度停办，抗战胜利后复办，但毓德的教育事业却在海外（如菲律宾等）有华人聚居的国家得到延续。

毓德在菲律宾的教育遗业

许多鼓浪屿人在海外创办教育。例如林叔娇女士，一位毓德的校友，于 1984 年在菲律宾的厦门姐妹城市宿务创办了毓德高中（贝塞尼基督学校）。从 20 世纪 70 年代起，大约有 70 名毓德老校友每年一度在宿雾相聚。但到了 90 年代，他们年事已高，难以继续维持聚会，于是在 1994 年召开了一次毓德校友和贝塞尼基督学校首届毕业生联席会议，将火炬传递给了下一代。

黄奕住于 1921 年设立的“慈勤女子中学”的校址即现在“厦门经贸干校”。

MacGowan, 1895

Amoy Women

John Ma (Ma Yuehan,马约翰)—**Gulangyu's Modern Sports Pioneer** Given Mao Zedong's lifelong preoccupation with health (he was 72 when he swam two miles across the Yangtze!), he must have really appreciated Gulangyu native Ma Yuehan (马约翰), China's 1st athletics coach and pioneer in sports.

纪念伟大领袖毛主席"七·一六"畅游长江十周年
16 July, 1966, 72-year-old Mao Swam 2 miles across the Yangtze

Mao Zedong on Sports

"In the educational system of our country, required courses are as thick as the hairs on a cow"… [but] Children become ill, or even die young, because of studying… Students feel that exercise is shameful. According to my humble observation, this is really their major reason for disliking exercise. Flowing garments, a slow gait, a grave, calm gaze — these constitute a fine deportment, respected by society. Why should one suddenly extend an arm or expose a leg, stretch and bend down? Is this not strange?" Mao Zedong, "A Study of Physical Education." 1917

John Ma (1882-1966) lived at #58 Zhangzhou Road, and led a tough life with his elder brother after losing his mother at age 5 and his father at age 7. When John was 13, friends and relatives helped him enter "Fumin Elementary School (福民小学). When he was 22 he entered preparatory classes in Shanghai's St. John's University and received a Bachelor degree in medicine at age 29.

Young John's swimming, and climbing Gulangyu's rocky peaks, gave him the physique to dominate the schools' soccer, swimming, tennis, baseball and track and field teams. He also had a strong will, as he showed in the Shanghai Y.M.C.A.'s "International Track and Field Sports Meet" (万国田径运动会). Angered by a haughty Japanese who was always a dozen yards ahead of him, Ma gave it everything he had and won the race, beating the Japanese by 50 yards.

Ma's degree was in medicine but he felt prevention, not cure, was the key to health, so he entered physical education. After studying in the U.S. he succeeded an American as Tsinghua University's P.E. director and led his students to 20 national track and field records—surpassing the former American's record. But university president Luo Jialun (罗家伦) saw no need for a "professor of fun and games" and demoted Ma from professor to coach.

马约翰 ——鼓浪屿现代运动先驱 从毛泽东一生对健康的高度重视就可以想像（他 72 岁时还横渡两英里宽的长江！），他一定很欣赏鼓浪屿人马约翰——中国的第一位体育教练和运动先驱。

毛泽东的体育观

"吾国学制，课程密如牛毛……"但是……"儿童缘读书而得疾病或至夭殇者有之矣……学者以运动为可羞也。以愚所考察，此实为不运动之大原因矣。夫衣裳襜襜、行止于于、瞻视舒徐而夷犹者，美好之态，而社会之所尚也。忽尔张臂露足，伸肢屈体，此何为者耶？宁非大可怪者耶？" 毛泽东《体育之研究》（1917）

马约翰（1882-1966)家住鼓浪屿漳州路 58 号，5 岁丧母、7 岁丧父，和他哥哥相依为命，过着艰苦的生活。在他 13 岁那年，亲戚和朋友资助他上了"福民小学"。22 岁那年，他进入上海圣约翰大学的预科班，29 岁毕业，获得医学学士学位。

年轻的马约翰经常游泳、爬山，这些锻炼造就了他一副健壮的体魄，使他成为学校的足球、游泳、网球、棒球和田径队主力。马约翰在参加上海 Y.M.C.A.举办的万国田径运动会时表现出了坚强的意志。有一位日本赛跑选手起初一直领先他十来码，态度骄矜。这激起了马约翰的愤慨，他拼尽全力，奋起直追，最终赢得比赛，而且把那个日本人远远地甩在 50 码以外。

马约翰所学的专业是医学，但他认为，达到健康的关键是防病而不是治病，因此他投身于体育教育。在美国进修课程后，他取代一个美国人，担任清华大学的体育部主任，带领学生创造了 20 项国家田径纪录，超过前任美国人的纪录。但是大学校长罗家伦却认为不需要一个"嬉闹游戏的教授"，因此把马约翰从教授降为教练。

Ma was undaunted. The next year, the Tsinghua Soccer Team won the championship in the North China Soccer Match (华北足球赛). The team returned home, ecstatic students carried John Ma onto the Tsinghua campus, and after the celebration President Luo reinstated Ma as a professor.

Many people tried to persuade Ma to leave Beijing just before Liberation but he said, "No matter what party or society we have, P.E. is necessary." Ma stayed at Tsinghua, and many followed his example. Ma promoted Chinese athletics right up until his death in 1966, and his family has carried on his work.

John Ma's son Ma Qiwei (马启伟), a champion volleyball player, was the dean of Beijing Sports College. Ma's son-in-law Mu Zuoyun (牟作云) played on the national basketball team, took part in the Berlin Olympic Games in 1935, and was a longtime chairman of the China Basketball Association.

Gulangyu's Jianqun Volleyball Team, 1930 Champs (Hong Buren)

"Because of the failure to develop a scientific method, and because of the peculiar qualities of Chinese thinking, China has been backward in natural science. I have confidence, however, that with the importation of the scientific method, and with adequate research facilities, China will be able to produce great scientists and make important contributions to the scientific world in the next century." Lin Yutang

马约翰没有泄气。第二年，清华大学足球队获得了华北足球赛冠军。足球队凯旋归来时，欣喜若狂的学生们抬着马约翰进入校园。庆祝活动之后，罗校长又将马约翰恢复为教授。

临解放时，许多人劝马约翰离开北京。他却说："不论我们有什么样的政党和社会，体育都是必要的。"马约翰留在了清华，很多人也以他为榜样。马约翰的一生促进了中国体育的崛起。1966 年他去世后，他的家人继续从事体育事业。

马约翰的儿子马启伟曾是一名得过冠军的排球选手，当过北京体育学院院长。马约翰的女婿牟作云是前国家篮球队队员，参加过 1935 年柏林奥运会，曾长期担任中国篮球协会主席。

Yang Xiuqiong
Swim Champ 1935
(Hong Buren)

(Hollister, 1932)

Girls' Basketball Team (not Xiamen)

"因为缺乏科学的方法，也因为国人的思想观念所限，中国在自然科学方面已经落后。但是我相信，一旦引进科学的方法，再配合以足够的研究设施，下个世纪中国必定能够培养出伟大的科学家并对科学界做出重大的贡献。"

——林语堂

"If characters don't perish, China must perish!" 汉字不灭，中国必亡！
Lu Xun, 鲁迅, 1936

Lu Zhuangzhang (卢戆章) Father of Pinyin & Punctuation Ever since Jesuit missionary Matteo Ricci published "Miracle of Western Letters" (Xizi Qiji, 西字奇迹) in 1605, scholars have debated Chinese characters' future. Fang Yizhi (方以智, 1611-1671) and others complained they were too numerous and too complicated. But change in tradition-bound China was more complicated than characters, and 200 years passed before any serious attempt at reform.

Song Shu (1862-1910) bemoaned China's high rate of illiteracy, especially for women (he estimated only 1 in 40,000 women could read!). Song Shu wrote:

> "With so few individuals able to read, how will the people ever be liberated from their accumulated distress? Now, we should emulate Japan and issue orders for education."

Song Shu was impressed with the impact of Kana[1], Japan's simplified syllabic writing system, and urged that Chinese too learn a spelling system before moving on to characters, but it was left to an Amoy boy to actually create what is known today as Pinyin Romanization.

Examine the granite stones as you ascend "Pinyin Path" (Gusheng Rd) from the beach to Anxian Hall and you'll discover, to your surprise, that many are engraved with punctuation marks, letters and Pinyin! These periodic carvings are an unusual but fitting tribute to Lu Zhuangzhang (1854-1928). A Tong'an native, Lu[2] studied English in Singapore and in 1928 returned to settle down on Gulangyu, where he helped an English missionary compile a Chinese/English Dictionary (英华字典).

Like many in his day, Lu was worried about the effect of China's dismally high rate of illiteracy, and he spent his entire life seeking reform. Inspired by the missionaries' Romanized Amoy dialect, which he learned as a youth, Lu developed wrote *Yimu liaoran chujie* (*First Steps in Being Able to Understand at a Glance*)—the first book by a Chinese proposing a workable spelling system for Chinese. The "Papa of Pinyin" also developed punctuation for characters (there had not been any!), and encouraged horizontal writing as opposed to vertical (though even today, the same page of a newspaper may have characters written left to right, right to left, and vertical!).

[1] Kana: comes from the Chinese words kan (jia, 假 false) and na (ming, 名 name).

[2] Interestingly, Trinity Church's 1st pastor was related to Lu.

“汉字不灭，中国必亡!”—— 鲁迅，1936

卢戆章——拼音和标点之父 自从耶稣会传教士利玛窦于1605年出版了《西字奇迹》，学者们就开始讨论汉字的未来。方以智（1611-1671）等人曾抱怨汉字太多太繁杂。然而，在深受传统束缚的中国，改革汉字却比汉字本身还要复杂。因此，200 年过去了，却不见有任何实质性的改革尝试。

宋恕 （1862-1910）曾为中国的高文盲率，尤其是妇女的文盲率（他估计40000名妇女中只有1人识字）而叹息。宋恕写道：

“只有那么少的人识字，人民如何从他们的深重苦难中解放出来呢？现在，我们必须赶超日本，为发展教育颁布政令。”

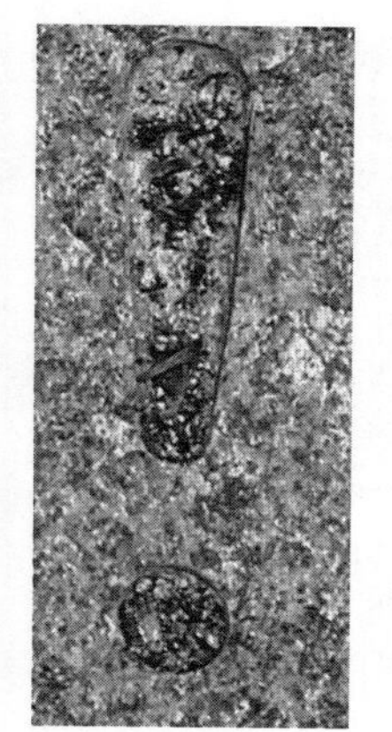

宋恕很推崇日本的假名[1]——简便音节构成的拼读系统，竭力主张中国人也应先学拼读系统再学认字。然而，今天我们所知的罗马字母拼音，实际上竟是由一位厦门人发明的。

当你从沙滩沿着小路往安献堂上行时，如果留意脚底的花岗岩，你就会惊奇地发现上面刻着标点符号、字母和拼音！这些有规律的雕刻是给卢戆章（1854-1928）的一份不同寻常却又恰如其分的献礼。

卢戆章[2]是同安人，在新加坡学习英语，于1928年返回鼓浪屿定居，帮助一位英国传教士编纂《英华字典》。

和别人一样，卢戆章也为可悲的中国高文盲率而忧虑，并且花费一生的时间和精力寻求改革。他记起年轻时传教士们所讲的罗马式闽南语，从中获得灵感，撰写了《一目了然初阶》，这是第一本由中国人撰写的，介绍适合中国人使用的中文拼音体系的书。这位“拼音之父”还发明了汉字的标点符号（当时还没有呢！），并鼓励用水平方向书写代替直行书写（即便是今天，还可以在一页报纸上看到有的汉字从左到右，有的从右到左，还有竖直成行的！）

[1] 假名 Kana：日本文所用的字母，多借用汉字的偏旁。楷书叫片假名，草书叫平假名。
[2] 有趣的是，三一堂的第一任牧师是卢的亲戚。

7th Day Adventists Sino-American School 7th Day Adventists were relatively late arrivals on Amoy (Perhaps because they waited until the 7th day?) Their work began with N. P. Keh, a Protestant pastor converted to SDA, who was joined by W.C. Hankins on Gulangyu in 1905. In 1906, Keh became the SDA's first ordained Chinese.

B.L. Andersen (安利逊)[1], an American born in Denmark in 1873, came to China in 1905 or 1907 (sources conflict) after earning a master's at the University of Colorado. He and his wife rented a place on Quanzhou Rd. and started the "Yucui Primary School" (育粹小学). Later renamed "Sino-American Primary School" (美华小学), it was unusual in having a Chinese president.

Dutch Milk Cows

Like most SDA missionaries, the Andersen's were on a shoe-string budget, so in 1910, the U.S. Consulate helped the Andersons buy inexpensive land from the Huang family in Wugepai (五个牌) and the enterprising couple set up farms and dairies to fund their school and to provide work-study programs. Mrs. Andersen taught English and ran the dairy, and in 1934, after decades of pinching pennies, the couple used their savings to build the magnificent three-storey granite "Girls' School" at #18 Jishan Rd (Chicken Hill Rd., 鸡山路).

Gulangyu's only 3-storey building constructed entirely of solid granite blocks, Anxian Tang (安献堂,"Andersen's Gift Hall") is now the Xiamen Sino-American (Meihua) Adventist Sanitarium and Retirement Center (基督教厦门美华老人院). See the Jishan Rd. chapter.

In 1938, the primary and girls' schools merged into the "Sino-American Three Studies Institute" (美华三育研究社), which provided only English, Chinese and math courses. It ceased operation after the start of World War II, and after Liberation, Anxian Hall was used as the "Kangtai Primary School" (康泰小学), which later became the "Gongnong Primary School" (工农小学), and then the Xiamen Music Academy.

[1] Source: Mrs. Eucaris Galicia, Research Assistant, SDA Archives and Statistic Office.

安息日会的美华学校 相对于其他进入厦门的教会，安息日会算是来得晚的了（兴许是因为他们等到安息日才来的缘故吧？）。 他们的工作始于N. P. Keh，此人原是个新教的牧师。1905年W.C. Hankins 也加入安息日会。1906年， Keh成为被安息日会任命为牧师的第一位中国人。

韩谨思•安利逊[1]，美国籍，1873 年出生于丹麦。他在科罗拉多大学获得硕士学位后，于 1905 年或 1907 年（资料冲突）来到中国。他和妻子在泉州路租了一所房子创办起“育粹小学”，后改名“美华小学”，不同寻常的是，校长居然是中国人。

如同多数的安息日会传教士，韩谨思•安利逊夫妇经济上并不宽裕。他俩于 1910 年在美国领事馆的帮助下，低价购得了黄姓族人在五个牌的地皮。富于创业精神的两口子创办了农场和牛奶场来为他们的学校提供经济来源，也作为供学生勤工俭学的一个项目。安利逊太太既教英语又经营牛奶场，经过几十年的省吃俭用，1934 年，夫妻俩终于攒足了钱在鸡山路 18 号建起了漂亮的花岗岩三层楼“美华女学”。

这座被称为安献堂（意为“安利逊的礼物”）的建筑物是鼓浪屿唯一完全以花岗岩条石砌成的三层方块建筑，现在是“基督教厦门美华老人疗养院”（详见“鸡山路”一章）。

1938 年，小学和女学并入“美华三育研究社”，只设英语、汉语和算术三门功课，二战爆发后停办。

解放后，安献堂被“康泰小学”用作校舍，后改名为“工农小学”。后又作为厦门音乐学校。

Anxian Hall B.B.

[1] 来源：Eucaris M. Galicia 夫人，助理研究员，安息日会档案和统计办公室

Dr. Lim Boon-keng/Lin Wenqing (1869-1957), "Sage of Singapore" Kipling said East and West would never meet, but they did meet in the 2nd president of Xiamen University, Dr. Lin Wenqing, who was called the Sage of Singapore by Chinese and foreigners alike. Xiamen University's founder, Tan Kak Kee, wrote that Lin was "well versed in Western materialistic sciences and Chinese cultural spirit."

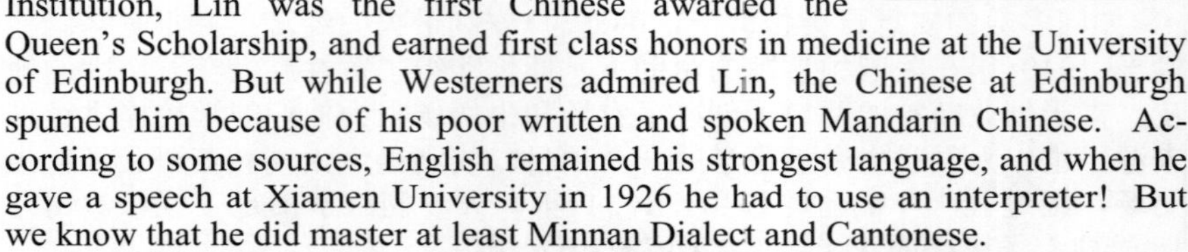

Educated first in a Hakka temple and then at Raffles Institution, Lin was the first Chinese awarded the Queen's Scholarship, and earned first class honors in medicine at the University of Edinburgh. But while Westerners admired Lin, the Chinese at Edinburgh spurned him because of his poor written and spoken Mandarin Chinese. According to some sources, English remained his strongest language, and when he gave a speech at Xiamen University in 1926 he had to use an interpreter! But we know that he did master at least Minnan Dialect and Cantonese.

In 1905, Lin set up a private hospital for prostitutes and founded the Anti-Opium Society (ironic, since both his father and China-born grandfather were opium farmers). Lin excelled at business, particularly the rubber industry, shipping and banking, and helped found the Singapore Chinese Chamber of Commerce. A pioneer Chinese financier, he partnered with Huang Yizhu to start the Hefeng Bank and Overseas Chinese Bank. Westerners and Chinese alike sought the Sage's wisdom. He was adviser to the British in the Legislative Council and the Chinese Advisory Board, and attended the coronations of King Edward VII in 1902 and King George V in 1911. Lin really showed his colors during World War I when he raised funds for the Prince of Wales relief fund and for war planes, and in 1918 was awarded the Order of the British Empire.

In 1900, Lin helped found the Straits Chinese British Association (of which he was elected president twice). He also started the Chinese "Philomathic" Society for the study of Chinese language, Western Music, and English literature, and the Singapore Chinese Girls' School. And perhaps because of his own difficulty in mastering Mandarin, he urged that Chinese children be taught in Mandarin, even going so far as to organize Mandarin language classes in his own home.

Lin was president of Xiamen University from 1921 until 1937, but after returning to Singapore he suffered greatly at the hands of the Japanese, who tortured his wife to force him into working for them. In 1949, Lin became the first president of the China Society, and supported that work until his death on New Year's day in 1957. He left 3/5 of his estate, including his Brush Mountain home, to Xiamen University. The estate is run down nowadays, but still holds a special place in the hearts of those grateful for this man who wrought great change in the lives of Chinese both at home and abroad.

林文庆博士（1869—1957）——“新加坡贤哲”

鲁耶尔·吉卜林说，东、西方永远碰不到一块儿。然而，厦门大学的第二任校长林文庆博士却能将这二者融会贯通。中外人士一致推崇他为 “新加坡贤哲”。厦门大学的创始人陈嘉庚评述林文庆时写道：“（他）能通西洋物质之科学兼具中国文化之精神。”

林文庆最早就读于福建会馆，而后升入莱佛士学院，成为获得女皇奖学金的第一个中国人。后来在爱丁堡大学学医，获得最高荣誉。正当西方人钦佩林文庆时，爱丁堡大学的中国人却因林文庆糟糕的汉语笔头和口头而对他嗤之以鼻。根据某些资料所说，英语仍是他最强的语言。1926 年他在厦大做演讲时还不得不靠人翻译呢！但我们知道，他至少懂得粤语和闽南语。

1905 年，林文庆开了一家为娼妓治病的私立医院，并创立了“反鸦片社团”（具有讽刺意味的是，他的父亲和出生于中国的祖父竟都是种鸦片的）。林文庆善于经营生意，尤其在橡胶、船运和银行等行业收入颇丰。他还参与创立“新加坡中华总商会”。作为华人金融家先驱，他和黄奕住合资创建“和丰银行”和“华侨银行”。中国人和西方人都推崇这位贤哲的智慧。他当过英国立法院顾问及中国顾问团顾问，出席过 1902 年爱德华七世和 1911 年乔治五世的加冕典礼。林文庆在一战期间表现出色，为威尔士王子救济基金和购置战斗机筹款，于 1918 年获得大不列颠帝国勋章。

1900 年，林文庆参与创立“海峡英籍华人公会”，两次当选为该会主席。他还创办了“华人 Chinese Philomathic 社团”，开展中文、西方音乐和英国文学等学科的学习活动，还创办了“新加坡华人女子学校”。也许是由于他本人汉语学得不理想，他竭力主张华人应从小开始学习汉语，甚至在自己家里组织汉语学习班。

从 1921 年到 1937 年，林文庆担任厦门大学校长。卸任后返回新加坡，却落入日本人之手，深受磨难。日本人拷打他的妻子，逼他为他们做事。1949 年，他成为“中华社团”的第一任主席，一直到 1957 年元旦他去世为止。他将五分之三的房产捐给厦大，鼓浪屿笔架山的房子也在捐赠之列。那座老房子如今已经破旧不堪了，但因其主人曾经谋求改善海内外华人的生活，在对林心存感念的人们心中仍占有特别的位置。

Dr. Lin in a Foreigner's Eyes

(by Averil Mckenzie, Gulangyu resident, 1920s)

"A year previously, Dr. Lim Boon Keng had been appointed President of the new University of Amoy. A graduate in medicine of Edinburgh University, he no longer practiced, but still lived part of the year in Singapore, where he had once done so, and it was there that we first met him and his wife. In Kulangsu, they and their family occupied a house delightfully set in a garden on one of the highest points of the island. A few days after our arrival we ate there. The Lim family's friendship endures to this day, so I cannot, with any certainty, recall of what we talked. I remember the catholic collection of English books on the ground floor, cockroach-scraped and silver-fish-nibbled, as all our books became, but all well-used and alive; and above, the billowing of white curtains, high and airily in white light; Mrs. Lim's dark hair and poised grace against white walls, and the agony of a mouthful of chili sauce which I mistook for tomato.

"Dr. Lim was short, square, with large, mild brown eyes, but he was a fighter of astonishing range and vigor. Apart from his continuous battle for Western concepts of hygiene against ignorant and superstitious colleagues when he was medical adviser to the Minister of the Interior and Inspector-General of the Peking hospital under the Chinese Government, he had championed any number of causes unrelated to his profession. One of these campaigns had been against pigtails. In this he was not alone but we felt that for him, as a Fukienese, it was particularly appropriate because, for more than two hundred years after the defeat of Koxinga and his supporters in 1683, the Fukienese peasants, forced to be 'tartarized' and to wear queues, coiled these symbols of subjection round their heads and hid them under turbans.

"Dr. Lim had traveled both to widen his own and other people's [views]...As a vigorous advocate for the adoption of kuo-yu, he had gone to Java to preach its benefits to the Chinese schools there. He and Mrs. Lim had explored Europe as well as attending the German, French and Italian medical conferences to which he was officially delegated. He was one of the first to urge his country-men in Malaya to plant rubber, and was always ready to pursue new ideas offered by friends or books. 'Reading,' he would say, 'and the cultivation of friends are as a fan to the flame of the mind and make it burn more brightly.' He had what I, as a European, can only call a Latin enthusiasm. It was, I suspect, as much for this comprehending eagerness as for his medical skill, that Sun Yat-sen had chosen him as a private secretary as well as physician. But with all his preoccupations for the future of his countrymen he never undervalued his country's past and her perennial philosophy. He had published various books on Confucianism, and a few years after we met, I was to engrave a frontispiece for his translation of the classic Li Sao [Dr. Lim died at the age of 88, in Singapore, shortly after I wrote this chapter]."

Nobel Prize Winner from Gulangyu! Walter H. Brattain, born on Gulangyu Feb.10, 1902, joined Bell Laboratories in 1929, and in 1956 shared the Nobel Prize for Physics for developing the transistor, which made possible the computer upon which I now type "Discover Gulangyu!"

一个外国人眼里的林博士

（《绿姜根》 Averil Mckenzie，1920 年代鼓浪屿居民）

“一年前，林文庆博士被任命为厦门大学校长。尽管他是爱丁堡大学的医科毕业生，但已不再行医了。仍像以前那样，一年当中他还是有一段时间在新加坡度过。也正是在新加坡，我第一次见到他和他太太。在鼓浪屿，他家拥有一座舒适的房子，坐落在岛上一制高点的花园里。我们到达后过了几天在那儿吃了一次饭。林家的友谊延续至今，所以我无法准确回忆起那天我们都谈了些什么。我记得，存放在一楼的各种英文藏书已被蟑螂咬出碎屑，也被蠹虫蛀过，就像我们所有的书那样，只不过因主人经常翻阅而显出生气。在高处，白色窗帘在白光中轻快地飞扬。林太太仪态典雅，乌黑的头发与白墙形成鲜明的反衬。还有，我错将辣椒酱当作番茄酱吃了一大口，痛苦不堪。

“林博士长得矮矮壮壮，一对棕色的大眼睛流露着温和的神情。但他在诸多领域却是个斗志旺盛的斗士。在担任中国政府内务部医学顾问和北京医院总监时，他坚持用西方的卫生保健观念来反击愚昧和迷信团体。除此之外，他还在一些与他的专业无关的领域为坚持真理而进行斗争。其中一项是反对留辫子。在这一点上，他并不孤立。但我们觉得，林文庆作为一个福建人，这样做是情理之中的事情。因为，在郑成功和他的支持者们 1683 年失利以后的两百多年里，福建的父老乡亲被迫‘满人化’、留长辫，他们将这意味着被异族统治的标志物盘在头上，包裹在头巾里。

“林博士游历各地，既为开阔自己的眼界，也为扩展别人的视野……作为一个极力推广国语的倡导者，他奔赴爪哇，向那里的华人学校宣传国语的种种好处。他被公派到德国、法国和意大利出席医学会议时，和他太太游历了欧洲。他是第一个力促马来亚的华人种植橡胶的，他也时刻准备探讨朋友或书本所提供的新思想。他说，读书和交友如一把扇子，可以使思想的火苗燃烧得更亮堂。以我作为一个欧洲人看来，他具有一种拉丁式的热情。我猜想，孙逸仙选择他作为机要秘书兼医官，不单是看重他的医学技能，同样也器重他追求真理的那份渴望。他关心国人的未来，从未轻视自己国家的历史及其世代传承的民族哲学。他出版过诸多关于儒家思想的书。在我们认识几年后，我曾打算为他的译作古诗《离骚》雕刻一幅卷首插图。[在我写完这章不久，林博士在新加坡去世，享年 88 岁。]”

来自鼓浪屿的诺贝尔奖获得者！ 沃尔特·布拉顿，1902年2月10日出生于鼓浪屿，1929年进入贝尔实验室当研究员，因为开发晶体管和研究半导体的特性（就是这些研究使电脑的发明成为可能，我才能用它来写出“Discover Gulangyu!”）而于1956年与他人并获诺贝尔物理奖。

Chapter 5
Gulangyu's Medical Pioneers

"I am a daughter of Gulangyu Islet. In my dreams I often return to the shores of Gulangyu, where the sea is boundless, blue and beautiful." 我是鼓浪屿的女儿 ,我常常在梦中回到鼓浪屿的大海边。那海面真辽阔，那海水真蓝，真美。 Dr. Lin Qiaozhi (林巧稚)

Lin Qiaozhi's stethescope

For such a minor islet, Gulangyu has played a major role in developing modern medicine. On Gulangyu, "The Cradle of Tropical Medicine," Sir Patrick Manson made his great medical discoveries, and little Gulangyu gave birth to Lin Qiaozhi, "Mother of China's Modern Obstetrics and Gynecology."

Gulangyu's trailblazing medicine began in 1842 with the arrival of Dr. Cummings, who lived with Amoy's first missionary, David Abeel (Yabili, 雅裨理), in the old home at #23 Zhonghua Rd. The two later moved to Liaozihou (寮仔后) and then to Zhushujiao (竹树脚), where in 1843 they founded a clinic that was forerunner of "Chibao (赤保) hospital" (later part of Hope Hospital).

Gulangyu's honor roll of medical missionaries includes pioneers like Dr. J.C. Hepburn (1843-1845), Dr. James Young (English Presbyterian Mission, 1850-1854), Dr. Hirschberg (London Missionary Society, 1853-1858), and Dr. John Carnegie (1859-1862). But my favorite of the lot is Dutch-born American Dr. John Abraham Otte (Yu Yuehan, 郁约翰), of the American Reformed Mission[1] (Guizheng Jiao, 归正教).

John Otte—Missionary doctor, architect, and carpenter Dr. Otte not only founded but also designed and built (with his own hands) three hospitals, including Gulangyu's historic Hope Hospital (救世医院). During Otte's copious free time he designed such Gulangyu edifices as the islet's most conspicuous landmark, the red-domed "Eight Diagrams Building" (Bagualou, 八卦楼).

---

1 ARM, known as the Reformed Protestant Dutch Church from 1816-1826

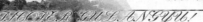

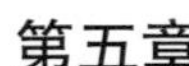

鼓浪屿医疗事业先驱

“我是鼓浪屿的女儿，我常常在梦中回到鼓浪屿的大海边。那海面真辽阔，那海水真蓝，真美。” ——林巧稚

鼓浪屿这个弹丸小岛在现代医学的发展过程中扮演了重要的角色。正是在这“热带医学的摇篮”，帕特里克·曼森先生取得了重大的医学发现；小小的鼓浪屿还诞生了“中国现代妇产科之母”林巧稚。

鼓浪屿对医学的贡献始于 1842 年。那年，鼓浪屿来了两个人——甘明医生和第一个进入厦门的传教士雅俾理。他俩合住于现在的中华路 23 号一座旧屋。这对搭档后来搬到寮仔后，之后又搬到竹树脚。在那儿，于 1843 年开设了一家诊所，就是“赤保医院”的前身（后来成为“救世医院”的附属医院）。

早期在鼓浪屿悬壶济世的传教士包括 J.C. Hepburn（1843-1845）医生、James Young 医生（英国长老会，1850-1854）、Hirschberg 医生（伦敦差会，1853-1858）和 John Carnegie 医生（1859-1862）等先驱者。不过，所有人中，我个人最为推崇的是生于荷兰的美国人，归正教[1]的郁约翰博士。

郁约翰——传教士医生、建筑设计师和木匠 郁约翰博士不仅创立，而且还设计和建造（有时他亲自动手）了包括鼓浪屿上具有历史意义的“救世医院”在内的三座医院。郁约翰还倾注大量的业余时间，设计了鼓浪屿岛上最引人注目的标志性建筑物，红色穹顶的“八卦楼”。

[1] ARM，在 1816-1826 年间被称为荷兰基督教改革宗教会

From his youth Otte wanted to preach, but diphtheria hurt his voice, and since he loved science more than seminary, he became a missionary doctor instead. After graduation from the University of Michigan, he did a year of post-graduate work in Holland, which gained him experience, as well as the financial support of the Dutch, who valued his selfless service to their community.

Otte and his wife Frances Phelps Otte arrived in Amoy on January 13, 1888, and began medical work in the backwater village of Xiaoxi (Pinghe County) which had a small but thriving church under the Chinese pastor Iap Han-cheong.

While Otte would have preferred Amoy or Gulangyu, he put his heart into his work. He designed and helped build the two-storey brick hospital, and lacking a capable local carpenter, built the wooden furniture himself. Locals initially opposed him, but the energetic missionary doctor/architect/carpenter quickly won not only their hearts but also their financial support. Mandarins and wealthy Chinese happily augmented Otte's meager $1,200 building fund, and peasants volunteered their labor. On March 5, 1889, pastor Iap dedicated Neerbosch Hospital, which was named after a Dutch town that donated funds for the hospital because Otte had cared for Dutch orphans during a measles epidemic.

Eighty Chinese patients arrived the first day, and within weeks patients were lining up at 2 a.m. each day for the 5 a.m. opening. Otte wrote,

> "All classes came: the well-to-do and the beggar; the proud scholar; the attaché of the Mandarin as well as the untutored toiler of the soil... In the first three months of operation, 1,500 different patients visited the hospital and received treatment 7,000 times."

By the time of Otte's 1895 furlough, Neerbosch hospital had doubled in size and Otte had treated 50,000 out-patients, over 2,400 in-patients, and performed over 1,500 operations. A Chinese doctor from Zhangzhou whose son Otte had treated donated a microscope and the local mandarin funded a refuge for addicts of opium, which Otte called one of humanity's greatest curses. Otte wrote,

> "England forced opium upon China. Not a single intelligent native doubts this from Li Hung Chang down. This is England's sin for which all the thousands poured into the coffers of the various missionary societies cannot atone."

Otte tried to reduce addicts' suffering by gradual reduction of opium intake, but this did not lessen the agony and only prolonged the pain. Otte described their pain as "indescribable...if ever I have been able to conceive what the sufferings of hell must be," [it was their suffering].

Otte treated 66 addicts from July 1891 to July 1892, but wrote that even if they stayed off the drug, they would suffer physically for the rest of their lives with indigestion, neurasthenia, bowel problems and impotency. They would be so miserable that many would return to opium to alleviate the pain. Still, many remained off the drug—and even returned with addicted friends in tow.

郁约翰从小就想要从事布道，但他患过白喉，伤了嗓子。由于他热爱科学甚于神学，他成了传教士医生。他毕业于密歇根大学，尔后在荷兰工作了一年。这让他不仅获得实践经验，还因无私地为当地服务而得到荷兰人民经济上的赞助。

郁约翰和他的妻子 Frances Phelps Otte 于 1888 年 1 月 13 日抵达厦门，一开始在偏僻、落后的“小溪”村（平和县）从事医疗工作。在那儿，有一座由中国牧师 Iap Han-cheng 负责的人气兴旺的小教堂。郁约翰其实更喜欢厦门或鼓浪屿，但他却专心做他的工作。

郁约翰设计并参与建设砖结构的两层楼医院。当时他找不到能干的当地木匠师傅，干脆亲自操刀做家具。起初当地人反对他，但这位精力充沛的传教士医生兼建筑设计师、木匠很快就赢得了民心，而且还得到百姓的经济赞助。郁约翰本来只有微薄的 1200 美元的建设基金，但中国的达官贵人为他雪中送炭，慷慨解囊，农民则不吝出力帮工。在荷兰的一次麻疹病流行期间，郁约翰帮助照料过一些孤儿，所以荷兰的 Neerbosch 小镇也捐资建院。因此，1889 年 3 月 5 日，在医院的落成仪式上，Iap 牧师将医院命名为 Neerbosch 医院。

医院开业的头一天来了八十名中国病人。在接下来的几个星期里，病人们每天从凌晨 2 点就开始排队，等候到 5 点医院开门接诊。郁约翰写道：

> “各阶层的人都来：富人，乞丐，清高的学者，官吏大员，还有目不识丁的、处于社会底层的苦力工……最初的三个月共有 1500 名病人来医院看病，接受治疗 7000 次。”

截止至 1895 年郁约翰休假，Neerbosch 医院的规模已经扩大到两倍，他也累计诊治了 50000 名门诊病人和 2400 多名住院病人，并做了 1500 多例手术。一位来自漳州的中国医生因为郁约翰为他儿子治病而捐献了一台显微镜。一名当地的官员提供了一处鸦片戒毒所。郁约翰说，鸦片是人间最深重的灾孽之一。他写道：

> “在李鸿章以下的任何一个明智的中国人都知道，是英国强制向中国输入鸦片的。这是英国犯下的弥天大罪。就算倾尽各教派钱柜里所有的钱，也无法代为补过。”

郁约翰试图通过逐渐减少鸦片吸入量的办法来减轻上瘾者的痛苦，但这减轻不了痛楚却反而延长了病痛。郁约翰这样记述他们的痛苦：“难以描述……如果我能想像地狱里是如何受煎熬的，那一定就是这情形了。”

从 1891 年 7 月到 1892 年 7 月，郁约翰治疗了 66 名瘾君子。他写道，即使戒掉毒瘾，他们的余生也将深受种种身体不适的折磨，如消化不良、神经衰弱、肠道问题、体虚、性无能。他们痛苦难忍，以至有些人重吸鸦片来缓解痛苦。尽管如此，还是有不少人戒毒成功，甚至还带着毒友回来接受戒毒治疗。

Otte's "Opium Refuge"

"For the first five days these patients are considered and treated as maniacs. They are locked up, and their food is handed them through a barred window. It is only in this way that they can be kept in the hospital.

[Of five patients] "The first day all went well, but the next day they became raving maniacs. Night and day they did nothing but crawl on the ground and howl like wild beasts; their room became filthy, and, when the coolie went in to clean it, four men [were needed] at times to watch the room to keep the patients from escaping...Whenever the physician or assistant appeared, they would beg on their knees to be let out, if only for a few minutes. When reasoned with, they said they were doing their best to keep quiet, but they seemed to have lost all control. Knowing this, they were patiently and kindly treated. When left alone, they made strenuous efforts to escape, and finally succeeded in wrenching off a foreign lock from the door. This was discovered in time, and heavy iron staples were clenched on the inside, and the door secured on the outside with a padlock. But on the fifth night they bent the staples with their fingers, so as to open the door. They then jumped down from a verandah twelve feet high and made their escape."

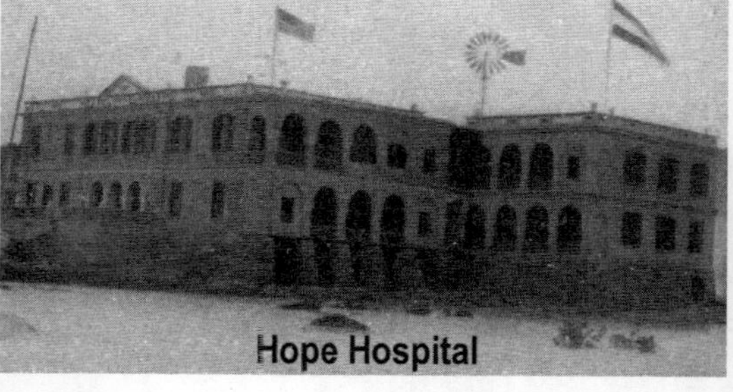
Hope Hospital

Hope Hospital, #82 Guxin Rd Otte was keen on training Chinese in medicine, but only three students survived his severe examinations and hands-on practice for the first graduation in 1893. It was a tough program, but the waiting line of students never ended, and Otte's legacy of medical training continued even after his death, when Hope Hospital started South Fujian's first nursing school in 1926.

Otte built Hope Hospital after returning from his U.S. furlough, and as with Neerbosch, he both designed the hospital and helped build it himself.

Otte initially considered refurbishing the English Presbyterian Hospital, which was on ARM land and had closed in 1894, but repairs would have been too costly, and a foundation for a new building on the site would have required costly pilings. At the suggestion of the American Consul General, Otte selected a site at the base of Swallow Tail Mountain (Yanweishan Hezai, 燕尾山河仔).

While Chinese had opposed Otte's Sio-khe hospital, his opponents on Gulangyu were foreigners, who feared patients would bring disease to their exclusive international settlement.

郁约翰的“鸦片戒毒所”

“开头五天，这些病人被当成疯子一样来对待。他们被锁在屋里，给他们的食物是从带栅栏的窗口递进去的。只有用这种办法才能把他们留在医院里。”

[五个病人的情况]“第一天一切都好，但第二天他们就变成了胡言乱语的疯子。夜以继日，他们别的不做，只是像野兽般在地上爬滚、嚎叫；他们的房间变得脏乱不堪，当工人进屋打扫时，四条汉子（有此必要）同时看住屋子，以防他们逃走 。每当他们看到医师或助理医师，就会跪在地上请求放他们出去，哪怕只给几分钟。当别人劝解时，他们说自己已尽量保持安静了，但是看上去他们处于完全失控的状态。了解到这一点，院方就耐心、友善地对待他们。 ”

“没人看管的时候，他们便为逃脱而使尽浑身解数，终于拧掉了门上的一把进口锁。还好，这事被发现得早。于是，大号的 U 形铁钉从里面将门扇钉死，再用一面挂锁从门外锁好。但第五天晚上，他们用手指头弄弯了 U 形铁钉，然后把门打开，从十二英尺高的阳台跳下，逃之夭夭。”

鼓新路 82 号救世医院　郁约翰积极、热心地为中国人培训医务人才。他教学严谨，1893 年他的第一期毕业班学生中只有三人闯关通过他的严格考试和实践考核。完成课程是很难的，可是排队报名的学生却不绝于庭。郁约翰传医授业的精神至死犹存，1926 年，救世医院设立了闽南第一所护士学校。

郁约翰从美国休假返厦后，就着手修建救世医院。与 Neerbosch 医院一样，他既设计又亲自动手帮工。

起初，郁约翰考虑翻修大英长老会医院。该院盖在归正教的土地上并于 1894 年关停。可是，翻修费太昂贵了。如果在原址上重挖地基，那花费成本就更吓人了。因此，郁约翰听从美国总领事的建议，选择了燕尾山河仔下的一块地。

不仅中国人反对郁约翰的 Sio-khe 医院，鼓浪屿上的外国人也反对。他们担心病人会把疾病带到他们专属的国际社区。

The foreigners appealed all the way to Peking and Washington, D.C., but without success, and in the end Otte mollified them with the promise of special hospital rooms for foreigners and wealthy Chinese.

Otte described Hope Hospital, which opened April, 1898:

> "Hope Hospital is a substantial two story brick structure, situated on the water's edge, and at high tide, surrounded on three sides by water. It contains a chapel, dining room, kitchen, two servants' rooms, office, dispensary, dark room for eye work, four student's rooms, and seven wards, in which are forty-five beds."

Otte Raises the Roof!

Otte personally laid the hospital roof to ensure it was done right! He wrote, "It took me two weeks of hard work, but finally it was all done and then I simply crowed. You ought to have seen me when at work. I was covered from head to foot with sticky asphalt. Even my baby, when she came with her mother one day to the hospital said, 'This is not my papa.'

"…Sometimes right in the midst of my work I would be called out on a serious case. Then I would hurriedly wash my hands in kerosene, change my clothes, and go to the case. Think of having to operate on the eye under such circumstances."

On the day of Hope's dedication, Otte laid the cornerstone for a women's hospital named after Queen Wilhelmina because the initial $2,518 in funds and $800 for maintenance came mostly from Dutch supporters, who created the "Netherlands Society for Building and Maintaining Missionary Hospitals in China."

Hope's "first come, first served" policy meant that many patients spent the night on the street to make sure they received a coveted bamboo entry slip. In 1900, Otte had over 10,200 patient visits to the two hospitals, treated 1,206 in-patients, performed 631 operations and extracted 155 teeth.

A busy man, Otte still found time to pursue architecture as well—but he contracted the plague from a patient and died in 1910. A monument erected by Otte's students was destroyed during the Cultural Revolution. The foundation and stone are now behind the former Pulmonary Hospital, which is just off the Gulangyu Ring Road past the U.S. Consulate. The inscription is in Dutch, English (barely legible), Chinese and Latin.

Otte Memorial

外国人通过各种途径闹到北京和华盛顿，但还是告不倒他，最后郁约翰为了平息众怒，许诺医院将为外国人和中国富豪提供专门的房间。

郁约翰这样描述开办于1898年4月的救世医院：

“救世医院是一座坚固的两层楼砖结构建筑，濒水而立，海水高潮时三面临水。内设有教堂、食堂、厨房、两间仆人房、办公室、药房、透视室、四间学生房、七间病房，共四十五张病床。”

郁约翰盖屋顶

为了确保万无一失，郁约翰亲自为医院盖屋顶。他写道：“我苦干了两个星期，终于大功告成了！我不禁畅然欢叫。你该来看看我干活时的样子，我从头到脚沾满了沥青。有一天，我幼小的女儿跟她妈妈来医院，居然说，‘这个人不是我爸爸。’

“……有时候我手上活儿正好干一半，却被告知有急症候诊。于是我匆忙用煤油洗手，换衣服，出去接诊。想想看吧，这种情况下还得做眼科手术呢。”

在救世医院落成典礼的那天，郁约翰以荷兰女王薇赫明娜的名字为医院立了一块奠基石。因为荷兰的支持者们创立了“中国教会医院建设与维护之荷兰社团”，并捐献了最初的2518美元建设基金和800美元维护基金中的大部分。

救世医院奉行“先来者先看病”的原则，因此许多病人天没亮就在街上排队，以确保能挂上号——领到一支来之不易的竹签。1900年这一年，郁约翰的两座医院共接待病人10200名，治疗1206名住院者，实行631例手术，拔牙155颗。

这么一个大忙人却还挤出时间来钻研建筑学，实在是难得。不幸的是，他被一个病人传染得病，于1910年去世。约翰的门生为他立了一座纪念碑。石碑在“文革”期间被毁，但碑基和碑石现在还在原肺科医院后面，也就是在鼓浪屿环岛路边，而原美国领事馆也在同一边，相距不远。碑文有荷文、英文（难以辨认）、中文和拉丁文。

Colonel Frank Otte, Dr. Otte's son, was born on Gulangyu and with General Chennault's 14th Air Force in Guilin he helped fight the Japanese. The Japanese, in turn, wreaked greater havoc on his father's Hope Hospital than just about any other Gulangyu building, destroying everything they couldn't steal. The hospital was restored after the war by director Dr. John Holleman, who also built the home at #75 Fuxing Rd.

Incidentally, in 1957 Holleman became director of Taibei's McKay Memorial Hospital （马偕纪念医院), and my wife Susan Marie was born at McKay the following year!

After 1949, Hope Hospital merged with Gulangyu Hospital on Fujian Road, and Hope became a pulmonary hospital. Gulangyu Hospital was renamed "Fandi (反帝) Hospital", and in 1971 became "Xiamen #2 Hospital."

Text of Otte Memorial
Reverend Johannes Abraham Otte, M.D. 1861-1910

"Born in Holland, educated in America, labored in China.

"The faithful use of his learning and skills in unwearied service made him a man of far-reaching influence. He left his homeland to give himself to the people of Amoy. Among them he labored with whole-hearted devotion for twenty years, preaching the gospel of Jesus Christ, healing the sick, building three hospitals, and training more than twenty medical students.

"We honor him as a man of great worth and unbending purpose. To accomplish his purposes, which were large, he gave all his strength in life, he spared not himself, and when he died his body was buried not in his homeland but, as he wished, among the scenes of his labors. This monument is raised by his students in memory of his character and deeds. This stone may crumble, his bones may become dust, but his character and deeds are imperishable."

Sir Patrick Manson, Father of Tropical Medicine Gulangyu is known to Western doctors as the "Cradle of Tropical Medicine" because it was here that Sir Patrick Manson (1844–1922), "Father of Tropical Medicine," made discoveries that helped tackle leprosy, malaria, and other diseases that 150 years ago made Xiamen a "white man's graveyard."

Surgeons or Sorcerers?

In his 1873 report of the Amoy Missionary Hospital, Patrick Manson noted that in 1871, it was rumored throughout Amoy that Western doctors gave out magical, poisonous pills that created diseases only they could cure. Pamphlets and posters accused Western doctors of using Chinese' eyes and hearts for potions, and of drugging and raping Chinese women. When patients died, doctors were accused of murdering them to harvest body parts. When patients survived, doctors were accused of resorting to magic to affect their miraculous cures. In the beginning, theirs was a thankless occupation!

弗兰克上校 弗兰克上校是郁约翰的儿子，出生于鼓浪屿，曾服务于陈纳德将军驻桂林的第 14 飞行队，帮助中国抗日。日本人作为报复，在鼓浪屿的诸多建筑物中，对他父亲的救世医院进行了最丧心病狂的浩劫，凡是他们偷不走的设备，一概砸毁。战后，夏礼文博士重建了这座医院。夏礼文还在复兴路 75 号建了一座住宅。无巧不成书，1957 年，他就任台北马偕纪念医院院长，而我太太苏珊·玛丽则在次年降生于马偕纪念医院。

鬱約翰牧師美國人
也，醫學博士。學稱厥名，
志宏厥名，志宏厥學，僑
廈敷教施診，精心毅力，
廿載靡濡。手創醫院三，
授徒成業二十餘輩，功效
聿著，愿力彌宏，以身殉
志，生不遺力，歿不歸骨
卒踐誓言，葬于兹邱，追
念功德，表石以紀。石可
泐，骨可朽，先生功德不
可沒。諸學生仝泐石。

1949 年以后，“救世医院”与“鼓浪屿医院”合并，院部在福建路，原“救世医院”改为“肺科医院”。“鼓浪屿医院”曾改名为“反帝医院”，1971 年以后叫“厦门第二医院”。

帕特里克·曼森先生——热带医学之父 对于西洋医生来说，鼓浪屿以“热带医学的摇篮”著称。因为正是在这里，“热带医学之父”帕特里克·曼森先生（1844—1922)找到了有助于对付麻风、疟疾等疾病的办法。而这些疾病在 150 年前曾使厦门一度成为“白人的坟场”。

是外科医生还是巫师？

在 1873 年“厦门传教医院”的报告中，帕特里克·曼森记录道，1871 年，厦门到处在谣传，说西洋医生开给病人神秘的毒药丸，导致的疾病只有他们才能治。传单和大字报指责西洋医生拿中国人的眼和心去制药，还迷奸中国妇女。如果病人死了，医生就被指责为图谋器官而害人命。如果病人被救活过来，医生则被指责故弄玄虚以标榜其医术不凡。至少刚开始时，他们的工作没人领情。

Manson the Tiger Hunter

Manson on Tiger Hunt, 1874

"Life in Amoy in those days in a mixed community of Europeans in China was far from dull. There was a gay social life, and also from time to time sporting events, such as pony races, and shooting expeditions into the surrounding countryside where excellent snipe grounds were provided by the numerous paddy-fields.

"Farther field were the wild highlands where every now and again tigers were bagged. Manson was foremost in these adventures and soon gained the reputation of being the best snipe-shot in China.

"But, as he became more familiar with the Chinese and their ways and won their confidence, work began to accumulate.

"Sometimes he was too busy to sleep, as his services were in constant demand." Sir Philip Manson-Bahr

The oldest of nine children, Manson gave up a lucrative career to study medicine. After obtaining his medical degree in 1866 from the university at Aberdeen, he spent 24 years in China, where he tackled not only mosquitoes but also Amoy tigers (he was an avid hunter).

Locals were slow to trust the sporting Scotsman. For centuries, Chinese had spread tales of foreigners eating Chinese babies and using their eyeballs to line mirrors, and many believed Western doctors' medicines were poison.

Manson gained their trust by opening his clinic to the street so everyone could see that his surgeon's scalpel didn't come in a set, with knife and fork.

Manson was dismayed by Western doctor's ignorance about the tropical diseases he faced. He estimated 1 in 450 people in Xiamen were lepers, but Western medicine had no answers. When he asked the British Museum for information on mosquitoes[1]; they wrote back six months later to say they had nothing on mosquitoes but were sending a book on cockroaches they hoped would help.

When Manson moved to Hong Kong in 1883 he found that Western doctors could not discern typhoid from malaria, calling it "typho-malaria". Malaria had wiped out nearly an entire regiment right after Britain occupied Hong Kong in 1841, and for years, 3% of British troops died from the dread disease.

[1] Earth's most deadly creature, mosquitoes kill over 2 million people yearly!

曼森在九个兄弟姐妹中排行老大。为了学医，他放弃了一个有利可图的职业。1866 年获得阿伯丁大学的医学学位后，他在中国呆了 24 个年头。在中国，他不仅对付蚊子，还对付厦门虎（他爱好狩猎）。

老虎杀手曼森

“那时候，欧洲人在中国已形成了一个混居的社群，他们在厦门的生活一点也不乏味。那儿有着五光十色的社会生活，而且还不时有体育活动，如赛马或是到附近乡下稻田遍布的区域狩猎水禽。

“再走远些则是荒山野岭，时而可以猎杀到老虎。曼森是从事这些冒险活动最为出色的人，所以他很快便被誉为中国最佳猎手。

“随着他越来越熟悉中国人及其他们的习俗，他渐渐赢得了他们的信任，他的工作也开始加重了。

“由于病人不断找他看病，有时候他忙得连睡觉都顾不上了。”

Sir Philip Manson-Bahr

当地人开始并不信任这个爱好体育的苏格兰人，因为几百年间，中国人流传着关于外国人吃中国婴儿并拿他们的眼珠子做镜子里衬之类的奇谈，许多人还相信西洋医生的药有毒。

曼森临街开了一间诊所，以便让众人都看清他用的是外科手术刀而不是餐用刀叉。他因此赢得了当地人的信任。

西洋医生对热带疾病一无所知，曼森对此感到吃惊。他估计在 450 名厦门人中有 1 人是麻风患者，但西医学里没有任何针对性的治疗方案。他向大英博物馆索要关于蚊子的资料[1]，6 个月之后，人家回信说，他们没有关于蚊子的书，倒是寄来了一本关于蟑螂的书，他们希望这本书能多少帮点忙。

1883 年曼森搬到香港时，他发现西洋医生不懂得将伤寒与疟疾相区分，称伤寒为“肠热性疟疾”。英国于 1841 年刚占领香港时，疟疾几乎消灭掉整整一个团的人数。数年之间，英军有 3%人数死于这种可怕的疾病。

[1] 地球上最致命的生物，每年因蚊子叮咬而死的人口超过 200 万！

Western medicine was impotent in the face of tropical disease, and Chinese medicine fared no better. In 1877, 2% of Xiamen's population died of cholera, and to Manson's frustration, traditional Chinese doctors treated the disease with alum, stimulants, hot poultices, shampooing, and "pinching." But Manson discovered that, in fact, some Chinese treatments *did* work.

Chinese cured a woman's anemia with pills concocted from a black chicken's dried liver. Western doctors did not learn to treat pernicious anemia with liver until 1926. Perhaps Chinese medicine's occasional successes helped spur the Scotsman on to the research that gave birth to modern tropical medicine.

Pioneer or Drunken Scotsman? In his quest to conquer China's diseases, Manson dissected everything from mosquitoes to corpses (in the dead of night, in graveyards, because Chinese frowned on carving up corpses). But it was a lonely life, and in 1877 the discouraged young pioneer wrote to a friend in London,

> "I live in an out of the world place, away from libraries, out of the run of what is going on, so I do not know very well the value of my work, or if it has been done before, or better."

In fact, Manson's work was so far ahead of his time that other doctors ridiculed his discoveries. One doctor said Manson's claims represented "either the work of a genius or, more likely, the emanations of a drunken Scots doctor in far-off China, where, as everyone was aware, they drank too much whisky."

Manson was first to connect mosquitoes with elephantiasis (1878) and malaria (1894), and he discovered that only female mosquitoes suck blood (males live on fruit juices). Manson also invented new surgical techniques and instruments that even today bear his name (he had one elaborate device made by a local Chinese metal worker). He also helped introduce modern vaccination to China—ironically enough, since Taoists inoculated against smallpox almost 1,000 years ago. Ancient Chinese almost created surgery as well (see end of this chapter).

As news of Manson's medical prowess spread, patients flooded in. In 1871, Manson's first year at the Baptist Missionary Hospital, he treated 1,980 patients. His third year he treated 4,476 people. In 1877, he performed 237 elephantiasis surgeries alone. He removed over one ton of tumors and lost only two patients. He also got sued.

Suing the Surgeon!

One patient had so much excess tissue that he could not move and he was carted about town in a wheelbarrow. He made a living selling lemonade and peanuts, and created a table by spreading a cloth over his massive deformities. After Manson removed eighty pounds of tumors, allowing him to move freely once again, he promptly sued Manson and sought compensation. He complained that without his convenient table of deformed flesh he had lost his livelihood! Sir Philip Manson-Bahr, "Patrick Manson"

西医对于热带疾病无能为力，中医也没有更好的办法。1877 年，2%的厦门人口死于霍乱。令曼森失望的是，对于这种疾病，中国医生的传统疗法是用明矾、兴奋剂等材料，采取热敷、洗头和刮痧等手法。不过，曼森发现，有些中医疗法其实是管用的。

中医拿乌鸡肝烘干后制成药丸治好了妇女的贫血病。西医直到 1926 年才懂得用动物肝脏来治疗恶性贫血。也许是因为中医疗法偶尔的成功激励了这位苏格兰人从事探索，才诞生出现代热带医学。

是先驱还是苏格兰醉汉？在探索中国疾病疗法的过程中，曼森解剖了小到蚊子大到人的尸体（解剖工作是深夜里在坟地进行的。因为中国人忌讳解剖尸体）。然而，那是一种孤独的生活。1877 年，这位一时泄气的年轻的先驱者这样写给他一位在伦敦的朋友：

> “我住在世界之外，远离图书馆，不知外界正在发生什么。因此我不能确定我的工作价值所在，也许这份工作以前有人做过，甚至干得比我好。”

事实上，曼森的工作远远超过了他所处的年代，以至于别的医生嘲弄他的研究成果。一名医生说：“曼森的论断像是一位天才的工作成果，但更像是一个远在中国的醉酒的苏格兰医生所说的胡话。众所周知，他们在中国喝威士忌有多么凶。”

曼森是第一个把蚊子和象皮病（1878 年）及和疟疾（1894 年）联系在一起的人，他还发现只有母蚊子才吸血（公蚊子靠吸取植物的汁液维持生命）。曼森发明了外科新技术和新仪器，至今仍沿用他的名字（他有一件由一位中国当地金属匠精心打造的疗具）。他还帮助将现代的接种疫苗技术引入中国（颇具讽刺意味的是，大约一千年前道家就曾用接种手段预防天花，古代中国人还几乎开创了外科手术。请参阅本章结尾）。

曼森医术高超，渐渐声名远扬，病人也就纷沓而至。1871 年，也就是曼森在 Baptist Missionary 医院的第一年，他治疗了 1980 名病人，第三年他治疗病人 4476 名。1877 年这一年，单单象皮病手术一项他就做了 237 例。他切除的肿瘤达一吨多重，仅有两位病人丧生。他还吃过官司。

控告外科医生

有个病人身上赘生的息肉过度增长导致行动不便，出门得靠别人用小板车推着走。他卖柠檬水和花生度日，用一块布铺在他巨大的畸形部位，就能搭成一个桌面。当曼森将他 80 磅重的瘤子切除掉，使他重又行动自如后，他马上控告曼森，并要求赔偿。他抱怨说，失去了原来畸形部位这张随身桌子，他也就失去了生计！

Sir Philip Manson-Bahr，《帕特里克·曼森》

Manson, like Otte, knew that the way to combat disease was to multiply the medical warriors through medical education. In 1886, Manson established the Hong Kong College of Medicine, which boasted such alumni as Sun Yat-sen, first president of the Chinese Republic. In September, 1898, he opened the London School of Tropical Medicine, although he was adamantly opposed not only by the government but also, ironically, by the medical establishment (which perhaps still suspected his reams of insights were the work of a drunken Scotsman). After writing his bestselling "Manual of Tropical Diseases", Manson retired in 1912 to fish in Ireland, but returned to medicine at the beginning of World War I, and in spite of debilitating gout, he pursued medical education until his death in 1922.

Madame Dr. Lin Qiaozhi (林巧稚) **Pioneer Obstetrician and Gynecologist** Over 1000 years ago Chinese women transformed the male Guanyin into the "goddess of mercy" because male deities lacked compassion for the "weaker" sex. And male doctors, like male deities, were not especially known for sympathy with women's unique needs, so by the twentieth century, Chinese women were ready for Madame doctor Lin Qiaozhi—a product of Gulangyu's pioneering education of women.

Over Lin's 60-year career she personally delivered over 50,000 children, and her compassion and dedication won the hearts of men and women alike, many of whom named babies after her.

Lin was born on Gulangyu Islet on 23rd December, 1901, and grew up at #47 Huangyan Rd. She always excelled in school, perhaps because her parents were teachers. She said, "If boys can get a grade of 100, then I'll get 110!"

A teacher at the Gulangyu Girls Normal School saw Lin crocheting on a hot summer's day and said, "You have such great hands. You should be a doctor!" Lin blushed, but that comment helped set her course in life.

In 1921, Ms. Lin entered the grueling eight-year program at Beijing Union Medical College[1] (北京协和医科大学), and earned her doctor of medicine degree from New York State University (40% of her classmates never graduated). In spite of her diligence as a scholar she was very easy going, and loved singing with friends and reading English novels every night until 1 or 2 in the morning.

In 1932, Lin studied at the London Medical College and the Manchester Medical College, and the following year toured Vienna on a medical research trip. Seven years later, she studied in the Chicago Medical College. After returning to Beijing, she was appointed a hospital's director of obstetrics and gynecology—the 1st woman in China to have such a position.

[1] Started in 1906 by the Chinese government and several foreign religious agencies (hence the name "Union"), the Rockefeller Foundation re-organized and relocated it in 1917, and today it is China's most prestigious medical school.

如同郁约翰，曼森知道，与疾病作斗争就应该通过医学教育培养出更多的白衣战士。他于 1886 年创立了“香港医学院”，该学院为拥有民国第一任总统孙逸仙这样的校友而自豪。1898 年 9 月，他开设了“伦敦热带医学校”。他不仅遭到过政府的坚决反对，而且颇具讽刺意味地受到医学界的打压。他们可能还在怀疑这一大堆医学见解是一名苏格兰醉汉的酒后狂言。在写成他最畅销的《热带病指南》这本书后，曼森于 1912 年退休，到爱尔兰钓鱼消遣。但一战爆发后，他又重返医学。尽管痛风病使他日渐衰弱，他仍坚持从事医学教育，直到 1922 年去世。

妇产科先驱林巧稚博士（女士）

一千多年前，中国妇女因为男神缺乏对处于弱势的女性的同情心，而将男观音改为“慈悲为怀的女神”。如同男神，男医生无法从妇女的特殊需要出发去同情她们。于是到了二十世纪，中国妇女终于盼来了林巧稚博士——鼓浪屿女子先驱教育培养出的一位人才。

在林巧稚 60 年的职业生涯中，她一人接生了 50000 多名婴儿。她的关爱和奉献赢得了众多男人和女人的心，其中很多人用她的名字给自己的孩子起名。

1901 年 12 月 23 日，林巧稚出生于鼓浪屿，日光岩路 47 号是她的故居。也许是因为她的父母都是教师，她在学校总是成绩优秀。她说：“如果男生能考 100 分，那我就要考 110 分。”

一个夏季里的某天，鼓浪屿女子师范学校的一位老师看到林巧稚在用钩针做编织活，就对她说：“你有这么灵巧的一双手，以后应该当个医生。” 林巧稚一阵脸红，但那句评语却帮她确定了一生的轨迹。

1921 年，林巧稚进入教学要求异常严格的、学制八年的北京协和医科大学[1]。在那儿，她成绩优异，被纽约州立大学授予医学博士学位（她的同学 40%未能毕业）。尽管身为学者用功勤奋，但她平易近人，喜欢和朋友一起唱歌、每晚读英文小说都到凌晨一二点。

1932 年，林巧稚赴伦敦医学院和曼彻斯特医学院继续深造，次年前往维也纳做医学考察。七年后，她就读于芝加哥医学院。回北京后，她被任命为（协和）医院的妇产科主任，成为中国第一位担任这一职务的女医生。

[1] 由中国政府和几家外国宗教机构于 1906 年联合创办（故取名为“协和”），洛克菲勒基金于 1917 年迁址重建，成为当今中国最具影响力的医科学府。

Lin Qiaozhi never married but was close to her extended family. Her brother, Lin Zhenming [1](林振明), financed her studies at Beijing Union Medical University, and after her graduation she footed the bill for her older brother's four children to attend Yanjing University (燕京大学). After liberation, she made a list of her relatives in Fujian and sent money to them until she passed away.

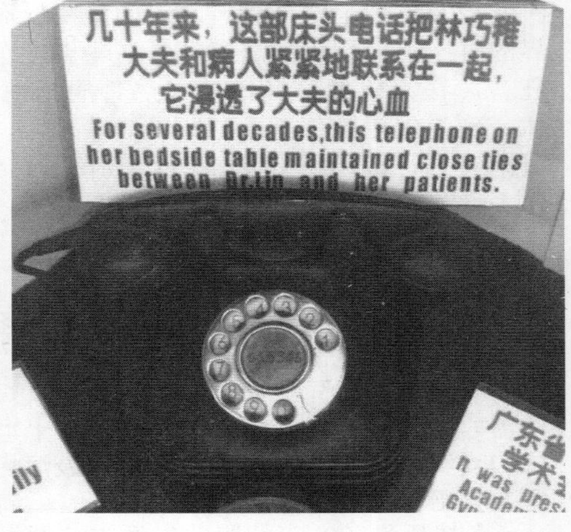

Dr. Lin was a model teacher, as well as writer and editor of such books as *Advice on Family Health.* She also chalked up many firsts. In 1955, she became the first female member of the Learned Department of Academia Sinica. In 1956, she was appointed vice-chairwoman of the China Medical Association. In 1959, she took up the position of director of the Beijing Maternity Hospital, as well as deputy director of the Chinese Academy of Medical Sciences.

In 1978, Lin became vice chairwoman of the National Women's Federation of China, and visited four West European countries as the deputy head of the Chinese People's Friendship delegation. But while in Britain, she suffered a brain hemorrhage, and was hospitalized for half a year before returning to China.

In 1980, Dr. Lin suffered another hemorrhage. On April 22nd, 1983, she passed away at the age of 82, having devoted her entire life to thousands of mothers and babies at the Beijing Union Medical College Hospital and, indirectly, to millions of women and children throughout China.

In 2001, famous doctors and prominent health officials and government leaders gathered in Beijing to celebrate the 100th anniversary of Lin's birth. Officials unveiled a copper statue of the doctor, and announced the new Lin Qiaozhi gynecological and obstetrics research institute at the Chinese Academy of Medical Sciences. Premier Li Peng wrote an inscription that reads, "Forever cherish the memory of outstanding medical scientist, Lin Qiaozhi."

---

[1] Lin Zhenming managed Gulangyu's Carbonated Drinks Factory (鼓浪屿汽水厂), and later moved to Taiwan, where he passed away in the 1970s.

林巧稚终生未婚，但与她的大家庭关系密切。她的哥哥林振明[1]曾资助她读北京协和医科大学，她毕业后则出钱供她大哥的四个孩子上燕京大学。解放后，她将福建的亲戚列成通讯录，给他们汇钱，直到她离开人世。

林博士是个优秀教师，也撰写和编辑诸如《家庭卫生顾问》这样的书。她还创下很多个第一：1955 年，她成为中科院第一位女学部委员；1956 年，她被任命为中华医学会副会长；1959 年她担任北京产科医院院长兼中国医学科学院副院长。

1978 年，林巧稚成为中国妇联副主席，以中国人民友好代表团副团长的身份访问西欧四国。在英国，她突发脑溢血，住院半年才回国。

1980 年，林巧稚再次脑溢血，于 1983 年 4 月 22 日去世，享年 82 岁。在北京协和医院，她把自己的生命奉献给了成千上万的母亲和婴儿，也间接地奉献给遍布全中国的数以百万计的妇女和儿童。

2001 年，著名的医生和健康专家以及政府领导云集北京纪念林巧稚诞辰 100 周年。领导人为一尊林巧稚铜像揭幕，并宣布中科院设立新的林巧稚妇产科研究中心。李鹏总理题词：“永远怀念杰出的医学家林巧稚。”

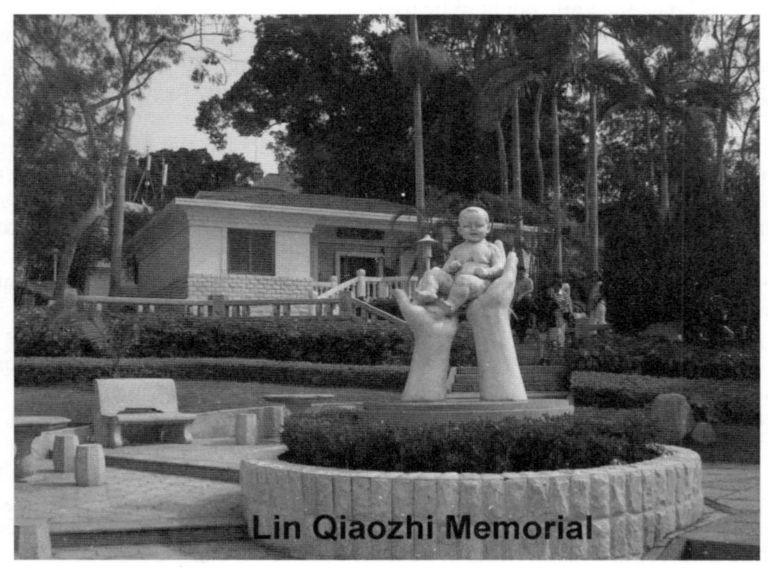
Lin Qiaozhi Memorial

[1] 林振明曾经营鼓浪屿汽水厂，后迁居台湾，70年代在台湾去世。

Learn more about Dr. Lin at the Lin Qiaozhi Memorial Hall on Zhangzhou Road, just past Fuxing church. This beautiful garden, with its sculptures of children and white marble statue of Lin, was built the year after Dr. Lin passed away, in 1984. The Exhibition Room tells her life story. A row of stone "books" along Zhangzhou Rd. shares such Lin quotes as:

"During the times I am not working, I feel lonely and isolated and as if life has no meaning." 我一闲下来就会感到寂寞、孤单,生命就会完结。

Supplement

How Ancient China Discovered (and lost!) Surgery

(From McGowan, 1913, pp.176-9)

"...There was not a doctor in the Empire who knew anything of anatomy and for any one of them to have performed a serious surgical operation would have meant certain death to the patient. [But]...

"Tradition tells the story of one famous doctor [华佗, Huatuo], who lived in the misty past, and whose prescriptions form part of the medical library of every regular practitioner, that is intensely interesting. He seems to stand out more prominently than any of the others who have become conspicuous in the history of medicine, because he evidently had the ambition and perhaps the genius to inaugurate a new system in the treatment of diseases. He evidently felt there were occasions when the knife ought to be used if life were to be saved.

"On one occasion a military officer had been severely wounded in the arm by a poisoned arrow in a great battle in which he had taken part. The doctor, who for long centuries has been a god, and shrines and temples have been erected in which his image sits enshrined, was summoned to his assistance. He saw at a glance that unless heroic measures were at once adopted the man would die of blood-poisoning. Contrary to the universal practice then in vogue, he cut down to the very bone, extracted the arrow, and scraping away the poison that might have been injected into the flesh, he bound up the gaping wound, using certain soothing salves to assist Nature in her process of healing.

"The result proved a great success, and might have been the means of introducing a new era in the treatment of diseases throughout China.

"Not long after a high mandarin [曹操, Caocao], who had heard of the wonderful cure, summoned the same doctor to prescribe for him. He had been greatly troubled with pains in his head, and no medical man that had attended him had been able to give him any relief. His case having been carefully diagnosed, the doctor proceeded to tell him what he thought ought to be done.

"I find," he said, "that what really is the matter with you is that your brain is affected. There is a growth upon it, which, unless it is removed, will cause your death. Medicine in this case," he continued, "will be of no avail. An operation will have to be performed. Your skull must be opened, and the growth that is endangering your life must be removed.

"The thing, I think, can be safely done, and your health will be perfectly restored, and you may continue to live for a good many years.

在位于漳州路复兴堂过去一点的林巧稚纪念馆，可以了解到更多林博士的生平。这座美丽的花园里有林巧稚的汉白玉大理石塑像以及儿童群雕，建于 1984 年，即林博士逝世的翌年。展览室则介绍了她的生平事迹。沿着漳州路旁，有一排石书，向众人展示林巧稚的语录，如：

“我一闲下来就会感到寂寞、孤单，生命就会完结。”

附录

古代中国外科手术的发明与失传

(From McGowan, 1913, pp.176-9)

“……在中国古代，没有一个医生对解剖学有所了解。医生如果要对病人动大手术，就意味着将病人推向死亡。（然而）……

“这是一个世代相传的很有趣的故事，它讲述了一位生活在不明年代的著名医生——华佗，他开的药方后来成了每个正规医生都遵循的药典的一部分。他似乎比医学史上其他任何名医更为卓越，因为他显然有雄心，或许还有创立一套治病新疗法的天赋。他显然认为，有时候动刀才能使病人获得重生。

“有一次，一位将军在一次恶仗中胳膊中了毒箭，病情严重。这位医生（后来几百年被奉为神仙并被雕塑成像供于庙宇）被召来为将军疗伤。他瞥了一眼就知道，除非采取大胆的措施并立即处理伤口，否则将军就会因血液中毒而死。有悖于当时通行的治病常规，他用刀切入伤口，直达骨头，取出箭头，刮掉毒汁，避免毒入肌里。他给伤口敷上了些止痛膏，将开裂的伤口包扎起来，以便更好地痊愈。

“结果这一疗法非常成功，只可惜没能推广普及全中国并开辟医疗新时代。

“不久后，曹操听人说起华佗出神入化的医术，就召他来为自己看病。曹操患的是严重的头疼病，先前为他看过病的医生没有一个能减轻他的病情。华佗对他作了认真仔细的诊断，然后把治疗方案告诉他。

“‘我发觉’，他说，‘您的真正问题所在，是您的大脑受到侵害，长了瘤子。因此必须将瘤子切除掉，否则您将性命不保。对于这样的病症，’他接着说，‘药物是起不到作用的，所以得做一次手术。您的头颅必须得打开，威胁您生命的瘤子才能得以切除。我想，手术是安全的，您的健康可以顺利地恢复，您还能活很久。

"If you are pleased to confide in me, I have full confidence in myself that I can do all that is needed to restore you to perfect health.

"Whilst he was talking a cloud had been slowly gathering over the mandarin's face. His eyes began to flash with excitement and a look of anger to convulse his face. In a voice tremulous with passion, he said: 'You propose to split open my skull, do you? It is quite evident to me that your object is to murder me. You wish for my death, but I shall frustrate that purpose of yours by having you executed.' Calling a policeman, he ordered him to drag the man to prison, whilst he gave orders to an official who was standing by that in ten days hence the doctor should be decapitated for the crime of conspiring against his life.

"During the days he was in prison he so won the heart of the jailer by his gentleness and patience that he showed him the utmost devotion and attention. The evening before his execution, he handed over to him some documents that he had been very carefully preserving, and said, 'I am most grateful to you for the kindness you have shown me during the last few days. You have helped to relieve the misery of my prison. I wish I had something substantial to give you to prove to you my appreciation of the sympathy and tender concern you have manifested towards me.

"'There is one thing, indeed, that I can bestow on you, and that is the manuscripts of all the cases I have attended. These,' he said, handing them to the jailer, 'will raise your family to wealth and honor for many generations yet to come. They explain the methods I have employed in the treatment of disease. Never part with them; neither let the secrets they contain be divulged by any of your posterity, and so long as your descendants are faithful to them poverty shall never shadow the homes of your sons and grandsons nor of their children after them.'

"Next day this great medical genius was foully put to death merely to satisfy the caprice of an ignorant official, and the first dawn of surgical enterprise was eclipsed by his death, and many a tedious century would have to drag its weary way along before the vision that had died out in blood would again appear to deliver the suffering men and women of China."

如果您信得过我，我会尽全力来让您完全恢复健康。’

“他话还没说完，曹操的脸色便阴沉了下来，目光如芒，容颜不悦，声音因激动而颤抖，‘你建议剖开我的头颅，是吗？这就足以说明你的目的是要害死我。既然你想让我死，我就先将你处死，让你不能得逞。’说完，他喊来卫兵，命令将华佗拖进牢里。同时他命令站在边上的一位官员，在十天之内以图谋杀官的罪名将华佗斩首。

“在被关押的日子里，华佗的温厚和忍耐赢得了狱吏的心，因此狱吏对他照顾入微。在被执行死刑的前一天晚上，华佗把自己精心保存的一些资料交给狱吏，说，‘十分感谢最后这几天来你对我的细致关心，你帮我减轻了牢中之苦，我想送你件重要的东西以表达我的感激之情。’

“‘我确实有一样东西可以送你，那就是记录我所有临床病例的手稿。这些，’他边递给狱吏边说，‘会给你的家庭和子子孙孙带来财富和荣耀。这些手稿阐述了我治病所运用的方法。要好好保管，让你的后裔千万别泄漏其中的秘密。只要你的子孙后人对它们忠心不二，他们的家庭乃至后代都不会受贫穷所困。’”

“第二天，这位伟大的医学天才就被一个昏官因一时狐疑而卑鄙地杀害了。他的死令中国外科事业的第一缕曙光黯然无色。在那血淋淋的杀戮之后，中国的男男女女还在继续遭受病痛无尽的折磨，不知还要经历多少个冗长的世纪才能迎来获救的希望。”

Streetside Doctor **(MacGowan, 1914)**

Chapter 6
Pioneering Music, Arts, & Literature

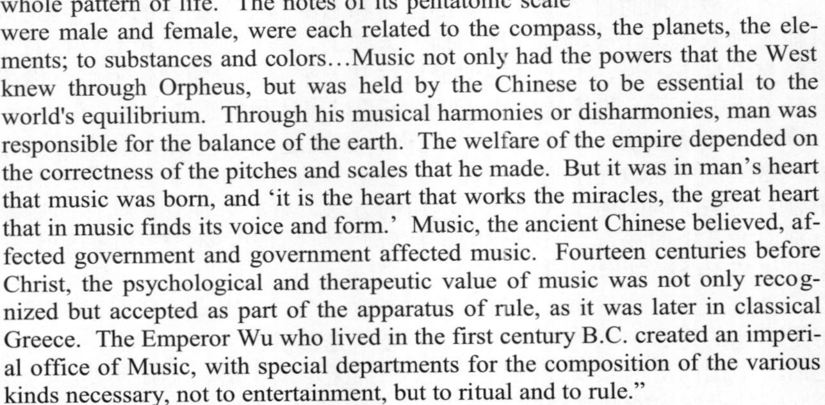

Music as Life in China

"In China, music had been inextricably woven into the whole pattern of life. The notes of its pentatonic scale were male and female, were each related to the compass, the planets, the elements; to substances and colors…Music not only had the powers that the West knew through Orpheus, but was held by the Chinese to be essential to the world's equilibrium. Through his musical harmonies or disharmonies, man was responsible for the balance of the earth. The welfare of the empire depended on the correctness of the pitches and scales that he made. But it was in man's heart that music was born, and 'it is the heart that works the miracles, the great heart that in music finds its voice and form.' Music, the ancient Chinese believed, affected government and government affected music. Fourteen centuries before Christ, the psychological and therapeutic value of music was not only recognized but accepted as part of the apparatus of rule, as it was later in classical Greece. The Emperor Wu who lived in the first century B.C. created an imperial office of Music, with special departments for the composition of the various kinds necessary, not to entertainment, but to ritual and to rule."

Anne-Averil McKenzie, "A Race of Green Ginger," 1920s

The Sounds of Music Gulangyu folks have been hooked on pianos ever since missionaries arrived with Bibles in one hand and pianos in the other (very big hands!). China's "Piano Islet" now has more pianos per capita than anywhere else in China, as well as Asia's largest piano museum[1] and what will soon be the world's largest organ museum.

Gulangyu's dozens of famous pianists and musicians have included Zhou Shuan in the '20s, Lin Junqing in the '30s, Wu Tianqiu in the '50s, and Xu Feixing in the 60s. Gulangyu is also the hometown of acclaimed conductor Chen Zuohuang, and Yin Chengzong, whom the New York Times has deemed the best Chinese pianist on the planet. In the 80s, Mr. Xu Feiping, a postgraduate student of the Juilliard School of Music, won many international prizes, including the Gold Medal in the 4th Arthur Rubinstein International Piano Master Competition in 1983 in Israel. And Gulangyu is still churning out globally acclaimed prodigies, thank to the Xiamen Music Academy.

---

[1] The Piano Museum is in Shuzhuang Gardens; the Organ Museum is in Bagua Lou

第六章

音乐、艺术和文学的先驱

在中国，音乐是生活的一部分

“在中国，音乐是生活不可分割的一部分。五声音阶的音符被赋予雄性和雌性的含义，每个音符都与罗盘、行星、元素，与物质和色彩相联系。对于中国人而言，音乐的力量已超出了西方人对俄耳甫斯神的了解范围，它还对保持万物均衡至关重要。音律的谐调或不调，会影响世界的平衡；编制的音阶与音高是否精确，会关系到帝国的福祉。但是，唯有在音乐中能发现声音与形态的心灵，能创造奇迹的伟大心灵，才能产生音乐。古代中国人相信，音乐能影响社稷，反之亦然。早在公元前 14 世纪，中国人就认识到音乐在心理与医疗方面的效果，并将它作为统治工具，就像后来的古希腊一样。公元前 1 世纪，吴王建立了宫廷音乐部门，专门谱写朝廷所需的各种曲子，并非用于娱乐，而是用于仪式和社稷统治。”

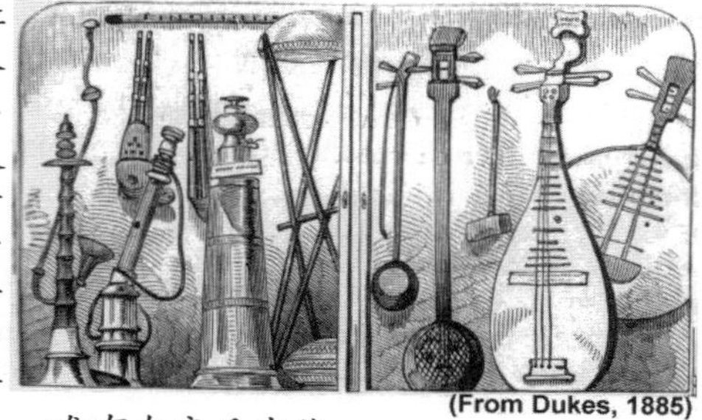
(From Dukes, 1885)

——Anne-Averil Mckenzie《绿姜根》，上世纪 20 年代于鼓浪屿

音乐之声

自从早期的传教士们一手捧着圣经、一手带着钢琴（这手可真够大的）来到这里，鼓浪屿人就与钢琴结下了不解之缘。

目前这座中国的“琴岛”人均钢琴拥有量为全国之最，同时还有着亚洲最大的钢琴博物馆[1]。（马上会有世界最大的风琴博物馆）

从鼓浪屿走出的几十位著名钢琴家和音乐家中，有活跃于上世纪 20 年代的周淑安，30 年代的林俊卿，50 年代的吴天球和 60 年代的许斐星。鼓浪屿也是殷承宗的家乡，《纽约时报》曾称他为世界上最棒的中国钢琴家。著名指挥家陈佐煌也是鼓浪屿人。上世纪 80 年代，从茱莉亚音乐学院硕士毕业的许斐平屡获国际大奖，包括在 1983 年以色列举行的第四届鲁宾斯坦国际钢琴大赛上夺得金奖。目前，位于岛上的厦门音乐学校还在不断培养输出国际知名的音乐人才。

---

[1] 钢琴博物馆位于菽庄花园，风琴博物馆位于八卦楼。

Xiamen Music Academy (Xiamen Yinyue Xuexiao, 厦门音乐学校), founded in 1988, has a staff of over 100 experienced teachers and professors teaching over 500 students of keyboards, strings, wind instruments, Chinese instruments, and vocals.

The school has fruitful exchange programs with schools and organizations in Australia, Japan, America, Germany, Russia, Malaysia, and Singapore, and has recruited prodigies from throughout the world. One of the school's first students, Miss Yao Lan (姚岚) is typical of Gulangyu's newest talents.

Yao Lan moved with her parents from neighboring Jiangxi Province to Xiamen and, intrigued by the home's large piano, began lessons at age four. She won first prize in a children's piano competition at age ten and was accepted into a primary school attached to Beijing's Central Conservatory of Music (中央音乐学院). She received a scholarship for the Royal Academy of Music in London and during graduate and postgraduate studies won several competitions in Britain. A Polish company produced an album of her performance in the 14th International Chopin Piano Competition.

After Yao Lan gave a performance in Xiamen in 2004, she said she hopes to eventually settle down on the island that today, more than ever, deserves the name "Isle of Music."

Zheng Xiaoying—the Isle of Music's Favorite Daughter The brightest star today in Gulangyu's firmament of musical talent is Madame Zheng Xiaoying, who according to Western media is "the best woman conductor in the world". Madame Zheng has performed at home and throughout Hong Kong, Taiwan and Macao, as well as in Russia, Japan, Australia, the U.S., Italy, Finland, Singapore, France, Holland, Germany, the U.K., Sweden, Estonia and Thailand.

Madame Zheng is the first Chinese musician to make popularizing the symphony her lifelong goal, and she has given over 2,000 performances with lectures to an estimated 300,000 people in mainland China.

厦门音乐学校

厦门音乐学校成立于 1988 年，拥有教授和老师 100 多人，学生 500 多人，主修科目有键盘乐器、管弦乐器、民族乐器及声乐。

学校与澳大利亚、日本、美国、德国、俄罗斯、马来西亚和新加坡等学校及团体的交流活跃而有成效，还在全球范围招收有才华的学生。姚岚，就是从学校最早的一批学生中走出的一颗新星。

姚岚小时随父母从邻省江西迁到厦门，四岁时迷上家里的大钢琴并开始学习。十岁时她在一次少儿钢琴比赛中获一等奖，并进入北京的中央音乐学院附小读书。后来她得到奖学金远赴伦敦的皇家音乐学院深造，在英国攻读学士及硕士期间在比赛中多次得奖，一家波兰公司还将她参加第十四届国际肖邦钢琴比赛的演奏录音制成专辑。

2004 年，姚岚在厦门演奏后曾说，希望将来能在鼓浪屿上安家。今天的鼓浪屿，比以往任何时候都更配得上“音乐岛”的美名。

Xiamen Music School

郑小瑛——“音乐岛”最心爱的女儿

在鼓浪屿音乐之星的天穹中，郑小瑛是最亮的一颗，被西方传媒誉为“全世界最好的女指挥家”。郑小瑛不仅在祖国大陆及港、澳、台地区演出，还曾远赴俄罗斯、日本、澳大利亚、美国、意大利、芬兰、新加坡、法国、荷兰、德国、英国、瑞典、爱沙尼亚和泰国执棒。

郑小瑛是国内第一个把普及交响乐作为毕生目标的音乐家。至今，她已经在祖国大陆举办 2000 多场带讲解的音乐会，观众总计超过 30 万人。

In a concert just days before her 75th birthday Madame Zheng still exemplified the exuberance that helped generations of her Hakka forebears succeed in China and abroad. And like all traditional Hakka, she values education, and uses her "Zheng Xiaoying System" to teach not only musicians but audiences to better understand and enjoy symphony. And as she learned early on in Xiamen, audiences do indeed need that education.

Before Madame Zheng was invited to Xiamen in 1998 to create China's first international model professional orchestra, Xiamen's symphony orchestra performances were lucky to get a couple dozen attendees a week. But with funding from local enterprises, Madame Zheng left her position as chief conductor of China's Central Opera Theater and Dean of the Department of Conducting at China's Central Conservatory of Music to create the Xiamen Philharmonic Orchestra. It was a blind leap of faith, but in just 6 short years her 30-member orchestra has grown to over 80 members, and has made a name for itself both in China and abroad. As of this writing, the Xiamen Philharmonic has given over 450 performances with a repertoire of over 100 symphonies and symphonic suites, 100 concertos for various instruments, and over 200 overtures, symphonic poems and other pieces.

Madame Zheng was the first nationally recognized female conductor in China, and the first Chinese conductor to take the podium of an opera theater abroad or to conduct a foreign opera company. She took advanced studies at the National Conservatory of Music in Moscow, where she received the French Literature and Arts Medal of Honor. Madame Zheng founded the Women's Philharmonic Orchestra (Ai Yue Nu,), which became China's first women's chamber and symphony orchestra, and in 1995 in Beijing, she conducted both the orchestra and the chorus as they performed Beethoven's "Ode to Joy" for the opening of the United Nations 4th World Conference on Women.

On November 23, 2002, in Middletown, Connecticut, Madame Zheng conducted the Wesleyan University Orchestra in "Echo of Hakka Earthen Buildings". She was accompanied by the symphony's composer, Liu Yuan, and two famous Fujian folk musicians—mountain vocalist Li Tiansheng ("King of W. Fujian Mountain Songs") and Qiu Shaochun, the famous Fujian "leaf player," who blew the audience away with music produced with nothing more than a natural leaf (I wonder how often he has to turn over a new leaf?).

郑小瑛 75 岁生日前夕，还执棒一场音乐会，显示出客家人特有的丰沛活力，而祖祖辈辈的客家人就是靠着这种精神在海内外取得了成功。和所有传统的客家人一样，郑小瑛重视教育，并运用她的“郑小瑛模式”引导音乐家和观众更好地理解和欣赏交响乐。她早先在厦门就了解到，观众们确实需要这样的教育。

1998 年，在郑小瑛受邀来厦组建中国第一个国际模式的职业乐团之前，厦门每周的交响乐演出门可罗雀。当得知本地企业同意出资后，郑小瑛毅然辞去中央歌剧院首席指挥和中央音乐学院指挥系主任的职务，组建厦门爱乐乐团。当时凭着信念放手一搏，现在短短 6 年之后，乐团就从 30 人发展到 80 多人，在国内外有了名气。截至撰写此书时，厦门爱乐乐团已演出 450 多场，演奏曲目包括 100 多部交响乐和交响组曲，100 多首不同乐器的协奏曲，以及 200 多首序曲、交响诗和其他作品。

郑小瑛是中国第一位闻名全国的女指挥家，也是第一个在国外执棒外国乐队的中国指挥。她早先在莫斯科的国立音乐学院深造，获得法国文学艺术荣誉奖章。郑小瑛还成立了爱乐女乐团，这是中国第一个全部由女性组成的室内交响乐团。1995 年在北京，她指挥“爱乐女”和合唱团，为联合国第四届世界妇女大会开幕式演出贝多芬的“欢乐颂”。

2002 年 11 月 23 日，在美国康涅狄克州的中镇，郑小瑛指挥韦斯利安大学乐队演出“土楼回响”。在场的还有该曲的作者刘湲及两位著名的福建民乐家——一位是山地歌手李天生（“闽西山歌王”），另一位是叶笛演奏家邱少春，他仅用一片普通的树叶就能吹出醉人的曲调。（我好奇的是他得多长时间换一片新树叶呢？）

Madame Zheng Xiaoying--a Daughter of Gulangyu

The Wesleyan orchestra spent half a year preparing, but Madame Zheng had only one week for on-site rehearsals, and the chorus rehearsed the finale, "A Song of Hakka (in Hakka dialect, no less!) only once, for one hour. The performance still earned a standing ovation, and Madame Zheng returned home, happy she had helped forge another link between East and West by teaching Americans about China, and helping Chinese better appreciate symphony.

A music student wrote of the Wesleyan concert, "Mixing a Western-looking orchestra with Asian feel was very emotional and thought-provoking, especially because it involved aspects of Europe, Asia and America." Another student said, "The music evoked a sense of awe and pride."

While Madame Zheng has had a busy professional life she has always kept her family as a high priority—and music appears to run in her family even as it has the Yin's for the past seven decades. Her daughter Su Zheng is a highly regarded ethnomusicologist.

Gulangyu's First Family of Music—the Yin's (殷家) The Yin family, led by its banker patriarch, arrived on Gulangyu in the '30s and settled easily into the world of privilege that the International Settlement afforded foreigners and wealthy Chinese. The Yins were Christians, and since all Gulangyu churches had at least one piano, they quickly took to music, producing decades of talented musicians and vocalists. A female soprano made Christian recordings in the 1930s, and a male Yin became a famous baritone and settled in Los Angeles in the 1980s. Yin Chengdian (殷承典) is a music teacher and a founder of the Xiamen Music School. But the most famous member of the family is Yin Chengzong (殷承宗), whom the New York Times has said is "China's best pianist", with an "absolutely beautiful command of piano color."

Yin was born on Gulangyu in 1941 and began piano at age 7—virtually self-taught. He gave his first recital at age 9, and at 12 enrolled in the Shanghai Conservatory of Music. At 18 he won a gold medal in the piano competition of the World Youth Peace and Friendship Festival in Vienna. He enjoyed quite a reputation—until the Cultural Revolution's Red Guards denounced all things Western, including philosophy, literature, and music—and those who indulged in such decadence. The savvy Yin rolled a piano into Tiananmen Square and for three days played revolutionary tributes to Chairman Mao, saving not only his own hide but also his prized bourgeois instrument. This, perhaps more than anything else, not only stopped Red Guards from beating pianists and violinists but also moved China to adopt these instruments for the revolutionary cause.

Mr. Yin helped write the revolutionary "Yellow River Concerto," which is popular even today, but after the Cultural Revolution he was again persecuted and banned from playing for several years.

Yin Chengzong moved to the U.S. in 1983, settled down in Manhattan, and put politics, but not China, behind him. In 2003, Chengzong made a concert tour of China, and now plans to help Gulangyu's renovation of architecture and emphasis of its musical heritage. Visit the Yin's Villa at #16 Jishan Rd.

韦斯利安大学乐队花了半年时间来准备这场音乐会，郑小瑛到场与乐队排练的时间只有一个星期，与合唱队排练终曲“客家山歌”（必须用客家方言演唱）的时间只有一个小时。尽管如此，演出结束后观众们都起立鼓掌。郑小瑛满意而归，因为此行使东西方之间的联系更加紧密，不仅让美国人更多地了解中国，也让中国人更好地理解了交响乐。

那场音乐会后，一位音乐专业的学生写道：“用一支西方人的乐队传递出亚洲人的感觉，这真令人激动，浮想联翩，特别是它还融合了欧洲、亚洲和美洲的各方文化。”另一位学生则说：“音乐表现了一种自豪感，令人肃然起敬。”

郑小瑛忙于事业的同时，也一直很注重家庭，她的女儿郑苏是位杰出的民族音乐学家。音乐成了郑小瑛家庭生活的一部分，就像在过去的七十多年间，它也是殷家生活的一部分一样。

鼓浪屿第一音乐之家——殷家

殷家早先从事银行业，上世纪 30 年代在鼓浪屿定居，并很快适应了这个外国人和富有中国人共同居住的优越环境。殷家人都是基督徒，因为岛上的教堂都配有钢琴，他们很快就爱上了音乐，并在之后的几十年间培育了许多才华横溢的演奏家和歌唱家。其中就有一位在上世纪 30 年代灌录基督教歌曲的女高音歌唱家，还有一位著名的男中音歌唱家在上世纪 80 年代定居洛杉矶。殷承典是位音乐老师，他参与创建了厦门音乐学校。但家族中最负盛名的要数殷承宗，《纽约时报》称他为“中国最好的钢琴家”，“对音色的驾驭已经炉火纯青”。

殷承宗 1941 年出生在鼓浪屿，7 岁开始学琴——几乎是自学成才，9 岁举办首场演奏会，12 岁进入上海音乐学院。18 岁时，在维也纳举办的世界青年和平与友谊节的钢琴比赛中，他获得金奖，从此声名鹊起。直到“文化大革命”开始，红卫兵批判所有西方的东西，包括哲学、文学和音乐，也批判那些沉迷其间的人。头脑灵活的殷承宗把钢琴搬到天安门广场上，连着三天演奏献给毛主席的革命颂歌，不但救了他自己，也使这架资产阶级乐器免遭横祸。有人评价说，此举意义不同凡响，它使红卫兵停止迫害钢琴家和小提琴家，也让当时的中国把西洋乐器用于革命事业。

殷承宗参与谱写的革命作品“黄河协奏曲”，直至今日仍备受欢迎。“文革”后他受到牵连，有几年不能登台演出。

1983 年，殷承宗移民美国，定居曼哈顿。他心怀祖国，但不再过问政治。2003 年，殷承宗在中国作巡回演出，目前他正计划协助鼓浪屿的建筑改造和音乐传承。欢迎前去拜访位于鸡山路 16 号的殷家别墅。

Conductor Zuohuang Chen The world famous conductor Zuohuang Chen was born in 1947 in Shanghai but grew up on Gulangyu Islet—so we claim him. Chen graduated from the Central Conservatory of Music's middle school in 1965—just in time to be sent to the countryside during the Cultural Revolution. Western literature and music were banned, so he toiled in fields by day and by night furtively studied music he'd smuggled from Beijing.

Chen received his conducting degree in 1981, and took a master's class with Seiji Ozawa, music director of the Boston Symphony Orchestra. He then studied in the U.S. at the Tanglewood Music Center and the University of Michigan's School of Music. In 1985, at the University of Michigan, he became the first Chinese to earn a Doctor of Musical Arts. In 1986, during two years of directing the University of Kansas Symphony Orchestra, he received the HOPE award for outstanding teaching.

In 1987, Chen became conductor of the Central Philharmonic Society in Beijing, and after touring 24 U.S. cities he led this orchestra, as well as the China Youth Symphony Orchestra and the China Junior Symphony Orchestra, on six highly successful tours of European and Asian countries.

Chen was music director and conductor for the Wichita Symphony Orchestra from 1990 to 2000, conductor of the Rhode Island Philharmonic Orchestra from 1991 to 1996, and received the Art Award and a Citation from the governors of both Kansas and Rhode Island.

In 1996, Chen became the first artistic director and principal conductor of the China National Symphony Orchestra—China's first professional orchestra to adopt a contract system and professional management of performances.

Chen has visited over 20 countries as guest conductor for 30 orchestras, including the Mexico National Symphony Orchestra, Colorado Symphony Orchestra, Zurich Tonhalle Orchestra, Vancouver Symphony Orchestra, Hungary State Symphony Orchestra, Pacific Symphony Orchestra, Hamburg Youth Symphony Orchestra of Germany, Russia Philharmonic Orchestra, Slovak Radio Symphony Orchestra, Haifa Symphony Orchestra of Israel, Hong Kong Philharmonic Orchestra, and the Taipei City Symphony Orchestra.

Gulangyu Music Hall (and former foreigner's cemetery) 番仔墓与鼓浪屿音乐厅 Please turn to the Huangyan Rd. chapter.

Xiamen Gulangyu Piano Museum (厦门鼓浪屿钢琴博物馆) Given Gulangyu's musical heritage, it is no surprise that Australian Overseas Chinese Mr. Hu Youyi chose his ancestral home for Asia's largest piano museum, which has over 70 pianos from the U.K., France, U.S., Germany, Australia, and Austria, and over 100 priceless piano lamps.

The Gulangyu Piano Museum's two halls are set within the tropical flowers and trees of a 2,000 square meter tract of land on the hill overlooking Shuzhuang Garden and the sea.

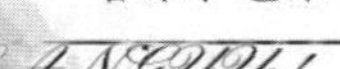

指挥家陈佐煌

闻名世界的指挥家陈佐煌 1947 年出生于上海，但他是在鼓浪屿长大的，所以也算上一个。陈佐煌 1965 年从中央音乐学院附中毕业，正好赶上“文化大革命”上山下乡。由于西方文学和音乐都在被禁之列，他只好白天在地里干活，晚上偷偷学习从北京带去的音乐材料。

1981 年陈佐煌获得指挥学位，并在时任波士顿交响乐团音乐总监小泽征尔的大师班里学习。接着他在美国檀格渥音乐中心和密歇根大学音乐学院就读。1985 年在密歇根大学，他成为第一个获得音乐艺术博士学位的中国人。1986 年，在执棒堪萨斯大学交响乐团的两年间，他还因教学成果突出获得 HOPE 奖。

1987 年，陈佐煌在北京成为中央交响乐团的指挥。在美国 24 个城市巡回演出之后，他又率该团和中国青年交响乐团、中国少年交响乐团在欧洲和亚洲作了六次非常成功的巡演。

1990 年至 2000 年，陈佐煌任威屈塔交响乐团指挥和音乐总监；1991 年至 1996 年，任罗德岛交响乐团指挥，并获得过堪萨斯州和罗德岛州州长颁发的艺术奖和嘉奖各一次。

1996 年，陈佐煌成为中国国家交响乐团第一个艺术总监和首席指挥，该乐团是中国第一个实行合同制和职业化管理的专业乐团。

作为客座指挥，陈佐煌去过 20 多个国家和地区，执棒过 30 多个乐团，包括墨西哥国家交响乐团、科罗拉多交响乐团、苏黎世唐霍乐团、温哥华交响乐团、匈牙利国立交响乐团、太平洋交响乐团、德国汉堡青年交响乐团、俄罗斯爱乐乐团、斯洛伐克广播交响乐团、以色列海法交响乐团、香港管弦乐团以及台北交响乐团。

鼓浪屿音乐厅与番仔墓

请参见晃岩路一章。

厦门鼓浪屿钢琴博物馆

鼓浪屿的音乐文化积淀深厚，难怪澳大利亚籍华人胡友义先生选择在他的家乡鼓浪屿上，建立亚洲最大的钢琴博物馆。该馆目前收藏有来自英国、法国、美国、德国、奥地利和澳大利亚的 70 多台钢琴以及 100 多盏珍贵的琴灯。鼓浪屿钢琴博物馆的两个展厅位于可俯瞰菽庄花园和海景的一座小山上，掩映在两千平方米的热带花木丛中。

Pasquale Street Piano (London, 1899) Also called "barrel piano," because it used a barrel filled with different lengthed nails, they were used downtown for monkey shows and street performances.

A perfect way to finish the museum tour is to sit on one of the piano benches before the ceiling-to-floor plate glass windows and savor the scenery while listening to piped in classical piano pieces.

Mr. Hu's collection includes a French street musician's barrel piano (I half expected to see an organ grinder and a monkey), the Broadwood & Sons piano that won a golden medal at the Paris International Fair, a grand piano with ivory keys from an English palace, and a piano cherished by president Lincoln.

The first of the two halls, opened January of 2000, has the collection's oldest piano. Few pianos were actually built by pianists, but this instrument was crafted in 1801 by visionary composer Muzio Clementi (1752-1832).

Clementi crafted both uprights and grands on which to perform his more than 106 sonatas (46 were for violin, cello or flute), as well as countless smaller pieces. Clementi is also remembered for the horrifying tale in which George Grove visited Clementi's nephew, a vicar in south-east England, and found the maid lighting a fire with Clementi's manuscript! I wonder if she was fired?

Hall #1 also has the world's tallest upright piano (an 1824 Broadwood & Sons, from London), and Hall No. 2 showcases the development of the piano with exhibits like the 1928 Haines. The most expensive piano of its era, this American marvel was completely automatic, able to perfectly imitate the styles of many well known pianists. As of this writing, the Haines is played for visitors daily at 4 pm. Address: No.45 Huangyan Rd (Shuzhuang Garden)

Gulangyu Organ Museum[1] The only such museum in China and soon to be the largest of its kind in the world, it opened in early 2005 in the red-domed Bagua Building with exhibits donated by the Piano Museum's founder, Mr. Hu Youyi. Vivian Zhang quoted Hu as saying at the museum's opening concert,

> "Pipe organs are acclaimed as the most sublime and divine musical instrument in the west. I hope one day organ lovers from all over the world will come on a music pilgrimage to my hometown, Gulangyu, to appreciate its beauty."

---

[1] Some info adapted from Vivian Zhang's "The Sound of Heaven," in Xiamen Daily's English weekly "Common Talk," March 16-22, 2005 Organist Paul Carr also provided invaluable information on the organ's history, and how it was transported to Gulangyu.

参观展馆的最佳方式莫过于坐在整面落地窗前的琴凳上，边欣赏美景，边聆听播放的古典钢琴曲。

胡友义的藏品包括一台法国卖艺人用的手摇风琴（我猜想那位街头手风琴师还有只猴子作伴），一台曾在巴黎国际博览会上获金奖的布罗伍德钢琴，一台有象牙琴健的来自英国皇宫的大钢琴，还有林肯总统钟爱的一台钢琴。

展馆中较早的一座于 2000 年 1 月开放，摆放有藏品中最古老的一台钢琴。很少有钢琴家自己制作钢琴，而这台钢琴就是由富于幻想的作曲家克莱门蒂（1752—1832）在 1801 年制造的。

克莱门蒂亲手制作立式钢琴和三角钢琴，并用它们谱写了 106 首奏鸣曲（其中 46 首为小提琴、大提琴或长笛奏鸣曲），以及数不清的较小作品。人们还记得有关他的一个可怕的故事：一次乔治·格鲁夫去英格兰东南部看望克莱门蒂当牧师的侄子，却发现女佣正用克莱门蒂的曲谱生火！不知后来她有没有被炒鱿鱼。

在一号展馆，有世界上最高的直立式钢琴（1824 年产的布罗伍德钢琴，来自伦敦），二号馆则展示了钢琴的发展过程，其中有一台 1928 年产的美国汉斯钢琴是当时最贵的钢琴，绝妙之处在于它是全自动的，能逼真地模仿许多著名钢琴家的演奏风格。现在每天下午四点钟，馆方会为参观者弹奏这台钢琴。钢琴博物馆地址在晃岩路 45 号（菽庄花园）。

鼓浪屿风琴博物馆[1]

这是中国唯一的，也将会是世界最大的风琴博物馆。它位于有着红穹顶的八卦楼，2005 年初向公众开放，全部藏品都由钢琴博物馆的创建人胡友义先生捐赠。下面是厦门日报《双语周刊》记者张薇薇在她文中摘录的、胡先生在风琴博物馆开幕式上的讲话：

> “管风琴是西方最崇高而神圣的乐器，我希望全世界爱好音乐的人们都能带着朝圣的心来到我的家乡鼓浪屿，欣赏她的美。”

[1] 部分信息来源于《厦门日报》英文周刊《双语周刊》2005年3月16日一期张薇薇写的“The Sound of Heaven”。风琴演奏家Paul Carr也提供了有关该风琴的历史，以及风琴如何运到鼓浪屿的宝贵信息。

The organ played at the opening concert was a historic "Norman & Beard" made in 1909. The 6 meter high instrument has 1,350 pipes, 3 layers of keyboards and 21 organ stops, and took Ian Wakeley, an Australian organ technician, over a month to restore and tune. Ian explained why the organ was in such good shape:

> "It is made of the best materials by the best builders with the best techniques and is representative of the highest level at that time. And that is why, after nearly a century, it still remains in amazingly good condition while most other instruments of its age have long since decayed."

This organ was formerly in England's Cradley Heath Methodist Church, where Paul Carr gave his 100th and final concert on it in June 2003. Carr seems happy with its new home. He wrote, "as the organ will not be squashed into a corner, as it was at Cradley Heath, it could sound up to 50% louder!"

Paul Carr at his 100th recital on the Norman and Beard (in England)

The church was to be closed, so organist Mark Checkley spread the word on the internet that the venerable instrument needed a home, but after 18 months and 250 responses, the best offer was from a local organ builder who wanted to dismantle the beauty and salvage pipes and parts for a future organ. But finally they heard that Ian Wakeley was seeking an organ for a Chinese client, and within a couple of weeks the organ was destined for Gulangyu.

The day after the church's final service on Sunday, July 18th, Ian and two assistants began 4 days of carefully dismantling the instrument and packing the components into crates custom made on the spot. Organist Paul Carr said it took four men six hours just to load the parts onto the truck, where it was hauled to Southhampton Dock, loaded onto the slow boat to China—and reassembled on Gulangyu.

Visit this remarkable instrument—and ask the attendants to play it for you!

在开幕式上演奏的是一台具有历史意义的 1909 年造的 Norman & Beard 风琴，高 6 米，有 1350 根音管，3 层键盘和 21 个音栓。澳大利亚的风琴技师伊安·威克利花了一个多月的时间进行组装和调试。当问及这台风琴为何状态良好时，伊安解释说：

“它是由最好的工人用最好的工艺和材料制成的，代表了当时最高的水平。尽管过了将近一百年，同时期的乐器早就腐朽了，而它却得以保存完好。”

这台风琴早先是摆放在英格兰的卫理公会派教堂。2003 年，风琴家保罗·卡尔在这里举行了他第 100 场，也是最后一场音乐会。卡尔对风琴的新家很满意，他写道：“这台风琴将不再像以前那样，被挤在教堂的一个角落，这样它的音量会增加一半。”

当时因为教堂将被关闭，风琴家马克·切克雷在因特网上登出这台古风琴寻找新家的信息。此后的一年半里，共有 250 个答复，但最好的也不过是一个本地的风琴制造商想把这个杰作拆除，好利用它的音管和部件。最后，他们终于听说伊安·威克利正为一位中国客户物色风琴，于是几个星期后，决定把这台风琴运往鼓浪屿。

7 月 18 日是星期天，教堂举行了最后一次仪式。在之后的四天里，伊安和他的两位助手小心翼翼地拆卸风琴，把所有部件当场装箱。据保罗·卡尔说，4 个工人花了 6 个小时才把箱子装好车，然后开到南汉普顿码头，用慢船运往中国，最后在鼓浪屿组装。

快去参观这台令人叹为观止的乐器吧——记得请工作人员为你弹奏一曲哦！

Inside the Intricate "Norman and Beard" Organ

An Amoy University Concert

by Anne Averil McKenzie, Gulangyu resident in the 1920s

(Dukes, 1885)

"The University looked quiet and purposeful in the grey afternoon. The large plain blocks were lifted from monotony by the upcurved, green-tiled roofs, an excellent blend of Eastern and Western idioms. Its situation, between the granite rocks and the sea, had an austere dignity. It was hard to associate the place and the quietly animated students, drifting about the still raw quadrangle and gardens, with riots and rabbles; with histrionics perhaps, but not with hysterics. Yet, all over China, it was the students who supplied the most ardent and fanatical agitators, as well as the political spearheads of revolution...

"In one of the smaller halls we gathered to hear the 'se' players. The first performer already sat behind the table which bore his instrument, a kind of psaltery, and was there a single orchid in a vase--or am I in another picture? He wore grey brocaded silk beneath his short black satin jacket and bent gravely over the silk strings.

"'I hope,' he eyes us solemnly, 'you, my honoured audience, will not emulate the Emperor Huang Ti who, you will remember, was so deeply moved by the Lady Su's playing of the "se" that he forthwith ordered the number of strings to be halved in order that he might suffer less.'

"The audience was delighted.

"From the first, the music was between the player and his 'se.' He seemed to be privately communing with the strings. Then I had the sensation that he and the "se" were one, and that their utterances were too subtle for me to understand... Its idiom was entirely strange, too baffling for immediate enjoyment, but it left us both with an aftermath in memory as strong and elusive as the aroma of Chinese tea on the palate.

"In China, from legendary times, music was written for poetry and poetry written to be sung. Both spoke a language I could not understand, using age-old symbols, classic repetitions and allusions to which I had not been educated to respond either intellectually or emotionally."

一场厦门大学的音乐会

（Anne Averil McKenzie 著，20 世纪 20 年代居于鼓浪屿）

Roadside Theater (MacGowan, 1912)

这是一个灰濛濛的下午，学校显得安静又有意境。简朴的大楼因向上弯曲的绿瓦屋顶而不再单调，体现了东西方风格的完美融合。它位于花岗岩石和海之间，彰显出一种简朴的高贵。活泼的学生们安静地出入于庭院和花园，很难把他们及这样一个地方与暴乱闹事联系起来，就算有大概也是演戏，而不是真的歇斯底里。然而在全中国，确实是学生们充当了革命最狂热的鼓动者和政治先锋。

我们聚在一个稍小的礼堂里准备听瑟的演奏。第一个表演者已经坐在桌子后面，桌上摆放着他的乐器，这是一种古代弦乐器，边上一朵兰花插在花瓶里——莫非我是置身在画中吗？他外穿黑色缎子短袄，内着灰色锦缎马褂，神情庄严地专注于琴弦。

“我希望大家，”他说话时眼神严峻，“我尊敬的听众，不要像黄帝一样。众所周知，他被苏夫人的瑟深深打动之后，立刻命令将琴弦的数量减半来减少自己的痛苦。”

听众闻之动容。

演奏一开始，音乐存在于演奏者和 “瑟”之间，他似乎在和琴弦喁喁私语。后来我感觉他和“瑟”融为了一体，两者间的交谈太玄妙令我难以理解……这种语汇是全然陌生，令人困惑的，不能给人即时的愉悦，但却给我们留下一段回忆，就像中国茶留在腭间的芳香一样强烈而又难以捉摸。

在中国，从传说中的年代开始，音乐就为诗而作，诗又为了歌而作。它们都传递着我无法理解的语言。对于那些古老的符号、经典的重复和暗示，在理性上和感性上我都不知如何产生共鸣。

Magic Horizons

"Each day the hill-ranges of the mainland presented us with a fresh expression. In league with the light and shadow, they cunningly rearranged their contours, played tricks on our eyes, held us with an hallucinatory magic. They floated, dissolved, redrew themselves on the pearly distances with an infinite variety of emphasis. I began to understand the fascination of this bare-boned landscape, the spell which it had laid on generations of Chinese poet-painters."

Averil Mackenzie-Grieve, Gulangyu Resident in 1920s

Teng Hiok Chiu—Gulangyu's Rediscovered Artist[1] Gulangyu's main claim to fame is music but recently we've learned the islet has also produced at least one internationally acclaimed artist!

Chiu's youth was a time of political turmoil, but the beauty of Gulangyu opened his eyes to art. He wrote,

"Since I used to play amidst the beautiful temples and pine trees or on the sandy beach, I have wanted to appreciate the best in nature and to be able to help everyone else to do so."

At age 14 Chiu was sent to the London Missionary Society's Anglo-Chinese College in Tianjin. After graduating he moved to the U.S. in 1920, studied art history, architecture and archaeology in Harvard for a semester, and then moved on to the Museum School of Fine Arts in Boston. He went to Paris in 1923, and in 1925 won a royal family-funded scholarship for the Royal Academy of Arts. Over the next five years, Chiu won every art competition he entered.[2] (He was also a member of Britain's Olympic basketball team!)

---

[1] Adapted from Vivian Zhang's "Immersed in Chinese Art," "Common Talk", March 17, 2004; "Path of the Sun—the World of Teng Hiok Chiu," by Dr. Kazimierz Z. Poznanski; and "Bold Comeback," by Rose Tang, Weekend Standard, June 26-7, 2004

[2] Tang wrote Chiu "was the 1st foreign artist to win the Turner Gold Medal and the Royal Academy Gold medal for his paintings." Queen Mary attended his 1929 solo exhibition in London, and he was the first foreign Associate of the Royal Society of British Artists.

梦幻天际

每天，陆地上的山峦都看上去焕然一新。在光与影的配合下，它们捉弄人的眼睛，巧妙地变换着轮廓，似有一股魔力让我们入迷。在远处珍珠色的天际，它们时而飘浮，时而消融，时而聚集，变幻无穷。我开始理解清隽的中国山水画的魅力，它附着在中国的诗画家们身上代代相传。 Averil Mackenzie-Grieve, 上世纪 20 年代居于鼓浪屿

周廷旭——被重新发现的鼓浪屿画家[1]

鼓浪屿主要以音乐闻名于世，但是最近我们了解到，岛上至少曾出过一位闻名世界的画家。

周廷旭的青年时代政局动荡，但鼓浪屿的美丽还是启迪了他的艺术灵感。他曾写道：

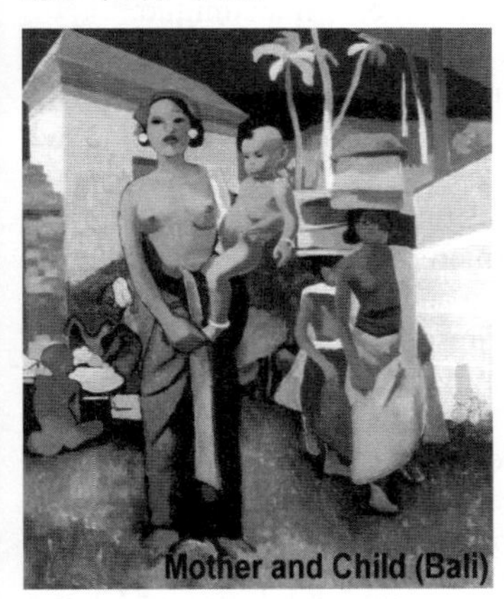
Mother and Child (Bali)

“我常常在宏伟的庙宇里、松林中和沙滩上嬉戏，我一直想见识自然界最好的东西，也希望能让别人见识到。”

14 岁时，周廷旭被送进由伦敦差会在天津办的英华学院。毕业后，他于 1920 年去了美国，在哈佛大学读了一学期的艺术史、建筑和考古学，之后又进入波士顿的美术馆学院。1923 年他去巴黎，并于 1925 年获得一项由皇室家族提供的奖学金，在皇家艺术学院学习。在之后的五年间，他每次参加艺术比赛都得了奖[2]。（他还曾是英国奥林匹克篮球队队员呢。）

[1] 该文的许多信息来源于《双语周刊》2004年3月17日一期张薇薇写的“Immersed in Chinese Art”；卡兹教授写的“Path of the Sun——the World of Teng Hiok Chiu”；以及Rose唐写的登在2004年6月26-27日“Weekend Standard”上的《雄归》。

[2] 据Rose唐所说，周廷旭是第一个因油画获得Turner金奖和皇家学院金奖的外国画家。玛丽女王还参观了他1929年在伦敦的个展，他还是第一个入选英国艺术家皇家协会的外国人。

But Chiu never courted fame, and after his death in 1972 the once celebrated artist's masterpieces were sold off at auctions and even garage sales, his paintings in China were destroyed by Red Guards, and the world forgot him. I was fortunate enough to learn about Chiu only because Xiamen University's Professor Tang Shaoyun gave me Rose Tang's article, "Bold Comeback," which recounted Dr. Kazimierz Z. Poznanski's rediscovery of Chiu when he came across 4 small black and white photos of Chiu's paintings in an auction catalogue.

Like many foreigners, Dr. Kaz cared little for classical Chinese paintings, and thought modern Chinese art was just a poor imitation of Western Art. He told Common Talk's Vivian Zhang, "But in the West, people don't give much attention to Chinese oil painters, assuming that Chinese artists using western techniques are just imitating instead of creating original art." But Dr. Kaz was captivated by the beauty and harmony—the innate "Chineseness"—of Chiu's Western-style oils, which he says rivals or even surpasses the best of Cezanne and Gauguin.

Dr. Kaz collected over 70 of Chiu's paintings, as well as all of the documents, letters and photos he could find, and has studied Taoist philosophy to enhance his appreciation not only of Chiu's works but of Chinese art as a whole. He has even taken up Chinese-style water-color painting on rice paper in his own attempt to marry elements of both Chinese tradition and Western technique.

Dr. Kaz appreciates Chiu's middle of the road approach, avoiding both imitation of classic Chinese and mindless copying of modern Western art. Professor Tang Shaoyun told Rose Tang,

> "[Chiu] was a typical Chinese artist, who was depicting the elegance and tranquility of an ideal world where humans are in harmony with nature. He was in constant dialogue with nature. He painted his calm and relaxed mood.... He was in his own fantasy world. He painted for himself. Supported by a rich family and scholarships, he didn't have to make a living by painting. One can tell from his pictures that he had little interest in wealth or fame.
> "...This is why he was so rare. He kept his style by refusing to follow trends when even Picasso had to keep changing his styles to stay on top. Today China is full of avant garde artists who chase Western trends to grab attention."

In 2004, over 50,000 people attended Dr. Kaz's 3-month exhibition of Chiu's works in Seattle's Fye Art Museum. The record-breaking attendance for that museum suggested that many Americans would like to know more about Chinese art, artists, and culture. If Dr. Kaz' succeeds in opening his Gulangyu museum for Chiu's works, we too will have a chance to better appreciate this almost forgotten artist.

但是周廷旭从不追求名望。1972 年去世后，他那些曾受到好评的画作被拍卖甚至贱卖，他在国内的画也被红卫兵捣毁，全世界都忘了他。我之所以有幸了解他，全有赖于厦门大学教授、知名艺术家唐绍云给我看了 Rose 唐写的一篇文章《雄归》，文中描述了卡兹教授在拍卖目录上看到周廷旭四幅作品的黑白样照后，如何重新发现这位画家的。

和多数外国人一样，卡兹教授本来对中国人作的古典油画不感兴趣，认为当代中国油画艺术只是对西方艺术的拙劣模仿。他曾对《双语周刊》的张薇薇说："西方人不关注中国的油画，觉得中国油画家运用西方绘画技巧只是在模仿，而不是创造艺术。"但是周廷旭油画中蕴含的中国因素——美与和谐，却使卡兹教授折服了，认为它们完全能与切扎尼和高更最好的作品相媲美，甚至还在其之上。

Dr. Poznanski

卡兹教授收藏了周廷旭的 70 多幅作品，以及能找到的所有资料、信件和照片。为了能更好地欣赏周廷旭及所有的中国艺术品，他还研究起道家哲学。他甚至还试着在宣纸上画中国风格的水彩画，力图将中国传统与西方技巧结合起来。

卡兹教授欣赏周廷旭的折中路线，既不一味模仿中国传统艺术，也不盲目抄袭西方当代艺术。唐绍云教授曾对 Rose 唐说，

"周廷旭是不折不扣的中国画家，他描绘的是人类与自然和谐共处的理想境界所拥有的优雅和宁静。他常与大自然交流，他画的是自己平和闲适的内心状态……他一直生活在个人的奇妙世界里，为自己而画。家境殷实又有奖学金，使他不必为谋生而作画。从他的作品中可以看出，他对名利非常淡泊。

"……正因为如此，他才那么的难能可贵。毕加索为了保住顶级大师的盛名都得常常变换画风，而他却能坚持自己的风格，不随波逐流。今天的中国却有太多为引人注目而追逐西方潮流的先锋派画家。"

2004 年，卡兹教授在西雅图的菲耶艺术馆展出周廷旭的作品，在三个月的展期内，观众达五万多人，创下该艺术馆的纪录，也说明许多美国人渴望更多地了解中国画家，以及中国的艺术和文化。如果卡兹教授在鼓浪屿上建造周廷旭作品展馆的计划得以实现，那我们就有机会更好地了解这位几乎被人遗忘的画家。

Lin Yutang—an "International"Chinese Writer Lin Yutang, who was schooled on Gulangyu and taught at Xiamen University from 1926-1927, was the first Chinese author to reach the top of the New York Times bestseller list. Pearl S. Buck had to urge the anxious author to publish his 1935 bestseller "My Country and my People," but Lin went on to do more than any one in his generation to bridge the gulf between East and West.

> "However inclined one may be to regard the Chinese as strange, peculiar, fantastic, or impossible, for no other reason than that one has never been fortunate enough to gain their friendly, intimate acquaintance, the reading of Mr. Lin's book will very soon dissipate any notion of uncertainty and assure one of the truth[s] of the Confucian statement, that 'Within the four seas all men are brothers.'" "The East Speaks to the West," *The New York Times* review of "My Country and My People" 8 December, 1935

Born the seventh of a Presbyterian minister's eight children in Longxi (龙溪) on October 10th, 1895, Lin wrote, "One of my earliest memories as a child was that of sliding down the roof of the church."[1] Lin, like his father, read everything he could lay his hands on. An Amoy missionary, Abbe Livingston Warnshuis[2], ardently promoted higher education to develop leaders for the new China he believed was coming, and fueled the family's intellectual fire by sending them books and pamphlets on both Christian and scientific issues. It was a blessing for young Lin Yutang, but led to tragedy for his second oldest sister and best friend, Mei-Kung.

Lin's father refused to let Mei-Kung attend college because, as Lin wrote, "college education for a girl was a luxury which our family simply could not afford." Denied an education, the bright girl married at age 22, and when Lin left for college she gave him forty cents and said,

> "...you are going to college. Don't waste your opportunity. Be a good man, a useful man, and a famous man... That is your sister's wish for you.' Knowing her desire so well, I felt the full force of these simple words. It made me guilty about the whole thing. They burned into my heart with the oppressive weight of a great load, so that I had the feeling I was going to college in her place."[3]

---

[1] "From Pagan to Christian," The World Publishing Company, Cleveland, Ohio, 1959, Page 19).
[2] Warnshui: a Reformed Church of America missionary in Xiamen from 1900—1905
[3] Lin Yutang, "Memoirs of an Octogenarian," Mei Ya Publications, Inc. Taipei, 1975

林语堂——一位“国际化”的中国作家

林语堂早年在鼓浪屿上读书，1926 年至 1927 年在厦门大学任教。他是第一个高居《纽约时报》畅销书排名榜首的中国作家。尽管是在赛珍珠的促使下出版了成为 1935 年畅销书的《吾国与吾民》，林语堂为跨越东西方鸿沟所作的贡献，在同辈中还是无人能及。

> 只是因为无缘与中国人成为亲朋好友，外国人往往认为中国人陌生、独特、古怪或是难以忍受。不管这些见解多么顽固，只要读了林先生的书，马上就会消除所有模糊的观念，并相信孔子说的一句话，“四海之内皆兄弟”。
>
> ——R. Emmet Kennedy 著的《The East Speaks to the West》，该文作为《吾国与吾民》的书评刊登于 1935 年 12 月 8 日的《纽约时报》第六部分，pp. 1～2。

林语堂 1895 年 10 月 10 日出生在龙溪一个长老会牧师家，是八个孩子中的第七个。林语堂曾写道：“孩提时最早的记忆之一就是从教堂的屋顶上滑下来。”[1] 和父亲一样，林语堂什么书都看。一个在厦门的牧师 Abbe Livingston Warnshuis[2]，相信新中国将要建立，并为培养领袖人物而热心推动高等教育。他还为孩子们提供有关基督教和科学问题的书和小册子，提高他们的智力。这对于年少的林语堂是件幸事，却造成林语堂的二姐、也是他最好的朋友的悲剧。

林语堂曾写道，父亲不让二姐上大学是因为“大学教育对一个女孩来说是奢侈的事，我们家实在负担不起。”这个聪明的女孩上不了学，在 22 岁时结了婚。林语堂离家读大学时，二姐给了他四毛钱，并对他说：

“你就要上学了。别浪费这个机会。做个好人，做个有用的人，做个名人……这就是我对你的希望。”我知道她多么渴望读书，因此格外感受到这些话的分量，在心里沉甸甸的，并产生一种负罪感，我觉得自己是在代替二姐上大学。[3]

---

[1] 《从异教徒到基督徒》第 19 页，该书 1959 年由俄亥俄州克利夫兰的世界出版公司出版。

[2] Warnshui: 1900至1905年在厦门的一间美国传教士的归正教堂。

[3] 林语堂著的《八十自叙》，1975年由台北美亚图书公司出版。

Just a year later, the 7-months pregnant Mei-Kung died of the plague, and a haunted Lin strove to become not only "useful and famous" but also to fight injustice, especially against women.

When Lin was ten, he and his two brothers studied in Amoy at the American Reformed Mission's Yangyuan Elementary School (养元小学) and the Xunyuan School (寻源书院). In 1912, he entered the Theological School of Shanghai's St. John University (上海圣约翰大学). He excelled at athletics, and even participated in the 1916 Far Eastern Olympics in Shanghai, but he was an unorthodox scholar. He often skipped classes, and though he gained a reputation as an avid reader, the books he devoured often had no relation to his classes (he wrote of how he secretly read history books during a civil law class).

Lin gradually came to resent that Western education had denied him his Chinese roots, and as he dove into Chinese studies, he abandoned his Christian faith[1]. He left the Theological School, though he remained in St. John's until his graduation in 1916, after which he taught at Beijing's prestigious Tsinghua University. He wrote,

> "To live in Peking then was to come into contact with authentic Chinese society, to see, as it were, ancient China made manifest....Peking was China, authentic China, with its yellow-roofed palaces and terra-cotta temple walls and its Mongolian camels and nearness to the Great Wall and the Ming tombs."[2]

Lin longed for the East but never quite let go of the West. He continued teaching Christian Sunday School even while delving into Chinese philosophy. Torn, he wrote in a couplet,

"One mind seeks the learning of ancients and moderns;
Two legs straddle the cultures of East and West."

From "With Love and Irony" (Lin Yutang)

Lin went to Harvard in 1919 but before graduation left for Europe, where he completed his M.A. and, ironically, a Ph.D. in Chinese studies in the University of Jena in Leipzig, Germany. Lin enjoyed studying abroad, but he had qualms about Westerners' preoccupation with logic and scientific method. In "My Country and My People" he wrote,

---

[1] In "From Pagan to Christian", which he wrote in 1959 after returning to Christianity, he described this period of his life as a three decade "Grand Detour".

[2] Ibid. p. 33.

一年之后，怀孕七个月的二姐死于鼠疫。在二姐的影响下，林语堂一直努力奋斗，不仅成为“有用的名人”，还与社会不公、特别是针对妇女的不公待遇作斗争。

林语堂 10 岁时，他和另外两个兄弟一起在厦门美国归正教会办的养元小学和寻源书院读书。1912 年，他进入上海圣约翰大学神学院学习。在运动方面他成绩突出，还参加过 1916 年的上海远东奥林匹克运动会。但他又是个离经叛道的学生，时常逃课，书读得很多，可往往与课业无关（他曾描写在公民法的课上偷看历史书的情形）。

林语堂渐渐厌恶起西式教育，认为让他脱离了中国文化的根本，当他转而投入到中文学习中去后，他又摒弃了基督教的文化根本[1]。他离开神学院，但仍留在圣约翰大学直到 1916 年毕业。之后他在北京著名的清华大学任教。他写道：

“那时住在北京，能接触到真正的中国社会，原原本本地看到古国的风貌……黄色琉璃瓦的皇宫，红陶土做的寺庙高墙，蒙古骆驼，附近就是长城和明陵——北京代表了中国，真正的中国！”[2]

林语堂醉心于东方文化，也不忘西方文化，在钻研中国哲学的同时他继续在基督教礼拜日学校教课，还写下这样一副对联：

“两脚踏东西文化，一心评宇宙文章。”

林语堂 1919 年去哈佛大学读书，但毕业前又离开去了欧洲。具有讽刺意味的是，他在德国莱比锡的耶那大学取得了硕士和中国语言学博士学位。林语堂喜欢留学生活，但他又质疑西方人凡事注重逻辑和科学方法。他在《吾国与吾民》中这样写道：

---

[1] 在皈依基督教后，1959年林语堂写下《从异教徒到基督徒》，文中他将这段人生描绘成一个三十年的“大圈子”。

[2] 《从异教徒到基督徒》第33页。

"It is easy to see why the Chinese mind cannot develop a scientific method; for the scientific method, besides being analytical, always involves an amount of stupid drudgery, while the Chinese believe in flashes of common sense and insight. And inductive reasoning, carried over to human relationships (in which the Chinese are primarily interested) often results in a form of stupidity not so rare in American universities. There are today doctorate dissertations in the inductive method which would make Bacon turn in his grave. No Chinese could possibly be stupid enough to write a dissertation on ice-cream, and after a series of careful observations, announce the staggering conclusion that 'the primary function of sugar [in the manufacture of ice-cream] is to sweeten it'; or after a methodical study in 'Time and Motion Comparison on Four Methods of Dishwashing' happily perceive that 'stooping and lifting are fatiguing'….

"This sort of stupidity, although useful to business advertisement, could really be arrived at, I think, just as correctly by a moment of Chinese common sense and 'intuition.'".[1]

In his 1937 bestseller "The Importance of Living", Lin emphasized the "spirit of reasonableness" over logic.

"In contrast to logic, there is common sense, or still better, the Spirit of Reasonableness. …The Reasonable Age, if that should ever come about, will be the Age of Peace….The Sprit of Reasonableness is the best thing that China has to offer the West….Humanized thinking is just reasonable thinking. The logical man is always self-righteous and therefore wrong, while the reasonable man suspects that perhaps he is wrong and is therefore always right."[2]

Lin delighted readers around the globe with essays on such profound subjects as his love for loafing, and his insistence that, bottom line, we are all alike:

"I am interested only in presenting [in this book] a view of life and of things as the best and wisest Chinese minds have seen it and expressed it in their folk wisdom and their literature. It is an idle philosophy born out of an idle life, evolved in a different age, I am quite aware. But I cannot help feeling that this view of life is essentially true, and since we are alike under the skin, what touches the human heart in one country touches all."[3]

Lin wrote widely during the 20s and by 1930, the New York Times was writing commentaries on his works. Lin worked with Song Qingling (宋庆龄), widow of Sun Yat-sen (孙中山), to create the China Democratic Rights Insurance League, and after 1938 he lived and traveled in Europe, where he wrote a trilogy consisting of "Peking Cloud" (京华烟云), "Wind and Crane's Tear" (风声鹤唳), and "The Red Door" (朱门).

---

[1] My Country and My People, 85.
[2] Importance of Living, pp. 424-25.
[3] The Importance of Living, page 1

"在中国人的心灵中，科学方法不能得到发展的原因是很容易理解的，因为科学方法除了要求分析性思维之外，总是免不了要有一些枯燥的工作要做。而中国人则相信自己的庸见与洞察力的闪光。推理的方法在应用到人际关系（中国人最感兴趣的东西）时，常常导致一种愚蠢的结论，这在美国大学里并不罕见。今天有许多用推理方法写成的博士论文，会使长眠地下的培根感到不安。没有一个中国人会愚蠢到去写一篇关于冰淇淋的博士论文，并且在一系列的观察与分析之后得出令人瞠目的结论说'糖（在冰淇淋的制作中）最重要的功能是使冰淇淋发甜'，或者在对'四种洗碟方法的时间与运动方法比较'进行研究之后，很高兴地下结论说'弯腰提取物件的动作是很累人的'……

"这种愚蠢的方法也许有助于商业运作，但我想中国人如果用片刻的直觉与常识，也完全能得出同样正确的结论。"[1]

在 1937 年出版的畅销书《生活的艺术》中，林语堂强调了"近情精神"比逻辑重要。

"与逻辑相对的有常识，或更好一些的说法：还有近情的精神……这近情的时代，如果有来临的一天，则就是和平时代的来临……近情精神是中国所能贡献给西方的一件最好的物事……人性化的思想其实就是近情的思想。专讲逻辑的人是永远自以为是的，所以他是不近人情，也是不对的；至于近情的人则自己常疑惑自己是错的，所以他永远是对的。"[2]

林语堂那些主题深刻的文章受到全世界读者的喜爱，例如他热爱闲游，以及他坚信从根本上看，人们都是相似的。

"我只想（在书中）表现一种中国最优越最聪慧的哲人们所见到而在他们的文字中发挥过的人生观和事物观。我知道这是一种闲适哲学，是在异于现代时代里的闲适生活中所产生。我总觉得这种人生观是绝对真实的。人类心性既然相同，则在这个国家里能感动人的东西，自然也会感动别的国家的人类。"[3]

在 20 年代，林语堂著述广泛，到了 30 年代，对他作品的评论文章不时见诸《纽约时报》报端。林语堂和孙中山的遗孀宋庆龄合作，成立中国民权保障同盟。1938 年以后他在欧洲游历，写下小说三部曲《京华烟云》、《风声鹤唳》和《朱门》。

---

[1] 《吾国与吾民》第85页。

[2] 《生活的艺术》第424～425页。

[3] 《生活的艺术》第1页。

Lin returned to the U.S. in 1936 and in 1959 began attending New York City's Madison Avenue Presbyterian Church. He wrote:

Looking back on my life, I know that for 30 years I lived in this world like an orphan. I am an orphan no longer. Where I had been drifting, I have arrived. The Sunday morning when I rejoined the Christian church was a homecoming.[1]

Lin settled down in Taiwan in 1966 and passed away in March, 1976, at the age of 80. The New York Times obituary noted,

Lin Yutang, poet, novelist, historian and philosopher, had no peer as an interpreter to Western minds of the customs, aspirations, fears and thoughts of his people and their country, China, the great and tragic land.[2]

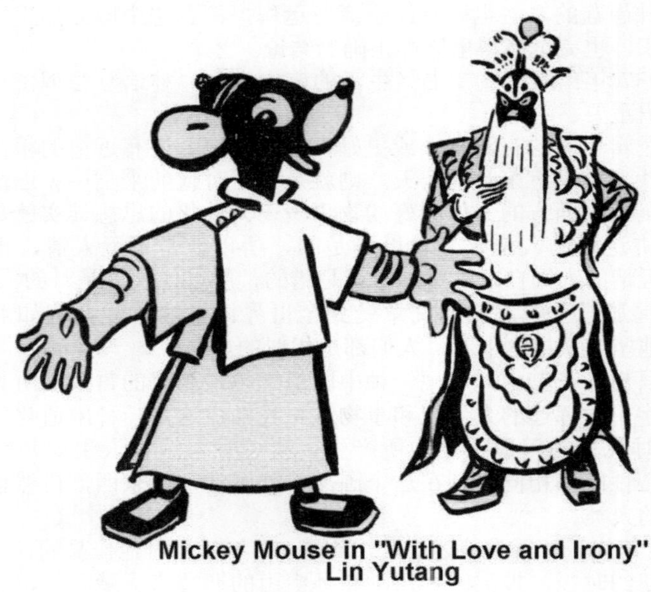

Mickey Mouse in "With Love and Irony"
Lin Yutang

"One of the most difficult things for me to put over to my Chinese-reading public is to convince them that humor is a part of life and therefore should not be shut out even from serious literature. This is as difficult as it has been for me to convince them that Confucius was a human being and always loved a good joke, even at his own expense." Lin Yutang, "With Love and Irony."

[1] "Why I Came Back to Christianity," in Presbyterian Life (April 13, 1959), 13-15.
[2] "Lin Yutang, 80, Dies; Scholar-Philosopher," *New York Times*, 27 March 1976

1936 年，林语堂回到美国。从 1959 年起，定期去纽约麦迪逊大街的长老会教堂。他写道：

“回顾我的一生，30 年来我就像个孤儿般活在人世。从现在起我不再是孤儿了，我又回到迷失的起点。重新参加礼拜的那个星期天早晨，对我而言就像回到家一样。”[1]

林语堂 1966 年在台湾定居，1976 年 3 月逝世，享年 80 岁。《纽约时报》的讣告这样评价他：

“林语堂，诗人，小说家，历史学家，哲学家。他向西方诠释中国这个多灾多难大国的风土人情，以及中国人的所盼、所虑和所思，在这方面他成绩卓著，无人能比。”[2]

“最难的事之一就是让我的中国读者们接受这样的观念：幽默是生活的一部分，即使在严肃文学中也应该占有一席之地。这和下面这件事一样困难重重：我一直在说服他们相信孔子是个爱开玩笑的普通人，甚至会拿自己开涮。”

摘自林语堂的《讽颂集》

[1] “Why I Came Back to Christianity”，1959年4月13日出版的“Presbyterian Life”第13-15页。

[2] “Lin Yutang, 80, Dies; Scholar-Philosopher”, 1976年3月27日《纽约时报》。

Chapter 7
Gulangyu Churches

Tung-A-Be Chapel (Dukes, 1885)

"Scarcely had the smoke from the battleships of the British fleet, that captured Amoy on the 27th of August 1841, cleared from the horizon when Rev. David Abeel [Yabili, 雅俾理] landed on these shores,—six months before the signing of the Nankin treaty. Rev. Wm. J. Boone, Bishop of the American Episcopal Church arrived at the same time, but as we shall see presently he remained here one or two years only. They were the first Protestant missionaries in Amoy."

Rev. Pitcher, "In and about Amoy," 1912, p.299

Minnan Dialect and Missions Fujian's endless mountains and valleys, have blessed us with an abundance of everything except flat farmland. Thus centuries of Fujianese were forced to either terrace mountains top to bottom or to emigrate abroad—which is why most Overseas Chinese are from Fujian—and why Christian missions came first to Xiamen.

As early as 1728, the Emperor threatened wannabe emigrants with the death penalty, but nothing stemmed the tide of emigrating Fujianese—and not everyone was sad to see them go. An 18th century Canton prefect, applauded the mass exodus, saying, "Only scum and riff-raff emigrated, the population was eased and beggars lessened." But the "riff-raff" thrived!

By the 1850s, there were 2 ½ times as many Overseas Chinese of Xiamen origin as there were inhabitants of Xiamen. In 1920, Paul Hutchinson wrote that over 60,000 went out of Xiamen each year. Today, our little island is the ancestral home of over 350,000 Overseas Chinese, including industrial tycoons throughout Southeast Asia.

Since most Chinese overseas were from South Fujian they spoke Minnan (S. Fujian) dialect. The missionaries to these Chinese abroad also learned Minnan Dialect, and after the 1st Opium War forced China open to trade and missions, missionaries headed for the one place they could speak the language: Xiamen.

第七章

鼓浪屿教堂

“1841年8月27日英国军舰攻占厦门不久，《南京条约》签订前半年，雅俾理就坐船来到这里。美国圣公会主教文惠廉也同时到来，但据我们所知，他在这只住了一两年。他们两位是首批来厦门的基督教传教士。”

——选自毕腓力1912年著的《厦门方志》，第299页。

闽南话和传教

福建界内高山丘陵密布，生态地貌多样，同时物产丰饶——唯独缺乏平整的耕地。几百年来耕地的匮乏迫使福建人要么开垦梯田，要么移民海外。这就是为什么多数海外华人祖籍福建，以及基督教传教士会率先来到厦门。

早在1728年，当时的统治者就威胁要将出洋的人处以死刑，但是什么也阻止不了福建人的出洋潮——有人还乐见其出，如18世纪的广东行政长官。他说：“出洋的都是些乌合之众，他们走了，人口就精简了，乞丐也少了。”可就是这些“乌合之众”后来都发了财！

到19世纪50年代，在海外的厦门人是厦门本地居民人数的2.5倍。保罗·哈金森在1920年写道，“每年有6万多人从厦门出洋。今天，有超过35万海外华人祖籍厦门，其中就有许多东南亚的工业巨头”。

大部分在东南亚的华人来自福建南部，说闽南话，为他们布道的传教士们也得学说闽南话。第一次鸦片战争后，中国开放贸易，允许传教士进入，传教士们就来到能说闽南话的地方——厦门。

London Mission House, Gulangyu (Dukes, 1885)

On April 5th, 1846, Fujian's first Chinese Protestants, Oug-Hok-kui, age 71, and Lau Un-siaage, 68, were baptized, and Xiamen is now known as the birthplace of Chinese Protestantism. China's oldest Protestant Church is Xinjie Church (behind the drugstore on the corner of South Siming and Zhongshan Roads), and one of her most beautiful historic churches is Gulangyu's Trinity Church.

Rev. Carstairs Douglas (杜嘉德, Du Jiade)
Pioneer in Minnan Dialect

THE ABOVE PHOTOGRAPH IS COPIED FROM ONE TAKEN WHEN HE WAS ABOUT 42 YEARS OF AGE.
your loving brother
Carstairs Douglas

Missionary linguists such as Carstairs Douglas and Elihu Doty (如罗蒂) tackled widespread illiteracy by romanizing the Amoy dialect. Doty published the gospel of John in Romanized Amoy in 1852, and James Laidlaw Maxwell (马雅各, Ma Yage) published the first Amoy Bible in 1884.

The "Dictionary of the Vernacular or Spoken Language of Amoy," published by Rev. Carstairs Douglas in 1873, remains a standard reference work even today. But Douglas never witnessed the fruits of his work; he died only 4 years later of cholera, at the age of 46 (22 years of which were spent in China).

"By overwork he had worn himself out, and made himself an old man while he was yet comparatively young in years. He came to China quite young and at the time of his death was only about forty-six years of age, and yet men who had recently become acquainted with him thought him over sixty… he did more work during the twenty-two years of his missionary life than the most of men accomplish in twice that time…

"Recently, especially during the last year, it was manifest, at least to others, that his physical strength was fast giving way. Yet he could not be prevailed upon to leave his field for a season for temporary rest, or even to lessen the amount of his work.

"I never knew a more incessant worker. He was a man of most extensive general information. I think I have never met with his equal in this respect. He was acquainted with several modern European languages and was a thorough student of the original languages of Holy Scripture, as witness the fact of his study of the Hebrew Bible, even after his last sickness had commenced. As regards the Chinese language, he was already taking his place among the first Sinologues of the land."

"40 Years in China"

1846 年 4 月 5 日，福建的首批中国基督徒，时年 71 岁的王福桂和 68 岁的刘殷舍接受了洗礼。厦门如今也被认为是中国基督教的诞生地。中国最早的基督教堂是新街礼拜堂（在中山路和思明南路拐角的药店后面），而鼓浪屿上的三一堂是最漂亮和最具有历史意义的教堂之一。

杜嘉德，闽南语的先锋

当时人们普遍都不识字，于是传教士、语言学家杜嘉德和如罗蒂用罗马拼音标注厦门话来扫盲。1852 年如罗蒂出版了用罗马拼音注厦门话的《约翰福音》，1884 年马雅各出版了第一部用罗马拼音注厦门话的《圣经》。

杜嘉德于 1873 年出版的《厦英大辞典》，至今仍有重要的参考价值。不幸的是，杜嘉德没能享受到他的劳动成果，出书 4 年后他死于霍乱，时年 46 岁（他在中国住了 22 年）。

“超负荷工作令他疲惫不堪，虽然年纪不大，看上去已像个老人。他年轻时就来到中国，去世时也才 46 岁，但最近认识的人都以为他已六十开外。在过去 22 年的传教生涯中，他做的工作比大部分人在双倍时间里完成的还要多……

最近一段时间，尤其是去年，大家都明显看到他的体力迅速衰竭。但他仍不肯听从劝告去休息片刻，甚至不愿减少工作量。

他是我见过的工作最勤勉的人。他知识渊博，这方面无人能及。他通晓数门当代欧洲语言，并全面攻读用希伯来原文著述的《圣经》，直到最后发病时，人们看到他还在学习这本书。至于汉语，他早已跻身第一批汉学家之列了。”

——选自《40 Years in China》

"Xin" ("Faith", Dukes, 1885)

Trinity Church #71 Anhai Rd China's 1st Protestant Church, Xinjie Church (新街礼拜堂), was followed closed by the Bamboo Church (竹树堂) and a church at Xiagang (厦港), near Xiamen University. But these churches were inconvenient (and dangerous during bad weather) for Gulangyu Christians, so around 1927 the above three churches joined to build a new church and bought a downtown Gulangyu potato field for 8,000 silver Yuan. (For that price, the field must have been a real hot potato!)

The American Reformed Mission gave 4,000 silver Yuan, the English Presbyterians 14,000, and the rest came from individuals. The name, "Three-in-One Church" (Sanyi Tang, 三一堂), reflected the Holy Trinity of Father, Son and Holy Spirit, as well as three churches cooperation.

Considered the most beautiful Protestant church in Fujian (perhaps all of China), this red brick beauty was designed by Chinese architect Lin Rongting (林荣廷) after his return from Germany. Lin designed the church for only 300-400 worshippers, but the committee expanded this to 1000 seats and added a new wall—all without consulting Mr. Lin. The miffed Mr. Lin refused to modify his design, so construction of the roof was transferred to the Dutch Zhigang (治港) company, which had constructed the Lujiang (鹭江) embankment. The frame's steel girders were imported from Hong Kong because they were too large to make in Xiamen. Steel-reinforced concrete pillars and an octagonal central belfry gave further reinforcement. The roof was still incomplete in 1936 when Trinity Church hosted the National Missions conference, and in fact was not completed until 1945—almost 20 years after construction began.

Trinity Church was confiscated during the Cultural Revolution and used as a government hall for 13 years, but on a Saturday morning in 1979, Pastor Chen was told that the church was being returned and he could begin services the following day. He was excited, but also worried that with only one day to get the word out no one would show up. A local official dropped by the next morning to see if anyone came, and was surprised to find the 1000 seats packed out and over 800 people waiting outside—the largest attendance since 1934!

Trinity has several pastors and evangelists, a congregation of 2,000, and is famous for its music (befitting a church on the "Isle of Music"). Trinity has an adult choir, young adult choir, youth choir for 12-16 year olds, and children's choir for under-12s, as well as a 50-strong orchestra and a toddlers' orchestra. Christmas music performances are so popular, that services must be held on both the 24th and the 25th of December, and sometimes on the Sunday of Christmas week as well.

三一堂，安海路 71 号

中国第一座基督教堂新街礼拜堂建成后不久，竹树堂和厦门大学附近厦港的一座教堂也落成了。但是对于鼓浪屿上的教徒们来说，去这些教堂不太方便（天气不好的时候还不安全）。于是在 1927 年左右，上述的这三所教堂的教友们联合起来要建一座新教堂，并花了 8000 银元在鼓浪屿的中心区域买下一块番薯地。（价格这么高，这块地还真是抢手！）

美国归正教会拨出 4000 银元，英国长老会拨出 14000 银元，其余款项由个人捐献。教堂的名字“三一堂”除了有圣父、圣子、圣神三位一体的含义，还有三个教堂合作的意思。

这座红砖建成的教堂被认为是福建（也许是全中国）最漂亮的一座基督教堂，它是由德国归来的中国建筑师林荣廷设计的。他设计的教堂容量是 300～400 人，而筹委会未和他商议，就擅自把座位增加到 1000 个，还加了一堵墙。林荣廷一气之下拒绝修改自己的设计方案，于是屋顶的工程就由曾建造鹭江防护堤的荷兰治港公司接手。做支架用的钢制梁太庞大了，得从香港进口。用钢筋水泥柱子和一个中间的钟阁来加固屋顶。1936 年，中国基督教全国查经会在三一堂举行时，天花板还未完工，直到 1945 年工程才完毕，这时距开工时间已近 20 年。

“文化大革命”期间，三一堂被没收，其后 13 年间被用作政府会堂。1979 年一个星期六的早晨，陈牧师被告知教堂已归还，第二天他就可以举行礼拜式了。陈牧师很激动，但是又担心没有人会来，因为只有一天的时间来通知大家。第二天，一位当地官员路过教堂想看看是否有人来，结果他吃惊地看到 1000 个座位都坐满了，教堂外面还有 800 个人在等候——这是自 1934 年以来人数最多的一次礼拜式！

三一堂有几位牧师和福音传教士，2000 名会友，并以其美妙音乐而闻名（不愧是“音乐之岛”上的教堂）。三一堂有一个成人唱诗班、一个青年唱诗班、一个 12 岁至 16 岁青少年组成的唱诗班，一个 12 岁以下的儿童唱诗班，还有一个 50 多人的乐团和一个少儿乐团。圣诞节期间的音乐演出十分受欢迎，因此除了 12 月 24 日和 25 日都有礼拜之外，有时在圣诞周的周日也会安排。

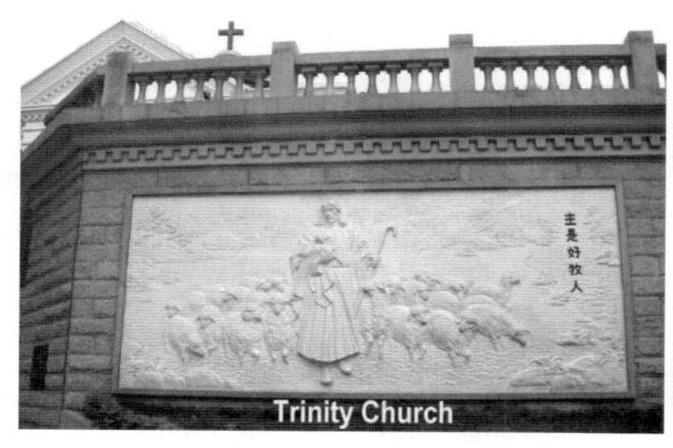

Trinity Church

The Gospel Hall #40 Sunlight Rock Rd. (Fuyin Tang, 福音堂) Built by the London Missionary Society in 1880 on the corner of Quanzhou Rd. and Chicken Hill (Jishan) Rd., this was originally the Memorial Hall for Carstairs Douglas (Du Jiade, 杜嘉德), the missionary linguist who spent 22 years in Amoy. After termites destroyed the church it was rebuilt in 1905 on Sunlight Rock Rd.

An Englishman designed the Gospel Hall, which was financed by overseas Chinese Christians, but by the '30s it had outgrown its 1000 seat capacity; in 1930 a sister church for believers in the Neicuo'ao area (内厝澳) was built on Gongping Road (公平路).

The Gospel Hall hosted China's All Christian Council in 1935 but was too small to accommodate the 4,000 attendees for the 1936 convention. The Council was moved to Trinity Church, which was also too small, and so the meeting was held in the Yinghua Middle School (英华中学).

By the 1940s, the Gospel Hall had over 800 foreign and Chinese members and attracted guest ministers and theologians from all over China, including the "Billy Graham of China," John Sung (see next page). The members were very active in the community, helping to establish "Fumin (富民) Elementary School," a school for housewives, various singing groups, and mission outreaches. The church was used as a factory during the Cultural Revolution, when dormitories were built on the grounds, but in 1987 the factory relocated and the church was returned to the Christians. Today it is a beautifully kept facility for retirees run by the Xiamen Christian Council.

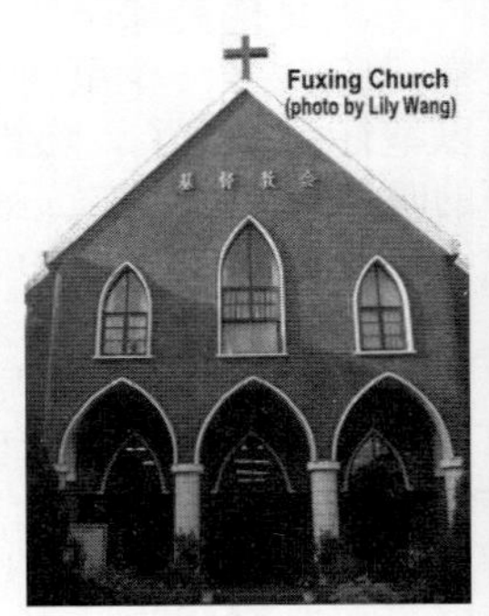
Fuxing Church (photo by Lily Wang)

Fuxing Church (Fuxing Tang,复兴堂), was originally near a ferry but recently moved to this garden-like triangular plot sandwiched between Fuxing and Lujiao (鹿礁路)roads. Fuxing is of the "Little Flock" sect founded in Fuzhou in the '30s by famous Chinese evangelist Watchman Nee, who wrote his "The Messenger of the Cross" on Gulangyu in January, 1926.

How the Little Flock Took Flight

The "Little Flock" sect (or "Assembly Hall") began as a reaction against Western domination of Chinese Christianity. Watchman Nee (Nee Tuosheng) chafed at the rigid hierarchy and formalism of Fuzhou's Anglican Trinity College, where he studied, so he joined Dr. Leland Wang's informal home worship services. Nee's subsequent call for an indigenous Chinese church was readily embraced during the 20s and 30s as many Chinese, including Christians, became anti-Western. Under Nee's guidance the Little Flock flew, in spite of opposition by Western mission agencies, some of which dismissed missionaries who showed sympathy with the fledgling group that claimed to be neither Catholic nor Protestant but Christian.

福音堂，晃岩路 40 号

该教堂是由英国伦敦差会于 1880 年在泉州路和鸡山路路口建造的，开始是作为传教士、语言学家杜嘉德的纪念馆，他在厦门居住了 22 年。后来教堂遭白蚁损毁，1905 年重建于晃岩路。

新教堂由一个英国人设计，资金则由海外的中国基督徒捐助。到 1930 年，1000 个座位已经不够用了，于是 1930 年在内厝澳的公平路又为信徒建了一座教堂，作为该堂的支会。

1935 年中国基督教理事会在福音堂召开。本来 1936 年的会议也要在福音堂举行，但是容不下 4000 名与会者，只好移到三一堂，但是三一堂也太小了，最后还是在英华中学开的会。

到了 40 年代，福音堂有 800 多名来自海内外的中外教友，还吸引了全国各地的牧师和神学家来访问，其中包括著有《中国的比利·格雷汉姆》的宋约翰。（见下页）

教徒们的社区活动很活跃，他们帮助建立了福民小学，为家庭主妇、合唱团体，以及教堂以外的传教服务。“文革”时期，教堂被征为工厂，底层建起了宿舍。1987 年工厂迁走了，教堂又回归基督徒所用，现在它成了为退休人员服务的场所。

复兴堂

复兴堂早先是在黄家渡附近，但最近迁到复兴路和鹿礁路之间花园式的三角地带上。复兴堂是上世纪 30 年代由中国著名的传教士倪柝声在福州创立的“小群教会”的分支，这位传教士 1926 年在鼓浪屿著有《十字架的使者》。

小群教会的起源

遍布世界的“小群教会”最初成立的原因，是反对西方势力把持中国基督教。倪牧师不满于他就读的福州英国圣公会三一学院等级森严形式僵化，参加了王立纶博士的非正式的家庭礼拜式。倪牧师随后发出建立本土化中国人教堂的号召，在 20 年代和 30 年代得到许多反西方势力的中国人的响应，其中就有基督徒。在倪牧师的引导下，小群教会冲破西方传教势力的阻挠得到发展，它宣称自己既非天主教，也非新教，而是基督教。一些同情小群教会的传教士则被西方教会所驱逐。

John Sung
20th Century's Greatest Preacher?

Photo from Trinity Church

John Sung (Song Shangjie, 1901-1944) born in Putian, Fujian, (莆田笏石镇刘厝坑北村人) was one of a Methodist minister's 11 children, and earned the nickname "Little Pastor" when at age 13 he began standing in for his father (even preaching for him!).

A brilliant scholar, John completed his B.A., M.A. and Ph.D. in only 5 years, even while working to support himself. But his faith foundered when he attended New York City's Union Theological Seminary, which he called a "theological cemetery."

After learning that God was dead and Christ had not risen, John turned to Buddhism, Taoism, and the Koran, but became depressed rather than enlightened.

He was on the verge of suicide when, on the evening of Feb. 10, 1927, he had a vision of Christ, who forgave him and changed his name to John (as in John the Baptist). John straight away told his favorite teacher, the famous Harry Emerson Fosdick, "You are of the devil! You made me lose my faith!" The "theological cemetery" promptly committed John to an insane asylum for 193 days.

The fiery youth got a crash course in patience during his incarceration, and claimed later that he read the bible cover to cover 40 times. After release he sailed back to China, and tossed his awards and degrees into the ocean, keeping only his doctorate (for his father's sake). Like Carstairs and countless others, John Sung burned the candle at both ends and died young, on Aug. 18, 1944, but not before establishing an unparalleled reputation. William E. Schubert said,

> "Dr. John Sung was probably the greatest preacher of the 20th century. I have heard almost all of the great preachers from 1910 until now, including R. A. Torrey, Billy Sunday, Henry Jowett, and Billy Graham. Yet John Sung surpassed them all in pulpit power, attested by amazing and enduring results."

宋约翰，20 世纪最伟大的布道者？

宋约翰（宋尚杰，1901—1944）出生于福建莆田（莆田笏石镇刘厝坑北村人）一个循道公会牧师家庭，家里共有 11 个孩子，他 13 岁时就代替父亲出席礼拜式，（甚至替他布道！）大家都称他“小牧师”。

他是一个才华横溢的学者，在半工半读中，只花了五年时间就完成学士、硕士和博士学位的攻读。但是在进入纽约市联合神学院后，他的信仰幻灭了，他把这所学校称为“神学墓地”。

他认为上帝已死，基督还未出现，便转而研究起佛教、道教和伊斯兰教，但是这些宗教没能启迪他的灵魂，反而令他倍感沮丧。他一度想要自杀，但就在 1927 年 2 月 10 日的晚上，他目睹了基督显灵，基督宽恕了他，并将他的名字改为约翰（正如施洗者约翰的名字）。宋约翰立即对他最敬爱的老师、赫赫有名的哈里·埃默森·佛斯迪克说：“你是邪恶的！你让我失去了信仰！”于是这座“神学墓地”立即将他送进疯人院，关了 193 天。

在羁押期间，这个血气方刚的年轻人经受了对耐心的极度考验，据他后来说，他总共通读了四十遍《圣经》。出院后宋约翰坐船回中国，在途中他将奖章证书都抛进大海，只保留了博士学位证书（为了他的父亲）。就像杜嘉德和其他无数人那样，宋约翰透支身体英年早逝，死于 1944 年 8 月 18 日，但他去世前就已享有无人可及的声誉。

威廉·E·舒伯特说过：“宋约翰博士也许是 20 世纪最伟大的布道者。从 1910 年至今，我聆听过几乎所有杰出布道者的宣讲，包括 R·A· 托利，比利·桑迪、亨利·祖耶特和比利·格雷汉姆。但是宋约翰在讲坛上的表现力超过了他们所有人，其影响深远，令人惊叹。”

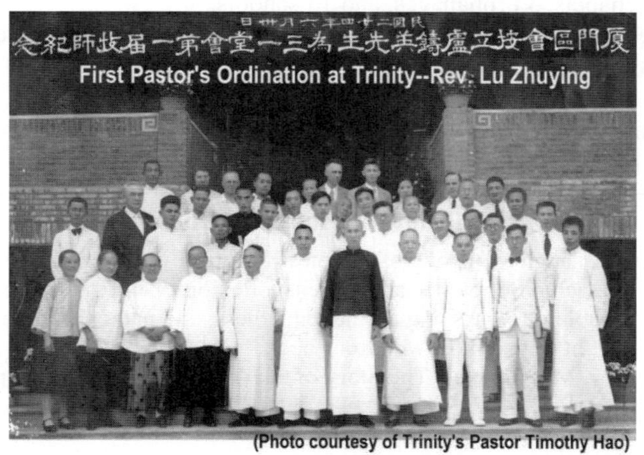

(Photo courtesy of Trinity's Pastor Timothy Hao)

Catholic Church, #34 Lujiao Rd (Tianzhu Jiaotang, 天主教堂) This neo-Gothic church built between 1912 and 1917 is a vision of Old World beauty. Resembling a cross from above, the church's delightfully aesthetic interior has two rows of columns along the central hall and an intricate green wooden polyhedral ceiling.

Photo by Lily Wang

The church was designed by a Spanish architect and built by Mr. Lin (林) from Zhangzhou (漳州). Mr. Lin built many other South Fujian churches, including a similar Catholic church near a Longhai (龙海) hillside on the way to Longhai's volcano and beautiful white beaches.

It's surprising that Fujian has so few Catholic churches because Catholics made it to Fujian centuries before the Protestants. Franciscans were in neighboring Quanzhou in the early 1300s, within a century of St. Francis' death. Spanish Catholic priests reached Fujian by the end of the 17th century, and Catholicism was introduced into Amoy from the Philippines in the mid 18th century. The Xiamen and Fuzhou Diocese were established in 1883, and the Vicariate Apostolic of Amoy (Dominican), which included Taiwan in its domain, oversaw 11 European and 8 Chinese priests, 32 churches or chapels, 3 orphanages, and 13 schools.

After the Opium War, Catholic priests rented a villager's house for worship, and then moved services to the Spanish Consulate in Lujiao（鹿礁 ）until the Spanish Gothic church was built between 1912 and 1917.

Today, the Vicariate Apostolic of Amoy has over 80 churches in Amoy, Zhangzhou (漳州), Quanzhou（泉州), and Putian（莆田).

The Beauty of Mandarin Chinese

"The Chinese language is one of the most beautiful in the world in which to enshrine the sacred Scriptures, and there is a flexibility and grace about it, that render it capable of expressing all the tenderness, and pathos, and poetry, and sublime thought of that most wondrous book."

Rev. MacGowan, "The Story of the Amoy Mission," 1889, p. 17

天主教堂，鹿礁路 34 号

这座新哥特式的教堂建于 1912 年至 1917 年间，旧世界残留下来的美丽影子。教堂的俯视图像是个十字架，内部装饰华美，中间大厅有两排圆柱，屋顶是繁复的绿色木质多面形。

教堂由一位西班牙建筑师设计，由漳州的林先生承建。林先生在闽南还建了其他很多教堂，其中一座风格类似的天主教堂就坐落在去龙海火山和白色海滩的路边山坡上。

令人费解的是，天主教徒早于基督教徒数百年来到福建，而福建的天主教堂却很少。14 世纪初，在圣方济各死后不到一百年，天主教的修士们就已经在附近的泉州了。17 世纪末，西班牙的天主教牧师们就来到福建，18 世纪中叶，天主教从菲律宾传到厦门。厦门和福州的教区成立于 1883 年，厦门天主教会的辖地包括台湾，共有 11 名欧洲牧师和 8 名中国牧师，32 所教堂或小礼拜堂，3 所孤儿院，以及 13 所学校。

鸦片战争以后，天主教牧师们租用了一所村民的房子来做礼拜，随后又迁到鹿礁路的西班牙领事馆，直到 1912 年至 1917 年间西班牙人的哥特式教堂建成。

现在，厦门天主教会在厦门、漳州、泉州和莆田共有 80 多所教堂。

汉语的魅力

汉语是世界上诠释《圣经》最优美的语言之一。它优雅灵动，能充分表达所有细腻的、悲悯的、诗意的情绪，以及最奇妙书籍的崇高思想。

摘自麦嘉湖 1889 年著的《The Story of the Amoy Mission》第 17 页。

Chapter 8 Gulangyu Festivals & Folklore

"May we all live long, And share the same moon,
Though you dwell 1,000 miles away."
Su Dongpo, Poet of Song Dynasty (960-1279)

Gulangyu is a delight year round, but even more so on festivals like Chinese New Year and Lantern Festival. And Gulangyu really springs to life on Mid-Autumn Festival, when locals haul out the bowls and dice to play the merry Mooncake Game.

Mad about Mooncake Game! Chinese claim Koxinga's greatest feat was liberating Taiwan from the Dutch, but I think his chief achievement was using the mooncake game to keep homesick troops happy.

Since 1988, our family has delighted in the mooncake games, which are held at Mid-Autumn Festival (the 15th day of the 8th Lunar month). Our sons Shannon and Matthew loved the game so much they made cardboard mooncakes so they could play year round!

Prizes used to be cookies and mooncakes, which range from bite-sized to the 3.934 ton monstrosity created by Nanning chefs in 2001. Fortunately, prizes are more practical nowadays—items like toothbrushes, thermoses and towels. We're so used to winning hoards of toothpaste each Fall that if we ever miss a Mid-Autumn Festival our dentist will be the first to know.

I suspect some of Xiamen's Laowai, especially new arrivals, may be as homesick as Koxinga's troops were in Taiwan, but the cure is coming! This Mid-Autumn Festival, as the brightest moon of the year illuminates our enchanting little island, and the night resounds with the sound of laughter and dice ringing in porcelain bowls, chances are you'll be playing the game yourself in the homes of Chinese friends and colleagues. But before you roll the bones[1], bone up[2] on the game by reading the rules in Amoy Magic—Guide to Xiamen (pages 374-375). And if you win Zhuangyuan, the Grand Prize, share it with me!

---

[1] Roll the bones: roll dice (dice used to be made of bone)

[2] Bone up: familiarize yourself with something; refresh your memory

DISCOVER GULANGYU!

第八章

鼓浪屿的节日与传说

“但愿人长久，千里共婵娟。”
苏东坡，宋朝（960—1279）诗人

上鼓浪屿玩是件令人愉快的事，尤其是在农历新年、元宵这样的节日，最好是在中秋节，因为那时岛上生气勃勃，人人都用碗和骰子在玩博饼游戏。

为博饼着迷！

Bill battles Koxinga's Troops!

“中国人都说郑成功最大的贡献是从荷兰人手中收复台湾，而我却以为，他的头功之一是让博饼游戏使士兵们乐不思蜀。”

博饼是在每年农历八月十五举行。从 1988 年至今，我们家就一直好玩它。我的儿子神能和马太对它非常着迷，他们在小时候甚至用卡片做成月饼，这样一整年都可以博饼。

游戏的奖品以前是月饼和饼干，有小到一口一个的，也有 2001 年由南宁厨师制作的 3.934 吨重的“巨无霸”。幸好现在奖品实用得多——像是牙刷、热水瓶、毛巾什么的。每年中秋，我们都能博回成堆的牙膏，要是哪年没有过上中秋节，我们的牙齿就该出毛病了。

我猜想厦门的老外，特别是新来的，会像郑成功的军队在台湾时一样，患上思乡病，而博饼就是一方解药！今年中秋，当一年中最明亮的月光普照着我们这个可爱的小岛，欢笑声、掷骰声此起彼伏，你很可能在中国朋友或同事家中亲身体验这个游戏。但是扔骨骰[1]前，请先温习[2]一下《魅力厦门》（第 374～375 页）中的游戏规则。如果你博到了头奖状元，记得要与我分享哦！

---

[1] 掷骨骰（骰子过去是骨头做的）。

[2] bone up：熟悉某种事情，唤起记忆。

Mooncake Game's Origin & Rules

Mooncake Game was started about 1500 years ago by scholars craving success in imperial exams. The total of 63 prizes, based on various dice combinations, was named after imperial titles earned from the exam:

One prize for **#1 Scholar** (Zhuangyuan) The seven prize levels:

Highest 1. Hongliubo (6 fours)

2. Zhuangyuan with Gold Flower
3. Yaodianliubo (6 ones)
4. Heiliubo (6 of the same, except fours)
5. Wuhong (5 fours)
6. Wuzi (5 of the same, except fours)

Lowest 7. Sihong (4 fours)

Two prizes for **No. 2 Scholar** (Duitang) A straight.
Four prizes for **No. 3 Scholar** (Sanhong) Throw 3 fours
Eight prizes for **No. 4 Scholar** (Sijin) Throw 4 of the same, except fours
Sixteen prizes for **No. 5 Scholar** (Erju) Throw 2 fours
Thirty two prizes for **No. 6 Scholar** (Yixiu) Throw 1 four

Rules and names of dice combos have changed little over the centuries, but chips have changed, from common coins to Zhuangyuan chips and Zhuangyuan cakes (Gulangyu's are most famous). Oddly, some people in N.E. Fujian's Fuding County speak S. Fujian dialect, and still use "Zhuangyuan Chips".

Legend has it that one of Koxinga's officers adapted dice game rules to create the mooncake game in order to preoccupy homesick soldiers, and according to many Qing Dynasty writers (like Zheng Dajiu, in "Taiwanese Folk Customs"), for centuries afterwards Taiwan folk stayed up all night shouting and tossing dice to compete for the large flour cake with a red "Yuan" character in the center.

Today the mooncake game is found not only in S. Fujian and Taiwan but also, it appears, wherever you find overseas Chinese of Xiamen ancestry. A reader of "Amoy Magic—Guide to Xiamen" e-mailed me to say, "We play the Mooncake Game in the Philippines too!" But only in Xiamen is the game preserved virtually unchanged. Even during the "Cultural Revolution," when all "old" thinking and practices were frowned upon, Xiamen folk tossed the dice for mooncakes—though furtively!

In 2003, Gulangyu's first annual Mooncake Game Cultural Festival attracted crowds of locals, as well as domestic and overseas visitors and the media, and since then the game has become more popular than ever—though mooncakes are no longer the prize of choice (mooncakes, like fruitcake in America, are traditional but not necessarily all that tasty). Prizes today are usually more practical, like shampoo, towels, thermoses, blankets, or cutlery.

博饼的起源与规则

掷骰游戏是由大约 1500 年前为求功名参加科举考试的读书人发明的。共有 63 个奖，根据骰子的不同组合以科举名词来命名。

第一名状元一个　　七种状元分别是：

最高级别　1 红六朴（六个四点）

2 状元插金花（四个四点带两个一点）

3 幺点六朴（六个一点）

4 黑六朴（六个一样的点数，除了四点和一点）

5 五红（五个四点）

6 五子（除五个红四以外的任何五个一样

最低级别　7 四红（四个四点）

第二名对堂两个　一到六点每个都有

第三名三红四个　有三个四点

第四名四进八个　有四个一样，除了四点

第五名二举十六个　有两个四点

第六名一秀三十二个　有一个四点

这些游戏名称和规则几百年来几乎一样，只是筹码变了，从普通钱币到状元筹再到状元饼（以鼓浪屿生产的饼最有名）。奇怪的是，居住在福建东北部福鼎的一些人现在还讲闽南话，玩“状元筹”。

传说中，郑成功手下的一个官员为了安抚士兵的思乡情绪，修改掷骰规则，改进了博饼游戏。据很多清朝作者（例如郑大枢在《台湾风物吟》中）的记述，之后的几百年间，台湾人往往通宵达旦地叫喊掷骰，争夺那块中间有个红色“元”字的大面饼。

今天，不仅闽南和台湾地区有博饼游戏，只要有厦门籍海外华人的地方都可以看到。《魅力厦门》的一位读者给我发邮件说：“在菲律宾我们也玩博饼！”但是只有在厦门才是最地道的玩法。即使是在“文革”时期，当所有传统思想和做法都被批判的时候，厦门人还在偷偷地掷骰博饼！

2003 年，鼓浪屿年度中秋博饼文化节首次举行，吸引了大量本市居民，及海内外的游客和媒体参加，从此这项活动更是盛况空前——虽然月饼不再作为奖品（月饼就像美国的水果蛋糕一样属于传统食品，但味道并不总是那么好）。现在的奖品往往实用得多，像是洗发水、毛巾、暖水壶、毯子或餐具。

Prof. Gong Jie Goes for Zhuangyan!

How Mooncakes Minced the Mongols Folks start munching mooncakes a full month before the festival, and children carry brightly colored lanterns of all shapes and sizes. And back in 1376, these lanterns and mooncakes helped overthrow the Mongol's Yuan dynasty!

Liu Bowen sent messengers bearing lanterns and mooncakes to friends and family—but the cakes concealed the time and place of the midnight massacre of the Mongols.

The Lady in the Moon Chang-er, the Lady in the Moon, is offered mooncakes and round fruits symbolizing the fullness of the moon, and many women pray for her to bless them with good husbands—though given Chang-er's marital woes, I don't see why she's considered an expert!).

There are many legends about Chang-er. One says she was married to the celestial archer Hou Yi, who saved the earth from a fiery fate by shooting down nine of the ten suns. The Queen Mother of the West (Britain?) rewarded him with the elixir of life, but he was a tyrant, so to keep him from becoming immortal Chang-Er stole the potion and drank it herself. When her furious husband came after her she flew to the moon and has lived there ever since in the company of a furry rabbit. I've no idea how the rabbit got there.

Another companion on the moon is the woodcutter Wu Gang, who was banished to the moon and became Chang-Er's friend and servant. The Jade Emperor punished Wu Gang by ordering him to fell an immortal cassia tree that grew back each time it was chopped down.

Since the Song Dynasty (960-1279), common folk and emperors alike have worshiped the moon, and imperial chefs created mooncakes over a meter in diameter, which they stamped with designs of Chang'er, the moon palace, and the immortal cassia tree.

Common folk made do with small cakes, which they munched while sipping tea and admiring the fullest moon of the year, and hoping to catch the reflection of the moon in their teacup.

月饼推翻蒙古人统治

中秋节前一个月，人们就开始吃月饼了，孩子们也提着大大小小、各种各样、色彩鲜艳的灯笼。这个习俗公元 1376 年时就有了，那年蒙古元朝的统治被推翻，其中还有月饼和灯笼的一份功劳呢！

据说刘伯温曾派信使带着灯笼和月饼前往各家各户，而在饼里就藏着半夜歼灭蒙古人的具体时间和地点。

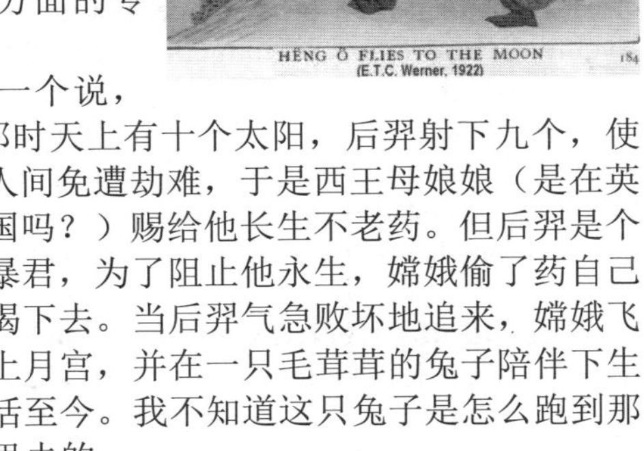

(E.T.C. Werner, 1922)

月中嫦娥

嫦娥是月中仙子，人们用月饼和象征满月的圆形水果供奉她，许多女子还求她保佑嫁个好丈夫。（嫦娥和她丈夫之间问题不少，真不明白她怎么会是这方面的专家！）

关于嫦娥的传说有很多。有一个说，她是天上的弓箭手后羿的妻子。那时天上有十个太阳，后羿射下九个，使人间免遭劫难，于是西王母娘娘（是在英国吗？）赐给他长生不老药。但后羿是个暴君，为了阻止他永生，嫦娥偷了药自己喝下去。当后羿气急败坏地追来，嫦娥飞上月宫，并在一只毛茸茸的兔子陪伴下生活至今。我不知道这只兔子是怎么跑到那里去的。

Gulangyu's Biggest "Bobing" Bowl
"Strange World Museum" #2 Zhonghua Rd.

另一个伙伴是伐木人吴刚，他被放逐到月亮上成为嫦娥的仆人和朋友。玉皇大帝命令吴刚砍倒一棵桂花树，以此来惩罚他——但这棵桂花树是不会死的，每次被砍倒后又会恢复原样。

自宋朝（960—1279）以来，无论是当朝皇帝或寻常百姓都要拜月。皇宫里的御厨做的是直径一米多的大月饼，上面印着嫦娥、月宫和那棵桂花神树的图案。

普通人家则制做小月饼，边观赏一年当中最圆的月亮，边品茶吃饼，并试图用茶杯接住月亮的倒影。

Legend of "Longing for Brother" Rock (Wang'ge Shi, 望哥石) The large and small rocks on the peak of Tongwen Hill, just opposite Xiamen's Heping Harbor (和平码头), are said to be sisters gazing into the distance, hoping for the return of their brother—hence the name Wang Ge Rocks.

Many centuries ago, an orphaned boy and his sister lived in a small village at the foot of Tongwen Hill and survived by fishing. One day, while rowing home to escape a fierce wind, they saw a 13-year-old girl flailing about in the sea. They rescued her and she told them that she was named Amei, and was from a family of Taiwanese fishermen whose boat had sunk the previous day. She survived by clinging to a board, but did not know her family's fate.

Amei and the brother and sister lived a happy life together for three years,--until the villagers built a large boat to trade with Taiwan, and the brother joined the crew. When he left, he promised Amei he would look for her parents, but the day after his departure, the weather began deteriorating. Skies darkened, seas raged, and many a boat went to a watery grave during the 3 day storm. Amei and the sister raced to the top of Tongwen Hill and for days neither ate nor slept, but gazed into the distance, hoping to see some sign of the brother's ship. Eventually the worried villagers ascended the hill to check on the two girls, and were shocked to find they had both turned into eastward-facing stones.

From then until the end of the Qing Dynasty, people stood on Wang Ge Rock in hopes of a reunion with family and friends. And given that so many Fujianese have sailed abroad and not returned, Wang Ge Rock has come to symbolize hopes for reunification not only with loved ones but also with Taiwan.

Legend of Inverted Cauldron Rock, Seal Rock, and Sword Rock Before Koxinga left Gulangyu to wrest Taiwan from the Dutch, he burned his bridges behind him by ordering his men to dismantle their cooking stove and toss the great iron pot into the sea to show his determination that he would not return from Taiwan alive unless he succeeded in driving out the Dutch.

Koxinga hurled his mighty sword and it impaled the ground where land and sea met. He then threw his personal jade seal, a gift from the king, into the waves to show that his heart, like this seal, would always remain with the people of Xiamen.

No sooner had Koxinga set sail than three rocks emerged from the sea where the three objects had fallen. One resembled a sword, one a seal, and the third a cauldron, and they are there to this day.

望哥石的传说

在厦门和平码头对面的同文山顶，有一大一小两块石头，传说这是两姐妹正遥望远方等待兄长归来，因此得名望哥石。

好几百年前，一对孤儿兄妹住在同文山脚下的一个小村庄里，靠打鱼为生。一天在划船回家避风时，他们看见一个女孩在海面上挣扎。女孩获救后告诉他们说，她 13 岁，名叫阿梅，是台湾的捕鱼人家出身，一天前船沉了，她抓着一块木板幸存下来，还不知道家里人怎样了。

之后的三年间，阿梅和这对兄妹一起幸福地生活。后来村民们造了条大船要和台湾做生意，哥哥就当了船员。临走时，他答应阿梅帮她寻找父母的下落，但就在他走后的第二天，天气变坏了。天空阴沉，海水滔天，在三天的暴风雨中，许多船都沉了。阿梅和妹妹跑上同文山顶，几天几夜茶饭不思眺视远方，盼望能看到哥哥的船。最后，村民们不放心，登上山顶看望两个女孩时，却惊愕地发现她们已经变成面朝东方的石头。

从那时起到清末年间，盼望和亲朋团聚的人们都会登上望哥石。许多福建人乘船出洋一去不归，因此望哥石不仅象征着与亲朋团聚，还象征着与台湾统一的愿望。

覆鼎岩、印斗石和剑石的传说

郑成功离开鼓浪屿从荷兰人手中收复台湾之前，他命令士兵把烧饭的炉灶拆了，将大铁锅扔到海里，自断后路，以此表达他不把荷兰人赶走誓不生还的决心。

郑成功将长剑一挥，剑端正好刺在陆地和海水交汇的地方。他又将皇帝赐给他专用的玉玺扔到海里，表明他的心将和这玉玺一样，永远和厦门人民在一起。

郑成功启航不久，三块礁石就从这三样东西落水的地方升了起来。一块像把剑，一块像印斗，一块像倒扣的铁锅，至今还在那里。

Legend of Gulangyu's Drum Rock Egrets & Goshawk Long ago, two egrets built their nest upon Drum Rock, where they passed their days contently until a lonely and jealous goshawk on nearby "Fiery Islet" (Huoshan Dao, 火山岛) decided to kill them.

On a dark, stormy night, the goshawk attacked the happy pair and carried off the male. The female searched far and near for days, and at last the exhausted bird settled upon Sunlight Rock and died of grief. Her white feathers were borne by the wind into the sea, and when seagulls saw her feathers in flight, they knew she had died, and grieved. For years, the gulls cried plaintively as they flew about the island searching for her. At last their cries moved the heart of Neptune, god of the sea. He stirred up the sea so the waves lashed upon the rock, making the sound of a drum to call the female egret. And hence the origin of the magical Drum.

Acacia—Tree of Longing It is no wonder that locals have created a legend about the acacia. Like Xiamen people, who have long clung to life in the face of adversity, this evergreen with fragrant white or yellow flowers survives upon little water and clings tenaciously to rocky peaks like Sunlight Rock.

And so it is said that many centuries ago, a poor husband went abroad to seek his fortune. Before he left, he planted an acacia tree beside the sea and promised to return three years later. From the day of his departure, the faithful wife stood by the tree every day, gazing upon the vast and empty sea, hoping in vain for her husband's return, but she never saw him again.

After her death, people dubbed the acacia the "Tree of Longing (xiangsi shu). The blossoms are said to represent the wife's tears, and the red dot on the flower's stamen and pistil is said to be a magical drop of the woman's blood, as her heart broke and bled for her husband.

Koxinga Legends—Please check the Koxinga chapter.

Afterword Given that most overseas Chinese come from South Fujian, it is no surprise that locals have so many stories of separation, or that a common theme of literature, festivals, songs and poetry is reunification, whether of lovers, of family members, or of Fujian and Taiwan, which for centuries have been joined by close blood ties and trade.

鼓浪石、白鹭及老鹰的传说

很久以前，有两只白鹭在鼓浪石上筑巢，幸福地生活。附近火山岛上孤单的老鹰嫉妒它们，想害死它们。一个暴风雨的夜晚，老鹰袭击这对伴侣，掳走了公鹭。母鹭连着几天到处寻找，最后精疲力竭地栖在日光岩上悲痛地死去。她白色的羽毛被风吹到海上，被海鸥看见，知道她已经死了，非常伤心，连着好几年它们哀怨地啼叫，围着岛屿飞行寻找母鹭。最后它们的叫声感动了海神，他搅动海水，波浪冲刷岩石，发出击鼓一样的声音呼唤母鹭，这就是奇妙的鼓浪石的来历。

金合欢——相思树

怪不得当地人要为金合欢树编一个传说。与厦门人总是直面逆境热爱生活的精神相似，这种开着或白或黄香花的常青植物只要一点点水，就能紧贴在像日光岩那样的大石壁上顽强生存。

传说几百年前，一位贫穷的丈夫出洋闯天下。离家前，他在海边种下一棵金合欢，发愿说三年后回来。自从他走后，忠贞的妻子天天在海边树下注视着茫茫大海，盼着丈夫回来，却再也没有见到过他。

她死后，人们把金合欢树叫做“相思树”。据说树上开出的花是妻子的眼泪，花蕊上的红点是她的心为丈夫破碎后流血，滴在上面而成的。

郑成功的传说

请参见郑成功一章。

后记

大多数的海外华人来自福建南部，因此当地有那么多骨肉分离的故事也就不足为奇。而团聚早已成为文学、节日及诗歌的一个常见的主题，团聚的主体有时指恋人，有时指亲人，有时则指几百年来血脉相连、贸易不断的福建和台湾。

Eastern Tortoise, Western Hare!

By Rev. MacGowan, 1913

> This boat race (true story!) between the "powerful" British soldiers and their "scrawny" Chinese competitors had an unexpected outcome !

"The Chinese as a race are on the whole a robust and healthy people. I have no doubt in my` own mind that this is largely due to the fact that they have to work for their living…One is surprised in traveling through China at the tireless activity of this people, and I have often wondered how they have been able to endure the wear and tear of successive ages and to be the strong and sturdy people that they are today. The simple food they are compelled to live upon, and the health-giving force of daily labor have had the effect of producing a race of people that seem to have all the elements of strength and endurance wrought into the very fiber of their lives.

"On one occasion a race had been arranged for between two cutters —one managed by an English crew and the other by ordinary Chinese boatmen. The former were men who had been selected with great care from a British man-of-war, whilst the others were men who were daily getting their living by rowing passengers across a broad river. The contest was a peculiar one, for, it was meant to be a test of the powers of endurance of the men of the East and the West, and so it was decided that the course should extend to a large village in the interior nearly twenty miles distant.

"Looking at the crews as they sat in their boats waiting for the signal to start, one felt that there could not be the least doubt as to which would be the winner. The bluejackets [British] in their well-known uniform looked the very picture of strength. They were big, brawny men, with thews and muscles that seemed to be made of iron. These men could never tire, one thought, and there was a proud and confident look on their faces that made one feel that there was no doubt in their hearts as to who should gain the victory.

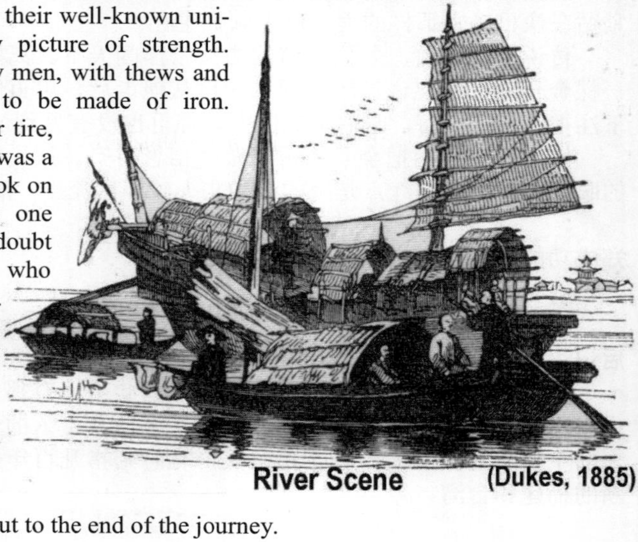

"The Chinamen, on the other hand, with the careless, indolent way in which they are accustomed to hold themselves, gave on the impression that they could never hold out to the end of the journey.

River Scene **(Dukes, 1885)**

东方龟，西方兔

麦嘉湖写于 1913 年

注：这是一个真实的故事，讲的是强壮的英国士兵和骨瘦如柴的中国对手之间的一场划船比赛，结局出人意料。

——潘维廉

中国人总体来说是精力充沛和健康的民族。我很肯定，这主要是因为他们为了谋生工作不息。在中国旅游时，中国人劳动不知疲倦令人惊叹，我常想他们是如何承受岁月的折磨而变得像现在这样强壮和坚毅。赖以糊口的粗陋食物，超强的日常劳动，造就了这样一个民族，他们的强健和坚韧在生活中随处可见。

一次有人安排了一场比赛——参赛的一方是英国水手，另一方是普通的中国船夫。前者是从一艘英国军舰上精心挑选出来的，而后者的工作是每天把行人摆渡到大河对岸。这是一场罕见的竞赛，因为它是东西方男人之间耐力的较量，赛道的终点定在大约 20 英里外的一个内陆的大村庄。

看着水手们坐在船上等待出发信号，毫无疑问英方将取胜。身穿著名蓝色水手服的英国人看起来充满力量。他们身材高大，肌肉发达，像是钢铁铸成，仿佛永远不会疲倦，脸上流露出的骄傲和自信表明，他们将赢得绝对胜利。

相反，那些中国人一如平时所表现的那样随意懒散，让人感觉他们肯定坚持不到终点。

MacGowan, about 1900

"They had never been made to sit upright, and they lounged on their seats as though the whole thing were a vast joke. There was an amused smile on their faces, and they were, no doubt, tickled at the idea that they were going to compete with the famous English, whose deeds of prowess had often been exhibited, to the detriment of their Empire.

"At last the signal was given, and away the boats started on their long race. The English got away with a swing, and soon they were far ahead of their Chinese competitors, who continued to row with an even, steady pull upon their oars as though they were quite unconcerned at the rapid progress that the English were making ahead of them.

The beat and the rhythm of the sounds that came from their boat never quickened, nor was there any excitement in the faces of the men, but with a calmness and serenity typical of the East they kept on with their measured strokes, apparently indifferent whether they won or not.

"By the time that they had gone ten miles the English crew began to show signs of distress. Their faces were flushed, and their clothes were wet with perspiration, whilst the vigorous swing and dip of their oars with which they had begun the race had lost their naturalness, and were the result of a strained effort that had begun to feel the stress that was laid upon their powers. The Chinese, on the other hand, seemed absolutely unchanged from what they were when they first started. There was no sign of distress on the faces of any one of them, and their pull was steady and regular as though the men were pieces of machinery that were being moved by some invisible force that brought no fatigue upon the rowers.

"In the meanwhile the boats were drawing nearer to each other, apparently without any special effort on the part of the Chinese, and finally the latter took the lead and easily came in victors without any signs of strain or fatigue such as were seen in the English crew when the long, exhaustive race was ended.

"The Chinese are a strong, sturdy race, with vast physical powers, which have enabled them to successfully endure the wear and tear of constant labor for countless ages. The many days of relaxation that ease the working-men in England are entirely unknown in China. As a Sunday does not exist in that country, they cannot claim the rest of one day in seven which that Christian holiday gives to men in England. There are, indeed, a half dozen or so festivals during the year when people, by universal custom, drop their work and take a holiday, but beyond these labor is continued on every other day in the year…

"…But whilst it is perfectly true that the nation on the whole are a healthy, vigorous people, and show no signs of decay in consequence of the incessant toil which every class of worker willingly carries on until old age creeps over him and compels him to take life more easily, it is equally the fact that there is a very considerable amount of sickness to be found existing in any district through which one may be traveling. The casual passer-by would never discover this, for in the bearing of pain and disease the Chinaman is a hero who shows the fiber of which he is made by the quiet endurance with which he suffers and dies if needs be without revealing the agonies that may have made life a torture to him."

他们从不坐直身体，而是斜靠在座位上，好像整个比赛不过是一场儿戏。在中国，经常可以见到这些赫赫有名的英国人“累累战功”的破坏痕迹，和他们比赛，着实令中国人感到讽刺，于是大家都面露笑意。

A Chinese Boat (Darley, 1903)

信号终于发出，两条船开始了漫长的赛程。英国人“一桨当先”，很快就把中国人远远地甩在后面。中国人则始终平稳匀速地划桨，仿佛一点也不关心英国人正在拉开距离。

他们划船的节奏一点也没有加快，脸上也看不到丝毫兴奋的表情，而是以东方人特有的平和冷静整齐地划桨，显然他们不在乎输赢。

船到 10 英里处，英国水手颓势初现。他们的脸变得通红，衣服被汗水浸湿，出发时有力的摆臂划桨动作也开始变形了，这可不是因为他们感到比赛压力而在故作努力。相反，那些中国人看起来和出发时没什么两样。他们脸上都看不到沮丧，划桨也是坚定有序如同机器一般，仿佛有种无形的力量将他们的疲劳一扫而光。

其间，中国人并没有特别卖力，但两条船越来越近了，最后中国人反超并轻松取胜。经过漫长艰苦的比赛，英国人看上去非常紧张疲劳，而中国人却一点事也没有。

中国人是健壮刚毅的民族，体能强大，这让他们能够年复一年地承受持续劳作带来的磨难。英国工人赖以休闲的众多假日在中国是不存在的。这里没有礼拜天，不能像英国人那样，每七天享有一天基督教的休息日。虽然一年中依照民俗，确实有几天节日可以停止工作休息一下，但除此之外的每天，人们劳动不息……

有两种现象在中国是并存的。一方面，全国人民大都健康充满活力，每个阶层的劳动者都任劳任怨，直到上了年纪才不得不干点轻活；另一方面，大量的病患存在于各个地区，但偶然经过的路人永远也不会发现这个事实。因为在忍受病痛方面，中国人堪称英雄。如果需要，他们会默默地承受痛苦和死亡，而不会将烦恼流露，否则生活对他们而言就成了一种折磨。

Chapter 9
Gulangyu Gardens

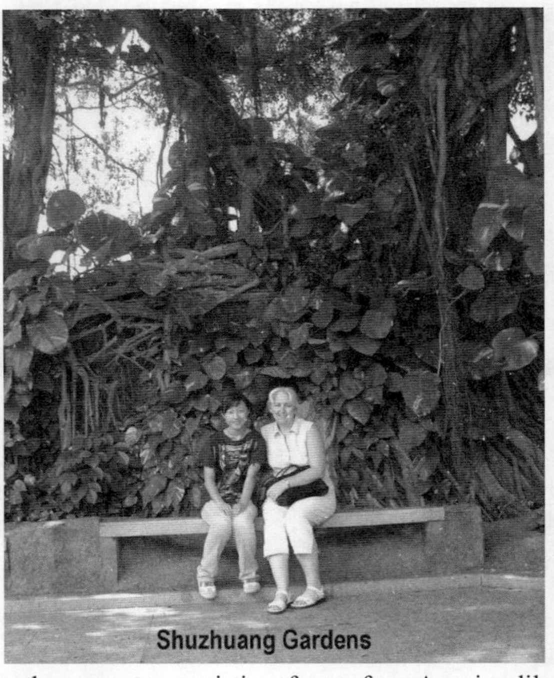
Shuzhuang Gardens

"Trees are found about temples and private residences. The gigantic banyan flourishes everywhere. It often reaches the extraordinary age of one thousand years. There are pines and bamboo, species of India-rubber, cotton, and tallow tree, erythrina, eucalyptus, and the pride of India. Aloes, cacti, and night-blooming cereus abound.

"Among the flowers that grow wild may be found the white cluster rose, white dog violet, blue harebells, pink oxalis, myosatis, vetches, goldenrod, sow-thistles, and ferns of many varieties, including maidenhair, bracken, and harefoot. Among the cultivated flowers there are many varieties of roses from America: lilies, camellias, chrysanthemums, magnolias, iris, geraniums, heliotrope, phlox, and mignonette. Creepers too abound; ivy, honeysuckle, bankinia, racemosa, a large purple flowered thunbergia, and four varieties of the begonia, and the wine flower with its quaint clusters of blossoms opening a creamy white and passing thro all the shades of red, till, before they finally die, they are a deep crimson. Crotons, brought from Singapore, are also cultivated…"

Rev. Philip Wilson Pitcher, "In and about Amoy", 1912, p.154

第九章

鼓 浪 屿

——海上花园

“寺庙和私宅，绿树掩映。高大的菩提树枝繁叶茂，而千龄古树亦非罕见。松树、竹子、种类繁多的印度橡胶树，木棉树，乌桕，桉树，还有檀香，芦荟，仙人掌，昙花随处可见，数量繁多。”

“在这鲜花盛开的世界里，野花也自摇曳吐芳，白玫瑰丛，野生紫罗兰，蓝铃花，红粉酢浆草，勿忘草，野豌豆，秋麒麟，蓟，还有多种蕨类植物，包括铁线蕨，欧洲蕨，和西印度野兔足。而人工栽培的花，有来自美洲的各种玫瑰、百合、茶花、菊花、玉兰、鸢尾、天竺葵、向日葵、福禄考，还有木犀草。‘爬藤比比皆是，常春藤，忍冬，bankinia，总状花序的植物；带紫花的黑眼苏珊。就连秋海棠都有四种；葡萄花，奇怪的一簇簇，刚开花时是奶油色，慢慢变成红色，到花谢时就成了深红色。’这儿也有从新加坡引进的巴豆。”

毕腓力 《厦门方志》 1912 年版 154 页

Gulangyu Islet is a riot of floral colors and scents, of gardens large and small at every turn. Even the smallest households display choice potted plants on balconies and rooftops, and larger villa gardens offer endless varieties of trees and exquisitely sculpted bougainvillea, roses, and azaleas.

Gulangyu gardens reflect their owner's tastes, temperaments, and education—or lack thereof. Some gardens' intricate detail overpower the senses. Others are elegantly simple. Still others are simply in bad taste (though even the gaudier gardens are worth a gander—at least once). On the following pages we'll explore some of the key private and public gardens.

Gulangyu Gardens at a Glance

Some Private Parks and Gardens

Li Qingquan Villa（李清泉别墅） Delightful garden & rockery

Huang Rongyuan Villa (黄荣远堂别墅)—#32 Fujian Rd. Expansive garden; rockery, best view of Catholic Church.

Yang Family Garden（杨家园）—#.27,29,31 Guxin Road, #4 Anhai Road.

Popular Public Parks and Gardens

Zhangzhou Rd. (漳州路) Gulangyu's "most garden-like" road

Shuzhuang Garden (Shuzhuang Huayuan, 菽庄花园)—Gulangyu's largest garden, including Asia's best piano museum (Gangqin Bowuguan, 钢琴博物馆). Read about the Piano Museum in the Arts & Music chapter.

Bright Moon Garden (Haoyue Yuan, 皓月园) & Koxinga Statue

Qin Garden

Yanping Park (Yanping Gongyuan,延平公园) & Koxinga's Well

Gulangyu Aviary (Bainiao Yuan,百鸟园) Beautiful tropical foliage, over 100 types of birds, bird performances, large-screen theater

Xiamen Overseas Chinese Subtropical Plant Nursery

鼓浪屿是花的海洋，花香四溢，大小花园密布。即使是最小的住家，也会在阳台上、屋顶上养着几盆花。若是大户人家，就更不用说了，绿树成阴，灌木丛，经过梳剪而造型奇特的植物，还有玫瑰和杜鹃。

岛上的花园折射出各家主人的品位、性情，还能看出他们是否有教养。那些错综复杂的花园甚至已超越了感观，有些简单而雅致，当然也有品位较差的（不过即使是俗丽的花园也值得一览，看上一回）。

接下来我们就去最主要的私人住宅和公园探探路。

鼓浪屿花园一览

李清泉别墅 其花园、假山园林令人心情舒畅

黄荣远堂 福建路 32 号 宽敞的庭院，假山，欣赏天主教堂，视野极佳

杨家园 鼓新路 27、29、31 号，安海路 4 号

受欢迎的公园和花园

漳州路 鼓浪屿最典型的花园式马路

菽庄花园 岛上最大的花园，包括亚洲最大的钢琴博物馆。欲了解钢琴博物馆，请参阅艺术与音乐一章。

皓月园与郑成功雕像

琴园

延平公园和国姓井

百鸟园 美丽的热带植物，超过 100 种鸟类，可欣赏鸟类表演，还有宽银幕影院

厦门华侨亚热带植物引种园

Private Gardens

Li Qingquan Villa

Li Qingquan Villa（李清泉别墅）, just off Fuxing Rd is Xiamen ace photographer Mr. Bai Hua's favorite Gulangyu mansion.To get there,turn left at the Gulangyu Ferry, stroll along Lujiao Rd.(鹿礁) past the army sanatorium, and bear right onto Fuxing Rd. (复兴路).

Take the left fork at Fuxing Church, turn left into the narrow lane ascending Flag-Raising Hill (Shengqi Shan, 升旗山). Li Qingquan Villa is at the top.

Read more about Li Qingquan and his Villa in the Fuxing Rd. chapter.

Huang Rongyuan Villa (黄荣远堂别墅), #32 Fujian Rd.. This large garden's rockery offers the best view of the Spanish Gothic catholic church next door. (It's tricky getting to the top; ascend from the right side, not the left).

Mr. Huang watched soccer games and sports meets from his balcony, and wandered among the garden's fig trees, elms (青榆), red date trees, the tung trees (刺桐, genus aleurites), Chinese cedar (香椿)，with their small pendulous flowers, the fragrant calyx canthus (腊梅)，camphor (香樟)，lotus (芙蓉)，and bamboo (修竹). (Please turn to the Fujian Rd. chapter).

Yang Family Garden（杨家园) is a four building complex on the slope of Brush Stand Hill at the corner of Guxin and Anhai Roads. The home of photographer Bai Hua, it has a typical walled Gulangyu garden, but Bai Hua complains the gardens and trees are now so unkempt and overgrown that they obscure the view of Sunlight Rock. Still, with a little imagination one can appreciate Yang Villa's past grandeur. (Please turn to the Anhai Rd. chapter).

私家花园

李清泉别墅，离复兴路不远，是厦门一流摄影师白桦最钟爱的鼓浪屿建筑。从鼓浪屿码头上岛后，向左沿着鹿礁路，经过陆军疗养院，朝右拐到复兴路上。

到复兴堂前的岔路时朝左走进一条狭窄的小巷，该巷朝上则通往升旗山。李清泉别墅就建在山顶。

欲知李清泉其人及其别墅，请参阅复兴路一章。

黄荣远堂，位于福建路 32 号，花园极大，假山顶上欣赏隔壁美丽的西班牙哥特式天主教堂视野极佳。（奇怪的是，得从右边而不从左边爬到假山顶上）

黄先生经常在阳台上观赏足球赛和运动会，或在花园里漫步。年代悠远的无花果树，青榆，红枣树，刺桐，香椿，花朵在风中摇曳，腊梅，香樟，还有芙蓉修竹散发的清香弥漫庭院。（请参阅福建路一章）

杨家园 位于笔架山坡面上的四幢楼群，即今天的鼓新路和安海路交界处。著名的摄影家白桦儿时就住在这里，杨家园拥有岛上最典型的筑墙花园。不过，他感到可惜的是，而今园内的花木由于疏于打理，参差不齐，已干扰到从阳台上观赏日光岩的景致。当然，只需稍加想象，你完全可以感受出杨家园昔日的繁华气息。（请参阅安海路一章）

Flowers of the Garden Isle

Myosotis

Bracken

Camellia

Begonia

Caladium

Azalea

Bougainvillea

Blue Harebells

Canna Lily

Chrysanthemum

Poinsettia

Geraniums

Pink Oxalis

Magnolia

Calyx Canthus

Harefoot

Phoenix Tail

Honeysuckle

Zinnia

Lily

Phlox

Maiden Hair

Acacia

Thunbergia

Gulangyu's Endless Parks

Bishan Park (Gulangyu's Wilderness)

Bright Moon Park

Jishan Christian Cemetery
(A very peaceful park!)

Dr. Lin Qiaozhi Memorial Garden

Seaside Garden and Sculpture

Cable Car Between
Sunlight Rock and Aviary

Public Gardens

Zhangzhou Rd. (**漳州路**) Gulangyu's most "garden-like road," was a coveted residential area for the former International Settlement's wealthy Chinese and foreigners. This delightfully shaded lane winds past the Koxinga statue in Bright Moon Garden (Haoyue Yuan, 皓月园), Xiamen Music Academy, and the former residences of folk like internationally known writer Lin Yutang (林语堂) and China's sports pioneer John Ma (马约翰).

Shuzhuang Garden, Gulangyu's Premier Garden (Shuzhuang Huayuan, 菽庄花园) #45 Huangyan Rd. The garden's creator, Mr. Lin Shuzhuang, （林菽庄）also called Er Jia (尔嘉), was born in Taibei, Taiwan about 1874 and is one of Gulangyu's favorite sons—primarily because of his Shuzhuang Garden (though both he and his ancestors had long made numerous contributions to both the mainland and Taiwan province).

In 1913, Lin built Shuzhuang Garden on Caozai Mountain （草仔山), modeling it after the elder Lin's Banqiao （板桥）villa in Taiwan, with back to the hill and facing the sea and their lost home of Taiwan.

Lin spent 10,000 Yuan to have president Xushichang（徐世昌）engrave a plaque for the garden, but the plaque was lost, and the one now on display bears the calligraphy of Mr. Luodan（罗丹）.

In 1913, Lin Erjia set up a Recital Club for composing and reciting poems, and after the Anti-Japanese War, he left Shanghai for Taiwan, where he died in Taibei on 8 November, 1951, at the age of 77.

Please turn to the Lujiao Rd. chapter to read more about Lin's home, the Octagonal Building, at #11-19 Lujiao Rd.

Improve Mountain, Hide Sea Shuzhuang's hillside area is called Bushan (补山, "Improve Mountain"), implying that man has improved upon natural beauty. The seaside area is called Canghai (藏海, "Hide the Sea"), because Er Jia deliberately built a low wall so that nothing is seen but hills and flowers, the sea springing into view only after one passes the Moon Gate.

公园

漳州路 鼓浪屿岛上花园式的路段，当年中外富豪竞相云集的寓居之地。此地氛围清幽，蜿蜒而过皓月园的郑成功雕像、厦门音乐学校，别忘了沿路还有不少名人故居，如蜚声中外的作家林语堂故居，还有中国体育运动先驱马约翰故居。

菽庄花园 岛上第一名园，园主人林菽庄，名尔嘉，可算是鼓浪屿最钟爱的孩子之一，首要原因是他所创建的菽庄花园（当然他的先祖和他本人长期以来对大陆和台湾省的贡献颇大）。

1913 年，林菽庄在草仔山下建起了菽庄花园。这是他仿照其先祖在台湾的板桥别墅（即林家花园）格调而修建的。该建筑倚山而建，面朝大海，以此纪念失去的台湾故居。

他还特地花了一万银元的润笔费，请当时的大总统徐世昌题写菽庄园匾，此匾已经遗失，现匾为罗丹先生手书。

同年，林尔嘉成立“菽庄吟社”，吟诗作赋。抗战胜利后，他从上海返回台，1951 年 11 月 8 日逝世，享年 77 岁。

若对于位于鹿礁路 11-19 号的林氏府八角楼想知道更多，就请翻阅鹿礁路一章。

补山藏海 菽庄花园靠山的部分命名为“补山”，其含义是指人类可以人工构筑补缀天然山景之不足。靠海的一侧是“藏海”，林尔嘉构思巧妙，特意建了一堵矮墙，如此一路走来不见海，唯有青山和鲜花相伴左右，待到转过月洞门，突然“海阔天空”，大海奔腾骤至，一览无遗。

Canghai Garden's 5 Main Attractions

44 Bridge（Sishisi Qiao, 四十四桥), Shuzhuang's most famous site, snakes across an inlet like a befuddled bamboo viper. I thought the bridge had 44 angles until I read it was so named because it was completed on the owner's 44th birthday.

Lin originally intended the bridge to be longer, connecting the garden with the neighboring Sea View Garden, but the Danish Great Northern Telegraph Company objected it would have crossed a submerged cable (the cable itself was illegal, but in those days Chinese laws did not overly inconvenience foreigners).

The characters "Haikuo Tiankong (海阔天空), meaning Vast Sky, Open Sea, are engraved upon a stone in the bridge's center. The phrase is from a poem carved upon Sunlight Rock by the famous Ming Dynasty calligrapher Zhang Ruitu (张瑞图). The two characters on the back of the boulder, Zhen Liu (枕流), have something to do, I'm told, with resting and listening to the waves.

The 44 Bridge's small pavilion has two vertical couplets:

明月浮空十二栏 (Mingyue Fukong Shi'er Lan, "bright moon floats over 12 bridge lengths")

长桥支海三千丈 (Changqiao Zhihai Sanqian Zhang, "long bridge spans 3,000 *zhang* across the sea"). Note: one *zhang* is about 3½ meters.

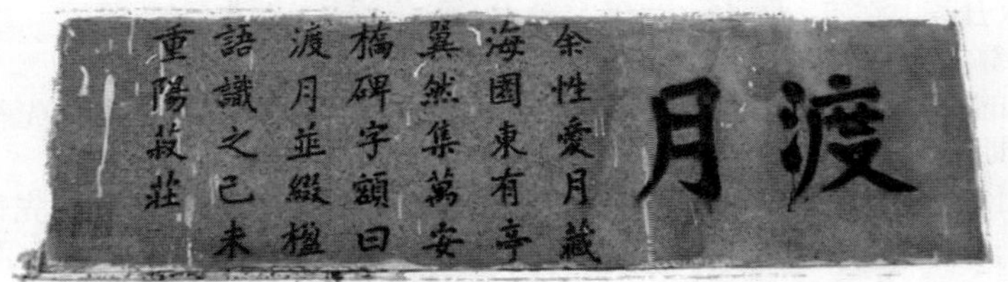

渡月 (Du Yue), read right to left, means "moon crossing".

Meishou Hall (眉寿, or "Long Life"), originally built of brick and wood but later remodeled, lies near the beach facing Nan Taiwu Mountain[1] (南太武). It was also called "Tan Ying Xuan" (谈瀛轩) because Mr. Lin, homesick for relatives and friends in Taiwan, relaxed here, composed poems, and drank wine and tea with companions.

Renqiu (壬秋) Pavilion, completed in the autumn of 1922, has a fish pond.

Zhen Shuai (真率, "Truthfully, Heartily") Pavilion was built as a place for friends to bare their souls with one another.

Zhao Liang (招凉) Pavilion is shaped like a Chinese fan. The name means "Catching Wind"—as indeed it does, thanks to its location at the cliff's base.

[1] Read more about the "Great Southern Warrior" in the Tianwei chapter intro

藏海园五景

四十四桥 菽庄花园一大名景，曲桥蜿蜒，犹如一条竹叶青盘旋于小海湾上。我曾以为该桥之所以命名为四十四桥是因为它转了四十四道弯，后来才知道是因为该桥落成适逢园主四十四岁生日。

林尔嘉最初的设想是要建得更长些，将花园与邻近的观海别墅相连。但是丹麦大北电报公司反对，认为可能会穿过铺设在海底的电缆（其实该条电缆亦属非法，但是当时的中国法律无权约束外国人）。

桥的中段刻着“海阔天空”四个汉字，其意为天空开阔，大海无垠。该成语取自刻于日光岩上明朝著名书法家张瑞图的诗句。石头的背面刻着“枕流”二字，人家告诉我，其意为休憩之余倾听涛声为乐。

四十四桥上有座小亭，亭上有副楹联：明月浮空十二栏，长桥支海三千丈（一丈约等于 3.5 米）。

横批“渡月”，读的顺序是从右到左，意思是“月亮从此经过”。

眉寿堂(长寿)，最初是砖木结构，后重建，坐落于海边，面朝南太武[1]；亦名“谈瀛轩”，原因是林尔嘉思念台湾的亲朋好友，经常在此邀友小酌，泡茶吟诗，放松心情。

壬秋阁　1922 年秋天落成，有一鱼池。

真率亭　朋友在此坦诚交心。

招凉亭　形似一把中国扇子，意为“迎风”。由于亭子位于崖壁之下，确实名副其实。

[1] 请参阅《田尾路》一章了解“南太武”更多相关信息

Bushan Garden's Five Main Attractions

Wanshi (顽石, or Stubborn Rock) Hillside House, behind the Monkey Caves, was Mr. Lin Er Jia's study area. He used the name "Stubborn Rock" to encourage himself, and others, to seek wisdom through diligent study.

Monkey Caves, an artificial rockery, has 12 caves, each representing one of the "Twelve Earthly Branches" (which with the Heavenly Stems designate years, months, days and hours). Each cave is unique, and together form a labyrinth.

Yi'ai Wulu (亦爱吾庐) Pavilion, in one of Lin Shuzhuang's favorite areas, was for meeting with friends. Yi'ai Wulu meant "I love my home."

Xiao Lan (小兰) Pavilion was another gathering place for friends. On the day it was completed (March 12, 1924), he invited 12 poets to compose and recite poems. Unfortunately, the 1959 typhoon that created the swimming resort on Gangzihou Beach also destroyed Xiao Lan Pavilion.

Ting Tao Xuan (听涛轩), or "Listening to the Tides Tower," on the bluff above the garden, now has Asia's largest piano museum, and is a great place to relax, sip tea, and contemplate the view. (See the chapter on Gulangyu Music).

After enjoying Shuzhuang's pavilions, flowers and shrubs, take in the sea view from the tea house, and then either visit the Piano Museum on the bluff or enjoy golden Gangzihou Beach right next door—just as Gulangyu's elite enjoyed it in the Roaring '20s…

(Fullerton, 1910)

"I used to stand fascinated and wondering, looking at the changing gray-purplish hues of the mountainsides and at the fanciful, wayward meanderings of the white clouds on the mountaintops. It gives one a contempt for the lowly hills and for all that is artificial and small and made by men. Those high mountains have become a part of me and my religion, for they give me a richness and inner strength and sense of independence which no man can take away from me." Lin Yutang, "From Pagan to Christian"

补山五景

"In a Gentleman's House: (Dukes, 1885)

顽石山房 倚山而建，在猴洞之后，为林尔嘉的书房。取名顽石，“勤能补拙”之意，既是自勉，也是共勉。

亦爱吾庐亭 该地是林尔嘉最喜爱的处所之一，所以他在此处建亭会见朋友，取“我爱我家”之意。

小兰亭 朋友聚会之所 1924 年 3 月 12 日乃亭子落成之日，林尔嘉邀请了 12 位诗人聚此吟诗赋词。可惜的是，1959 年的台风虽然造就了港仔后海滨浴场，却也摧毁了小兰亭。

听涛轩 建于花园崖壁上，而今是亚洲最大的钢琴博物馆，更是放松、品茶、观景的好去处。（请参阅鼓浪屿音乐一章）

漫步在花木扶疏的园子里，逛了这么多的亭子，不妨去茶楼里喝喝茶，看看海景，还可以去参观断崖上的钢琴博物馆或者去隔壁的港仔后沙滩上走走——风云四起的 20 世纪 20 年代鼓浪屿上的上层人士热衷于此。

> “我常常站着遥望那些山坡灰蓝色的变幻，及白云在山顶上奇怪的，任意的漫游，感到迷惑和惊奇。它使人轻忽矮山及一切人为的、虚假的、渺小的东西。这些高山早就成为我及我信仰的一部分，因为它们使我富足，心里产生力量与独立感，没有人可以从我身上带走它们。”
>
> 林语堂《从异教徒到基督徒》

Gangzihou Beach 港仔后

"As Amoy lies in the track of typhoons there are times when there is decidedly too much breeze." Rev. Pitcher, "In and About Amoy," 1912

Gangzihou Beach has bathrooms, tea rooms, flower nurseries, bumper cars and a roller-skating rink. You can also rent jet skis, or have tea on a floating platform.

Legend of the Gold Belt Gangzihou Beach used to be called Gold Belt Waters (金带水, Jindai Shui) because of a legend dating back to 1276 A.D. Yuan Dynasty troops from Zhejiang Province invaded Fujian, which was ruled by the Southern Song Dynasty. The 11-year-old king Zhao Shi (赵昰), escorted by prime minister Lu Xiufu (陆 秀夫) and general Zhang Shijie （张世杰), fled to Xiamen, where he planned to escape to Guangdong Province. When violent swells threatened to capsize the small escape craft, the miniature monarch tossed his golden belt into the sea, whereupon the ocean became calm and he crossed safely. From that day onwards, locals called that area, "Gold Belt Waters."

Gangzihou Beach

Gulangyu Laowai Beach Party (1920s)

"Even in high summer noons, the small bay was not always left to the beating sun. On Saturdays and Sundays there would be bathing parties to which all the residents in the immediate neighborhood were, perforce, invited, since otherwise to observe the polite conventions and preserve the privacy of the party was almost impossible. The satisfaction of dispensing hospitality was preferable to the mood engendered by social coercion....

"By an unwritten code, only we of the bay assumed the rights of party-giving. Guests were exclusively European. In a temperature of rarely less than ninety degrees Fahrenheit, emerging from a lukewarm sea, it was customary for the bathers to be offered cherry-brandy on a silver salver by their hostesses' house servant." Anne Averil Mackenzie, "Green Ginger"

港仔后

“由于厦门位处台风必经之地，自然不时地会狂风大作。”

毕腓力 《厦门方志》 1912 年版

港仔后有一个海滨浴场。1959 年还在这里建起了淋浴房、茶室、花房、碰碰车游乐和溜冰场。你还可以租艘滑艇（水上摩托）过过瘾，或者在浮排上泡茶。

金带水的传说 港仔后海滩原名金带水，还有一个传说可追溯到公元 1276 年。当时，南宋小朝廷蜗居闽地，元军由浙攻闽，11 岁的小皇帝赵昰由宰相陆秀夫和张世杰将军护卫，逃到厦门，准备由此假道广东。突然，海浪暴起，即将吹翻逃生的小舟，这时小皇帝解下金腰带扔进海里，于是风平浪静，安然渡海。从那时开始，当地人就把这片海域叫做“金带水”。

鼓浪屿上的老外海滩宴会 （20 世纪 20 年代）

“即使是盛夏的中午，小小的港湾也并不是只有明晃晃的大太阳。一到周六周日，海滩上都是浴场宴会。既然那种彬彬有礼的交谈和保有隐私的宴会几乎是不可能的，邻近的居民必然受邀，齐聚一堂。盛情款待之下，宾客尽欢，最适宜这一强制性社交而形成的氛围……”

“出于不成文的规定，只有我们才有权在海滩上举办宴会。客人全都是欧洲人。气温很少低于华氏 90 度，那些从温热的海水中出来的浴者习惯喝上一杯樱桃白兰地。而这些自然有女主人手下成群的家仆手持银托盘在侍候。” Anne Avril Mackenzie 女士，《绿姜根》

Gangzihou Beach

The Gardening Isle—circa 1920s
(by Averil Mackenzie-Grieve, Gulangyu, 1920s)

"The garden was riotous, flaming hotly with scarlet and orange cannas, vermilion lobelias, purple orchids and zinnias colored to match them all, as well as in their own peculiar biting pink. By contrast the kitchen garden was restful, foaming with a great tide of green from the successful germination of a quarter of a pound of parsley seed, inadvertently handed over to our old gardener with the packets of Australian flower seeds.

"Under his devoted care all the plants grew into enormous magnifications of their normal size.

"This unruly abundance, which delighted us, worried him beyond measure. Such indiscipline he held to be savage--no tribute to his skill, but a shame he was powerless to rectify while we insisted on herbaceous borders.

"Plants and flowers should be treated as individuals, savored and enjoyed for special qualities in an almost contemplative spirit.

"His was not the stricted purism of the Japanese, but he provided us with a fresh angle from which to view our own gardening tradition, a fresh example of the Chinese craftsman's respect for materials. In the damp hothouse atmosphere in which the flowers throve, we slept badly, cursing the koel which began its endless, five-note call before even the cicadas seamed up the early morning silences. It was a wonderful relief to shed the muffling air of the house, to feel the sea on hot, sticky skin. The bay was beautiful, too, in the colorless early morning light. The grey hills of the mainland rose out of the white mists, layer on layer, fading into a grey sky. The tentative fold and spread of the water's edge was the only movement.

"Huang Yizhu's garden wall looked severe from the sea, for the regimented flowers were sheltered behind it. Over the other side of the island was another and more beautiful, classically Chinese garden. The owner had taken the tall rocky headland, studied its character, and then collaborated with its contours, its cliffs, its trees. With the privilege of walking there, we learned to appreciate the subtle simplicities of Chinese garden planning: the full exploitation of each element, of each idiosyncratic growth. The owner was a rich scholar: Wei-ju was just rich." [See next

Yanping Park (延平公园), near Gangzihou Beach, was set up as a memorial to Koxinga, The park's Fujing Spring （拂净泉）, also called Guoxing Well (国姓井), is said to have been dug by Koxinga's troops. Read "The Legend of Koxinga's Well" in the chapter on Koxinga.

"The secret of contentment is knowing how to enjoy what you have, and to be able to lose all desire for things beyond your reach." Lin Yutang

海上花园——大约 20 世纪 20 年代

Averil Mackenzie- Grieve, 20 世纪 20 年代鼓浪屿居民

“整个花园姹紫嫣红，一派繁荣景象，深红的、橘色的美人蕉，朱红的半边莲，紫色的兰花，再加上抢眼的粉红鱼尾菊，颜色非常相配。相比之下，菜园显得悠闲些，绿浪起伏，其实那只是 1/4 磅的欧芹种子生根发芽，茁壮成长的结果。而且那袋花种还是无意中随澳大利亚花种交给我们的老园丁的。

“由于他的精心饲弄，菜园里所有的作物长势喜人，硕大无朋。

“这些作物肆意生长，茂盛繁密，喜了我们，愁煞园丁。他觉得，植物的生长不受拘束，随意蔓延会长疯的，也表现不出自己的才艺，他的无力矫正，对自己的技术更是一种羞耻。但是我们坚持以灌木为绿篱。

“植物和花朵都应是独立的个体，且在敛心默祷中品味他们的特质。

“然而园丁不像日本式的完全拘泥于园艺学的范畴，他倒是给我们提供了一个新角度看待传统园艺学，而且鲜活地说明中国花匠对花草的尊重。植物滋长繁盛，房子里又闷又潮，我们睡得也不好，气得直咒骂；噪鹃老早就开始无休止地啼叫，然后可怕的蝉鸣又打破了寂静的清早。屋子里空气实在令人压抑，能够逃离出来到海边去让粘热的肌肤自然呼吸，可说是一大快事。在清晨敞亮的光线下海湾无比漂亮，陆地上青山在薄雾中逐渐浮现，又渐渐没入天空。此时，唯有海边的浪花翻滚而已。

“黄弈住的花园围墙屹立于海边，护着墙内大片的花丛。而在岛的另一边，有一家更漂亮，中式古典风格浓郁的花园。园主将假山延伸入水，因势利导，与周边的环境，峭壁，树木，融为一体。有幸漫步其中，我们领略到中国花园的布局既微妙又朴素，物尽其用，特色鲜明。园主是位家境殷实的学者，而黄弈住只是有钱而已。” [见下页]

延平公园 靠近港仔后海滩，是建来纪念郑成功的。园内的拂净泉，也称国姓井，据说是郑成功部队挖掘的。请参阅郑成功一章“国姓井的传说”。

“满足的奥秘全在于知足常乐，对无法得到的切勿心存奢望。”

林语堂

A Rich Chinese' Gulangyu Garden

(Averil Mackenzie-Grieve, Gulangyu, 1920s)

"Wei-ju was the richest inhabitant of the [Gulangyu International] Settlement. A humble man who had, it was said, made his fortune in Javanese sugar, he owned several houses, pavilions and gardens on the island. The whole of the right-hand crescent of our bay belonged to him. The formal garden that he had laid out on the rocky point was open to the public. There was no custodian but, in spite of much great poverty, no one ever damaged or stole from the superb array of potted plants. No one left litter. But this was partly due to the shortage of fuel in a deforested land. Often it was rice alone that kept body and soul together, but rice had to be cooked. Thus, all over the island, thin little girls, often carrying babies too heavy for them slung in red cloths, scoured the paths and beaches like nesting birds, for every twig, leaf, straw and piece of paper. In the little pavilion overlooking the sea, Wei-ju was keeping his mother's corpse until such time as the geomancers had declared the Feng-shui of her burial place to be favorable. Since his continuing prosperity and that of his children depended upon it, the correct aspects of wind and water were essential.

"The house where Wei-ju entertained was set in another formal garden, neat and brilliant as an embroidery, with its seasonal, potted patterns of narcissi, zinnias, phoenix tail, crotons and chrysanthemums. Inside, the carved and lacquered Chinese furniture of the hall was enlivened by a complete set of white-painted European bedroom furniture, a gigantic stuffed orangutan in a glass case, and a discreetly draped marble woman with dove in the Alma Tadema tradition. The thirty or so courses of excellent food which he always provided, the crowd of gaping sightseers, the poor relations on the marble stairs, the indescribable cacophony produced by two bands of musicians playing against each other, the good humour, the throat-clearing, the spitting, were wholly Chinese. The returned emigrant, the successful, self-made man, deserved to enjoy his success. And why not with an orangutan, I said to myself, if he likes to be reminded of the jungles of the south?"

The Subtropical Botanical Garden, or "Xiamen Overseas Chinese Subtropical Plant Nursery," covers 1.3 sq. km. at the base of Sunlight Rock. The garden began with 280 kinds of plants of commercial value and now has over 1,000 species divided into several main areas, including a nursery for the introduction of new variations, an experimental nursery, a flower garden, a cultivation greenhouse, and a refrigerated room (perhaps for subtropical plants that can't take the heat?).

The garden was set up in 1959 by the Xiamen Overseas Chinese Association, and in 1962 was attached to the East China Subtropical Plant Institute of the China Academy. It was closed during the Cultural Revolution, but later reopened, and in July of 1984 the garden came under the control of the Xiamen Science Commission and the Xiamen Overseas Chinese Association.

中国富绅的岛上花园

Averil Mackenzie- Grieve,20 世纪 20 年代岛上居民

“黄奕住是岛上安家落户的居民中最有钱的一个。原本出身卑贱，据说在爪哇经营蔗糖发了财。他在岛上有多处房产别墅。我们海湾右手边的那块地就是他的。他曾在岩石顶上建起了花园还对外开放。虽然无人管理，而且穷人遍布，可是就没有人会去破坏或偷窃那些成排的盆花。也没人乱扔垃圾。但这也可能是因为岛上森林日稀，燃料短缺。通常米饭就能强身健体，当然米必须是煮熟的。因此，岛上到处都是瘦弱的小姑娘，背着裹在红襁褓里的婴儿，而且婴儿对她们来讲都太重了，不胜负荷。她们像筑巢的小鸟似的，一路‘扫荡’小路和沙滩，捡回任何一根细小的树枝，树叶，稻草，还有纸屑都不放过。黄弈住将母亲暂时安葬在可俯瞰大海的小亭里，直到风水先生找到风水宝地才移走。确实，他个人及其子孙的万世基业都需仰赖风水，可见风水的重要性。

“黄弈住娱乐消遣的处所则建在另一处花园里。园内犹如一匹刺绣，整洁鲜亮，处处点缀着当季的盆花，水仙，鱼尾菊，凤尾，巴豆，还有菊花。屋内，精雕油漆的中式家具在全套白色欧式卧室家具的映衬下，添了几分生动。玻璃柜里摆放着大猩猩，还有极具埃及风格手托鸽子的大理石雕美女。他通常会用 30 道左右的精美菜肴款待宾客，蜂拥而至的宾客，大理石阶上的穷亲戚，两支乐队演奏着完全不同的乐曲而产生难以描述的刺耳噪音，清喉咙的嗓音，吐痰的声音，人群混杂，颇具讽刺，这就是纯粹的中国特色。这位海外归来的华人，功成名就，有资格享受成功。那又为何与大猩猩相伴？我想，可能他想提醒自己别忘了在南洋丛林中的日子吧？”

亚热带植物园 也称厦门华侨亚热带植物引种园，位于日光岩山脚下，占地 1.3 平方公里。最初以 280 个品种起家，创造了一定的经济效益，而今已超过 1000 多个品种，分为若干区域，包括新物种引进区、试验区、花园、温室培育区、冷冻区（难道是亚热带植物无法抗热？）。

该园由厦门市侨联于 1959 年创办，1962 年归属于中国科学院华东亚热带植物研究所。“文革”期间停办，后复办。1984 年 7 月，又归回厦门市科委和厦门市侨联管理。

Chapter 10
Dining, Shopping, Entertainment, Hotels

RICE BOWL AND CHOPSTICKS. (Dukes, 1885)

Forks or Chopsticks?

by Duke (1885)

The point of greatest interest is always reached when the traveler begins his meal…

The laying out of plates, knives and forks is a great mystery. Much questioning goes on as to the way of using them.

They beg to know the reason why we prefer to employ a man to carry all our apparatus for dinner, instead of using their bowls and chopsticks… When we lift our food to our mouth, many hands move in a similar way, as they say quietly to one another, 'Look! He is doing like this!' Standing as closely around our small table that we feel inconvenienced, we entreat them to give us breathing room while we dine, and afterwards we will talk to them. Many voices break forth with pleasure at our speaking to them. 'The foreigner speaks our words,' says one; 'Yes, let him eat,' says another; 'stand back, you man without propriety,' says a third, whose zeal for good manner is evidently due only to his desire to secure a front place.

The first 'westren' building you see after disembarking the ferry, the Gulangyu Mall, was built not a century ago but in 2001, with the Tourist Info Center below and trendy shops and eateries above.

Gulangyu Visitor Information Center

Sample popcorn and cotton candy while enjoying live traditional music in the courtyard, or enjoy a nice buffet on the roof. The food is not 'on the house,' but the splendid view is.

The Mall is on Dragon Head Rd. (Longtou Lu, 龙头), which has Gulangyu's best shopping district and sites like the Gulangyu Aquarium. (For more shopping, try Zhonghua Rd., near the former Masonic Lodge, and check out its Weird World Museum, which also has puppets shows.)

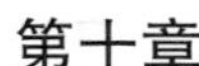

第十章

饮食，购物，娱乐和宾馆

刀叉还是筷子？

迪克 1885

一到游客吃饭的时候，大家就兴致盎然……

盘子、刀叉的摆设都显得极其神秘。大家争相问起如何使用这些东西。

他们好奇得不得了，为什么我们宁愿雇个人帮忙拿那些吃饭的家伙，而不用他们的碗筷……当我们将食物送到嘴里，马上很多只手都指到类似的方向。那些人在窃窃私语“快看，那个人这么吃饭。”那些看客把小小的餐桌围得密不透风，我们觉得很不舒服，求他们给我们留点空间吃饭。我们愿意吃完饭再和他们聊。我们一开口，立即说开了。他们显得很开心。“这个老外会说中国话。”“是啊，让他先吃吧。”“往后站，你们这些人太没礼貌了。”第三个人开口了，好像很懂礼节，其实他只是为了占个前排的好位子。

从码头一上岸，你所看到的第一幢西洋式建筑就是鼓浪屿商业中心。这可不是一个世纪前建的，2001 年才完工。楼下是鼓浪屿游客中心，楼上是时尚的店铺和吃东西的地方。

你可以在中庭里边品尝爆米花和棉花糖，边欣赏现场的传统音乐表演；楼顶上还有自助餐。在楼顶，你享受不到食物，却可以饱览佳景。

商业中心出来就是龙头路——鼓浪屿最好的商业街（想购物也可以去中华路，靠近原麻笋教厦门分会）。附近还有鼓浪屿海底世界，珍奇世界博物馆（里面还有木偶剧表演）。

Gulangyu Entertainment at a Glance

Wine & Dine

Enjoy Minnan Tea Ceremonies, local seafood specialties, and S. Fujian cuisine. For simple and cheap, try the Luzhou Hotel, just off the ferry, or the large seafood place on Huangyan Rd., just past the Music Hall. Also try the 4-star hotel beside Shuzhuang Garden (fine food, but pricey).

Entertainment

Underwater World, at #2 Longtou Rd.; one of China's fi with over 10,000 finned friends, offers daily shows.

Weird World, a "Believe it or not" style museum on Zhonghua Rd., also offers puppet shows. Lujiao Rd. also has puppet shows and wax works.

Museums: Piano Museum (Asia's largest) and Organ Museum (planet's largest?)

Cable Car—the ride from Sunlight Rock to Hero Hill gives a great view of Gulangyu architecture.

Gulangyu Aviary – over 100 kinds of birds; frequent bird shows

Rides & Cruises—cruise the islet ring road in comfort on an electric cart—or head to sea. The eight kilometer cruise around Gulangyu offers tantalizing glimpses of Monkey Isle, Baozhuyu (Pearl) Isle, and Huoshaoyu Isle (or 'Burning Isle," an extinct volcano).

Shopping

Laowai and Laonei alike pick up great buys on Gulangyu handicrafts. **Pearl World** (#115) is ***the*** place for China's famous cultured pearls. **Yogi's** shop (Longtou #11-6) offers amazing bottles and globes hand-painted on the inside. Former U.S. President Jimmy Carter had one word for them: "Miraculous!"

The #63-2 Longtou Rd. shop offers leather scrolls hand painted by Gulangyu art school students for a few dollars, and fine jade and stone jewelry, or pick up a traditional Chinese watercolor or modern oil painting.

Paintings can range from $5 to $500 (USD!), depending on the artist. I can't tell a master's work from those churned out cheaply by Xiamen art students. My advice is if it's worth it to you, buy it—but bargain! And pick up a Minnan tea set, and the fine Anxi tea that paved the way for American Independence (we tossed it in the sea during the Boston Tea Party!). And try Gulangyu specialties like Mooncakes, fish balls, and the dried meats from a family business dating from 1842! (#95 Longtou Rd.)

鼓浪屿娱乐一览

饮食

试试闽南茶道，本地的海鲜，闽南特色菜肴。要简单又便宜，那就去码头边上的绿洲酒店；或是音乐厅附近，晃岩路上最大的一家海鲜店。当然菽庄花园隔壁还有一家四星级的酒店（食物不错，价钱也不便宜）。

娱乐

海底世界　龙头路 2 号，中国最好的水族馆之一，拥有上万只鱼，每天都有表演。

“珍奇世界”博物馆　这个“信不信由你”类型的博物馆位于中华路上，还有木偶演出。

博物馆——钢琴博物馆（亚洲最大的），风琴博物馆，厦门博物馆

空中缆车　路线从日光岩到英雄山，一路上可观览岛上建筑。

鼓浪屿百鸟园　上百种鸟，经常有鸟类表演。

悠闲观光　可坐在电瓶车上，轻松地环岛而行，或开到海边。绕岛一圈 8 公里，一路上，猴岛、宝珠屿、火烧屿（死火山）都只能匆匆一瞥。

购物

无论是老外还是老内都喜欢在岛上大量采购手工艺品。珍珠世界是中国最著名的人工养殖珍珠销售点。龙头路 11 号之 6 出售瓶内手工绘画的中国瓶和地球仪，美国前总统吉米·卡特对此赞叹不已：“简直不可思议！”

龙头路 63-2 号的那家商店还出售手工绘制的中国风光皮制品，要价几美元。还有精美的中国传统水彩画及更现代的油画。价位从 5 块到 500 块（美金！）不等，看是谁画的。说实话，我自己是没办法区别出大师级的作品和厦门学艺术的学生批量的低价作品有何不同。我的意见是，如果值得你买，那就买吧——但一定要还价。

还可以买套闽南茶具，上好的安溪茶叶，那可为美国的独立战争开辟了道路（波士顿倾茶事件中被我们倒进了海里）。

此外，买点本地特色小吃吧，像馅饼、鱼丸，还有肉松——这可是家族经营，可追溯到 1842 年！（龙头路 95 号）

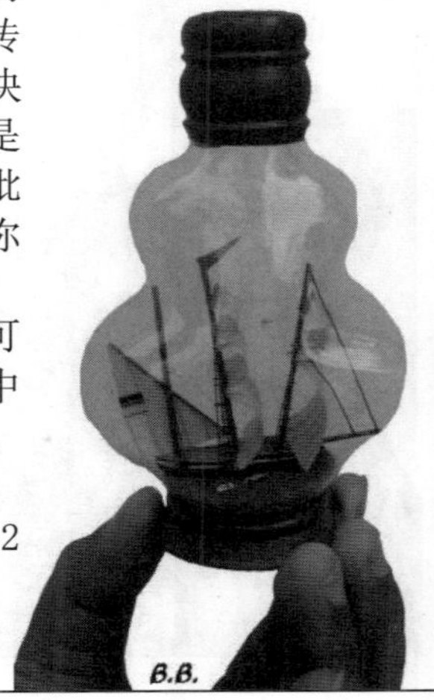

(Dukes, 1885)

Sleight of Hand- Puppets!

Marco Polo's fabled Quanzhou, just 70 miles north, is China's marionette capital, and just to the west is Zhangzhou, home of hand puppets, but Gulangyu also produces puppets and offers private performances.

Chinese puppets are nothing like our childhood toys. In the hands of a master, they are the closest thing you'll find in this life to real life little people!

One puppet puffs a long pipe and blows smoke out his mouth. Another pours a tiny cup of tea with a steadier hand than I'll ever have into a thimble-sized cup. Puppets perform dragon dances, and perform astonishing comic routines and acrobatics—throwing spinning plates into the air and catching them on two poles, or juggling a barrel on their heads, or even tossing and flipping each other!

No Puppets, No Fireworks A Chinese who was amused by the childlike delight I took in the puppets' antics told a friend, "It's because America doesn't have puppets."

His sage observation reminded me of the Longyan farmers who witnessed our family firing off half a ton of fireworks. He told his friend, "See how excited those foreigners are! Other countries don't have fireworks, you know."

B.

For the record, Americans do have fireworks, and puppets too. All we lack is the Chinese master's magic to bring them to life (I once snuck behind stage to reassure myself that the little folk were not alive!).

Arrange a puppet show on Gulangyu with Mr. Hong Mingzhang (洪明章), of the Weird World Museum（珍奇世界博物馆）, and take home a genuine made-on-Gulangyu Zhangzhou hand puppet. Phone: 206-9933, or 897-3331.

木偶把戏！马可·波罗笔下神话般的泉州，北距厦门 70 公里，号称中国的牵线木偶之都，而厦门以西的漳州则是手工木偶之乡。但鼓浪屿上也生产木偶，还有私人表演。

这些木偶一点都不像我们孩提时玩耍的普通木偶。在大师的手上，他们成了现实生活中最逼真的小精灵。

一个木偶吸了口旱烟，吐着烟圈。另一个木偶一手稳稳地抓起一只小茶杯（我还没办法呢），茶水直直地倒进另一个顶针大小的杯子里。木偶还会表演舞龙、喜剧和杂技，实在令人称奇——将旋转的碟子抛向空中，用两只竿子接住；或用头顶住圆木桶，时而抛起，时而相互空翻。

没有木偶，没有鞭炮 木偶滑稽可笑，看得我就像孩子般兴奋，一位中国人很吃惊，对他朋友说，“那是因为美国还没有木偶。”他的话使我想起龙岩的村民。看着我们一家放掉了半吨的鞭炮，其中一个对他朋友说，“你瞧那些老外兴奋的样子。你知道吗，只有中国才有鞭炮。”

事实上，美国也有鞭炮。木偶我们也有。我们所缺乏的是中国大师的魔力，赋予他们生命（我曾经偷偷跑到后台，去确认那些木偶真的没有生命！）

珍奇世界博物馆的洪明章先生可以安排木偶表演，还可以买个鼓浪屿产的漳州手工木偶带回家。电话：2069933，8973331。

Puppets Handcrafted on Gulangyu

So much to do on Gulangyu!

Sample Gulangyu's Famous Mooncakes

Visit Gulangyu Tourist Information Center

Have Yogi Transform Your Name into Art!

Count Sculptures (there are dozens!)

Enjoy a Minnan Tea Ceremony

Stroll Shady Lanes

Savor our Seafood

Shop for China's Famous Cultured Pearls

Play Koxinga's Mooncake Game!

Explore China's Narrowest Lanes!

See the Seal Show

Enjoy Water Sports

Take Electric Tram Tours

Rent a Boat for a Day

Sample Huangjin Jerky
Since 1842! (#95 Longtou)

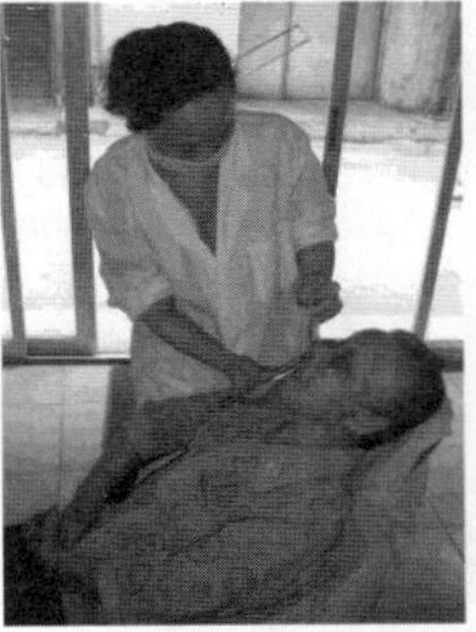
Have Your Teeth Pulled!
#177 Longtou Rd

Famous
Fishball Soup
#183 Longtou Rd.

Where to Start?

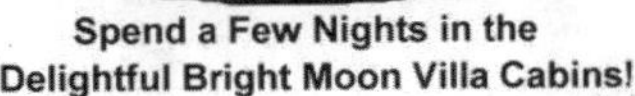
Spend a Few Nights in the
Delightful Bright Moon Villa Cabins!

Explore the old Chinese
Christian Cemetery

Take a Dinner Cruise

Yogi's Haindpainted bottles
#11-6 Longtou Rd

Gulangyu's Famous Pearls
#115 Longtou Rd

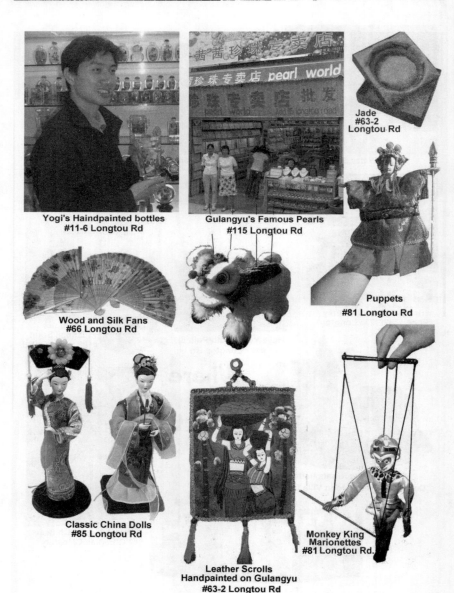

Jade
#63-2
Longtou Rd

Puppets
#81 Longtou Rd

Wood and Silk Fans
#66 Longtou Rd

Classic China Dolls
#85 Longtou Rd

Monkey King
Marionettes
#81 Longtou Rd.

Leather Scrolls
Handpainted on Gulangyu
#63-2 Longtou Rd

Shopping with Eyes *and* Hands　　购物，眼手并用

"Chen taught us more about the importance of touch, demonstrating his skill with beautiful, pale-olive hands….Chen had inherited from his father one of the finest collections of blue and white china in the country. In his pockets he carried broken fragments of the classic K'ang Hsi period.

"'I feel them,' he said, 'and my fingers learn more than my eyes. My fingers never betray me, but sometime my eyes will.'"

陈以那双漂亮、浅褐色的手向我们展示他的技巧，并反复强调手感的重要性。陈从其父那儿继承得到国内顶尖的一批青瓷收藏。他还随身携带康熙年间的瓷器碎片。

"我能感觉到，"他说，"我的手指比我的眼睛知道更多。我的手指从不会骗我，但眼睛可能会。"《绿姜根》，20 世纪 20 年代

Shark Feeding!

Underwater World Xiamen, #2 Longtou Road, is just to the right of the Gulangyu ferry, behind the giant octopus, and has more fish than you'll find in a Cantonese restaurant. Over 10,000 finned folk of 350 fresh and salt water species swim about in 17 large and small tanks, a rock pool, a cylindrical tank, and two immense shark and reef tanks.

Two 80-meter tunnels Plexiglas tunnels allow you to walk under the tanks (and sharks!) without getting soaked by one million liters of water.

It's especially exciting if you catch the diver feeding them. I marveled as he tossed fish to sharks, and repeatedly urged a moray eel to eat from his fingers. Also visit the Penguin and Freshwater Fish Hall, Ocean Fish Hall, Sperm Whale Hall, and Dolphin and Sea-Lion Performance Hall. Phone: 206-7668

厦门海底世界 龙头路 2 号，出了鼓浪屿码头，往右便是厦门海底世界，就在巨型章鱼雕像的后面。你会发现，比粤菜馆里的鱼多多了。在 17 个大大小小的鱼缸、一个池塘、一个圆柱体鱼缸，两个巨大的鲨鱼馆和礁石馆里生活着 350 种，上万只淡、咸水鱼。

两个 80 米长的有机玻璃隧道可让你在水下（还有鲨鱼呢！）自由漫步，而不会被 100 万升的水淹没。

如果刚好碰到潜水者在喂食物的话，你会更兴奋。看着他扔鱼给鲨鱼吃，还不断催促海鳗从他手指上咬吃的，这让我叹为观止。还有企鹅馆、淡水鱼馆、海洋鱼馆、抹香鲸馆、海豚海狮表演馆。电话：2067668

Gulangyu Hotels

> "Arthur Smith's renowned Chinese Characteristics has a chapter on 'The Absence of Comfort and Convenience,' recounting his experience and observations of Chinese dress, houses, pillows and beds, which all European readers find amusing. I wager it is ten times more amusing to Chinese readers to learn of Arthur Smith's account of his sufferings and discomforts. The white man's nerves are undoubtedly degenerate." Lin Yutang

Fortunately for us degenerated foreigners, Gulangyu has fine hotels!

Bright Moon Villas

Bright Moon Garden Villas (Haoyue Yuan, 皓月园) Our favorite! Let the crashing surf soothe you to sleep as you bed down in a small wooden villa perched on the bluff behind the massive Koxinga statue.

Luzhou Hotel （绿洲酒店), half a minute ahead of the ferry, has a fine little restaurant with simple, inexpensive food. They have an English menu but you must beg for it, because they delight in befuddling foreigners with Chinese menus. Large plate glass windows offer a nice view while dining—and offer the throngs of pedestrians a nice view of you as well.

Beautiful Island Hotel, #133 Longtou Rd. (Lizhi Dao Jiudian, 丽之岛酒店) – a five minute walk from the ferry. Rooms are small but clean and cheap. Phone: 206-3309

Piano Island Hotel (Qindao Jiudian, 琴岛酒店)—on Lujiao Rd., is just a two minute stroll to the left of the ferry.

Former U.S. Consulate, at #26 Sanming Rd.. Now the Jinquan Villa, spend the night in style—but don't expect to be fed unless you're a party of ten or more and arrange it in advance. Read more in the Guxin/Sanming Rd. chapter.

A 4-Star Hotel (4-star prices) is on the bluff overlooking Shuzhuang Gardens.

鼓浪屿的宾馆

> “阿瑟·史密斯在他的名作《中国人的特性》中有一章，称中国‘缺乏舒适与方便’。这里他叙述了自己对中国服装、住宅、枕头和眠床等等现象的观察与感受。所有的欧洲人都感到非常有兴趣。我敢打赌，中国读者听到史密斯叙述自己在中国的磨难与不舒适之后，会感到十倍的有趣。白人的神经毫无疑问是退化了。”
>
> ——林语堂

幸运的是，对我们这些感官退化的老外，今日的鼓浪屿上还是有好几家不错的宾馆！

皓月园临海别墅（我们的最爱）　随意下榻于坐落在断崖上的任何一间木制小别墅，宏伟的国姓爷雕像在前方守护，浑厚的海涛拂岸声必能伴你安然入眠。

绿洲酒店 码头朝前直走半分钟，有一家小小的饭店，还有英文菜单（但得向他们索要，他们总是乐意给外宾看中文菜单）。食物简单，也不贵，一面大大的钢化玻璃窗可以让你边用餐边看美景哦。

丽之岛酒店 龙头路 133 号——从码头向龙头路方向走五分钟。小房间，干净朴素——但很便宜。电话：2063309

琴岛酒店 鹿礁路上，码头向左仅需两分钟的路程。

原美国领事馆 三明路 26 号，而今是金泉宾馆。可在此气派地过上一宿（不过，他们只为十人以上的团队准备饮食，还得提前预订）。请翻阅鼓新路和三明路一章。

四星级酒店（和四星级的价位）坐落在崖壁上，可俯瞰菽庄花园。

Chapter 11
Architectural Overview

Stroll our shady serpentine lanes past high-walled gardens and imposing red-roofed mansions and you'll see why Xiamen spent over 76 million Yuan protecting Gulangyu's architecture.

The former Gulangyu International Settlement had consulates from 13 countries, and during the heyday of the late 19th and early 20th centuries, elite foreigners and Overseas Chinese built hundreds of delightful buildings such as the French style Lin House, the former American consulate (now a hotel), the neo-Gothic Spanish Catholic church, the geometric Art-Deco[1] court building, the Filipino Huang Rongyuan Mansion, and Gulangyu Shifan University, which was designed by American architect Henry Murphy, who was famous for marrying Chinese and Western architecture.

Treaty Port Architecture

"Square, stuccoed, with its solid arched verandas facing a big garden, our house was typical of the early Treaty Port architecture. The Portuguese must have been originally responsible for it, how it evolved I do not know. Although clumsy, it was yet practical for a climate which ranged from coal fires in winter to fans which hardly mitigated the sweltering summer heat. The houses, moreover, symbolized the solid dignity of the mid-nineteenth-century merchants who settled on the island to develop British trade. They were not incongruous, for they suited their purpose and possessed a character of their own." Averil Mackenzie-Grieve, Gulangyu, 1920s

"Many a Sino-European partnership, matrimonial or commercial, has been wrecked on the European's impatience with Chinese stodgy smugness and the Chinaman's impatience with the European's inability to keep still." Lin Yutang

[1] Art Deco originated in the 20s, inspired by the discovery of King Tut's tomb, with its highly stylized Egyptian motifs. Art deco employed clean, streamlined designs with such elements as cubic forms, zigzags, and ziggurats.

第十一章 建筑概览

#42 Zhangzhou Rd.

漫步在鼓浪屿上任何一条小巷，都是浓阴匝地，蜿蜒曲折，花园高墙耸峙，红屋顶的建筑巍峨壮丽，你就会理解为什么厦门要花上7600多万人民币保护岛上的建筑。

先前，岛上老外云集，先后有13个国家在岛上设领事馆。19世纪末20世纪初达到顶峰，华侨和外国精英纷纷来此购地置业，建起了数百座别墅，如法国风格的林屋、原美国领事馆（现在成了宾馆）、西班牙新哥特式天主教堂、几何艺术装饰[1]的庭院建筑、菲律宾黄荣远堂、鼓浪屿师范学院（由美国建筑师亨利·墨菲设计，其擅长中西建筑风格合璧）。

通商口岸建筑

“我们的房子，方方正正，灰泥粉刷，牢固的拱形阳台面对着一个大花园，属于典型的早期通商口岸建筑。最早是葡萄牙人的风格，后面是如何改良的我就不清楚了。虽说看起来有点傻，但很实用。非常适合当地的气候，这里的冬日需要炉火御寒，而到了酷暑，扇子也无济于事。而且，房子也成为19世纪中期定居小岛发展英国贸易的商人的尊严体现。这并非不合时宜，因为这切合了他们的目的，也展示其特色。”

Averil Mackenzie- Grieve，鼓浪屿，20世纪20年代

“在许多中国人与欧洲人组成的伙伴关系中，无论是婚姻关系还是商业关系，欧洲人总是看不惯中国人那种令人生厌的沾沾自喜。中国人则看不惯欧洲人那种坐立不安的坏脾气。” 林语堂

[1] 艺术装饰：起源于20年代（19世纪），灵感源自埃及法老图坦卡门陵墓的发现，该陵墓具有典型的埃及特色。艺术装饰善于运用简练新型式设计，多采纳立体、Z字形、神塔式等元素。

How Gulangyu Architecture Got This Way Gulangyu's madcap marriage of Western and Chinese architecture did not evolve without some measure of resistance and ridicule.

This hodgepodge of houses was born of foreigners schizophrenically grasping at the East while clinging to the West, and of Chinese clinging to their roots while grasping all things 'modern', often resulting in what Laura Wild called "hideous duplication of the ugliest kind of brick structures America can produce."[1] Walter A. Taylor[2] wrote in 1924 that the missionaries who built churches, hospitals and schools, were,

> "the same people [who] fill their homes with all manner of thing Chinese [to] adapt themselves to Chinese customs…[but] ornament the outside of their buildings with poor copies of details ten generations removed from Europe, and 'milk bottle' columns which would make Vignola[3] turn in his grave."[4]

Taylor encouraged modern architects to blend Chinese style with modern foreign construction but warned, "We cannot carry on in the foreign 'rut' and we cannot go over into the Chinese 'ditch.'"

Fortunately, the American architect Henry Murphy, who designed Gulangyu Shifan University, avoided both rut and ditch with his Ginling College for Girls in Nanjing, which opened in October, 1923. Laura Wild wrote, "Buildings well adapted to modern laboratory work and furnished with the conveniences of life have been crowned with beautiful roofs and decorations characteristic of China."

A mere three years later, Tan Kah Kee followed Murphy's lead in designing Xiamen University, claiming that his own blend of East and West represented his vision of modern education rooted in traditional Chinese values.

Amazed at the Maze? Gulangyu architecture is amazing. It's also a maze. Narrow lanes twist and turn, up and down hills, and four or five lanes may share the same name, as long as they intersect or are in the same general area (see Guxin Road chapter). Some estate gates do have official brass plaques but these tell you little more than the address (which you already know, if you've found it) and a title such as "Historical Building" (which you could guess).

To help you solve the maze, I've introduced architecture and sites by road, giving one page overviews at the beginning of each chapter.

Getting About Electric carts service the main routes, but a leisurely stroll with frequent stops for tea is the best way to savor scenery and sites.

---

[1] Laura H. Wild, "Higher Education for Women in China," China Christian Advocate October, 1923, p.5 (she was not writing on Gulangyu but in general).

[2] Walter A. Taylor taught at Ohio State University's College of Engineers from 1920-21, and then attended the Harvard-Yenching School of Chinese Studies in Beijing.

[3] Giacomo da Vignola, 1507-1573, influential Italian architect best known for writing the "Rule of the Five Orders of Architecture in 1562

[4] Chinese Recorder, October 1924

鼓浪屿建筑的由来 鼓浪屿建筑是中西合璧的产物，在发展过程中也伴随着人们的抵制和奚落。建筑中外合璧的原因，一方面是老外紧跟的是西式风格，但神经质地融入东方的特色；另一方面，中国人难舍自己的根，又不愿舍弃那些“现代”的东西。因此，就形成了劳拉•维尔德所谓的“那种最丑陋的美国式砖结构建筑在世界上的令人恐怖的不断复制”。[1]1924年沃尔特 • A • 泰勒[2]这样描写那些广建教堂、医院和学校的传教士：

> “同样的，他们总是让自己的房子里充满了各种各样的中国特色，以便让自己更适应中国的习俗……（然而）再用离欧洲原型十万八千里的建筑细部的可怜复制品以及能让维诺纳[3]在墓地里也会作呕的‘奶瓶’式柱子来装饰自己房子。”[4]

泰勒鼓励，现代建筑确实可以结合中外风格，但他警示说，“我们不能一味地按自己的惯例来操作，我们也不可以完全陷入中国化的深沟。”

幸运的是，设计鼓浪屿师范学院的美国建筑师亨利 • 墨菲避免了这两种情况。已于 1923 年 10 月开学的南京金陵女子大学就是他负责设计的。劳拉•维尔德写道“既满足现代实验所需、又非常方便生活的建筑，而且它们都有着具有中国特色的美丽的屋顶和装饰。”

仅三年后，陈嘉庚遵循墨菲的风格设计厦门大学，声称其建筑中西合璧，表明自身的现代教育眼光依然根植于中国传统价值观。

迷惑于迷宫？鼓浪屿上的建筑非常地神奇，同样也令人迷惑。小巷七拐八弯，上坡下坡不断，可能四五个巷子共用一个名字。只要他们互为交叉或同在一个区域（请参阅鼓新路一章）。某些建筑的门上会很正式地镶嵌着黄铜色的金属薄片，可惜上面的信息几乎都只有地址（你肯定知道的，如果你能找到地方的话）和一个称号“历史性建筑”（你完全可以猜出来的）。

为了帮大家走出迷宫，我已经在每一章的开头用一页来介绍沿路的建筑和景点。

走动 电瓶车可通往每条主干道。但是品味风光与景点的最好方式是悠闲的漫步，偶尔驻足喝杯茶。

---

[1] 劳拉•维尔德，《中国女子的高等教育》，中国基督教的传播者 1923 年 10 月。第 5 页（这里她是泛指，并非针对鼓浪屿而写。）

[2] 沃尔特 • A • 泰勒，1920－1921 任教于俄亥俄州立大学机械系，后参与北京哈佛－燕京大学的建设。

[3] 维尼奥拉 • 维诺纳，1507-1573，意大利著名建筑家，著作有《五种柱式规范》，1562 年

[4] 《教务杂志》，1924 年 10 月

Take the 4 kilometer ring road for a scenic view of bay and beaches, then cut inland just about anywhere to savor the architecture, paying close attention to the delightful variety of gates, windows, verandas, roofs, columns, pillars (of which I give an overview later in this chapter).

Gulangyu Architecture at a Glance

Longtou Road (龙头路) Straight ahead of the ferry, Longtou's Tourist Info Center is your first stop; its endless shops are your money's last stop

Lujiao Road (鹿礁路) Turn left at the ferry: Bo'ai Hospital; Seashore Inn; Octagon Building; Earlier British Consulate; Former Japanese Consulate

Fujian Road (福建路) Some of the best architecture: Yi Garden, Huang Rongyuan Mansion; Catholic Church; Sea & Sky Mansion; Cat King's Villa

Zhangzhou Road The most "Garden-like Road": Bright Moon Garden; Koxinga Statue; Former British Consulate; John Ma's Former Residence; Lin Yutang's Former Residence; Xiamen Music Academy

Fuxing Road (复兴路) Fuxing Church; Dr. Clarence Holleman's Former Home; Dr. Lin Qiaozhi Memorial; Li Qingquan Villa on nearby Flag Hill

Quanzhou Road (泉州路) Lin House; Golden Melon Bldg; Qiu Jin's Former Residence; Former Inquest Law Court (later moved to Brush Hill Rd.)

Guxin Road (鼓新路)—Former Taihe Company Bldg; 8 Diagrams Bldg. (Xiamen Museum & Organ Museum); Maritime Affairs Residence; Hope Hospital

Tianwei Road (田尾路) International Club (1920s); Danish Telegraph Office; Seaview Villa; former Dutch Consulate

Anhai Road (安海路) Trinity Church; Yang Villa; Foreign Lady Villa (best gate); Pleasant Garden (Yiyuan Villa)

Zhonghua Road (中华路) Former Dutch Consulate; Dafudi (200-year-old Chinese residences; David Abeel lived here); "Strange World" Museum

Yongchun Road （永春路）Koxinga Memorial Hall; Kanqing Villa

Huangyan Road (晃岩路) Gulangyu Music Hall (former Foreign Cemetery); Dr. Lin Qiaozhi's childhood home; Huang Family Gardens, Gospel Hall, Sunlight Rock Temple.

Chicken Hill Road (Jishan Lu, 鸡山路) Yin Family Home (1st family of music); Anxian Hall; Pastors' homes; Chinese Christian cemetery

Brush Mountain Road (Bishan Lu, 笔山路) Former Residence of Lin Wenqing (former Xiamen University President); Scenic View Bldg; Yizu Villa; Chuncao Palace;

Sanming Road (三明路）Former U.S. Consulate (now a hotel)

Drumbeat Road (Gusheng Lu, 鼓声路) Drumbeat Rock; Hero Hill; Wave Listening Bluff (Tingtao Ya); Aviary and Cable Car to Sunlight Rock; Liaoxian Villa; Overseas Chinese Subtropical Plant Introduction Garden

4 公里的环岛路可欣赏沙滩、海湾的一派风光，随处都可以拐进去感受建筑的风格，亲密接触形形色色的门窗、走廊、屋顶、柱、梁。（接下来我将对此做一综述）

鼓浪屿建筑一览

龙头路 码头上岸直走，游玩第一站是游客中心，而购物区则是你钞票的最后一站

鹿礁路 码头左走：博爱医院，海滨旅社，八角楼，最早的英国领事馆，原日本领事馆

福建路 聚集了部分最好的建筑：怡园，黄荣远堂，天主教堂，海天堂构，陈国辉宅

漳州路 花园式马路：皓月园，国姓爷雕像，原英国领事馆，马约翰故居，林语堂故居，厦门音乐学校

复兴路 复兴堂，夏礼文医生故居，林巧稚纪念室，升旗山附近的李清泉别墅

泉州路 林屋，金瓜楼，秋瑾故居，原会审公堂（后迁至笔山路）

鼓新路 原泰和公司建筑，八卦楼（厦门博物馆、风琴馆），船屋；救世医院

田尾路 万国俱乐部（20 世纪 20 年代），丹麦大北电报公司，观海别墅，原荷兰领事馆

安海路 三一堂，杨家园，番婆楼（门楼第一），宜园

中华路 原荷兰领事馆，大夫第（200 年历史的中国古民居，雅俾理曾居住于此），“珍奇世界”博物馆

永春路 郑成功纪念馆，瞰青别墅

晃岩路 鼓浪屿音乐厅（原番仔墓），晃岩寺，黄家花园，福音堂，林巧稚故居

鸡山路 殷宅（音乐第一家），安献堂，牧师楼，中国基督徒墓地

笔山路 林文庆故居（厦大已故校长），观彩楼，亦足山庄，春草堂

三明路 原美国领事馆（而今是宾馆）

鼓声路 鼓浪石，英雄山，听涛崖，百鸟园和缆车可通往日光岩，了闲别墅，华侨亚热带植物引种园

Classic Architecture

(From Rosengarten, 1891)

Find these on Gulangyu!

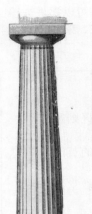

Doric Column

Temple of Neptune at Paestum (Built 470 - 460 B.C.)

Romanesque Ornamented Shaft

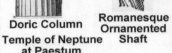

Corinthian Capital
Temple of Apollo at Didyma
(about 300 B.C.)

Ionic Capital, Temple of Apollo at Bassae
(about 420 - 410 B.C.)

Ionic Column in Athens' Erechtheum

Corinthian Column

Romanesque Capital
Cathedral in Speyer, Germany
(Built 1030 - 1061 A.D.)

Ionic Capital
Temple of Minerva Polias
in Priene

Byzantine Capital
Church of Theotokos
Constantinople
(Modern Istanbul)

Ornamented Roman Astragal

Egyptian Capital
Temple at Edfu
(Built 237-57 B.C.)

Ionic Capital in
Athens' Erechtheum
(Built 421-405 B.C.)

Classic Architecture

(From Rosengarten, 1891)

Find these on Gulangyu!

Ionic Entablature
Priene's Temple of
Minerva Polias

Part of Facade of Florence's
Rucellai Palace (Rennaisance Style)
(1452 - 1470 A.D.)

Corinthian Capital
with Entablature
The Pantheon, Rome

Rennaisance
Style Window

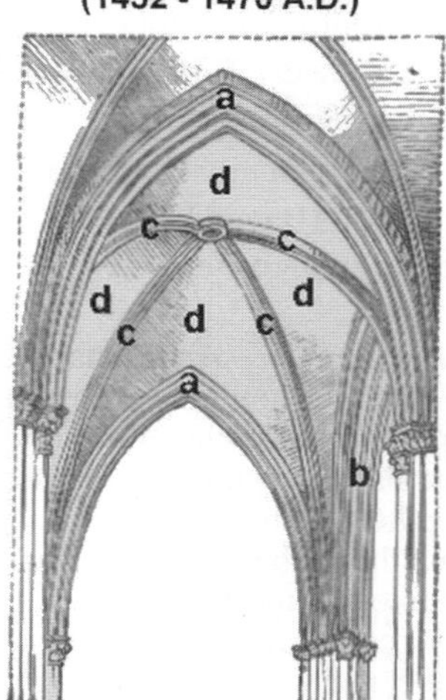

Gothic Vault

a=transverse ribs
b=pier-arches
c=diagonal ribs
d=vaulting ceilings
(ogives)

Bonn Cathedral
(Romanesque Style)

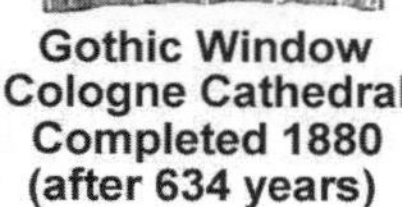

Gothic Window
Cologne Cathedral
Completed 1880
(after 634 years)

Gulangyu Windows, Gates, Verandas, Roofs…

Gulangyu has an astonishing variety of intricately detailed roofs, porches, windows, verandas, columns, pillars. Some photographers have entire albums of just windows, or gates—or even pillars!

#36 Anhai Rd.

Gulangyu Verandas (廊) Most Gulangyu villas have colonnaded verandas enclosing one or more sides of the building. With their ornate pillars, columns and arches, these verandas were both decorative and practical, allowing hosts a place to meet guests or to chat, protected from the tropical sun or the pounding rains that frequent our sub-tropical island. Samples include:

Single-Sided Verandas--Yang Home, at #4 Anhai Rd. (杨家园) and Liqing Quan Villa (李清泉) on Flag Hill Rd. (see Fuxing Rd. chapter).

Two-Sided Verandas—Foreign Lady Building, at #36 Anhai Rd. (番婆楼). Two-sided verandas were usually on the east, south and southeast to provide maximum shade in summer and sunlight in winter.

Three-sided Verandas— Seaview Villa (观海别墅), Huifeng Residence (汇丰公馆) and Yanhuo Building (验货楼).

Four-sided Verandas—Huang Family Mansion (Huangjia Huayuan, 黄家花园) and Eight Diagram Building (Bagua Lou, 八卦楼). Bagua Bldg's largest column reaches almost one meter in diameter.

Gulangyu Attached Buildings (陪楼) Traditional Chinese extended families preferred large homes but Gulangyu homes were even larger than normal because they also had very large families. They not only had many children (and many wives to bear them) but also welcomed (or endured) an influx of rural relatives who wanted to live on elite Gulangyu Islet.

In addition to family, wealthy Chinese needed quarters for the small armies of servants who undertook domestic and business affairs. Most mansions also had separate kitchens, laundry rooms, and storage rooms, all of which were similar, at least externally, to the main building, though internally they were of much simpler design, reflecting servants' lower status in Gulangyu highly stratified society.

The best insights on the lifestyle of servants are seen in photographer Bai Hua's childhood home, Yang Family Villa. Externally, the attached buildings are similar to the main building, but the rooms are small and narrow. Also note the narrow alleyways between buildings. These were used primarily by servants, who were expected to attend to their duties as unobtrusively as possible.

鼓浪屿的窗、门、走廊、屋顶……

鼓浪屿上，屋顶，门廊、窗户、走廊、门柱、柱，千姿百态，各种各样，令人惊奇。有些摄影师仅以窗或门，甚至是柱子就可出整本的图片册。

鼓浪屿建筑的廊 大部分的鼓浪屿别墅都有列柱的单面廊或多面廊。那些走廊，配上装饰华丽的柱子和拱门，既美观又实用，非常适合主人在此招待宾客聊天，还可遮阳挡雨，这些可都是我们这个亚热带小岛常有的事。典型的例子包括：

单面廊——杨家园，安海路 4 号；李清泉别墅，升旗山路（参阅复兴路一章）。

双面廊——番婆楼，安海路 36 号。双面廊大多设于东、南、东南方位，夏可纳阴，冬可吸阳。

三面廊——观海别墅，汇丰公馆和验货楼。

回廊——黄家花园和八卦楼。八卦楼最粗的大圆柱直径近一米。

鼓浪屿建筑的陪楼 中国传统的大家庭喜欢大房子，而鼓浪屿上的房子更大，因为家庭人口更多。他们不仅儿女成群（当然抚养孩子的妻妾也是成群），还欢迎（或忍受）那些渴望来鼓浪屿过优裕生活的农村亲戚的涌入。

Lin House
#82 Quanzhou Rd.
Photo by Scott Ballantyne

除了家庭人口众多，有钱人还需要地盘，让那些帮忙打点家务和生意的下人有容身之处。大部分的陪楼都有独立的厨房、卫生间、储藏室。从外形看，与主楼没什么两样。但其内部装饰更为简单，反映了在鼓浪屿等级森严的社会里下人地位的卑微。

而最能看出仆人生活状态的应是摄影家白桦幼年居住过的房子——杨家园。其陪楼外观与主楼相似，但房间窄小。请注意，主楼与陪楼间常有狭小的通道连接。这主要是为了仆人听候主人使唤更为方便。

Gulangyu Roofs Sunlight Rock's peak affords an excellent view of the orange and red Jiageng (嘉庚瓦) roof tiles that contrast yet oddly harmonize with the deep green forested hills of Gulangyu Islet. The most unusual roofs are:

Sunlight Temple (Riguangyan Si, 日光岩寺) Part of the roof's a rock!

Eight Diagrams Building at #43 Guxin Road (Bagua Lou, 八卦楼). Gulangyu's most conspicuous roof (inspired by Middle Eastern mosques).

Golden Melon Building (金瓜楼), at #99 Quanzhou Road. Some say the "Golden Melons" reflect Romanesque influence; others say they are Chinese. A place in Kangle Village (康乐新村) has two similar golden melons.

Lin House, at #82 Quanzhou Road (Linwu, 林屋) These intricately sloping red and orange roofs seem Dutch to me but experts say they are North European. The designer, Mr. Lin Quancheng (林全诚), also designed the roof of Gulangyu Island Water Supply Company to resemble an unfolding red tulip bud.

Catholic Church （天主教堂), at #34 Lujiao Rd. has a beautiful neo-Gothic roof (geteding, 哥特顶), white steeple contrasting starkly with the deep greens of the magnificent old trees guarding its perimeter.

Scenic View Villa (观彩楼), #6 Bishan Rd. —my favorite, this Dutch designed roof is said to resemble a Chinese sedan, hence the nickname "bride's sedan," but the windows look to me like Pluto's house in Disneyland.

Sea & Sky Palace Complex, at #38 Fujian Road (Haitian Tanggou, 海天堂构), is said to be like no other building in China. Notice the carved phoenix and other mythical creatures on the rooftop of the intricately detailed central building.

鼓浪屿的屋顶 登上日光岩，放眼四顾鼓浪屿，在苍翠欲滴的绿树掩映下，屋顶上橙红的嘉庚瓦分外显眼，但又极其和谐。最突出的应是：

日光岩寺 岩石也成了屋顶的一部分

八卦楼 鼓新路 43 号 鼓浪屿最显眼的屋顶（灵感来自中东的清真寺）

Photo by Lily Wang

金瓜楼 泉州路 99 号 有人说那两个金瓜是罗马式的，也有人说是中国特色的。康乐新村某地也有两个与此类似的金瓜。

林屋 泉州路 82 号 屋顶使用坡折屋面，配以嘉庚瓦。我觉得是荷兰风格，但行家认为是北欧风味。林屋的设计师林全诚还将鼓浪屿自来水公司的屋顶设计成一株含苞待放的红色郁金香。

Sea and Sky Palace

天主教堂 鹿礁路 34 号 哥特式屋顶，白色的尖塔在绿阴里颇显个性，犹如守卫着自己的地域。

观彩楼 笔山路 6 号——我的挚爱。这个荷兰人设计的屋顶，酷似中国的花轿，故有别称“新娘轿子”。但我觉得，窗户就像迪斯尼乐园里的狗——布鲁托的家。

海天堂构 福建路 38 号，据说在中国是独一无二的。请注意看，细致入微的中楼屋顶上雕饰着凤凰和其他神话里的飞禽走兽。

Gulangyu Gates Ancient villages and modern factories all bear witness to Chinese' love affair with grand gates, but Gulangyu's extravagant gates are in a class by themselves.

Gates with Greek columns are embellished with 18th and 19th century European artwork and mythic Chinese dragons and phoenixes, and capped by Chinese "flying sparrow" eaves, with an Art Deco lintel right out of 1930s' Chicago thrown in for good measure.

Golden Melon (99 Quanzhou Rd.)

Many gates retain the traditional double central door flanked by smaller doors on either side. Side doors were used on a daily basis and the central door was reserved for dignitaries or very special occasions.

The best gates are on Fujian Road（福建路), Anhai Road（安海路), Lujiao Road（鹿礁路), Brush Mountain Road（Bishan Lu, 笔山路) and Chicken Hill Road (Jishan Lu, 鸡山路).

Gulangyu's Three Most Magnificent Gates

Sea & Sky Palace, #38 Fujian Rd. (Haitian Lou, 海天堂)

Golden Melon Building, #99 Quanzhou Rd. (Jingua Lou, (金瓜楼)

Foreign Lady Building at #35 Anhai Rd. (Fanpo Lou, 番婆楼)

Many Gulangyu gates once bore inscriptions with construction date and family name, but most were chiseled off during the Great Proletariat Cultural Revolution, often replaced with a hastily scrawled "Long Live Chairman Mao!"

#28 Fujian Rd.

The lights on the less ostentatious gate in front of the former Electric Light Company（电灯公司）on Fujian Road（福建路）supposedly resemble those in such classical French films as Camille (茶花女). I also enjoy the humbler Chinese gates still to be seen here and there (try Fuxing Road or Haitan Road).

鼓浪屿的门楼 无论是古老的乡村还是现代的工厂，皆可看出中国人对大门无比钟情。但鼓浪屿的门楼豪华奢侈，自成一族。

古希腊柱式的门楼，沿袭 18、19 世纪欧陆建筑风格，又加以中国神话传说中的龙凤为装饰，云雀檐，艺术装饰的门楣，融入了 20 世纪 30 年代芝加哥的流行款式。

许多门楼一般是中间双扇的正门和设于两侧的边门。边门供日常进出，正门只在贵客临门或特殊场合才开启。

以福建路、安海路、鹿礁路、笔山路和鸡山路的门楼最具代表性。

鼓浪屿上最壮观的三处门楼：

海天堂构，福建路 38 号

金瓜楼，泉州路 99 号

番婆楼，安海路 35 号

鼓浪屿的许多门楼上都曾刻有建造的时间和主人的姓氏。然而绝大多数在无产阶级文化大革命中都被铲去文字，再极其草率、潦草地写上“毛主席万岁！”

有人告诉我，福建路上原电灯公司的门楼，比较朴实，少装饰，门楼上的灯就像法国经典影片《茶花女》中的灯。当然那些较为简陋的中式大门也随处可见（不妨去复兴路或海坛路走走）。

#36 Anhai Rd. Fan Po Villa

Gates on Gulangyu
by Lily Wang

Architectural Embellishments

by Lily Wang

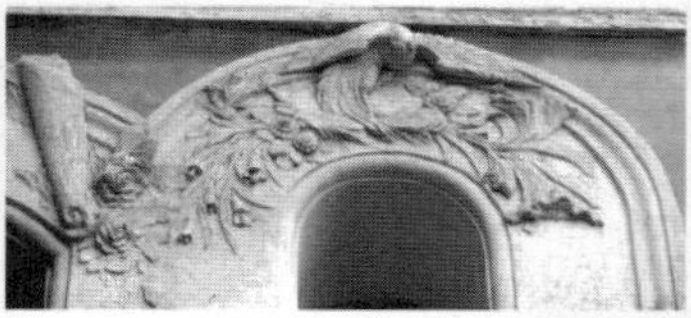

Gulangyu Columns Gulangyu architects had a fetish about columns, employing not only traditional Doric (陶立克式), Ionic (爱奥尼克式), and Corinthian (科林斯式) styles but also a few of their own. Classic Greek columns are adorned with carved Chinese unicorns and phoenixes, or Taoist "taiji" diagrams, and a single column may employ Doric, Ionic and Corinthian, with Chinese ceramic trim.

For amateur architecture buffs like myself, who confuse "roof" with "ceiling", I give a brief description of the main columns you'll encounter.

Corinthian columns, the most decorative of Greek columns, are most popular in the West, and employ entasis (columns bulge slightly) so they appear straight, even though they are not. Classic Corinthian columns have fluted shafts (carved vertical lines) and flowers and leaves on the capitals (Chinese columns have Taoist diagrams and auspicious Chinese animals). Corinthian columns are also different from Ionic or Doric in that the cornices are flat, rather than slanted.

Doric columns, like those of Athens' Parthenon, are plain but powerful, with no bases and unfluted 20-sided shafts.

Ionic columns, the most common on Gulangyu, appear taller than Dorics because they are slenderer and, like Corinthians, employ entasis to avoid appearing smaller at the top. Large bases resemble stacked rings, and capitals are a scroll above a fluted shaft. Like Corinthians, Doric friezes are unadorned.

Tuscan columns are plain, with unadorned shafts and simple capitals, bases and friezes. **Composite columns** are a combination of Ionic and Corinthian.

鼓浪屿的柱式

鼓浪屿的建筑对柱式无比钟爱，有陶立克式、爱奥尼克式、科林斯式，还有中国式的。古希腊柱式上还装饰着中国的麒麟和凤凰，或道家的太极八卦图。甚至一根柱子上也可能同时用上陶立克式、爱奥尼克式和科林斯式，再用中国的陶瓷挑檐。

Yang Villa

对于和我一样还分不清“屋顶”和“天花板”的建筑爱好入门者，我特别提供了一份你可能会遇到的主要柱式的简要描述。

#85 Lujiao Rd

科林斯式柱 古希腊柱式，装饰最为繁多，在西方最受欢迎。使用凸肚（柱子略微凸起）让柱子看起来更笔直，即使柱子本身并非如此。古典的科林斯式柱还有槽轴（凿出竖线），顶端以花叶修饰（中国式还会用道家的八卦图或代表吉祥的兽类）。科林斯式柱与爱奥尼克式柱或陶立克式柱的不同之处在于前者的楣是平面而非斜面。

陶立克式柱 和帕台农神庙中的柱子相同，看起来更平实也显得更威严，没有基座，虽有 20 面的轴却没有半道凹槽。

爱奥尼克式柱 鼓浪屿上最常见的柱式，显得比陶立克式柱高，因为它们更苗条，也像科林斯式柱采用凸肚，顶端看起来就不会那么小。巨大的基座就像叠加的环，顶部槽轴上是带卷形的。和科林斯式柱一样，陶立克式柱中楣也不带修饰。

托斯卡纳柱 非常朴实，不带修饰的轴，朴实的顶部，基座和中楣。所谓的合成式则是糅合了爱奥尼克式和科林斯式。

Gulangyu Columns and Capitals

by Lily Wang

A Window on Gulangyu
by Lily Wang

"As eyes are windows on the soul, so windows illuminate a building's soul."
Professor Gongjie (龚洁教授) , Curator of Xiamen Museum

Windows on Gulangyu Gulangyu's endlessly varied windows can be European, American, Colonial, Chinese, Gothic, Art Deco, Art Nouveau, etc. And some buildings, like Fujian Road's Huang Rongyuan Villa (黄荣远堂) have 3 or four styles and shapes of windows on the very same wall.

Gulangyu windows are every shape, size, color, and material. They are wood, stone, concrete, or brick; single or double; wide or narrow; shuttered or unshuttered; steeply arched, or semi-circular. Some are plain and others are heavily ornamented with Eastern or Western designs (or both). Many have small balconies and rows of potted plants reminiscent of German country homes. The sheer variety is beyond my ability to describe, so you must settle for the photos below.

My Favorite Windows

Scenic View Building (观彩楼), #6 Bishan Rd. I love this Dutch home's Disneyesque dormers!

#21 Zhonghua Road These are "iron anchor and owl" windows.

Yang Family Home (杨家园忠权楼) Flanking "bottleneck" designs.

Lin's Octagonal Tower (林氏府八角楼)

Seaview Villa

"宛如人的眼睛是心灵的窗口一样，窗是别墅楼房的灵魂窗口。"

龚洁教授，厦门博物馆馆长

鼓浪屿的窗 鼓浪屿上的窗，有欧洲的、美洲的、殖民地的、中式的、哥特式的、艺术装饰的、新艺术主义的样式，可谓五花八门，千姿百态。如福建路上的黄荣远堂，一面墙上，窗户的风格和样式就有三四种。

窗户的样式、尺寸、颜色和材料都各不相同。有木头的、石头的、水泥的、砖头的；单层或双层；或宽或窄；百叶窗或非百叶窗；尖拱或圆拱的。有些很朴实；有些则有繁复的装饰，或中或西或混合。很多都自带小阳台，摆着成排的盆栽，让人想起德国的乡舍。款式种类之多已非我能描述，所以你一定会满意以下的照片。

我最喜爱的窗户

观彩楼，笔山路 6 号。我最喜欢的是这幢荷兰人住家里迪斯尼动漫风格的天窗。

中华路 21 号 窗户酷似"铁锚和猫头鹰"。

杨家园忠权楼 侧面"颈瓶"设计窗

林氏府八角楼

#21 Zhonghua Rd.

Chapter 12
Longtou Rd
Gulangyu's Mainstreet

(Dukes, 1885)
"Chinese Shoemaker"

"The foreigners generally live on Kulangsu, a small island in Amoy Harbor, with a shore line of about 3 miles, and one of the most picturesque places to be seen on the whole coast of China." Hutchinson, 1920, p.160

A century ago, Dragon Head Rd. (Longtou Lu, 龙头路) teemed with diplomats, missionaries, tourists, and Chinese and foreign businessmen trading in the infamous but extremely lucrative "pigs 'n poison trades."[1]

Longtou Rd. is still the heart of Gulangyu, a rich mix of old and new, with everything from the famous Huangjin Xiang Jerky Shop (Supposedly family-owned since 1842!) to the new multi-story Sanyou Mall, tourist shops, Xinhua bookstore, Pearl World, Gulangyu Aquarium, Music Hall (actually on Huangyan Rd.), etc.

Start your tour at the Gulangyu Tourist Information Center, about 180 meters from the ferry. Review the bilingual displays, get your bearings from the topographical model of the islet, and then try your hand with the dice in the Mooncake Game Hall. While you're in the area, read up on the Wang Brothers, who not only helped develop the area but actually wrested it from the sea.

[1] Pigs: Coolies (from the Chinese "kuli" 苦力, meaning "bitter labor"); poison: opium

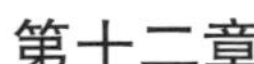

第十二章

龙 头 路

——鼓浪屿的主干道

“老外大都住在厦门港内的一个小岛——鼓浪屿上，虽说海岸线大约只有 3 英里，但风景如画，可说是中国沿海最美的地方之一。”

——哈钦森，1920 年版，160 页

一个世纪前，龙头路上人烟辐辏，外交官，传教士，游客，当然还有中外商贾云集，忙于恶名昭彰却利润丰厚的猪仔和毒品贸易[1]。

今天的龙头路依然还是鼓浪屿的中心，新旧交汇。从“老字号”黄金香肉松店（据传家庭作坊始于 1842 年！）到新近多层的三友假日旅游城，旅游纪念品商店，新华书店，珍珠世界，鼓浪屿海底世界，音乐厅（实际上在晃岩路），等等。

不妨从鼓浪屿游客中心开始你的行程。那里离码头大约 180 米。可参阅中英双语的景区游览展示区，全岛的山地模型，可帮助你搞清方位。还可以到博饼民俗馆试试手气。身处游客中心，还可以了解王氏兄弟的故事，他俩不仅促进了鼓浪屿的发展，实际上还将土地面积拓展到海上（围海造田）。

[1] 猪仔：苦力（来自中文）；毒品：鸦片

Longtou Road at a Glance

Your First Stop—**Gulangyu Tourist Welcome Center** Located below McDonalds. Excellent bilingual exhibits about Gulangyu sites, culture, history, and festivals—like famous Mooncake Games.

#1 Longtou Rd Luzhou Hotel (绿洲酒店) One minute from ferry, it has our favorite small restaurant; good food, good prices.

#2 Longtou Rd Underwater World Xiamen Marvelous aquarium and shows.

#11-6 Longtou Rd Yogi's Shop—Art and handpainted bottles

#19 Longtou Rd Historic house, circa 1891.

#63-2 Longtou Rd Handpainted leather scrolls; jewelry, crafts

#89 Longtou Rd Gulangyu Mooncake Shop (famous old shop)

Gulangyu Bookstore (on corner) Offers a broad selection of maps, music books, tour guides—and Amoy Magic—Guide to Xiamen! ☺

#95 Longtou Rd Huangjin Jerky Shop (Huangjin Xiang, 黄金香)—family owned ***since 1842!*** Many varieties and flavors.

#115 Longtou Rd Gulangyu Pearl World（鼓浪屿茜茜珍珠专卖店）—Foreigners' either save a fortune here or spend one (depends on perspective!). Ms. Li Qian (李茜), a 5th generation pearl merchant, hawked pearls at Sunlight Rock in the 80s, and in 1992 moved to this shop, which once housed Gulangyu's most famous tailor. Phone: 206-3620

#133 Longtou Rd Beautiful Island Hotel (Lizhidao Jiudian, 丽之岛酒店). Simple, clean, cheap; only 5 minutes from ferry, 1 minute from Music Hall, ½ a minute (and ¾ of your wallet) from Pearl World. Phone: 206-3309. Website: http://www.lzd-hotel.com

#177 Longtou Rd Famous Local Dentist! Crack your teeth on rocky rice? Mrs. Xie Xiujuan (谢秀娟) will fix you right up.

#183 Longtou Rd Fish Ball Snackshop (龙头鱼丸店). Before liberation Ms. Chen Yalan's （陈亚兰) father toted these tasty treats around town on baskets slung across his shoulders. Eat in the tiny shop or buy a few *jin* and boil them up at home.

#277 Longtou Rd Antique Shop (古玩店) One man's junk is another man's treasure!

Bai Hua and his antiques

龙头路一瞥

游客中心 就在麦当劳楼下，内设展区，双语介绍，超级棒，涉及鼓浪屿建筑、文化、历史，还有节日——如著名的博饼。

龙头路 1 号 绿洲酒店，离码头一分钟，里面有我们最喜爱的小餐馆，东西好吃，价格实惠。

Family Owned--Since 1842!

龙头路 2 号 厦门海底世界，令人称奇的水族馆和海洋动物表演。

龙头路 11-6 号 工艺品店——手工绘制工艺瓶

龙头路 19 号 历史性建筑，大约建于 1891 年。

龙头路 63-2 号 手绘皮革卷；珠宝，工艺品

龙头路 89 号 鼓浪屿馅饼店（老招牌）

鼓浪屿书店（拐角处）书籍琳琅满目，可选择范围广，地图，音乐书籍，旅游册——还有《魅力厦门》！

龙头路 95 号 黄金香肉松——1842 年开始的家庭作坊。口味繁多，选择多多。

龙头路 115 号 鼓浪屿茜茜珍珠专卖店，老外的最爱，可省很多钱，也会花很多钱（取决于你的鉴赏力）。李茜小姐，第五代珍珠商，80 年代在日光岩上兜售珍珠，1992 年搬到这家店，此前该店住的是鼓浪屿最出名的裁缝。电话：2063620

龙头路 133 号 丽之岛酒店。简洁、干净、便宜；距码头 5 分钟，离音乐厅 1 分钟。1 分半钟（你的钱包只要 3/4 分钟）到珍珠专卖店。
电话：2063309
网址：http://www.lzd-hotel.com

龙头路 177 号 本地有名的牙医！饭粒硬到牙齿崩裂？谢秀娟会帮你搞定。

龙头路 183 号 龙头鱼丸店。解放前陈亚兰的父亲可是肩挑这些美味的东西沿街售卖。就在小店里吃也行，或是买几斤带回家自己煮。

龙头路 277 号 古玩店。一个人的垃圾对另一个人来说可能是宝贝！

MacGowan (1912)

The Wang Brothers Ziru Wang (王紫如) and Qihua Wang (王其华), the youngest two of an impoverished Burmese Chinese' three sons, eked out a living pulling rickshaws in Burma until they learned about Shanghai rickshaw's labor-saving geared wheels (滚珠花鼓筒). The Wang Brothers' "Quanshengzhan (泉胜栈) Jinrickshaw Company" made a fortune renting high-tech rickshaws. The entrepreneurial Wangs remind me of the American Wright Brothers, who were also bicycle buffs (though we must be careful not to confuse Wright and Wang).

The Wang brothers returned to their ancestral home of Hui'an[1] (惠安) to build two homes with traditional winged ceilings (护厝), and then settled down on Gulangyu to engage in various social and cultural and business endeavors—such as Gulangyu Market and Yanping Theater.

Gulangyu Market During the Ming Dynasty, the small bay by the Gulangyu dock extended to "Middle Street Park" (街心公园), Haitan Rd. (海坛路), and Market Road (市场路). This area was renamed "Heziqian" (河仔墘), which roughly means "riverside."

In 1929, the Wang Brothers established Gulangyu's "Ruhua Company" (如华公司). They bought the land around Heziqian, filled in the harbor, and developed stores on Haitan Rd. Local residents and farmers welcomed their single-floor marketplace, which was later replaced with the more modern Singapore-style "Gulangyu Market" (鼓浪屿市场), with high ceilings, wide and bright corridors, and simple Doric (陶立克式) columns.

Ingenious ceiling ventilation helped minimized odors and protect foods from the semi-tropical heat. The market sold everything from fresh fruit, veggies, and eggs to fish, fowl and other carcasses. After the Anti-Japanese War, the brothers declined a very generous bid of 50 kg. of gold for the marketplace, determined to leave their hard-won enterprise for their descendants.

[1] Hui'an: part of Quanzhou, is a 2 hour drive up the coast from Xiamen

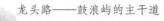

王氏兄弟 王氏三兄弟，家境贫寒，老二王紫如，老三王其华到缅甸仰光拉人力车谋生。后来，他们听说上海人力车出现使用滚珠花鼓筒以减轻劳动强度的新技术，便将其移植到仰光，开设泉胜栈，靠出租高技术人力车获利甚丰。王氏兄弟的发迹让我想到美国的赖特兄弟，他们是以自行车起家（当然我们须小心，不要将赖特和王氏混为一谈）。

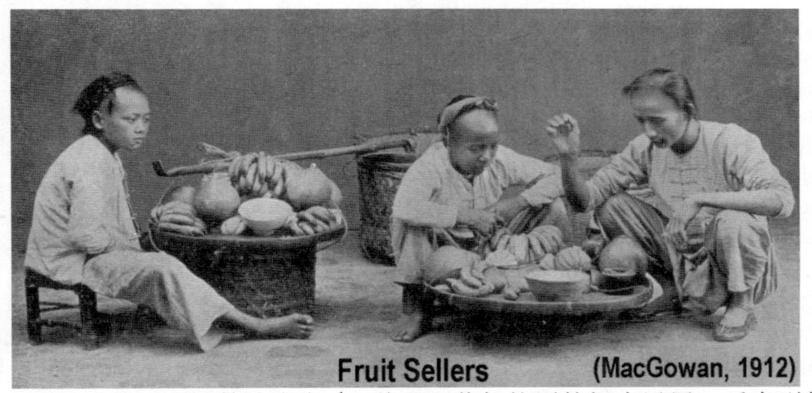
Fruit Sellers (MacGowan, 1912)

王氏兄弟回到祖籍地惠安[1]，盖了两落加护厝的闽南民居。后来到鼓浪屿定居，投身各种社会和文化产业，如鼓浪屿市场和延平戏院。

鼓浪屿市场 明朝鼓浪屿码头的小港湾，一直延伸到今天的街心公园、海坛路、市场路那里。后来，那里还被称为“河仔墘”，大意是“河汊”。

1929 年，王氏兄弟来到鼓浪屿，成立“如华公司”。他们买下河仔墘附近的地皮，将港汊填平，建成海坛路的店面。这种单层市场深受居民和菜农的欢迎。后来，拆除单层市场，在原址上按新加坡模式再建更现代的新市场，定名为“鼓浪屿市场”。该市场有挑高的天花板，宽敞明亮的过道，简洁的陶立克式柱。

精致的天花板，良好的通风，利于秽气疏导和食品保鲜，并少受亚热带炎热气候的影响。市场内瓜果蔬菜、鸡鸭肉蛋、生猛水产，一应俱全。抗战胜利后，有人出 1000 两黄金的高价要收购市场，王氏兄弟深感创业的艰辛，拒绝出售，决定留给后代。

[1] 惠安：隶属泉州，从厦门驱车沿海岸线北上仅需 2 小时。

Former Yanping Theater

Yanping Theater (延平戏院) The Wang Brothers imported an entire shipload of lumber and German stained glass to build the second-floor, 600-seat European-style two-level "Yanping Cinema."

In spite of state-of-the-art audio and visual equipment, dependable power from a downstairs generator, and original movies from many countries, the theater attracted few people other than wealthy foreigners and Chinese. The Wangs rented their theater to others, who fared no better and closed the theater in 1942 during the Pacific War. After the war, the "Hele Film Company" (和乐影业公司) rented the theater and renamed it "Gulangyu Cinema" (鼓浪屿戏院), but it closed again in 1949.

A complete overhaul between 1974 and 1978 raised the ceiling, expanded seating from 600 to 728, and introduced Xiamen's first automated ticket-punching machine. In 1979 it became the "Gulangyu Movie Center" (鼓浪屿电影院), but it closed after the "Gulangyu Music Hall" (鼓浪屿音乐厅) opened and in 1986 was turned over to the "Gulangyu Culture Center" (鼓浪屿文化馆).

During China's "Reform of Private Houses" (私房改造), Gulangyu Market and Yanping Theater were managed by the Housing Administration Department (房管局), but the "Oversea Chinese Housing Policy" (华侨房屋政策) put into effect after reform and opening up, led to much of the property being returned to the multitudinous offspring of the Brothers Wang (with the exception of some apartments in Gulangyu Market and Yanping Theater).

Other Wang Enterprises The Wang brothers helped build the "Zhangsong Highway" (漳嵩公路) connecting Zhangzhou to Songyu, in Haicang (海沧嵩屿), and established the "Fujian Tannery" (福建硝皮厂) which later became the "Gulangyu Lamp Factory" (鼓浪屿灯泡厂). The tannery's chief engineer, a famous Chinese chemist named Zhaoqing Lv (吕兆清), went on to become a big potato in the Shanghai upper class (上海政协委员).

Like most successful Chinese tycoons, the Wang Brothers were big on social and charitable endeavors. They helped build the "South Hui'an Middle School" (Huinan Zhongxue, 惠南中学) & "Jade Plate Primary School" (Yuban Xiaoxue, 玉坂小学), contributed towards construction of hospitals, bridges and paved roads, gave to the poor, and adopted and educated abandoned children (many of whom went on to become quite successful).

Laurel and Hardy hit Amoy!

延平戏院 王氏兄弟从国外运来整船木材和德国的压花玻璃，在市场的楼上建起欧式风格的“延平戏院”，内有两层，能容600名观众。

尽管备有优质的视听设备，楼下有发电机保障供电，并且引进诸多国家的原声片，然而除外国人和有钱的国人，观众甚少。王氏兄弟只好租给他人经营。生意还是不好，1942 年太平洋战争爆发后停业。抗战胜利后，被“和乐影业公司”租用，并改名“鼓浪屿戏院”，到 1949 年再次停业。

1974-1978 年,戏院彻底翻修，加高了屋盖，观众席的座位由 600 个增加到 728 个。同时是厦门第一个使用自动检票机器的电影院。1979 年改名为“鼓浪屿电影院”。1986 年，“鼓浪屿音乐厅”建成后，电影院停映，交“鼓浪屿文化馆”使用。

Gulangyu Movie Projector

在中国的私房改造期间，鼓浪屿市场和延平戏院均由房管局管理。改革开放后，厦门落实华侨房屋政策，大部分财产已归还王氏兄弟的众多后人（市场和延平戏院的部分房产除外）。

王氏兄弟的其他产业 王氏兄弟还参与建设漳州到海沧嵩屿的“漳嵩公路”，还建立了“福建硝皮厂”，后来，在硝皮厂址创办了鼓浪屿灯泡厂。硝皮厂的总工程师，中国著名化工专家吕兆清，后为上海市政协委员。

就像大部分功成名就的中国企业家，王氏兄弟热心社会公益，广办善举。他俩捐建了惠南中学，玉坂小学，还有医院，修桥铺路，资助贫民，还领养弃婴，为他们提供读书机会（其中不少人还大有出息）。

Qihua died in 1969 at age 69, and Ziru passed away in 1974 at age 77. The Wangs' 20+ sons (and daughters, I presume?) now pursue successful careers in the U.S., Canada, Singapore, Burma, Hong Kong, and Xiamen.

Meanwhile, yet another Wang (unrelated to the above Wangs) went from rags to riches in the Philippines and is now transforming not only Xiamen and Shanghai but also Gulangyu—one of his projects being Longze Garden.

Mr. Wang Fangze's Longze Garden（王芳泽的龙泽花园）Mr. Wang Fangze, director of an international business company in the Philippines, was born in 1938 in Anhai, Jinjiang（安海,晋江), just south of Quanzhou. He moved to Hong Kong in 1958 and to the Philippines in 1960, where he worked as an auto mechanic before setting up his own repair shop. A very driven auto mechanic, he quickly became an influential figure in Philippine business.

Wang Fangze began investing in Xiamen in 1980, just as the Special Economic Zone was getting into high gear. He erected 17 buildings in his Bailu Garden (白鹭苑), which is now Xiamen's premier cultural center, and in 1988 he invested 400 million RMB in building Longze Garden（龙泽花园), pledging at the opening ceremony to use 60% of profits for reconstruction of historic Gulangyu architecture.

Longze Garden (龙泽花园）faces the Lujiang Strait（鹭江道), with Sanqiutian Dock（三丘田）dock to the left and Ocean Park to the right. The 30,000 m^2 site has 45 buildings designed by experts from Tsinghua University and the City Architectural Design Institute, and includes a mall, tourist village, gardens, and parks.

Longze Garden's diverse architectural styles reflect European influence, but modified for Xiamen's sub-tropical climate and locals' aesthetic preferences.

Mr. Wang has set his sites far beyond Gulangyu. He built the Fengze（丰泽）industrial and commerce center in the Shanghai Pudong Waigaoqiao（浦东外高桥）bonded area, and plans several skyscrapers for Xiamen.

Not bad for an ex-auto mechanic!

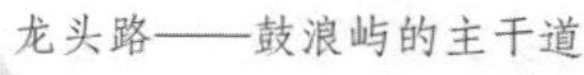

其华 1969 年去世，终年 69 岁；紫如 1974 年去世，终年 77 岁。兄弟俩有儿辈 20 多人（我猜还有女儿吧？）分别在美国、加拿大、新加坡、缅甸、香港和厦门创业，事业有成（颇为兴旺）。

此外，还有另一位王姓人士（与上述的王氏兄弟毫无关系哦）在菲律宾也是筚路蓝缕，最终发家致富，而今在厦门和上海都各有产业，鼓浪屿上也有他的产业——“龙泽花园”。

王芳泽的龙泽花园 王芳泽先生，菲律宾一家国际商业公司董事长，1938 年出身于泉州南面晋江安海。1958 年赴港，1960 年到菲律宾，先当汽车修配厂徒工，后自己开修理店。由于悉心经营，很快在菲律宾工商界独树一帜。

1980 年厦门经济特区起步之初，王芳泽就来厦门投资，兴建了 17 幢建筑组成的“白鹭苑”，而今已成为厦门重要的文化中心。1988 年，他投资 4 亿人民币兴建龙泽花园。在开工典礼上，王芳泽表示，花园所赚利润的 60%将捐给鼓浪屿的旧房改造工程。

龙泽花园面朝鹭江道，左邻三丘田码头，右倚海底世界，占地 3 万平方米，由 45 幢别墅、购物中心、旅游度假村、花园和公园组成，由清华大学和市设计院的专家共同设计。

龙泽花园建筑风格颇具欧陆风采，但同时也考虑到厦门亚热带气候与本地建筑的风格，稍作调整。

王芳泽在鼓浪屿外还有诸多地产。他在上海浦东外高桥保税区兴建丰泽工贸中心，还准备在厦门建多幢摩天大楼。

以一名汽车修理工起家而言，成就颇大。

Longtou Garden

Piano Quay 钢琴码头

Until the 1930s the only way to cross Xiamen bay to Gulangyu was by rowboat, sampan, barge—or a long swim. But in July, 1937, a ferry was opened from Xiamen's Daomei Rd., at the Zhongshan Rd. intersection (岛美路和中山路) to Gulangyu's Piglet Quay.

It was called Piglet Quay because it was used in the "Piggy Trade" (Coolie trafficking: see next page).

Piggie Quay was used as Yihe Shipyard's (义和船行) coal quay after 1894, and then as freight quay for Yongming Soap Works（永明肥皂厂), when it was known as Xuewen Quay（雪文码头). The Ferry Quay was finished on Oct 16th, 1937, but though it was so inadequate that the ferry could accommodate only 70 passengers, it wasn't until 40 years later, in 1976, that the Xiamen government extended the quay and built a 100 m^2 waiting room and a larger ferry.

Officials argued over which design to adopt, and in the end the dean of the design institute chose a "half-vaulted" plan by engineer Lin Jinyi（林金益). The designers first attempted a thin roof shell resembling the Sydney Opera House but lacked the technology, so modified it to a half vault, which was light, simple, aesthetic and economical. Lin Jinyi chose blue for the roof, shutters and eaves so the building would harmonize with the sea.

Lin intended the ferry to be simply a modern abstract building, but after completion, residents insisted it resembled a giant piano, and so today Gulangyu visitors' first site is the Piano Quay.

Note: It's a good thing Gulangyu gave up on the Sydney Opera House idea. After the Opera House (designed by 37-year-old Danish architect Jorn Utzon) was completed, an engineer said that had they known how hard it would have been to actually build it they'd have abandoned the project. It took five years just to figure out how to build the roof, and the final cost was $102 million—14 times the original estimate.

钢琴码头

直到 20 世纪 30 年代，厦鼓之间仍需靠双桨、舢板、驳船来往，游泳也行。1937 年 7 月，厦鼓轮渡开始运行，厦门一侧建在中山路口的岛美路头，鼓浪屿一侧建在猪仔码头旧址，因该地曾用于猪仔贸易（贩运苦力）而得名。

猪仔码头于 1894 年后作为义和船行的煤码头；后又作为永明肥皂厂的货运码头，称雪文码头。1937 年 10 月 16 日建成轮渡码头后，规模甚小，客容量仅为 70 人。一直到 40 年后的 1976 年，厦门市政府才扩建厦鼓轮渡，并建起了 100 平方米的站房和更大的渡轮。官员争论不休，究竟应该选择哪个设计方案，最终由设计院院长一锤定音，采用林金益工程师设计的“半拱顶方案”。

原想设计成悉尼歌剧院那种薄壳结构的建筑，但当时还不具备建造薄壳结构的技术，几经修改，建成了现在的半拱顶屋顶，既轻巧、简练，又经济、美观。林金益把屋顶、百叶、挑檐均设计为蓝色，与大海浑然一体。

至于建筑的外形——林金益希望是简练的现代抽象派设计。可是建成后，市民坚持说是像一架巨大的钢琴，因此今天钢琴码头就成了游客进入鼓浪屿的第一景。

注：鼓浪屿放弃悉尼歌剧院的想法是英明之举。悉尼歌剧院当时是由 37 岁的丹麦建筑师乔恩·伍重设计。这名建筑界翘楚后来感慨，如果当时有任何一个人想到真正建成这幢建筑是如何艰辛，他们肯定会放弃这项工程，整整花了 5 年的时间才敲定如何建屋顶，而最终的花费是 1 亿 200 万美金——大约是最初预算的 14 倍！

Pigs 'n Poison[1]

"Most coolies came from the southern, coastal provinces of China, especially Fukien… large numbers of men were shipped out through Hong Kong, Macau and other ports such as Amoy.

"They were, from the very start, exploited by Chinese coolie shipping agents and ships' captains – over a third of whom were Americans – then abused and treated atrociously by their employers. The trade in these unfortunate souls was known colloquially as the 'Pig Trade': the 'Poison Trade' was slang for the opium business.

"Crowded into corrals like slaves they were, as the British Consul in Canton observed in 1852, frequently painted with letters such as P, C or S meaning Peru, California or the Sandwich Islands.

"Whilst some were convicts on release or kidnap victims (we still use the contemporary expression, 'shanghaied'), over 95 per cent were indentured workers who, having had $50 paid for their sea passage on their behalf by would-be employers who regarded it as a loan against future income, were offered a wage they never saw for their loan and deductions for living expenses exceeded their earnings. Their traveling conditions were grim but because money had changed hands they were not legally slaves so no action could be taken against their shippers. Many died en route: one British-owned vessel, the John Calvin, lost 50 per cent of its passengers whilst American ships were often known to have 40 per cent mortality rates.

"Women were sometimes part of 'Pig Trade' cargoes. Under Chinese law females could not emigrate but coolie employers overseas wanted women: the aim was to make their indentured coolies settle in their new countries, thus alleviating the need to import more. The women were mostly either kidnapped or purchased under a Chinese system, known as mui tsai, which allowed for the sale of young girls as servants or concubines-in-training. This aspect of the trade was invidious: in 1855, the British vessel, Inglewood, hove to off Amoy with a cargo of female children all under the age of eight. The crew, disgusted at what comprised their cargo, reported it to the British consul who arranged for the children to be returned home."

"Opium – A History", by Martin Booth, St. Martin's Griffin, New York, 1996

猪仔与毒品

“多数苦力来自中国南方沿海省份，特别是福建……他们大批地从香港、澳门和像厦门这样的港口被贩运出去。

“他们一开始就被人贩子和船长盘剥一番——其中 1/3 以上是美国人。然后，又被雇主虐待、剥削。对这些不幸的苦力进行交易被称为‘猪仔买卖’，而‘毒品买卖’指的是鸦片生意。

“据 1852 年英国驻广东领事记载，这些苦力像奴隶一样被关进畜栏，被打上 P、C、或 S 的记号，分别代表秘鲁、美国加州和英国的三维治岛。

“除了一些是刑满释放或遭绑架的受害者（今天的英语里还有 shanghaied 一词，意指被绑架到船上做苦力），其他 95%以上的苦力都是签了契约的包身工。雇主为他们预支了 50 美元的船费，以后从薪水中扣除。但由于工资太低，他们永远都还不清这笔路费和生活费。海上旅行的条件实在很差，但由于金钱已转手，他们不受法律保护，也就无法追究船主的责任。许多苦力死在了路上：一艘名叫约翰·加尔文的英国船只，运送苦力，死了 50%；而美国船只的死亡率通常也高达 40%。

“妇女也是猪仔买卖的对象。依照当时的中国法律，妇女不能移民。但海外的雇主想要女苦力，这样可以让卖身的男苦力在那些新国家定居下来，从而减少进口中国苦力的需求。女苦力大多是被绑架或买来做下人或童养媳的。这种猪仔引起人们的不满：1855 年，一艘名叫英戈伍德的英国货船满载一船不满 8 岁的女童驶离厦门港时，船员十分不满船上所载的‘货物’，于是向英国领事馆报告。结果这批女童就被遣送回家。”《鸦片——一段历史》，马丁·布斯，圣马丁·格瑞芳出版社，纽约，1996 年版

Where to from Longtou Rd? Longtou ends at the "T" intersection with Huangyan Rd, just opposite Gulangyu Music Hall (built over the former foreign cemetery). Take a left and you'll come to the scenic gardens and architecture of Fujian Road, the neo-Gothic Spanish Catholic Cathedral, and the former Japanese Consulate, with its infamous underground jail and torture chamber.

Take a right on Huangyan Rd. for the People's Stadium and bust of modern sports pioneer John Ma, Gulangyu Guesthouse (where Nixon stayed), the Gospel Hall, Sunlight Rock, and the former residence of pioneer doctor Madame Lin Qiaozhi. Continue up and over the hill and you'll come to the cemetery and the magnificent 3-storey granite block 7th Day Adventist Anxian Hall.

Turn left at the People's Stadium for Shuzhuang Gardens and Piano Museum on the backshore. Turn right at the People's Stadium to explore Zhonghua Rd.'s fascinating architecture, including the former home of Amoy's 1st missionary, David Abeel (Yabili, 雅俾理), which is a beautiful block of traditional S. Fujian dwellings at what is now #23 Zhonghua Rd.

The Fine Art of Chinese Shopping

(A *Race of Green Ginger*, 1920s, p.154,5)

"There was no doubt that one had to learn technical as well as aesthetic discrimination; one was not born with it.

"We were gradually learning the feel and character of blanc de chine and celadon, but gained no judgment at all in blue and white while any fake bronze would deceive us.

"My Chinese women friends had taught me what to look for in embroidery: to pinch up the satin-stitched motifs which, they said, should bend smoothly and look as even as the silk itself, not showing a single loop; to look for fine tight Peking know-stitch--the aristocrat of stitchery--and to examine the twist of the threads themselves. They showed me how to discover whether chopsticks were made of genuine ivory. Putting them side by side, they would lay a bamboo sliver horizontally across a drop of water placed on the sticks. If they were ivory the sliver would immediately come alive, swing round vertically and stop. On any other substance it would remain motionless. But the skill by which they could infallibly distinguish carved lacquer from veneered composition, good cloisonné from pieces lifted and reassembled on modern bronzes by Japanese craftsmen, would, I knew, never be mine. It was their inheritance, compounded of discerning sight and the miraculously sensitive touch that, for them, made the incised mahjong tiles so easy to read with finger-tips alone."

"Besides the noble art of getting things done, there is the noble art of leaving things undone. The wisdom of life consists in the elimination of non-essentials."

Lin Yutang

龙头路通向哪？ 龙头路尽头为 T 形路口与晃岩路交汇，对面就是鼓浪屿音乐厅（建在番仔墓上）。朝左拐则是福建路，路上都是花园式建筑，西班牙新哥特式天主教堂，原日本领事馆，而且领事馆内还有臭名昭著的地下监狱和刑讯室。

右拐到晃岩路。路上有人民体育场、现代体育运动先驱马约翰半身像、鼓浪屿宾馆（尼克松曾下榻于此）、福音堂、日光岩、医学先驱林巧稚故居。继续往前走，翻过小山则是墓园和壮丽的三层花岗岩建筑——安息日会安献堂。

如果在人民体育场左拐，则通往鼓浪屿后面的海边，那儿有菽庄花园和钢琴博物馆。

如果在人民体育场右拐，不妨去看看中华路上的那些迷人建筑，包括厦门第一个传教士雅俾理的故居，那是一幢漂亮的闽南传统建筑，现为中华路 23 号。

中国人的购物艺术

（《绿姜根》，20 世纪 20 年代，154 页第 5 行）

“毫无疑问，技巧和美学的鉴赏力，没有人是与生俱来的；每个人都得学。

“我们逐渐学会手感和认识中国白瓷和青瓷的特性，但还是无法判断蓝白瓷器的真伪，因此任何青铜器的赝品都可以骗倒我们。

“我的女性中国友人教我如何鉴别刺绣的精品。她们说，用手摩挲一块缎子绣品，它会松松地弯曲，看起来就像绸缎一样光滑，连一道针脚的印痕都没有；去寻觅上好的京绣——刺绣中的精品——关键是看针脚弯曲的地方。她们还教我如何看筷子是不是用真正的象牙做的。将筷子并排放在一起，滴一滴水到筷子上，再水平放上一根薄竹条。如果是象牙筷，那竹条马上会轻微地上下颤动一下，然后停下来。如果不是象牙筷，那竹条就会毫无反应。而且他们还会区别真正的漆雕和其他装饰品的不同；质地上乘的景泰蓝瓷器与日本工匠抄袭再重新组装的现代青铜制品也区别得很清楚。我知道这些窍门与我无缘。那是他们的传家宝，辨识的眼力和不可思议的敏锐触觉，造就了他们只需用指尖就能轻而易举地摸出麻将上的纹路。”

“高雅艺术意味着有所为，有所不为。人生的智慧其实就在摒除那种不必要的东西。” 林语堂

Chapter 13
Lujiao Rd

Gulangyu in 1843

"The next morning (Sept. 7, 1843), Mr. Abeel and myself rose early for a walk round the island of Kulangsu. It is about three miles long, not quite a mile broad, and is wonderfully diversified with hill and dale. Small as it is, I have never seen so many beautiful prospects in the same place. Every hill-top is crowned with black and naked rocks, while every spot of ground that can be cultivated is used (or rather was used, for the Chinese are not now allowed to reside on the island, while it is occupied by the English troops,) either for houses, or rice grounds, or tombs. The population, previous to its being occupied by the British, has been commonly estimated at five thousand, but judging from the houses still standing, and the ruins of those torn down, I should say, this was a very moderate estimate. There may have been eight or ten thousand persons, and from the style of the houses, it may be inferred that many of the wealthier inhabitants of Amoy had their common residences on this island. There are a number of noble banyan trees, and my impressions of the island were very favorable.

"It was beautiful exceedingly. Perhaps it appeared more beautiful from its dissimilarity to the bare and rugged hills of Hong Kong and Macao, but it reminded me strongly of many scenes long since, perhaps forever, passed. It was melancholy to see the ruined houses, and to meet the English soldiers at every step, for they told of violence and war…" Lowrie, 1850, p.209

Historic Bayside Lujiao Rd A stroll down riverfront Lujiao Rd., which becomes Zhangzhou Rd., is quite an education—if you know what you're looking at. After the 1st Opium War forced open Xiamen as a treaty port, Lujiao (formerly Xizi Rd, 西仔路) became the key commercial and consular district.

Foreign merchants arrived in ships laden with opium and departed with cargoes of tea, silk, porcelain and piggies (Chinese coolies). The British set up their offices in Lujiao in 1844, and were followed by the Germans, Japanese and Spanish. Lujiao was also a key cultural center, with schools, churches, clubs, and hospitals.

第十三章

鹿 礁 路

1843 年的鼓浪屿

“第二天早上（1843 年 9 月 7 日），我和雅俾理先生起了个大早沿着鼓浪屿散步。小岛约三英里长、不到一英里宽，密布着形形色色的小山、溪谷。虽是弹丸小岛，我却从未在同一个地方看到如此多美景。每个山头都覆盖着裸露的黑色岩石，所有能开垦的土地都已被开发（确切地说是曾经被开发，因为现在这里已经被英国军队占领，不允许中国人居住在岛上），这里要么是住房，要么是稻田或是墓地。英军占领之前，岛上大约有 5000 多人。但是从那些尚存的房子和残垣断壁看来，我觉得这是一个很保守的估计，可能有 8000 甚至上万人。从建筑风格可以推断出当时许多有钱的厦门人在这岛上都有相似的房子。岛上还有许多茂盛的榕树，给我留下了很好的印象。

“鼓浪屿实在太美了。不同于香港、澳门的濯濯童山，鼓浪屿也许更美，但它同时也勾起了我对许多往事的回忆。那些废墟和无处不在的英国士兵诉说着暴力与战争，此情此景，让人心情沉重。”

娄理华，1850 年 第 209 页

风云海滨路——鹿礁路

如果你知道自己在追寻什么，那么在江边的鹿礁路（与漳州路交界）漫步也不失为一次很好的教育。第一次鸦片战争后厦门成为“五口通商”口岸之一，鹿礁路（原称西仔路）也因此成为重要的商贸和领事区域。

洋商的轮船带着鸦片而来，却满载着茶叶、丝绸、瓷器和“猪仔”（中国劳工）而去。英国于 1844 年在鹿礁路设立领事馆，随后德意志、日本、西班牙也接踵而来。鹿礁路也是一个文化中心，有学校、教堂、俱乐部和医院。

Lujiao at a Glance

#1 Lujiao Rd Bo'ai Hospital (博爱医院) Former Japanese hospital built with materials from Japanese-controlled Taiwan

#2 Lujiao Rd Seashore Inn (海滨旅社) 1920s; plain but historic. Japanese surrendered here; used in Chiang Kai Shek's Great Gold Robbery.

#5 Lujiao Rd This gate's carvings resemble British-style lions.

#7 Lujiao Rd Beautiful Garden (Meiyuan, 美园), circa 1920s; Eastern/Western, built by a Philippine Chinese; red bricks & white pillars.

#8 Lujiao Rd Piano Island Hotel (Xiamen Qindao Jiudian, 厦门琴岛酒店) a 3 minute walk from Gulangyu Ferry. Phone: 206-6668

#13, 15 Lujiao Rd Octagon Building, home of Lin Erjia (林尔嘉,林菽庄与八角楼). Lin Erjia founded Shuzhuang Garden.

#16 Lujiao Rd Earlier British Consulate, circa 1869) See Zhangzhou Rd. chapter for info on the 2,000 sq. ft. British consulate.

#19 Lujiao Rd Note the old well by this unknown vine-covered edifice opposite Fuxing Church. Water was precious on old Gulangyu.

Underground Japanese Jail

#24, 26, 28 Lujiao Rd Former Japanese Consulate (Riben Lingshiguan, 日本领事馆), now Xiamen University housing. Basement jail and torture chamber are seldom used now except for recalcitrant students. .

#38 Lujiao Rd Xu Family Villa (Xu Jiayuan, 许家园). Early 20th century 4-story villa. Note the ornate gate, unusual columns, red brick square pillars, and unusual roof carving.

#83 Lujiao Rd Private home, early 20th century.

#85 Lujiao Rd Pink House, circa 1933. My wife Susan's favorite—in spite of the clashing green trim.

#99 Lujiao Rd This Tudor style villa was prime beachfront property a century ago. The Old World sharply sloping colored roofs often used colored cement instead of typical Chinese roof tiles (Jiageng wa, 嘉庚瓦).

#111 Lujiao Rd New Bay Cultural Arts Company (厦门新湾文化游乐有限公司) Puppet shows, tribal dances, dioramas, portraits, wax figurines of historical Chinese. Phone: 206-4908 E-mail: xinwan188@vip.sina.com

#113 Lujiao Rd Circa 1930s; note unique windows, and ornate gate with the inscription "Sun Rises in the East" (Zhaogong Shengdong, 照拱升东).

鹿礁路掠影

鹿礁路 1 号：博爱医院，日本人创办，建筑材料取自日本人当时占领的台湾。

鹿礁路 2 号：海滨旅社，建于上个世纪 20 年代，朴实无华却很有历史意义。日军在此投降，蒋介石黄金大抢劫也与之有关。

鹿礁路 5 号：门上的雕刻类似英式的狮子。

鹿礁路 7 号：美园，大约建于 20 世纪 20 年代，中西结合的风格，红砖白柱，由菲律宾华侨兴建。

鹿礁路 8 号：厦门琴岛酒店，从鼓浪屿码头出发只需走三分钟。电话：2066668

鹿礁路 13、15 号：八角楼，林尔嘉故居，建于 20 世纪初。林尔嘉还建了菽庄花园。

鹿礁路 16 号：早期英国领事馆，大约建于 1869 年，占地面积 2000 平方英尺，详情请见漳州路一章。

鹿礁路 19 号：复兴教堂对面的这座不知名的大宅里，爬满藤蔓，有一口古井。水在以前的鼓浪屿比较珍贵。

鹿礁路 24、26、28 号：原日本领事馆，现为厦门大学教工宿舍。地下监狱和刑讯室现已基本荒废了，“除了用来对付一些不听话的学生”。

鹿礁路 38 号：许家园，20 世纪初建。这栋四层楼的别墅，有华丽的大门、独特的圆柱、红砖砌的方柱和奇特的屋顶雕花。

鹿礁路 83 号：民居，20 世纪初建。

鹿礁路 85 号：粉红的房子，大约建于 1933 年。这是我妻子苏珊的最爱——尽管绿色的镶边与之不协调。

鹿礁路 99 号：一个世纪以前，这座都铎式的别墅是海滨一流的房产。那时的坡面屋顶多为彩色水泥所建，而非典型的中式瓦（嘉庚瓦）。

鹿礁路 111 号：厦门新湾文化游乐有限公司。这里有木偶戏表演、部落舞蹈、透视画、肖像画和中国历史人物蜡像。电话：2064908，电子邮件：xinwan188@vip.sina.com

鹿礁路 113 号：大约建于 20 世纪 30 年代，独特的窗户，华丽的门楼上刻着“照拱升东”四字。

#1 Lujiao Rd Bo'ai Hospital (Bo'ai Yiyuan, 博爱医院) Left of the Gulangyu ferry and just past the Piano Hotel, at the "T" intersection is the historic two-story Bo'ai Hospital, which the Japanese built in 1918 and was run by a

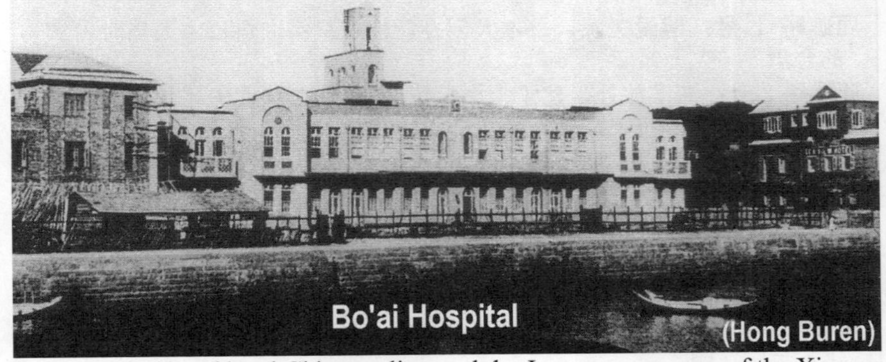

Bo'ai Hospital (Hong Buren)

board consisting of local Chinese elites and the Japanese manager of the Xiamen bank.

The Japanese began Bo'ai by renting Ye Qingchi Villa (叶清池), using the first floor for outpatients, the second floor for inpatients, and the third floor for a dormitory. In 1919, Bo'ai set up a medical college and taught courses (in Japanese, of course). The 60 graduates went on to become doctors in South Fujian and throughout Southeast Asia.

After outgrowing the Ye Qinchi Villa facility, the Japanese rented Lin Erjia's Villa, but quickly outgrew that as well (over 200,000 patients annually by 1932, surpassing even the missionary-run Hope Hospital), so they built a new hospital in the Japanese "Dahe" (大和) style of architecture using materials from Japanese-controlled Taiwan. The hospital, which was larger than the Hope Hospital, cost 800,000 Silver Dollars and took Chinese laborers one year to complete.

The hospital was shut down in 1937 during the war with Japan, but reopened after the Japanese occupied Xiamen. The Japanese navy took over and moved the hospital to Xiamen's Minguo (民国) Road (now Xinhua Road). After the navy left, this branch became a division of Bo'ai hospital.

The local government took over both Bo'ai Hospital and the division, which was used for freshmen in Xiamen University (during the war, Xiamen University had relocated for 8 years to remote Changting (长汀), in the far west of Fujian; during their absence the Japanese wreaked havoc on Xiamen University, which had to be rebuilt).

After 1949, the PLA turned Bo'ai Hospital into an army sanatorium. Today it is the Nanjing (南京) Military District's soldiers' sanatorium.

鹿礁路 1 号：博爱医院

在鼓浪屿轮渡码头往左拐，经过琴岛酒店，就来到了在丁字路口的博爱医院。这座两层楼高的建筑具有重要的历史意义，为日本人 1918 年创办。当时的董事会成员包括一些地方绅士和厦门洋行的日本经理，医院由他们管理。

Bo'ai Hospital Today

日本开办博爱医院之初，租用叶清池别墅，一楼为门诊，二楼为病房，三楼为宿舍。1919 年，博爱设立了附属“医学专科学校”并教授课程（当然是用日语）。这里的 60 个毕业生后来都成为了医生，遍布闽南和东南亚。

随着门诊患者不断增多，叶清池别墅的设施已无法满足要求，日本人继而租用了林尔嘉别墅，但很快也不够用了（到 1932 年，每年接纳患者 20 多万人次，甚至超过了传教士创办的救世医院），所以他们新建了一座日本“大和式”的医院，所用材料取自他们占领的台湾。这座医院比救世医院规模更大，花了 80 万银元，中国工匠用了一年的时间才完工。

1937 年抗日战争爆发，博爱医院停办，厦门沦陷后复办。因院址被日本海军占住，医院迁至厦门民国路(今新华路)。日本海军离开后，这里就成了博爱医院鼓浪屿分院。

后来当地政府接管了博爱医院及其分院，一度用作厦门大学新生院（抗日战争期间，厦门大学曾迁至偏远的闽西长汀 8 年；在这期间，日军摧毁了厦大，之后不得不重建）。

1949 年以后，解放军将博爱医院变成了军队疗养院，现为南京军区疗养院。

#5 Lujiao Rd Gate

#2 Lujiao Rd Seashore Inn (海滨旅社) Directly across from Bo'ai Hospital, the three-floor red brick Seashore Inn was built in the 1920s. The plain building lacked the ornamentation common on even the humblest Xiamen residences, but its prime seaside location made it accessible by boats at high tide.

After 1949, Seashore Inn became private residences, but today this nondescript building still has a special place in Xiamen people's hearts, not because of its appearance but because of its role in local history. It was not only the site of the Japanese surrender in Xiamen, but also played a role in Chiang Kai Shek's theft of an unimaginable fortune in gold and silver.

The Japanese Surrender at Seashore Inn On Aug 15th, 1945, Japan's Emperor accepted the " Potsdam Resolution"（波茨坦公告）and surrendered. Xiamen folk were thrilled to see an end to eight years of grievous Japanese occupation—but an argument arose amongst the Chinese as to whom should administer the liberated town.

Gu Zhutong（顾祝同）, commander of the 3rd military district, appointed the police chief Yan Zeyuan（严泽元), and Xiamen's new mayor Huang Tianjue（黄天爵), to take over, but the Navy Commander Chen Shaokuan（陈绍宽) saw Xiamen's importance as a strategic port and so appointed the commander of the 2nd fleet, Major General Li Shijia（李世甲), to take over Xiamen. Neither camp would budge, and so the Japanese surrender had to wait until the Chinese generals had quit fighting amongst themselves.

Eventually, the national take-over committee appointed Major General Liu Depu（刘德浦） as commander of Xiamen port to help Li Shijia（李世甲） take charge. The Japanese commander Lieutenant General Yuantian Qingyi（原田清一) formally surrendered on Sep. 28th in the Seashore Inn to Major General Li Shijia. Xiamen took 2779 Japanese captive and confiscated 4 Japanese naval vessels, over 1000 scatter-guns, and several cannon.

The American Army briefly used the Seashore Inn for R&R after the war, and then the Seashore Inn sank back into oblivion—until it played a small part in the Great Gold Robbery.

#5 Lujiao Rd (Facing former Japanese Consulate)

鹿礁路 2 号：海滨旅社

博爱医院的正对面就是三层楼的红砖海滨旅社，建于上个世纪 20 年代。尽管只是一座朴实的房子，甚至连最简陋的厦门民居那样的装饰都没有，但却坐拥绝佳的地理位置，临海而建，涨潮的时候划着小艇就能到这里。

1949 年以后，海滨旅社成为私人住宅，但现在这座本来名不见经传的建筑却在厦门人心中占据特殊的位置，并不是因为它的外观，而是因为它在厦门现代史上所演绎的角色。这里不仅是在厦门的日军向中国政府投降的旧址，同时在蒋介石卷走无数金银财富时曾扮演了一定的角色。

日本在海滨旅社投降

1945 年 8 月 15 日，日本帝国主义接受了《波茨坦公告》并投降。在日本人铁蹄蹂躏之下长达七年多的厦门人民无疑是人心振奋。然而对该由谁来接收获得自由的厦门，却引发了争议。

当时的第三战区司令长官顾祝同钦点了福建省保安纵队司令严泽元和厦门的新任市长黄天爵来接管，但是海军总司令陈绍宽认为厦门是海军要港，因此指派海军第二舰队司令李世甲来执掌。两方阵营谁也不愿意让步，所以投降了的日本人还不得不等待中国的长官们停止“内战”。

最后，全国统一接收委员会调刘德浦少将为厦门要港司令，辅助李世甲办理接收厦门事宜。9 月 28 日，李世甲少将在海滨旅社正式接受日本海军中将原田清一的投降。厦门接收了 2779 个日军战俘，没收了四艘战舰，千余挺机关枪和几尊大炮。

战后，海滨旅社曾作为美军教导团招待所，尔后逐渐被人遗忘，直至在蒋介石黄金大抢劫中扮演了一定的角色。

Chiang Kai Shek's Great Gold Robbery On the night of Jan. 1st, 1949, Chiang Kai Shek (Jiang Jieshi, 蒋介石) had the Central Bank ship 151 cases of gold accounted worth 572,899,487 liang（两） and 1000 cases of silver dollars worth 4,000,000 Yuan to the Xiamen Central Bank on the ship Haixing（海星号), accompanied by the Naval ship Meisheng（美盛号). On the 21st, the Central Bank secretly shipped another 4,500 cases of silver, worth 18 million Yuan, to Xiamen, and on the same day Chiang Kai Shek declared that the bank had, somehow, gone bankrupt.

President Li, who was short of funds, ordered gold and silver be returned to Nanjing, but Fujian Province's Chairman, Zhu Shaoliang（朱绍良), declared that precious metals could not be shipped out of Fujian without his permission—which he of course refused to give.

On the afternoon of April 15th, Song Ziwen（宋子文） and his wife Zhang Leyi（张乐怡） fled from Taiwan to Xiamen, where he took a boat to Gulangyu Islet and stayed in the Seashore Inn. He conveyed Chiang Kai Shek's order that the commander and mayor of Xiamen send the gold and silver to Taiwan, and fled to Hong Kong the next morning.

#15 Lujiao Rd **The Octagonal Building** complex (nicknamed Funei, 府内), was the early 20th century home of Lin Erjia (林尔嘉), founder of Shuzhuang Garden, and member of a family that had great influence upon both Taiwan and Southern Fujian.

Shuzhuang's grandfather, Lin Yingya（林应寅）was born in Bai Shibao, Longxi（白石堡, 龙溪）but during the Qing Dynasty moved from Xiamen across the Strait to Dan Shui, Taiwan. He began a school and accepted apprentices, and with a fortune earned through farming and the salt business, the family built the Lin Family Villa (林家) in Taibei. Mr. Lin's father, Lin Weiyuan（林维源), was Taiwan's agriculture and defense minister during the Sino-Japanese War （甲午, Jiawu), and respected for being an upright and just official, as well as for his simple lifestyle (though he was wealthy enough to live simply!).

Taiwan was ceded to Japan after the Sino-Japanese War in 1895, and Lin Weiyuan, loathe to become a Japanese subject, moved his family to Gulangyu.

The Pink House (#85 Lujiao Rd.)

蒋介石黄金大抢劫

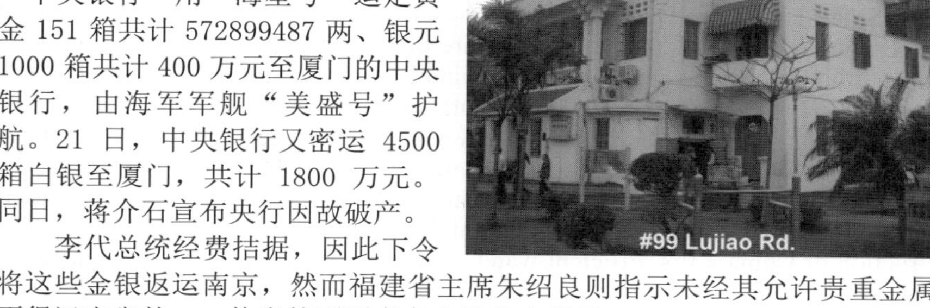

1949 年元旦当晚，蒋介石从“中央银行”用“海星号”运走黄金 151 箱共计 572899487 两、银元 1000 箱共计 400 万元至厦门的中央银行，由海军军舰“美盛号”护航。21 日，中央银行又密运 4500 箱白银至厦门，共计 1800 万元。同日，蒋介石宣布央行因故破产。

李代总统经费拮据，因此下令将这些金银返运南京，然而福建省主席朱绍良则指示未经其允许贵重金属不得运出省外——他当然不愿意交出这些金银了。

4 月 15 日下午，宋子文偕夫人张乐怡从台湾潜往厦门，乘船至鼓浪屿并下榻海滨旅社。宋面谕了蒋介石的指示，命令厦门要塞司令和市长将金银送往台湾，次日清晨逃往香港。

鹿礁路 15 号

八角楼（又称府内），为菽庄花园主人林尔嘉 20 世纪早期的住宅。林家在历史上对台湾和闽南都产生了重要影响。

菽庄（即林尔嘉）祖父林应寅出生在龙溪白石堡，在清朝乾隆年间跨越海峡移居台湾淡水镇。他在此开馆授徒。经营垦殖、盐业发家后，在台北修筑了林家别墅。中日甲午战争期间，林尔嘉父亲林维源官至台湾抚垦大臣兼团防大臣，因为官正直和生活简朴（虽富甲一方，却深居简出）而广受尊敬。

1895 年中日甲午战争结束后，台湾被割让给日本，林维源厌恶日本人的统治，因此林携一家老小寓居鼓浪屿。

The younger Lin became one of the richest men in China by helping his father set up credit banks in Xiamen and other places.

Erjia inherited the property after Weiyuan's death in 1905, but almost lost the "Small House" in December, 1914, when his son Gangyi's (刚义) chemical experiment exploded. The family empire blossomed, and the Emperor granted Lin a title. He became director of the Fujian Railway Company, Chairman of the Shanghai Huatong Marine and Fire Insurance Company, and Superintendent of the Xiamen Telephone Company. He was also thrice elected to Chair the Chinese Chamber of Commerce, and became the first Chinese Chairman of the Board of the Municipal Council of Gulangyu. A very pragmatic man, he used his powers to help modernize Xiamen, and was largely responsible for the construction of China's first efficient water works, telephone network, and electricity lines.

In 1914, Er Jia became a member of the national senate, and then head of the Xiamen political committee. He also served on the Fujian Legislature (福建省行政讨论会会长).

A proponent of modern Western education, Erjia helped establish and fund many schools, including the Xiamen Normal School, Overseas Chinese Girls School, Zhangzhou Normal School, the Tongwen Institute, and Hong Kong University.

After the success of the Anti-Japanese War, Shuzhuang returned to Taiwan with wives #4,#5 and #6 (四、五、六姨太), the Octagon building was occupied by relatives and the #3 wife, who died in 1972. Shuzhuang died in November, 1951 at the age of 77.

About Lin's Home When Weiyuan Lin (林维源) moved to Gulangyu he bought a two-floor villa (called the "Big House") in Lujiao, and built a smaller house ("Small House") next door for his son Erjia and others. A small cottage beside the "Small Building" was used by the cooks and servants. Weiyuan converted the vacant grounds behind the "Big House" into the small " Back Garden" (后花园). When wife #2 lay on her deathbed, they made a tiny door because the coffins of Little Wives (numbers 2 thru 6 in Erjia's case) were not allowed to go out the front door. Thus even in death she was forced to Zou Houmen[1] (走后门).

Erjia built the 5-floor "Octagon Villa" (#15 Lujiao Rd.) between the Big and Small Houses and connected them with corridors. The brick and wood structure is said to reflect French design, and Chinese claim the octagonal shape resembles a "noblewoman dressing for the ball." Personally, I can't see that (and think they should lay off the rice wine!).

---

[1] Zou Houmen: "use the back door" is a Chinese euphemism for using one's connections

年少的林尔嘉协助父亲在厦门等地设立“信用银行”，成为中国最富有的人之一。

1905 年，林维源辞世后，尔嘉继承父业，但是 1914 年 12 月其子刚义化学实验爆炸，几乎毁掉了他的“小楼”。林氏家族日益兴旺，清政府晋升林尔嘉为侍郎。他曾先后担任了福建铁路有限公司督办，上海华通水火保险有限公司总董和厦门一家民营电话公司创办人。他曾三次被推举为厦门总商会总理，同时也是鼓浪屿工部局的第一个华人董事。林是个务实的人，他充分利用职权把厦门朝现代化方向建设，并且负责兴建了中国第一家自来水、电话、电灯公用事业。

1914 年，林尔嘉被推选为全国参议院候补参议员，其后又担任厦门市政会会长。他还担任福建省行政讨论会会长。

尔嘉是个西方教育的拥护者，他参与捐资兴建了多家学校，包括厦门师院、华侨女子学校、漳州师院、同文学院和香港大学。

抗日战争胜利后，尔嘉携四、五、六姨太回到台湾，于 1951 年 11 月与世长辞，享年 77 岁。其亲戚和三姨太仍住在八角楼，三姨太 1972 年去世。

关于林氏府

林维源迁至鼓浪屿时，在鹿礁路买了一栋两层别墅（时称“大楼”），并在旁边修建了一座较小的楼房（时称“小楼”）供其儿子等居住。“小楼”一侧是厨师和仆人住的平房。维源在“大楼”后的空地修建了一个小花园，称“后花园”。尔嘉在二姨太病危时，修了一扇小门，因为姨太太们（即林的二姨太至六姨太）的灵柩是不能从正门抬出去的，只能走后门[1]。

尔嘉在“大楼”和“小楼”之间新建了五层高的八角楼别墅（鹿礁路 15 号），楼与楼之间有联廊相通。据说这里的砖木结构是法国人设计的，中国人声称八角楼形似“为舞会而盛装的贵夫人”。但我怎么也看不出来（我倒觉得他们应该戒米酒了）。

[1] 走后门：委婉语，利用关系网。

In the early 1980s, Erjia's grandson Weizhen (慰祯), a Canadian Professor, renovated the Octagon Building. Today, the building is in rather good shape, though the eyebrow pond (眉月池) is dry, the Back Garden is overgrown, the wisteria gazebo has collapsed, and the camphor trees and flowers have seen better days.

#16 Lujiao Rd Earlier British Consulate, circa 1869, (英 国 领 事 馆). See #5 Zhangzhou Rd. for later Consulate.

In August, 1841, an English fleet of 30 warships and 3500 soldiers occupied Gulangyu. On August 29th, 1842, China signed the first of many unequal treaties, the Nanjing Treaty (南京条约), and Xiamen became one of China's 5 treaty ports. The British army gave up the occupation of Gulangyu only after the Qing government reimbursed Britain for the opium that Commissioner Lin Zexu had destroyed in Canton (for a sobering but enlightening review of the opium wars and the century of nationalized drug trafficking inflicted upon China at gunpoint, read pages 397-411 in "Amoy Magic—Guide to Xiamen").

British Consulate Pitcher, 1912

The British set up the first foreign consulate in Amoy on November 2nd, 1843. They first built an office at #16 Lujiao Rd., and then a residence at what is now #5 Zhangzhou Rd.[1] The sloped roof one-storey dwellings were reminiscent of European country villas, with fine wooden floors, and beautifully detailed fireplaces and chimneys. The Lujiao dwelling was repaired in the 1960s to be used as a hotel, but damaged during the Culture Revolution.

Reports claim the consulate had six 7.5 square meter jail cells outfitted with the latest in fine instruments of torture. One of the consul's devoted dogs was interred in the annex grounds' canine crypt, from which a British flag flew proudly. But when Xiamen folk destroyed the foreign cemetery in July，1958 in protest of Britain's invasion of Egypt, they also destroyed the dog's tomb.

Today, the Oasis Hotel stands within the area once encompassed by the consulate walls, which were dismantled in 1958. Towards the end of the 1970s, shortly after the Industrial Design Institute moved into the former consulate, the red brick building was partly damaged by fire.

The German Consulate (德国领事馆), circa 1870, was built next to Lujiao Rd.'s British consulate, but closed after Germany's defeat in World War I, and the building was in ruins by the 1950s.

[1] The British built a consulate annex in 1870 at #6 Tianwei Rd.

20 世纪 80 年代初，尔嘉的孙子慰祯，一加拿大华裔教授，对八角楼进行了整修。今天我们看到的八角楼华彩依旧，尽管眉月池早已干涸，后花园杂草丛生，紫藤亭已经倾颓，香樟树和各色花儿却更风光了。

鹿礁路 16 号 早期英国领事馆，大约建于 1869 年（后期英国领事馆详情请见关于漳州路 5 号的章节）。

1841 年 8 月，一支由 30 艘军舰、3500 名士兵组成的英国舰队占领了鼓浪屿。1842 年 8 月 29 日，清政府签订了第一个不平等条约《南京条约》。厦门成为"五口通商"口岸之一，在清政府赔偿英国在林则徐"虎门销烟"中所受的损失后，英军才撤出鼓浪屿（想要知道更多关于鸦片战争和在枪口威胁下的全国范围的毒品走私活动，请参阅《魅力厦门——厦门指南》一书的第 397～411 页）。

英国于 1843 年 11 月 2 日在厦门建立了第一个外国领事馆。起初在鹿礁路 16 号设立了办公楼，然后又在漳州路 5 号[1]建了一座公馆。这两座坡式屋顶的单层建筑让人联想到欧洲的乡间别墅，精美的拼木地板，壁炉和烟囱装饰细致秀美。上个世纪 60 年代，鹿礁路的房屋经重新修葺后作为招待所，但"文化大革命"时遭到破坏。

据称英国领事馆处有六间 7.5 平方米的牢房并配备有最新的刑讯工具。一领事的爱犬就埋葬在楼前，而地面旗杆上的英国国旗，曾在那耀武扬威。1958 年 7 月，为了抗议英军入侵埃及，厦门人民捣毁了番仔墓，这座狗墓也未能幸免。

那些围墙在 1958 年被拆除，今天，原来的领事馆围墙以内的地方兴建起绿洲酒店。上个世纪 70 年代末，工业设计院迁入领事馆，不久，这座红砖楼部分毁于大火。

德国领事馆

大约建于 1870 年，与鹿礁路的英国领事馆比邻而建，第一次世界大战德国战败后关闭，上个世纪 50 年代这里成了废墟。

German Consulate　Pitcher, 1912

[1] 英国人于 1870 年在田尾路 6 号建了一座领事馆副楼。

(Hong Buren)
Japanese Search Chinese on Gulangyu Ferry

#24 Lujiao Rd Former Japanese Consulate (Riben Lingshiguan, 日本领事馆). The Japanese viceroy and soldiers landed on Gulangyu Islet in 1875, and established a consulate in the Yamato Club. In 1896, the Qing agreed to lease a district to the Japanese in Shanghai, Tianjin, Wuhan, and Amoy, and in 1898 the Japanese began construction of a new consulate building at 24 Lujiao Road.

A Chinese, Mr. Wang Tianxi (王天锡), designed and built the new structure to resemble a British residence. The 600m^2 20,000 Yen building had offices on the first floor and dorms in the second. In 1897, the Japanese forced the Qing to lease 360,000m^2 (roughly 1/3 of Gulangyu) to Japan. The U.S. demanded the remaining 2/3, but other nations fought for their share, and in the end settled for establishing an International Settlement.

In 1928 the Japanese added two more modern red brick buildings, resembling those in Tokyo University, to the right of the consulate. One was dorms and the other a police station (set up in 1915, replete with basement jail and torture chamber). Xiamen Museum has reproductions of the cells, replete with the victims' anti-Japanese Slogans scrawled on the walls.

> "Among 179 Chinese citizens tried in 79 cases by a Japanese quasi-military court during World War II in Southern China's Huanan region [Hong Kong and Amoy], 118 were handed the death sentence, a Japanese researcher told Kyodo News…among the 118 Chinese citizens given the death penalty, 25 were charged with concealment of weapons and hostile activities such as distribution of anti-Japanese handbills and participation in anti-Japanese rallies." *Asian Political News*, Sept. 3, 2001

The consulate was closed after the outbreak of the Anti-Japanese War in 1937, but reopened after the Japanese occupation of Xiamen in May, 1938 and the building became a residence in November. After Japan's surrender in August, 1945 in the Seashore Inn, the consulate was closed and all assets confiscated by the Chinese government. The Japanese consulate is now Xiamen University dormitories.

Where to now? Fujian Rd—the best collection of elegant old architecture!

鹿礁路 24 号：日本领事馆

日本 1875 年在鼓浪屿设立了日本领事馆。1896 年，清政府同意日本在上海、天津、武汉和厦门设立租界，随后 1898 年日本在鹿礁路 24 号的领事馆也破土动工。

中国人王天锡设计、承建该馆，以仿英式住宅为基调。该馆占地 600 平方米，一楼办公，二楼住人，造价 2 万日元。1897 年，日本企图迫使清政府割借给其 36 万平方米（约占了鼓浪屿面积三分之一）。美国想独占剩余的三分之二，但是其他国家也争着分杯羹，最后鼓浪屿成了公共租界。

1928 年，日本在领事馆右侧又新建了两栋现代红砖楼房，建筑风格类似日本东京大学。其中一座是宿舍楼，另一座则为日本警察署（建于 1915 年，内设地下监狱和刑讯室）。监狱墙上的抗日标语的复制件陈列在厦门博物馆内。

> "二战期间，华南地区（香港和厦门）的日本准军事法庭立案 79 次审判了 179 名中国公民，其中 118 名被判死刑。一名日本研究员曾告诉日本共同社，被判死刑的 118 名中国公民中有 25 名是因为藏匿枪支以及散发反日传单和参加反日集会等'敌对'活动。"
>
> 摘自《亚洲政治新闻》2001 年 9 月 3 日

1937 年抗日战争爆发后，日本领事馆被迫关闭，但是 1938 年 5 月日本再次占领厦门后又重开领事馆，同年 11 月，这里被转用为官邸。日本于 1945 年 8 月投降，领事馆也被关，所有的财产由中国政府没收。现在这里已经成为厦门大学的教工宿舍楼。

接下来去哪里？

福建路——一流的建筑群！

Chapter 14
Fujian Rd
Gulangyu's
Best Architecture

#28 Fujian Rd.

19th century Western colonial governments were increasingly leery of Over-seas Chinese who, by dint of diligence and thrift, accumulated great wealth and power throughout Asia. When these governments put the squeeze on them, many of the "Jews of Asia," headed for home, and those who could afford it chose Gulangyu because of its beauty, climate, and the security and vast trade opportunities afforded by its international settlement.

#40 Fujian Rd.

Mansions mushroomed on Gulangyu, and Fujian Road became a prime location for men like Huang Xiulang (黄秀烺), who built the startling Sea & Sky Palace. Fujian Road was also home to domestic dastards like the "Cat King" (Chen Guohui, 陈国辉), who terrorized the province in his efforts to get ahead but in the end only lost his head—literally.

Join me on one of my favorite Gulangyu strolls as we tour these mansions, the exquisite Spanish Catholic church, and the less than exquisite ex-Japanese Consulate and Jail, (technically, the Church and Japanese Consulate are on Lujiao Rd., but our Fujian Rd. tour takes us right by them).

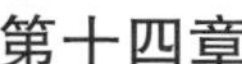

第十四章

福　建　路

——鼓浪屿最棒的建筑群

#38 Fujian Rd.

19 世纪西方殖民主义者越来越注意到海外华人凭借勤劳节俭，逐步在亚洲积累了大笔财富和权势。西方殖民者企图压制这些“亚洲犹太人”，很多华侨因此回到故土，一些较为富有的就选择了鼓浪屿，因为这里的景色优美、气候宜人，而且这个公共租界蕴藏着无限商机。

#28 Fujian Rd

一座座豪宅如雨后春笋般地拔地而起，福建路成为许多人的首选地，如令人称奇的海天堂构的主人黄秀烺。同时，一些土匪头头也曾居住在此，如陈国辉，又称“猫王”，他称霸闽南，希冀出人头地（最终的下场却是人头落地）。

与我同行吧，我最喜欢漫步在错落有致的房屋之间，还有精巧的西班牙天主教堂，略微逊色的原日本领事馆和带有刑讯室的监狱（严格地说教堂和日本领事馆位于鹿礁路，但是从福建路也能走到这里。）

#30 Fujian Rd

Fujian Road at a Glance

#24 Fujian Rd Yi Garden (林鹤年故居), circa 1895.

#26, 28 and 30 Fujian Rd Homes built in 1935 and 1936 are in a small side street to the right of Huang Rongyuan Villa. Note the balcony's colorful ceiling decorations, and Art Deco gates.

#30 Fujian Rd Modern architecture with western columns.

#32 Fujian Rd Huang Rongyuan Mansion (黄荣远堂), circa 1920. One of Gulangyu's best, owned by Vietnam Overseas Chinese Huang Zhongxun (黄仲训), designed by Filipino architect.

#34 *Lujiao Rd* Spanish neo-Gothic Catholic Church (Tianzhu Jiaotang, 天主教堂), Circa 1916, designed by a Spaniard. Actually on Lujiao Rd., but conveniently right next door to Fujian Rd.'s Huang Rongyuan Villa.

#37 Fujian Rd Cat King's Villa (陈国辉宅) Read his story in this chapter (it's to the left of the Music Hall)

#38 Fujian Rd Sea & Sky Palace (Haitian Tanggou, 海天堂构), early 20th century; five building complex built by Philippine Overseas Chinese, Huang Xiulang (黄秀烺).

#40 Fujian Rd Huang Nianyi Villa (黄念亿宅), early 20th century by Mr. Huang, a Philippine Overseas Chinese.

#43 Fujian Rd Former Christian Bookstore and Press (圣教书局)

#44 Fujian Rd No info on this stately red brick building.

#58 Fujian Rd Ye Qingchi Villa (叶清池)

#24 Fujian Rd Yi Garden (怡园), Lin Henian's (林鹤年) former residence, circa 1895. Anxi (安溪) native Lin Henian, aka Changyun (氅云), was considered one of Fujian's most famous late Qing Dynasty poets, though he was actually born in 1846 in Guangdong, not Fujian. Perhaps because his father was a Canton official, Henian virtually worshipped Lin Zexu (林则徐), the Commissioner who instigated the 1st Opium War when he tried to stop Western drug trafficking in Canton in the 1840s. Henian was also a fan of Koxinga (Zheng Chenggong, 郑成功), who drove the Dutch from Taiwan.

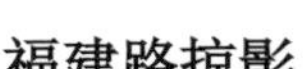

福建路掠影

福建路 24 号： 怡园 林鹤年故居，大约建于 1895 年。

福建路 26、28、30 号：民居，建于 1935 年至 1936 年间，位于黄荣远堂的右侧，中间仅隔一条小路。阳台天花板上的彩色装饰和门上的艺术装饰比较引人注目。

福建路 30 号：民居，一座现代化的建筑，还有西式廊柱。

福建路 32 号：黄荣远堂，约建于 1920 年。鼓浪屿最棒的建筑之一，归越南华裔黄仲训所有，菲律宾建筑师设计。

鹿礁路 34 号：西班牙新哥特式天主教堂，约建于 1916 年，由西班牙人设计，严格意义上说是位于鹿礁路，但是正好在黄荣远堂隔壁，从这走过去，非常便利。

福建路 37 号：陈国辉宅，在本章你就可以读到他的故事了(靠鼓浪屿音乐厅左边)。

福建路 38 号：海天堂构，20 世纪初建，五座楼构成的楼群，由菲律宾华侨黄秀烺所建。

福建路 40 号：黄念亿宅，菲律宾华侨黄念亿 20 世纪初建。

福建路 43 号：故圣教书局。

福建路 44 号：一座宏伟的红砖楼房，无其他详情。

福建路 58 号：叶清池别墅。

福建路 24 号： 怡园 林鹤年故居，大约建于 1895 年。

林鹤年，字氅云，祖籍安溪，他被誉为福建晚清最著名的诗人之一，实际上他是 1846 年出生在广东而非福建。鹤年的父亲为广东官员。林则徐 19 世纪 40 年代在广东的禁烟运动成了第一次鸦片战争爆发的导火线，鹤年因此对其仰慕有加。鹤年还崇拜把荷兰人驱逐出台湾的郑成功。

#24 Fujian Rd

Henian excelled in his studies, received his first official post in 1883, and was transferred to Taiwan in 1892, where the Qing government honored him for his work. After China lost the Sino-Japanese War in 1895 and turned Taiwan over to the Japanese, Lin returned to the mainland. Many Taiwanese people, officers and soldiers refused to give up the fight. Liu Yongfu (刘永福) fought back by forming the "Black Flag Army" (黑旗军), which Lin Henian supported. But Black Flag Army retreated to the mainland after only four months. When Lin Henian got the news, he promptly wrote 8 poems, and sobbed his eyes out in Koxinga Temple. On April 7, 1897, he climbed the peak of Sunlight Rock, gazed towards Taiwan, and wept.

Henian named his 2-storey red brick home Yi Garden (怡园) to express his longing for Taiwan, and created a garden for friends, which he called Small Peach Garden (小桃源), which for Chinese roughly connotes "paradise" or "Elysium." His friend, the noted calligrapher Lv Shiyi (吕世谊), inscribed a stone inscription for the garden.

After settling down on Gulangyu Island, Henian taught for several years in Anxi's Chongwen School (崇文书院, 安溪), and planned to go into business with his son but died on July 16, 1901 at the age of 55. In 1993, his granddaughter Wu Wanting (吴婉婷) returned to Xiamen from Canada, and retrieved his 16 volumes of poetry, which included 1936 poems.

Henian's offspring live in Yi Garden, but new houses have been built in areas of Small Peach Garden and the walls are crumbling, though the garden still retains a few of its famous Tai Lake stones (太湖石).

#32 Fujian Rd Huang Rongyuan Mansion (黄荣远堂), circa 1920, is directly opposite Sea and Sky Palace. The villa reminds me of antebellum mansions in the Deep South—though no Southerner ever had a garden like this, with its towering palms, shimmering pool, and Chinese pavilion and rockery to the left, from which you can snap a photo of the Spanish Gothic Catholic Church on the other side of the wall.

Huang Rongyuan Villa was designed by a Filipino architect and built in 1920 by Shi Guangchong, a Philippine overseas Chinese whose ancestral home was Jinjiang, and who was related to one of Gulangyu's most famous residents. His nephew's wife was the first daughter of Lin Erjia (林尔嘉), creator of Shuzhuang Garden (菽庄花园).

鹤年学业很出色，1883 年就投身仕途，1892 年调任台湾，他在台湾的政绩也倍受清政府赞赏。中日甲午战争中国战败，台湾被割让给日本，林鹤年回到大陆。不少台湾人民、官兵拒绝投降，刘永福组织了“黑旗军”抗击日本，受到了林鹤年的大力支持。但是仅四个月后，“黑旗军”就失败、撤回大陆。林鹤年闻讯，赋诗八首，在郑成功庙哭诉。1897 年 4 月 7 日，他登上日光岩，眺望台湾，潸然泪下。

鹤年将这座两层的红砖楼命名为“怡园”，以表达对台湾的思念之情，并且造了一座供友人聚会的花园“小桃源”，即中国人所指的“世外桃源”或“极乐世界”。其友——著名的书法家吕世谊还为“小桃源”手书石刻。

定居鼓浪屿后，鹤年曾到安溪崇文书院主讲多年，后与其子准备在厦从商，1901 年 7 月 16 日，林鹤年辞世，终年 55 岁。1993 年，其外孙女吴婉婷从加拿大回厦问祖，携回他的诗抄 16 集（含 1936 首诗）。

鹤年的后人现仍住在怡园，但是“小桃源”被新建房屋所占用，围墙斑驳不堪。不过园中仍有几块有名的太湖石。

福建路 32 号：黄荣远堂

大约建于 1920 年，就在海天堂构的正对面。这座别墅让我想起美国南北战争前南方的住宅——尽管那些南方人都没有这样的花园，园子里是参天的棕榈树，波光粼粼的池面，左边是中式的亭子和假山，在假山上还能抓拍到围墙另一侧的西班牙哥特式天主教堂。

黄荣远堂由菲律宾建筑师设计，菲律宾华侨施光从于 1920 年建造，施祖籍晋江，他和鼓浪屿的名人菽庄花园的主人林尔嘉还有一些渊源（林的长女为施的侄媳）。

While Gulangyu was a heavenly place to visit, by the 1930s the Japanese were making it a hell of a place to live in, and in 1937 Mr. Shi hightailed it back to the relatively safety of the Philippines. The villa was taken over by Mr. Huang Zhongxun, who then gave it to his younger brother, Huang Zhongping. He renamed the place Huang Rongyuan Villa, after the real estate company founded by Huang Wenhua (a Nan'an native who made a fortune in developing wilderness in Vietnam), and his son (the same fellow who walled in Sunlight Rock and made it his private garden; read more in the Yongchun Rd. chapter).

Huang Rongyuan Villa is pretty much a Western-style dwelling, with its "Southern mansion" two-storey curved front porch and Ionic columns. But few Western homes boast as many styles of windows on one front, and the upper floor, with its dozen or more columns, looks like it was added as an afterthought. Still, I appreciate the imagination that went into its design and construction, and find it astonishing that such a magnificent building was later used as the Deer Reef Kindergarten.

The Spanish Catholic Church (#34 Lujiao Rd.) is on the other side of the garden wall, just across from the former Japanese consulate.

#37 Fujian Rd The Cat King's Villa (陈国辉宅) Chen Guohui（陈国辉), one of Gulangyu's most inglorious residents, was named Cat King because of his pockmarked face, but on December 23rd, 1933, the 19th army resolved his complexion problem—permanently.

Gulangyu folk rejoiced when they read the Fuzhou St. placard announcing the villain's execution by Jiang Guangnai (蒋光鼐). He was not well loved.

Chen Guohui's father died before he was born in Nan'an's Xitou Village (西头,南安), and his mother remarried shortly after. Chen was poor, but nobody's fool. He joined the army at age 18 and became assistant to the head military officer. After his boss's death, he formed his own army and proceeded to loot the countryside, stealing provisions, weapons, and wives. In 1917, he was recruited by another army and became deputy head officer. After his attack on the Beiyang (北洋) army, he was promoted to deputy colonel and brigadier of the First Division of the provincial defense army.

After leading the Fifth Army in an attack on the rebel Chen Jiongming (陈炯明) in 1927, the Cat King became a junior general of the Beifa（北伐）army. In 1930, he gave his support to the provincial chairman, Fang Shengtao (方声涛), who gave him military and political power over the districts of Yongchun（永春), Dehua（德化), Anxi（安溪）and Nan'an（南安). Chen proved the axiom "Power corrupts." He grew more evil than ever, and when the Nineteenth Army came to Fujian, angry overseas Chinese demanded they execute the Cat King, who had stolen at least two of their wives.

鼓浪屿曾经是个天堂般的旅游胜地，但是在上世纪 30 年代日本人却把这里变成了人间地狱。1937 年，施先生匆忙逃离了鼓浪屿回到相对安全的菲律宾。这座别墅转入黄仲训名下，后来又转给其弟黄仲评。黄仲评将别墅改名为“黄荣远堂”，黄荣远堂是黄文华（南安人，在越南开发荒地致富）和其子（就是那个将日光岩圈为私家花园的家伙，在永春路章节你可以知道更多）创办的房地产公司。

黄荣远堂是一幢以西洋风格为主的建筑，有“南方大宅”的两层拱券和爱奥尼克式的柱子，但很少西式房子在前壁会有这么多各式各样的窗棂，二楼有十几根廊柱，看上去像是后来才添加上去的。不过我仍然颇为欣赏这座房子富有想像力的设计和结构，让我颇为惊讶的是，这座壮观的楼房后来成了鹿礁幼儿园。

西班牙天主教堂（鹿礁路 34 号）就位于黄荣远堂院子围墙的另一侧，在日本领事馆的正对面。

福建路 37 号：陈国辉宅

陈国辉是鼓浪屿最臭名昭著的居民之一，因脸上长满麻子被人戏称为“猫王”，但是 1933 年 12 月 23 日，十九路军将他击毙，为其永久解除了面部问题。

后来，福州街头张贴的布告宣告了这位恶人已经被蒋光鼐处决，鼓浪屿人心大快。他并不受欢迎。

陈国辉出生于南安西头村，父亲在他出生前就已去世，母亲随后很快就改嫁了。陈家贫却聪明机灵。他 18 岁投奔“民军”，给头人当勤务。头人死后，他自行组织了一支队伍，开始在乡下四处抢掠粮食、武器和女人。1917 年，他被另一支军队收编去当了副长官。后因袭击北洋军有功，被提升为副团长及省防军第一混成旅旅长。

1927 年，陈率第五路军讨伐叛军陈炯明，“猫王”因此摇身一变成了“北伐军”的少将团长。1930 年，他投奔福建省主席方声涛，方委任他为永春、德化、安溪、南安四县中将警备司令。陈应验了那句“权力导致腐败”的格言，他此后更加作恶多端。十九路军入闽后，愤怒的华侨们要求处死猫王，因为他至少强夺了两个华侨的妻子为妾。

In his youth, Chen had married a country girl, Wei Sanniang（魏三娘), and after her death he married Huang Rujuan（黄汝娟), from Yongchun（永春). But after coming to power the pockmarked privateer married three more girls by force. Lv Hanniang（吕罕娘), the "#2 Wife," had been married to an overseas Chinese (and later ran off with yet another Overseas Chinese). The "#3 Wife," Ye Xiulian（叶秀莲), had been the wife of a millionaire.

People the world over, from ancient Egyptians to modern Chinese, affirm that cats have nine lives. Apparently, so did the Cat King. He purchased his 3-storey red brick Western-style villa from an Anxi (安溪) landlord. The Cat King's guards used the other dwelling, which was connected to the main building so they could respond quickly to his needs or emergencies (furious wives, for instance; he certainly had his share). Ever mindful of enemies, Chen prepared many escape routes, such as the small gate entering the Foreigner's Cemetery (now the Music Hall), from which he could evade attackers from without and wives from within.

Eventually, the 19th army lured the Cat King to Fuzhou by asking him to participate in a military meeting, and executed Chen at East Lake. The bandit's underling, Xu Xianshi (许显时), who was head of the provincial construction bureau, returned Chen's body to Gulangyu and buried him in his garden, called "peace garden," perhaps in the hopes that all nine lives would rest in peace. The tomb was destroyed during the Great Proletariat Cultural Revolution.

Public Notice

Dec. 23rd, 1933

Chen Guohui, brigadier of No 1 troop of the provincial defense army, was a robber who lived in Minnan（闽南）and committed such evil crimes as robbery, looting, murder, and arson. His crimes were witnessed by society and were an undisputed fact. Our army came to Fujian and, in accordance with witnesses' testimony and the demands of the public, we executed Chen Guohui. In the past, I gave him opportunity for reform, but he refused to accept my advice and continued to commit evil acts. So today we executed him, and reported this to the government's military committee, which after serious consideration has condoned the execution. The criminal, Chen Guohui, was sentenced to death according to army, navy and air force criminal law, clauses 25, 27, 35, 47, and 63.

`This is official public notice that on the 23rd of this month, he was condemned, and sent to the execution grounds for execution.

Chen Guohui, 35 years old, was a native of Nan'an (南安), Fujian Province.

Signed, Jiang Guangnai (蒋光鼐) Head of Fujian Suijing Bureau (福建绥靖公署)

陈年轻时，娶了乡下妇女魏三娘为妻，魏死后，他又续娶了永春姑娘黄汝娟。后来有权势后，这满脸麻子的匪军头目又强抢了三个妇女为妻。二姨太吕罕娘原系一华侨之妻（后来又和另一个华侨私奔了）。三姨太叶秀莲，曾经是百万富翁的老婆。

全世界的人，从古埃及人到现代中国人，都坚信猫有九条命。显然，猫王也是。他从安溪房东那买下了一幢三层的红砖西式洋楼。猫王的警卫住在另一栋楼里，此楼和主楼相通，以便在有需要时和紧急情况下（比如说泼妇妻子）可以快速反应。因为担心敌人来犯，陈国辉准备了不少逃生通道，比如通往番仔墓的小门，这里外可避敌人内可防老婆。

最后，十九路军骗猫王至福州参加某军事会议，尔后在东湖将其击毙。这个土匪的尸体由他的部下、时任福建省建设厅长的许显时出面收殓，运回了鼓浪屿，葬在宅子花园内，并将其取名“息园”，也许是希望九条命能够安息。“无产阶级文化大革命”的时候，息园被毁。

布　告

1933 年 12 月 23 日

为布告事：照得福建省防军第一混成旅旅长陈国辉，系剽骑鸣镝之徒，因缘时会，啸聚闽南，暴戾恣睢，无恶不作。如庇匪掳勒，渎职殃民，横征暴敛，擅创捐税，勒种罂粟，屠杀焚村，摧残党务，拥兵抗命，种种罪恶，擢发难数，皆属社会所共见，无可掩讳之事实。当本军转师入闽之初，接受海内外民众团体及被害人控诉陈犯祸福文电，积存盈尺。本主任尤一再优容诫勉，冀其悔悟自新，不图该犯怙恶不悛，荼毒地方，拥兵抗命如故，如今拿办，业已呈奉国民政府军事委员会，电令组织军事法庭会审，并经详细研讯，罪证确凿，无法可宥。合依陆、海、空军刑法第 25、27、35、47、63 各条规定，合并论罪，判处死刑。即于本月 23 日，验明正身，绑赴刑场，执行枪决，以昭炯戒，切切此布！

计开陈国辉一名，年 35 岁，福建南安县人。

福建绥靖公署主任 蒋光鼐 （签字）

1933 年 12 月 23 日

#38 Fujian Rd Sea & Sky Mansion (Haitian Tanggou, 海天堂构), an early 20th century five building complex, was built by Huang Xiulang (黄秀烺), an overseas Philippine Chinese whose ancestors were from Jinjiang, returned to China and settled down on Gulangyu after World War I. His first dwelling was a 3-floor red brick building on Fujian Rd., west of the Spanish Catholic church and just south of Ye Qingchi (叶清池). Huang sold this to the Li family and in the early 1920s, Xiulang and a hometown friend, Huang Nianyi (黄念亿), built five buildings of Chinese and Western style to the south of the red brick building. Huang Xiulang lived in the central building, his Guangdong concubine lived in the right building, and Huang Nianyi occupied the other two villas (the right one for himself, the left one for his concubine.

The four Chinese characters above the main door, Haitian Tanggou (海天堂构), were later replaced with "Long live Chairman Mao."

These buildings are a hodgepodge of architectural styles, somewhat Western below but crowned with Chinese roofs. On one building, Putian (莆田) artisans crafted ornate turned-up Chinese eaves, and added what appear to be phoenixes on the corners. Window casings are primarily Western, but interior woodwork has a Chinese flavor.

Five decades later, the Gulangyu District Government used the central building as an office. The family hall's Buddhist paraphernalia and the Buddhist nuns who worshipped there were moved to the "Lin House." Soon after, the district office was moved back to the former Industry Bureau's building, and the house became the office of the Lujiao area Neighborhood Council.

Pay particular attention to the intricately detailed pavilion as you enter. While at one time it was no doubt colorful and attractive, it is now a dull concrete grey, rather like an ornate tomb—which is fitting, because Gulangyu must have plenty of ghosts (like that of the "Cat King" at #37 Fujian Rd).

Orient's Revenge?

Many Chinese articles quote American missionary Pitcher (Bifeili, 毕腓力), who said this blend of Chinese and foreign architecture is the "orient's revenge!" Westerners ran roughshod over Overseas Chinese, so Chinese built Western dwellings but crowned them with Chinese roofs. Interesting, but maybe not the true motive. Tan Kah Kee, who founded Xiamen University, said his mix of Eastern and Western architecture represented China's new foundation of modern education under the protection of traditional Chinese values and morals.

Where To From Fujian Rd? Like many Gulangyu streets, Fujian Rd is confusing because it is really three roads, and can be entered from Lujiao Rd, Fuxing Rd, (just past Fuxing Church) or Huangyan Rd. If you think this is confusing, wait till you get to the maze called Anhai Rd! While in this area, visit Li Qingquan Villa (Flag Hill Rd), Bright Moon Garden and Koxinga Statue, and the Lin Qiaozhi memorial.

福建路 38 号：海天堂构

#38 Fujian Rd's Gate

晋江旅菲华侨黄秀烺于 20 世纪初建了这五幢别墅组成的建筑群，他在第一次世界大战结束后归国定居鼓浪屿。起初，他住在一幢三层的红砖楼里，在西班牙天主教堂的西侧，福建路叶清池别墅南面。后来，他把这房子卖给了一李姓华侨。上个世纪 20 年代黄秀烺和老乡黄念亿在红砖楼的南边建了 5 幢中西合璧的别墅群。黄秀烺住在中楼，他的广东姨太太住在门楼右边的那栋，黄念亿使用另外两幢别墅（右边的为其自己居住，左边的为姨太太居住）。

楼群正门上书“海天堂构”四个大字，后来被“毛主席万岁”所代替。

楼群的建筑风格就像是一个大杂烩，西式的楼身，中式的屋顶。在其中一幢楼，莆田工匠建造了中式的翘角，角边有貌似凤凰的饰件。窗线脚洋味十足，内部木制工艺却是充满中国味。

50 年后，鼓浪屿区政府将中楼改为政府办公室。黄家大厅的佛堂和佛姑被迁往“林屋”。不久，区政府办公室搬回原工部局大楼，这里就成了鹿礁居委会的办公室。

进门的时候，你会注意到这里的亭子很精致复杂。毫无疑问，它曾经是色彩鲜艳、引人注目，但现在却是黯淡无光、毫无生气，更像一座华丽的坟墓——这么说很贴切，因为鼓浪屿一定有不少鬼魂（比如福建路 37 号的猫王）。

东方人的报复？

许多中文文章都引用美国传教士毕腓力说过的一句话：这种中西合璧的建筑是“东方人的报复”！西方人在华侨头上作威作福，中国人因此建造西式建筑并冠以中式屋顶。真是有意思，不过或许这不是真正的动机。厦门大学的创办人陈嘉庚建造了中西合璧的建筑则显示了中国的现代西方式教育是根植于传统价值观和道德观的。

看完福建路去哪呢？

福建路和鼓浪屿上的其他路一样，错综复杂，因为它其实是三条路，从鹿礁路、复兴路或晃岩路都能到达。比起迷宫一般的安海路来说，这里还不算是复杂的。在福建路区域，你可以去看看李清泉别墅（升旗山）、皓月园、郑成功雕像和毓园。

Chapter 15
Zhangzhou Rd—the Most "Garden-like" Road

"It was finally decided I was to go to Amoy, where I arrived with my wife and daughter in November 1923… The Consulate at Amoy was beautifully situated on a high bluff rising from the sandy bays of the outer harbor. The view extended for miles, beyond the huge outer harbor to the open sea with a small island, some twenty two miles away, in the distance. This natural harbor with the wooded hills on either shore was one of the finest typhoon anchorages on the coast, and could accommodate ships of all sizes and in great numbers. On one side of the bluff on which the Consulate stood was a lovely wood thick with firs and presenting a perfect specimen of the glorious Flame of the Forest. Poinsettias abounded, bougainvillea flourished in rich profusion. The house was bungalow style with wide verandahs on the south and west sides. Originally it possessed an upper story, but this had been damaged in a typhoon and was never rebuilt…The Consulate had its own bathing beach and the bathing was excellent." Sir Meyrick Hewlett, British Consul, 1922-25

#42 Zhangzhou Rd.

Zhangzhou Rd. begins at Lujiao Rd. (鹿礁路), to the left of the ferry, and winds past "Dadeji (大德记)" Beach, Koxinga Statue and Bright Moon Garden (Haoyue Yuan, 皓月园), and Signal Hill. It then bears right and arcs past the former British Consulate, former Tianwei Girl's school, Xiamen Music Academy, the former residences of Lin Yutang (#44 Zhangzhou Rd) and John Ma (#58 Zhangzhou Rd) and ends up at the People's Stadium (人民体育场) on Zhonghua Rd.

第十五章

漳 州 路

——花园式马路

“最后终于决定将我派往厦门。1923 年 11 月，我和妻子、女儿抵厦……驻厦领事公馆建在高高的崖顶，悬崖下就是外港沙滩，景致优美。这里视野可及数英里之外，巨大的海港之外就是开阔的大海，大约 22 英里的远处有一个小岛。这个天然海港两岸都有山林，是避风的优良港湾，可以停泊大量的大小船只。领事馆所在的崖顶一侧有一片秀丽、茂密的杉树林，还有一种理想树种——凤凰木。一品红、九重葛遍布山野。这座别墅南面、西面都带有宽大的走廊，原本有两层楼，但是二楼被台风摧毁后一直没有重建。主厅的地板为釉面砖，在我记忆中卧室地板是混泥土材料。领馆有专用的海滨浴场，在此游泳是件令人惬意的事。”

——梅里克·休利特爵士，英国领事，1922－1925

漳州路从鹿礁路起始（轮渡的左边），蜿蜒至“大德记海滨浴场”，皓月园和郑成功雕像，还有升旗山。这条路向右延伸至英国领事馆旧址，沿路蜿蜒而行，经过田尾女学堂旧址、厦门音乐学校、林语堂故居和马约翰故居，直至中华路的人民体育场。

Gulangyu's British Police (from Hong Buren)

Zhangzhou Road at a Glance

Bright Moon Garden & Koxinga Statue (Hao Yueyuan, 皓月园) Spend a few nights in delightful seaside cabins.

"Dadeji (大德记)" Beach

Huifeng Bank (汇丰银行) manager's former residence.

Gulangyu Water Supply Bureau; 2 villas, circa 1927, designed by Lin Quancheng (林全诚)

#5 Zhangzhou Rd Former British Consulate (Yingguo Lingshiguan, 英国领事馆)

#9 and #11 Zhangzhou Rd English-style two-storey villas, former residences for Xiamen customs officials; now the Guanhai Yuan tourist village (观海园).

#9 Zhangzhou Rd Former Xiamen Customs Office, designed by British and built in 1865; rebuilt between 1923-1924.

#20 Zhangzhou Rd English Commercial Bank, Xiamen Branch, 1920s (原英商厦门区)

#38 & 40 Zhangzhou Rd Li Family Home（李家庄).

#38 Zhangzhou Rd.

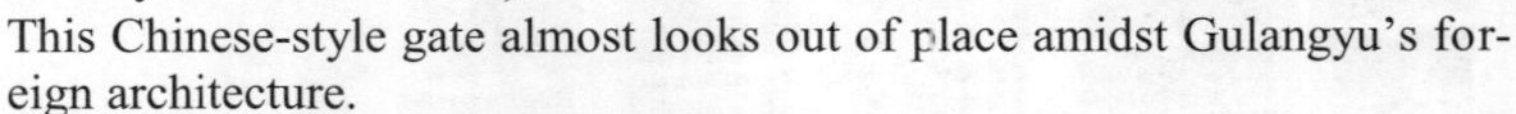

This Chinese-style gate almost looks out of place amidst Gulangyu's foreign architecture.

#42 Zhangzhou Rd Li Family Home (李家庄), around the corner from Lin Yutang's home, now rented out to six families.

#44 Zhangzhou Rd Lin Yutang's Former Residence

#50 Zhangzhou Rd No info on this well maintained old place. (also see #64)

#54 Zhangzhou Rd Red brick home built in 1932 by a Chinese from either Hong Kong or the Philippines.

#58 Zhangzhou Rd Former home of John Ma (Ma Yuehan, 马约翰), China's 1st Athletics Coach, built end of 19th century.

Xiamen Music Academy Former Xunyuan (浔源) School built in 1889; then used as Yude (毓德) women's school dorm.

The Li (李) Brothers' (Zhaoyi, 昭以 and Zhaobei, 昭北) Sino-European home is past the Music Academy. Note the spacious garden, and columns with flowers and Chinese ornaments carved by S. Fujian craftsmen.

漳州路掠影

皓月园和郑成功雕像：可以在海滨的小屋小住，度过一个愉快的夜晚。

大德记海滨浴场

汇丰银行经理的故居。

鼓浪屿供水局：有两幢约建于 1927 年的别墅，由林全诚设计。

漳州路 5 号：英国领事馆旧址

漳州路 9 号、11 号：英式的二层别墅，原厦门海关官员宿舍，现为观海园度假村。

漳州路 9 号：厦门海关办公楼，英国人设计，始建于 1865 年，1923－1924 年重建。

漳州路 20 号：原英商厦门区，建于上个世纪 20 年代。

漳州路 38、40 号：李家庄。这里的中式大门在鼓浪屿的西式建筑中显得很不合适。

漳州路 42 号：李家庄，在林语堂故居的拐角处，现在已出租给六户人家。

漳州路 44 号：林语堂岳父的廖宅。

漳州路 50 号：这座保存完好的老房子无详细信息记录（另见 64 号）。

漳州路 54 号：建于 1932 年的红砖房，可能是香港人或菲律宾华裔所建。

漳州路 58 号：马约翰故居，中国第一个体育教授，建于 19 世纪末。

厦门音乐学校：建于 1889 年的浔源书院旧址，后用作毓德女学堂的校舍。

过了厦门音乐学校，是李昭以和李昭北兄弟的中欧合璧的宅邸，有开阔的花园，柱子上有闽南工匠雕刻的花朵和中式装饰。

#54 Zhangzhou Rd.

#5 Zhangzhou Rd Former British Consulate (Yingguo Lingshiguan, 英国领事馆). The 2,000m^2 British Consulate, Gulangyu's earliest and most beautiful European building, was built in 1847 and a prison annex was added in 1870. The British Consulate was first at #16 Lujiao Rd. (Read the story in the Tianwei chapter!).

Zhangzhou Rd Xiamen Music Academy The former Xunyuan School (浔源书院), Lin Yutang's alma mater, was built in 1881 and after it moved to Zhangzhou in 1925, the building was used as a Yude (毓德) Women's School dormitory. After liberation, it became the Xiamen Women's Middle School, the Xiamen #2 School dorms, and the Xiamen Weaving School. The old buildings were then razed and replaced by the new Xiamen Music Academy (厦门音乐学校). Read more in the Gulangyu Music and Arts chapter.

#44, 48 Zhangzhou Rd Lin Yutang's Former Residence (林语堂岳父的廖宅). Lin Yutang, one of the most influential Chinese writers of the 20th century[1], lived in a relatively simple British-style home nestled beneath camphor and eucalyptus trees near the Xiamen Music Academy. The simple yet elegant Liao House (廖宅), #48, one of Gulangyu's oldest European-style buildings, belonged to the parents of Lin's wife, Liao Cuifeng (廖翠凤).

To the right of the Liao House is the 2-storey Liren Villa (立人宅), with its elegant broad veranda and solid window shutters and doors. The second floor was decorated with the colored glaze once fashionable on the island. Lin's wedding took place in Liren Villa's front hall.

#44 Zhangzhou Rd.

[1] For more on Lin Yutang, see the Music & Arts chapter

漳州路 5 号：英国领事馆旧址。该馆占地 2000 平方米，是鼓浪屿最早最漂亮的欧式建筑，建于 1847 年。1870 年时，加建了一座副楼作为监狱。早期的英国领事馆在鹿礁路 16 号。请参见田尾路一章。

Former British Consulate (Lily Wang)

漳州路厦门音乐学校：这里为林语堂的母校浔源书院旧址，建于 1881 年，1925 年迁往漳州，后来被用作毓德女学堂校舍。解放后，这里先后成为厦门女子中学、厦门纺织学校和厦门第二中学的校舍。这些老建筑被夷为平地后，就新建了厦门音乐学校。在鼓浪屿音乐和艺术章节，你可以获知更多详情。

#38 Zhangzhou Rd.

漳州路 44 号、48 号：林语堂[1]岳父的廖宅。林语堂是 20 世纪中国文坛最有影响力的作家之一，他的故居在厦门音乐学校附近一座相当简朴的英式宅子里，房子掩映在香樟和桉树林中。漳州路 48 号这座简朴却不失雅致的廖宅，是鼓浪屿最古老的欧式建筑之一，也是林语堂夫人廖翠凤的娘家。

廖宅的右边是二层楼的立人斋，有雅致的宽廊、牢固的百叶门窗。二楼饰以彩色玻璃镂空花格，这在当年的鼓浪屿算是时髦的。林语堂就是在立人斋的正厅举行婚礼。

[1] 林语堂简介请参见音乐艺术章节

#58 Zhangzhou Rd

#58 Zhangzhou Rd Former residence of John Ma (马约翰故居,1882-1996), China's 1st Athletics Coach. The two-story Western-style former residence of John Ma was built at the turn of the end of the 19th century. Check the Gulangyu pioneer educators chapter for more on John Ma.

Where to from Zhangzhou Rd? Zhangzhou Rd ends at Zhonghua Rd by the People's Stadium and John Ma's memorial. To the left are Shuzhuang Garden and beaches; to the right are such sites as the Dafudi Residence. From Zhonghua Rd, take a left on Haitan Rd for a shortcut to Sunlight Rock and the Koxinga Memorial, or continue on Zhonghua Rd to Quanzhou Rd, bear left onto Anhai Rd, and visit Trinity church and the beautiful architecture and scenery of the once-exclusive Bishan Mountain.

The Sedan Chair

"The sedan chair is an instrument of torture to the uninitiated. It consists of a box-like contrivance swung on two long bamboo poles each about fifteen feet in height. It is usually carried on the shoulders of two men, unless the person occupying it weighs over 175 pounds when three men are employed. Next to the *kago* of Japan the sedan chair is about as uncomfortable a contrivance as could be imagined...Never were the marks of an 'injured being' more manifest than those written on the face of the traveler who has for the first time been carried ten miles in one of the back-breaking and head-splitting arrangements. It is a journey he will never forget." Rev. Pitcher, "In and About Amoy," 1912

"This I conceive to be the chemical function of humor: to change the character of our thought." Lin Yutang

漳州路 58 号：马约翰故居，建于 19 世纪末，马约翰为中国第一个体育教授。

马约翰故居是一座两层西式洋楼，建于 19 和 20 世纪之交（欲知马约翰的详情，请参阅鼓浪屿教育先驱章节）。

看完漳州路接下来去哪里呢？

(Dukes, 1885)

漳州路的终点在中华路人民体育场和马约翰纪念碑。往左走可以去菽庄花园和沙滩，往右走是中华路的一些景点，如大夫第。中华路往左途经海坛路，即可抄近路到日光岩和郑成功纪念馆，或者在中华路继续往泉州路走，左走至安海路，可以参观三一堂，还有曾经独一无二的笔山的美丽建筑和景色。

轿子

“这种轿子对不习惯的人来说是一种折磨。这种像箱子一样的发明物在两根约 15 英尺长的竹竿上摇晃。通常由两人来抬轿，如果坐在轿子上的人体重超过 175 磅，那就需要三个人了。这种轿子不舒服的程度令人无法想像，仅次于日本轿子……一些游客第一次坐轿子十英里，落得腰酸背痛、头痛欲裂，他们脸上的表情比伤员的表情更能说明问题，这将是他们一生无法忘怀的旅程。” 毕腓力，《厦门方志》，1912 年

“我认为这是幽默发生化学反应的结果：改变人类的思维特征。”

——林语堂

Chapter 16
Tianwei Rd —High Ground & High Society

The Great Southern Warrior

"On the south the bay is bounded by a low range of mountains, from the midst of which rises abruptly Lam-tai-bu (Nantaiwu), the 'Great Southern Warrior.' This is the most beautiful sight in the whole of the landscape, for there is a never-ending charm in its varying moods, as seen in storm or sunshine. In fine weather its summit is bathed in great floods of light, and it stands out clearly against the sky as it looks down upon the blue waters of the bay, which dance and sparkle beneath the rays of the great eastern sun. When bad weather is coming on, dense masses of cloud, tumultuous and agitated, as if clinging to it for protection, gather round its head and far down its sides, and then the waters of the bay, dark with the shadows cast upon them, seem to be in sympathy with them, as though they feared the coming gale…"

Macgowan, "The Story of the Amoy Mission," 1889, p.25,26

Pitcher, 1912 Amoy Club

Elegant villas grace most of Gulangyu, but the heart of big money and high society was South Gulangyu's "Tianwei" (田尾, "tip of the paddy field"). And since locals believed this former rice paddy boasted some of the islet's best "fengshui," the British victors of the Opium War added insult to injury by erecting their majestic consulate upon a Tianwei bluff. But when a typhoon blew off the upper floor and forced England to settle for a less imposing one-storey consulate, the locals chortled that Tianwei's dragon and tiger[1] had knocked the Brits off their high horse, even if not off their high bluff.

[1] Dragon and Tiger: two hills flanking the consulate help create the excellent 'fengshui'

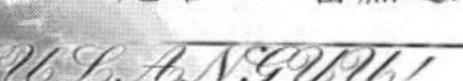

第十六章

田 尾 路

——富庶之地与上流社会

南太武

“海湾的南边是绵延的矮山坡，透过薄雾，突兀的‘南太武’（雄伟的南方护卫）隐约可见。这里的景色是最美的，在风雨和阳光下千变万化、魅力无穷。天气晴好的时候，山顶沐浴在阳光中，在天空的衬托下显得更加清晰，山峰俯视着蔚蓝的大海，海面在东方耀眼的阳光下波光粼粼。天气不好的时候，浓厚的云层变得骚动不安，乌云在山头密集，笼罩着整座山峰，似乎是要抱住小山寻求庇护，被乌云笼罩的海水仿佛也同情它们，好像惧怕正要来临的大风……”

——麦嘉湖 1889 年《The Story of the Amoy Mission》第 25～26 页

优雅的别墅几乎遍布整个鼓浪屿，但是富庶之地和上流社会却是在鼓浪屿南端的田尾。当地人认为这片曾经的稻田是岛上的风水宝地。鸦片战争的渔利者英国人在田尾悬崖边竖立起庄严的领事馆，伤害之余又侮辱了这里的风水。后来一场台风掀去了领事馆的顶楼，只剩一楼的大楼风光不再，英国人也不得不将就于此。当地人因此戏称是田尾的青龙白虎[1]让英国人从高高的马背上摔下来，纵然不是从悬崖上摔下去。

[1] 青龙白虎：领事馆两侧的山，是绝佳“风水”的体现。

Denmark's Great North Telegraph Company was in Tianwei, and Mr. Huang Yizhu (黄奕住) bought its Norwegian manager's home and transformed it into the Seaview Villa (Guanhai Bieshu, 观海别墅), which had terraces overlooking the ocean, and elaborate labyrinths in front of the home.

Tianwei was also the site of several of the Reformed Church of America's (Guizheng Jiao, 归正教) schools for girls and women, the French and Dutch consulates, and the French consul's villa, which he rented from Mr. Huang Zhongxun (黄仲训). The establishment of the International Club ("Club of 1 Million Nations") by foreign consuls and enterprises firmly ensconced Tianwei as the center of Gulangyu high society.

Tianwei's wealthy residents could afford the finest villas and expansive lawns and gardens, so estates weren't as tightly packed together as elsewhere on this tiny islet. A stroll along Tianwei's lanes, with the estate's high walls and ancient trees arching overhead, is like walking a tunnel back in time to opium-era opulence. The opium is gone but some opulence remains, because Tianwei is now a haven not for wealthy Laowai and Chinese but for high-ranking cadres who flock from all over China to the exclusive retreats and sanatoriums.

Tianwei Rd at a Glance

#1 Tianwei Rd Hong Tian'en's Home (洪天恩宅), early 20th century
#6 Tianwei Rd Former British Consulate Annex, built in 1870.
#16 Tianwei Rd International Club, 1920s. （原万国俱乐部）.
#21 Tianwei Rd Danish Telegraph Office, circa 1869 (原丹麦大北电报公司办公楼）
#17 Tianwei Rd Seaview Villa (观海别墅)
#27 Tianwei Rd Xiamen Customs, circa 1865, (厦门海关)
#38 Tianwei Rd Foreigner's home (原外国人住宅)
#40 Tianwei Rd Former Dutch Consulate

原丹麦大北电报公司办公楼就在田尾路，黄奕住先生买下了其挪威籍经理的住宅，并改装成观海别墅，在露台上可以眺望房前的大海和迷宫。

田尾路曾有美国归正教开办的“女学堂”，法国和荷兰领事馆，及法国领事从黄仲训先生那里租来的别墅。外国领事和洋商所建的万国俱乐部，使得田尾作为鼓浪屿上流社会中心的地位更加稳固。

(Johnston, 1907)

Amoy Women's School

田尾的有钱人买得起最好的别墅，带有宽大的草坪和花园，而不像这个弹丸小岛的其他地方一样房子都紧挨着。漫步在田尾的小巷里，周围是高大的围墙和参天的古树，仿佛是穿行于时间隧道回到那个鸦片充斥的年代。那些鸦片已经没有踪影，但这里还是一样富饶；这里也不再是中外阔佬的天地，但还是有不少来自全国各地的官员来此隐居、疗养。

田尾路掠影

田尾路 1 号：　洪天恩宅，建于 20 世纪初期
田尾路 6 号：英国领事馆副楼，建于 1870 年
田尾路 16 号：原万国俱乐部，建于 20 年代
田尾路 21 号：原丹麦大北电报公司办公楼，约建于 1869 年
田尾路 17 号：观海别墅
田尾路 27 号：厦门海关，约建于 1865 年
田尾路 38 号：原外国人住宅
田尾路 40 号：荷兰领事馆

Getting to Tianwei Enter Tianwei Rd. from either south of the Koxinga Statue on Seaview Rd. (Guanhai Lu, 观海路), or from Gangzihou Rd. (港仔后路) near the former Masonic Lodge and the Luhai Hotel（鹭海宾馆).

Former Dutch Consulate, early 20th century (#40 Tianwei Rd)

#16 Tianwei Rd International Club, circa 1920s. (原万国俱乐部). During the early 1900s, the Gulangyu foreigners' club was in the "consular district" consisting of consulates of Germany, Spain, Japan and Britain, but it was too far from their homes so in the 1920s they sold the club building to Xiulang Huang (黄秀烺).

A larger, more modern International Club, called the Lequn Building (乐群楼), or Great Globe building (大球间), was built between the British and French consulates in Tianwei. Only formally attired consular officials and other elite foreigners were admitted to the hallowed halls of this stately club, which offered a foreign language library, ball room, pub, and facilities for tennis, table tennis and cricket.

According to one local writer, it was within Lequn's hallowed halls that foreign devils hatched their hellish plans for the lucrative pig 'n poison trades, but by the International Club's day the coolie trade had pretty much cooled off (though Britain's opium trafficking continued well into the 1940s).

The Lequn's deft marriage of American and English architecture was elegant but simple, eschewing the elaborate carvings and statues prevalent in the villas of Gulangyu's nouveau riche. One can only imagine the splendor of the building, with its interior doors, windows, stairs and floors of finely crafted teak.

Alas, in the 60s the Lequn became the Fujian Provincial Officer's Rest Home (福建干部休养所), and in 1984 the elegant teak doors were replaced with "modern" aluminum, and the estate was reopened as the "Seaview Garden Vacation Village" (Guanhai Yuan Dujia Cun, 观海园度假村)

如何去田尾：从观海路郑成功雕像往南走，或者从港仔后路荷兰领事馆和鹭海宾馆附近出发都能走到田尾路。

田尾路 16 号：原万国俱乐部，建于 20 年代。20 世纪初期，鼓浪屿外国人俱乐部设在“领馆区”，包括德意志、西班牙、日本和英国领事馆，但是离这些老外的住所太远，所以 20 年代他们把俱乐部大楼卖给了黄秀烺。

后来，在田尾路英国和法国领事馆之间建起了一个更大、更现代的万国俱乐部，称为乐群楼，也叫大球间。这个高贵俱乐部只允许着装正式的领事馆官员和一些上等老外进入。俱乐部里设有外语书籍阅览室、舞厅、酒吧，还有各种运动设施如网球、乒乓球和板球场地。

据一个当地作家说，就是在乐群楼神圣的高墙内，这群洋鬼子密谋了高利润的“猪仔”和毒品贸易的罪恶勾当，尽管那时苦力贩卖已经接近消亡（但是英国的鸦片贸易一如既往，直至 20 世纪 40 年代）。

乐群楼美英合璧的建筑风格优雅简约，没有鼓浪屿富人别墅流行的精致雕花和塑像。但是透过屋内工艺精美的柚木制成的门窗、楼梯和地板，你可以想像出这座大楼昔日的辉煌。

60 年代乐群楼成为福建干部休养所，可惜的是，1984 年，雅致的柚木门被“现代的”铝合金门取而代之，这里成为“观海园度假村”，重新对外开放。

Xiamen International Club Today

Gulangyu's International Club is long gone but Xiamen has a new International Club (国际会所) on the 7th floor of the Bank Center building #189 Xiahe Rd. Here you'll encounter the city's new business elite—including descendants of the overseas Chinese who made Gulangyu International Settlement one of the wealthiest places on the planet. Phone: 239-4222
E-mail: internationalclub@intclub-xm.com

Tung in Cheek A magnificent Chinese tung oil tree (Shili, 石栗) tree outside the Lequn building was planted when the Japanese seized Gulangyu. Tung oil trees can tower 12 meters, and the soft, dark green, heart-shaped leaves are up to 15 cm. wide. In the West we use Tung oil on wood, but Chinese have countless other uses for this versatile product: motor oil, artificial leather, wire insulation, greases, brake-linings, etc. Chinese also claim the oil would be delicious if the tannins (单宁) and poisonous saponin were safely removed. Given that Chinese eat anything edible (and what isn't edible they ingest and call medicine), I'm surprised they haven't found a way to eat it already!

Tung Leaf

During the early 1960s, the First Secretary of the Xiamen Communist Party, Mr. Yuan (袁改), learned of the many uses for the tung oil tree and promptly ordered the tree be planted all over Xiamen, and today The Garden Island's tung trees provide delightful shade for visitors to Yundang Lagoon (白鹭洲).

#17 Tianwei Rd Seaview Villa (观海别墅) was built in 1918 as the residence for the Norwegian manager of Denmark's Great Northern Telegraph Company. Indonesian Overseas Chinese Huang Yizhu[1] (黄奕住) bought the villa in 1926, remodeled it, built a small garden and labyrinth, and added a flat roof for viewing the sea—hence its name. It became one of Yizhu's favorite villas because the rhythmic sound of the surf resonated through the house each night, lulling even the worst insomniacs to sleep.

[1] Read more about the amazing barber-cum-businessman Huang Yizhu in the Sunlight Rock Rd. chapter.

今日的厦门国际会所

鼓浪屿的万国俱乐部已经尘封历史，但是在厦禾路 189 号银行中心 7 楼有一个新的国际会所。去那走一遭，你一定会遇见这个城市新的商业精英，包括那些华侨的后裔，正是这些华侨使得鼓浪屿这个国际聚居地曾是世上最富裕的地方之一。

电话：0592－2394222

电子邮件：internationalclub@intclub-xm.com

石栗

乐群楼外有一棵高大的石栗，是日本人强占鼓浪屿后栽种的。石栗可高达 12 米，柔软、墨绿的心形叶子宽可达 15 厘米。在西方，石栗榨的桐油用来涂在木制品表层，但是在中国桐油有无数种用途：电动机润滑油、人造革、绝缘体、润滑油、制动衬面等等。中国人还宣称，如果能安全剔除其中的单宁和有毒的皂角苷，桐油还很美味呢。因为中国人能吃的无所不吃（不能吃的，也当药咽下去），所以我感到有些吃惊，他们竟然还没有找到吃桐油的方法。

20 世纪 60 年代初期，厦门市委第一书记袁改先生得知石栗用途广泛后，便立即通知在全市培植广种，如今花园城市的石栗为白鹭洲游客提供了宜人的树阴。

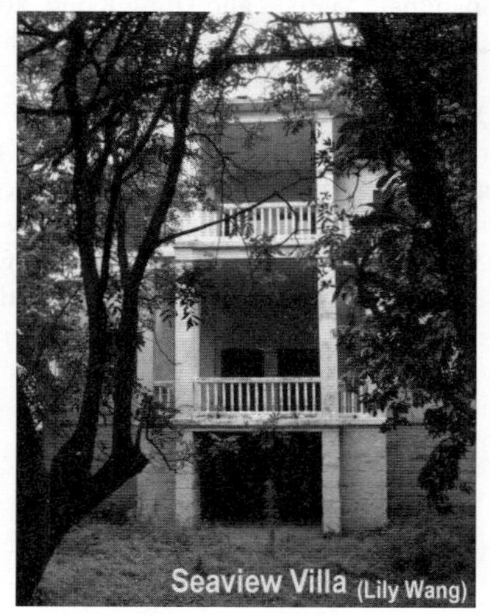
Seaview Villa (Lily Wang)

田尾路 17 号：观海别墅

观海别墅 1918 年建成，是原丹麦大北电报公司挪威籍经理的公寓。印尼华侨黄奕住[1]1926 年买下这座别墅并稍做修整，建了一个花园、迷宫，还加建一层作为观海台——观海别墅因此得名。这也成为黄奕住最心爱的别墅之一，因为每晚海浪有节奏地拍打着岸边，涛声回荡房内，即使是最严重的失眠患者也会被引入梦乡。

[1] 在日光岩路章节，有更多关于黄奕住这个原为剃头匠的商人的介绍。

The year before the Northern Expedition[1], Kuomingtang (KMT) key member Wang Jingwei (汪精卫), fearing assassination, hid out at Seaview Villa for 3 days. He showed his thanks to Huang Yizhu by writing a calligraphic inscription of a poem by the famous Tang Dynasty poet Libai.

In 1947, Seaview was the Haijiang Academy's "information center," and in 1950 the Guanhai Seaview Platform was a sentry post. Seaview's music has soothed decades of cadres to sleep since becoming a cadre's sanatorium in 1964.

Seaview villa was built in an airy multi-level French style, with a special subterranean insulation to combat the injurious sub-tropical humidity. The arches alternated red and white, and had Persian blinds. The bedrooms each had fireplaces, though given the tropical weather, I suspect they were more for atmosphere than warmth.

Yizhu planned to connect Seaview Villa with Shuzhuang Garden's "44 Bridge" but the Danes' Great Northern Company protested the bridge would disturb their underwater cables (ironic, since their cables were illegal). But Yizhu's protests in European courts were futile. Foreigners in China were above Chinese law, but Chinese were subject to foreign law.

#21 Tianwei Rd The Danish Telegraph Office, 1920s（原丹麦大北电报公司办公楼) The Danish set up a Gulangyu consulate in 1869 but had no consul, so affairs were run by the Great Northern telegraph company.

Established in April, 1874, its 1574 km-long undersea cable connected Shanghai, Xiamen and Hong Kong, and took in 20,000 silver dollars monthly.

The French consul tried to cash in on this lucrative business by setting up a 1481 km-long cable from French-occupied Vietnam to Gulangyu, but unlike the Danes, the French never bothered to seek permission, and refused Chinese entreaties to close the illegal business. After they went belly up, a local writer noted, "France tried to sell their rubbish cable to us but we refused to buy it."

The Chinese refused to renew the contract with Great Northern in 1928, and on January 1st, 1931, Xiamen cut off the company's land and sea line. Both the Xiamen and Gulangyu offices shut down February 12th.

[1] During the two-year Northern Expedition (1926-8), the Kuomintang overthrew Beijing's warlord government

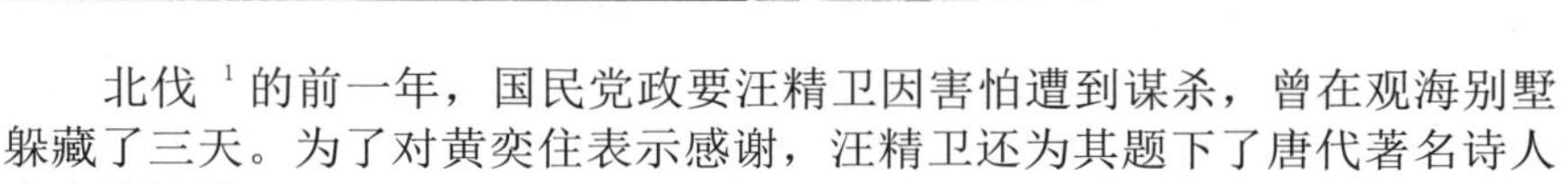

北伐[1]的前一年，国民党政要汪精卫因害怕遭到谋杀，曾在观海别墅躲藏了三天。为了对黄奕住表示感谢，汪精卫还为其题下了唐代著名诗人李白的诗歌。

1947 年，观海别墅用作“海疆学术资料馆”。1950 年，在观海台上又设立了观察哨。1964 年，这里变成干部疗养所后，几十年来，海边的催眠曲每天伴着疗养者进入梦乡。

观海别墅是通风的多层仿法建筑，设有特殊的地下隔潮层，以防止亚热带潮湿天气带来的损害。拱门红白相间，还有百叶窗。每个卧室都有壁炉，不过我怀疑在这样的亚热带气候里，这些壁炉只是一种装饰，而非用来取暖。

黄奕住原本打算将观海别墅和菽庄花园的“四十四桥”连接起来，但是丹麦大北电报公司抗议说大桥会干扰他们的海底电缆（讽刺的是，他们铺设的电缆是非法的）。黄奕住的申诉在欧洲法庭被判无效，因为当时在华洋人不受中国法律约束，而华人却得服从洋人的法律。

田尾路 21 号：原丹麦大北电报公司办公楼，约建于上个世纪 20 年代。

丹麦于 1869 年在鼓浪屿设立了领事馆，但却没有派驻领事，因此这里的事务都由大北电报公司负责。电报公司成立于 1874 年 4 月，铺设了长达 1574 公里的海底电缆，连接起厦门与上海、厦门与香港，每月营业收入可达两万银元。

法国领事看到这个行业有利可图，也千方百计地铺设了长 1481 公里的电缆，连接法国殖民地越南和鼓浪屿。但和丹麦人不同的是，法国人根本不操心能否获得许可，中国人要求关闭这个非法企业，法国人却置之不理。最终他们破产了，一个本地作家写道：“法国人异想天开要把那些废电缆卖给我们，但是我们坚决不买。”

1928 年，中国拒绝大北公司的续约请求。1931 年元旦，厦门截断了他们的水陆联络线。大北公司厦门和鼓浪屿两个办事处于同年 2 月 12 日一起关闭。

[1] 1926 年至 1928 年的北伐战争，国民党推翻了北京的军阀政府。

The Japanese closed the company for good during World War II and the building was vacant for years until the offices were renovated and used for training classes. The steel cables, which crossed the beach right into the 50s and 60s, have been removed, but Chinese still fume about the Danish violation of China's "telecommunications sovereignty," and one guidebook call the attractive Danish villa a "devil building that took 7 million silver dollars from Xiamen."

(Dukes, 1885)
A Chinese Officer

#27 Tianwei Rd Xiamen Customs (Bitulu, 吡吐庐), circa 1865. In 1683, General Shilang (施琅) deposed Koxinga's grandson and reunited Taiwan with the mainland. The General asked Emperor Kangxi (康熙) to establish a customs office in Xiamen, and the following year the Emperor established customs offices in both Xiamen and Fuzhou. In 1729 the Fujian governor took over all of Fujian, and sent the S. Fujian customs supervisor resident in Fuzhou to take over Xiamen customs.

Xiamen became one of China's five treaty ports after the 1st Opium War, and after the second Opium War Xiamen established its "New Customs" (新关), or Foreign Customs (洋关). Foreigners controlled Foreign Customs, and after 1901 Xiamen surrendered control of all customs to foreigners.

Xiamen's tax bureau rented an English captain's European-style two-story villa until purchasing it on July 1, 1865 for 6000 silver dollars, and renaming it Bitulu. The villa had an auxiliary residence for the small army of servants, which included sedan chair bearers, gardeners, doormen and kitchen personnel. The 3,300m^2 vegetable garden to the east of the servants' residence (at what is now #54 Tianwei Rd.) was later commandeered by the government and turned into a badminton court for the teacher-training school.

After the last British tax officer left on July 31st, 1949, Bitulu was vacant for several years until occupied by soldiers, and in 1956, the villa was rented out as the "workers' sanatorium." Xiamen Customs took the building back in 1992, demolished it in 1996, and built a Training Center on the site.

Where to Now? From Tianwei, head south to Shuzhuang Gardens and the Piano Museum, or head back up the coast to the Koxinga Statue, Bright Moon Garden, and the Ferry.

二战期间，日本人永远地封闭了报房，大楼从此空置多年，后来经过一番修缮，这里还办过学习班。那些纵横海底的电缆直到五六十年代才被清除。但是对丹麦人违反中国的“电信主权”，中国人仍愤愤不平，有一本旅游指南把这座引人注目的丹麦大楼称作“从厦门吸走700万银元的魔房”。

田尾路27号：厦门海关（吡吐庐），约建于1865年。

1683年，施琅将军废黜了郑成功之孙，再次统一了台湾，上疏奏请康熙皇帝在厦门设立海关。次年，康熙下旨设立闽海关厦门口、福州口。1729年，福建巡抚接管了整个福建，委派福建海关监察接管了厦门口，常驻福州。

第一次鸦片战争后，厦门成为“五口通商”口岸之一，第二次鸦片战争后，厦门建立了“新关”，又称“洋关”。洋关由洋人掌管，1901年后，厦门的整个海关都被洋人控制。

A Mandarin and Son (MacGowan, 1912)

厦门税务司租用英国船长的欧式二层别墅，并于1865年7月1日买下了这幢别墅，价银6000关平两[1]，改名为吡吐庐。别墅还有一幢副楼供仆人居住，这队人马包括轿夫、园丁、门卫和厨师。副楼东侧（现田尾路54号）有一片3300平方米的菜园，后来被政府征用，拨给师范学校用作羽毛球场。

1949年7月31日，最后一任英国税务司离去后，吡吐庐空置了多年，后由驻军使用。1956年起，这座别墅出租成为“工人疗养所”。1992年，厦门海关收回大楼，1996年将其拆毁并在旧址上重建了一个“培训中心”。

现在去哪里呢？从田尾路，往南可以去菽庄花园和钢琴博物馆，或者掉头沿着海边至郑成功雕像、皓月园和鼓浪屿码头。

[1] 即关银，旧中国海关征税时使用的记账银两，以纯银583.3英厘作为一海关两。1930年1月废除。

Chapter 17
Fuxing Rd & Flag Hill Rd

#77 Fuxing Rd

Getting to Fuxing Rd. Turn left from Gulangyu Ferry onto Lujiao Rd., walk past Bo'ai Hospital along the coast towards Koxinga Statue, and turn right where Lujiao meets Zhangzhou Rd. by the odd triangular house. The road forks at Fuxing Church, with Fuxing Rd. to the left and Fujian Rd. to the right. Further up Fuxing Rd. is the memorial to Lin Qiaozhi, the "Mother of Modern Chinese Obstetrics and Gynecology" (see Pioneer Medicine chapter).

Fuxing and Flag Raising Hill Rds at a Glance

#1 Fuxing Rd I've no idea what this aging yellow building used to be, but I like the 120-year-old tree (ficus microcarpa) growing right out of the wall.

#3 Fuxing Rd Note the exquisite gate of this early 20th century edifice opposite Fuxing church. It's now a government office.

Fuxing Church (Fuxing Tang, 复兴堂), a "Little Flock" church (read more in the Gulangyu churches chapter).

#4 Fuxing Rd Interesting gate, circa 1942.

#10 Fuxing Rd Unidentified but grand red brick building; interesting gate.

#47 Fuxing Rd Old Chinese home—one of few reminders that Gulangyu was Chinese's home long before Laowai showed up trading pigs 'n poison.

#75 Fuxing Rd Former home of American surgeon Clarence Holleman (Xialiwen, 夏礼文), 5th & 7th president of Hope Hospital. In 1957 he became head of Taipei's McKay Memorial Hospital （马偕纪念医院).

#77 Fuxing Rd Interesting columns and wooden shuttered windows on this two-storied yellow home.

#85 Fuxing Rd Nothing is visible but an overgrown gate shielding a walled-in jungle, but given the prestigious location, it must have stories to tell.

#96, 98 Fuxing Rd Bai Gewai residence & servants quarters, early 20th century (白格外宅).

Flag Hill Rd (The small lane to the left of Fuxing Church)

Li Qingquan Villa (李清泉别墅)—one of the most delightful estates.

第十七章 复兴路和升旗山路

前往复兴路 从鼓浪屿轮渡向左转，到鹿礁路，沿海边朝郑成功雕像方向走，穿过博爱医院，在鹿礁路和漳州路交汇处右转，这里有座三角屋。这条路在复兴堂路分为两叉，左为复兴路，右为福建路。复兴路往上是“中国现代妇产科之母”林巧稚纪念馆。（参见《医学先驱》一章）

复兴路和升旗山路一览

复兴路 1 号 我不知道这所老旧的黄房子以前是做什么用的，但我喜欢那棵长到墙外来的 120 年的老榕树。

复兴路 3 号 复兴堂对面这座 20 世纪初的建筑的精致的门楼值得留意，现为政府办公楼。

复兴堂是“小群教会”教堂(详情参阅《鼓浪屿教堂》一章)。

复兴路 4 号 门楼很有意思，约建于 1942 年。

复兴路 10 号 未经鉴定但很大气的红砖建筑，门楼很有意思。

复兴路 47 号 这座中国古宅提醒着中国人，在老外登陆此处贩卖鸦片和“猪仔”之前，鼓浪屿是中国人的家园。这样的建筑其实并不多。

复兴路 75 号 救世医院第五任、第七任院长，美国外科医生夏礼文的故居。1957 年夏礼文任台北马偕纪念医院的院长。

复兴路 77 号 两层的黄色建筑有很有意思的柱子和木制百叶窗。

复兴路 85 号 古老的大门，院内杂草丛生，除此之外，什么都看不到。但考虑到它坐落于显要位置，背后一定有番故事。

复兴路 96、98 号 白格外宅，建于 20 世纪初。

旧复兴堂 最初是在轮渡附近的一个“小群教会”教堂，详情参阅“鼓浪屿教堂”一章。

升旗山路 （复兴堂左面的一条小路）

李清泉别墅 鼓浪屿最令人赏心悦目的一处花园住宅。

Li Qingquan Villa (李清泉别墅), on Flag-Raising Hill to the left of Fuxing Church, is one of Gulangyu's most magnificent estates. Ascend the steps and enter the small side gate (traditionally, double gates were only for dignitaries).

After you get past the groundskeeper, note the "1926" inlaid into the sidewalk with pebbles. In 1926, lumber baron Li finished his 3-story mansion, with its towering columns reminiscent of "Gone With the Wind's" antebellum mansions.

He planted the four towering pines (Araucaria, 南洋杉), which can now be seen from across the bay on Xiamen, to show his 1st fortune came from lumber.

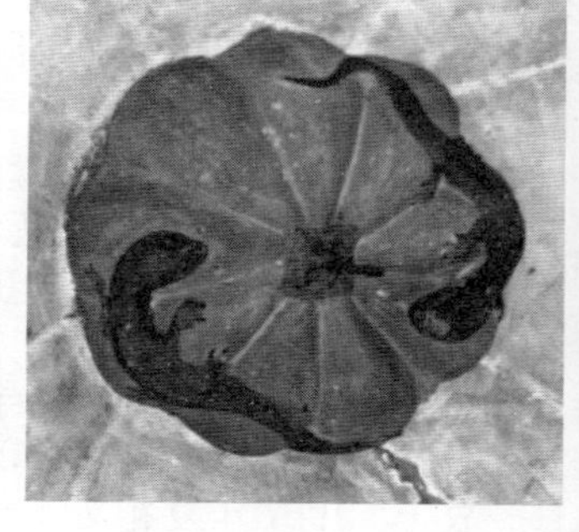

A central fountain dominates the villa's expansive garden, which includes barrel cacti. The cave-riddled concrete rockery is crowned by a Chinese gazebo with a delightful ornamental pumpkin and geckos in the ceiling. The rockery's peak gives a marvelous view of the bay and Xiamen's elevated Ring Road.

One can imagine the luxurious lifestyles led by rich Chinese and expats in the 20s and 30s as you take in the grandeur of the grounds, the towering columns, and the roaring '20s décor and furniture. The dining room ceiling fresco's bright pigments have not faded since applied with care back in 1926. No wonder film companies use the villa as a 20's period movie set.

李清泉别墅 位于升旗山路上，在复兴堂左面，是鼓浪屿最令人赏心悦目的花园住宅。拾级而上，沿侧门进入（中间的两扇门在古代只供贵族使用）。问候过看门人后，留意一下小道上用鹅卵石镶嵌的“1926”。这是这座三层建筑完工的年份。木材大王李清泉模仿电影“飘”中内战前高楼而建的。为纪念自己由木材生意起家，他种植了四棵南洋杉，现在它们已经长成参天大树，从对面的厦门岛就可看见。

Li Qingquan Villa

别墅有个大花园，中央是喷泉，以及成簇的仙人掌。迷宫似的土假山顶上是怡人的中式露台，饰以南瓜和壁虎的图案。登山顶极目远眺，厦门海湾和环岛路的迷人景色尽收眼底。

漫步园中，华丽的建筑、挺拔的廊柱和 20 年代的豪华家具装修风格，上世纪二三十年代中国富人和侨眷的生活便可略见一斑。

餐厅顶部的壁画颜料得益于 1926 年前后的保护而尚未剥落，难怪电影公司常把李清泉别墅作为20年代的背景拍摄地。

Lumber Baron Li Qingquan

Mr. Li, along with his father and brother, Li Zhaoyi and Li Zhaobei, moved from Jinjiang to Manila and started a lumber mill. In 1920, at the age of 32, Li Qingquan set up Manila's first commercial bank (马尼拉第一家私人商业银行——"中兴银行"). After becoming one of the Philippine's richest Chinese merchants, Li set up Xiamen's "Li Mingxing Real Estate Company".

Li invested millions of silver dollars in a landfill project, the Lujiang Road dike, and numerous real estate projects, including 6 buildings on Datong Road and Zhengbang Road, and 10 buildings on Zhongshan Road and Bishan Road. Some of the buildings were destroyed in the fire during the war against Japan.

In 1922, the politically and socially active Li established the "Radical Committee of Chinese Overseas in the Philippines". When the 19th Army mutinied in Fuzhou in November, 1933, and founded the "Chinese People's Revolutionary Government", Li collected 200,000 Yuan to support the fledgling government.

Li also tackled the infamous "Chinese Bookkeeping Act." On Feb. 21, 1921, the Philippines enacted a law requiring that bookkeeping be done only in English, Spanish, or one of the local dialects. The law was allegedly to stop Chinese firms from evading taxes, but in reality it was also an attempt to curb the growth of Chinese firms, which accounted for 60% of Philippines business (and most Chinese firms were too small to afford bookkeepers who knew English).

Li Qingquan led Chinese to disobey the law, and after appealing and losing in every Philippine court, he appealed to the U.S. Supreme Court, since the Philippines was a territory. Justice William Taft (later a president) ruled the law unconstitutional because it primarily targeted one class or race of people. Taft also praised the Philippine Chinese traders, whom he said could earn 100 pesos and save 150 pesos.

In Feb. 2005, I met journalist Wilson Lee Flores in Manila. His grandfather was 2nd cousin and best friend to Lee Qingquan, and is buried with Li in Manila's magnificent Chinese cemetery. Wilson's great grandfather and Lee Qingquan's grandfather were the closest of 7 brothers and are buried in one tomb. And Wilson's as feisty as his ancestors!

#15 Fuxing Rd. Bai Gecheng Residence and Servants Quarters, early 20th century. (白格外宅). In the 1850s an Anxi native, Bai Rui'an (白瑞安), began producing gold and silver foil in Xiamen, and later opened the Ruiji Bookstore (瑞记书店) and a publishing shop that produced "*Trimetric Classic*" (三字经), "*Thousand-word-articles*" (千字文), etc.

Bai Rui an changed the firm's name to "Cuijing Tang Publishing" (萃经堂), moved to #15 Fuxing Road, and printed Carstairs Douglas' famous "Dictionary of the Vernacular or Spoken Language of Amoy" (厦语注音字典) , as well as the hymnbook for Xinjie Church (China's 1st Protestant church). The business expanded further after passing on to Bai Rui'an's son, Bai Dengbi 白登弼, who became the first printer in Fujian to abandon hand-printing when he imported equipment from Britain and hired an expert from Hong Kong.

木材大王李清泉

李清泉早年与父亲李昭北一道从晋江移居马尼拉，并在那里开了一间木材厂。1920 年，32 岁的李清泉开设了马尼拉第一家私人商业银行“中兴银行”。李成为菲律宾最有钱的华商之一，之后他还在厦门还开办了李民兴房地产公司。

他还投资上百万银圆用于处理城市垃圾，开发修建了鹭江大堤以及许多房地产项目，其中包括大同路、镇邦路上的六处房产，中山路和碧山路上的十处房产，有些房子在抗日战火中被毁。

李清泉积极参与社会政治活动，在 1922 年成立了“菲律宾华人激进会”。1933 年 11 月，以 19 路军将领为首在福州发动并成立“中华共和国人民革命政府”，李筹措了 20 万元支持羽翼待丰的政府，他还出面解决了臭名昭著的“西文簿籍案”。

1921 年 2 月 21 日，菲政府出台法令，规定所有户口文档只用英文、西班牙文或当地文字记载。这部法令名义上是为了阻止中国商行逃税，实际上是要遏制已占菲律宾商业 60%份额的中国商行的继续增长。（大部分中国商行根本雇不起懂英文的会计。）

李清泉带领华人抵制该法，在菲律宾法庭屡诉屡败后，他上诉到美国最高法院，菲律宾当时是美国的殖民地。美国大法官威廉塔夫特（后来当选总统）当时判决此法无效，因为它主要针对某一特定阶层或种族。威廉塔夫特还称赞了菲律宾华商的勤俭节约作风，他说他们挣 100 比索能存 150 比索。

2005 年 2 月，我在马尼拉遇见记者威尔逊·李·劳伦斯(Wilson Lee Flores)。他祖父是李清泉的二堂兄兼好友，与李清泉合葬于华丽的马尼拉中国公墓。威尔逊的曾祖父和李清泉的祖父是七兄弟中关系最为密切的，也合葬一处。威尔逊和他的祖先一样个性鲜明，十分好辩。

复兴路 15 号　20 世纪初的白格外宅和下人房。1850 年，白格外是安溪人白瑞安的后人。白瑞安 1850 年在厦门开始生产金银纸箔，后来开了瑞记书店和一间出版社，出版《三字经》、《千字文》等书籍。

白瑞安后将出版社迁至复兴路 15 号，更名为“萃经堂”，出版了杜嘉德有名的《厦英大辞典》以及新街礼拜堂（中国第一座新教徒教堂）所用的赞美诗集。白瑞安的儿子白登弼接管父业后，生意更加兴隆，他从英国进口印刷机器，从香港请来专家，成为福建第一位摈弃了手工印刷的出版商。

In 1902, Bai Dengbi built the first of the Spanish-style homes on the west side of Flag Raising Hill (Shengqi Shan, 升旗山), and ten years later rented a similar building to foreigners, but Bai died of stomach disease only a couple years later, in 1914. His wife sold the printing business, which was moved to Xiamen Island's Galloping Horse Rd. (Da Zouma Lu, 大走马路), and the family survived on the two villas' rent until the children married and moved back into the villas. Bai Dengbi's offspring still live in the villas today.

Both buildings have long verandas in front and back, and simple arched windows. The gardens have such fruit trees as Dragon Eye and loquat, as well as holly, cypress, and lofty pine trees.

The original wicker windows have been replaced with glass, and electric lights have been installed. The iron hooks on the ceiling were for kerosene lanterns, as the area lacked electricity when the buildings were constructed.

#75 Fuxing Rd Former home of the 5th and 7th president of Hope Hospital (救世医院), the American surgeon Clarence Holleman (Xialiwen, 夏礼文). Built in 1947 on Flag Raising Hill (升旗山), this 1200 m^2 two storey home had reinforced concrete frames, a humidity barrier in the foundation, and elegant wooden floors. In 1957, Holleman took over Taipei's McKay Memorial Hospital (馬偕紀念醫院), where my wife Susan Marie was born in 1958! Read more in the "Gulangyu Medical Pioneers" chapter.

#83 Fuxing Rd.

#83 Fuxing Rd This white villa opposite the Lin Qiaozhi memorial belongs to Philippine Chinese Tan Tay Cuan (陈台村), whose firm Permex produces and exports canned fish. He's also the uncle of my friend Patrick Hsu, a coffee and cereal manufacturer whose ancestors owned vast tracts of Gulangyu. I'm waiting for Patrick to buy a fine villa for me to borrow on weekends!

Dr. Lin Qiaozhi Memorial – opposite #83. See Medical Pioneers chapter.

1902 年，白登弼在升旗山西面建起了第一座西班牙式家宅，十年后将一座风格相近的建筑出租给老外。1914 年时白死于胃病。他太太变卖了已搬迁到厦门岛大走马路的印刷社，全家人靠两栋别墅的租金生活，直到孩子成家后才搬回别墅。白登弼有个儿子白格外曾在荷兰安达银行厦门分行当华人经理，其后人现在仍居住于此。

两座别墅前后都有长长的走廊和古朴的拱窗。花园内种有龙眼、枇杷等果树，以及冬青树、柏树和高高的松树。

原来的柳条窗已经换成了玻璃窗，电灯也装上了（房子刚建好时，这个地区尚未通电，照明靠的是吊在天花板上的煤油灯）。

复兴路 75 号　约建于 1947 年，前救世医院第五任、第七任院长，美国外科医生夏礼文的故居。坐落在升旗山上占地 1200 平方米的这栋两层小楼的突出特点是用防潮的混凝土框架和精致的木地板。1957 年，夏礼文接管了台北的马偕纪念医院，我妻子苏珊就是 1958 年在那儿出生的！详见“鼓浪屿医学先驱”一章

Mr. Tan Tay Cuan (Tuna King!)

Dr Lin Qiaozhi Memorial

复兴路 83 号　林巧稚纪念堂对面的这座白色别墅的主人是菲律宾华侨陈台村，他的公司 PERMEX 生产并出口罐装鱼。我朋友帕特里克·苏 Patrick Hsu 是他的侄子。Patrick 是个咖啡、麦片商，祖先在鼓浪屿有大片地产。我盼着 Patrick 能买下一栋别墅，我好借来度周末！

林巧稚纪念堂　复兴路 83 号对面，请参见医学先驱一章。

Chapter 18
Guxin & Sanming Rds

"The great stream of Chinese emigration that flows and empties itself in might volume into the outer world finds its source in the two provinces of Fukien and Kwantung of South China.

"The Chinese are known in almost every land under the sun. Where other nationals can not live there they abide, opening mines and canals, building railroads which turn the deserts into blooming fields or prosperous towns and cities....A grand total of something like 10,000,000 of the Chinese abroad, and principally from the two provinces named....On an average about 65,000 leave Amoy annually..."

Pitcher, "In and about Amoy," 1912, p.159,160

Getting to Guxin Where on earth (or China?) is Guxin Rd? The easiest way to reach such Guxin Rd sites as Xiamen Museum and Yang Villa is to turn right where the Longtou Rd from the ferry crosses the Longtou Rd after the bookstore (not the Longtou **before** the bookstore, mind you, but the third Longtou Rd **after** the bookstore).

Confused? Join the crowd!

Gulangyu has many roads with the same name, intersecting one another and wreaking havoc with one's sense of direction. I suspect this is revenge against foreigners for wresting this beautiful islet from the Chinese and turning it into an international colonial settlement. As Confucius would have said had he been American, "Don't get mad, get even." The Chinese got even by giving so many roads the same name that the befuddled barbarians could not find their way home each night after a long day at the office pedaling pigs 'n poison. But never fear. It's a small island, so even wrong turns turn up unexpected delights.

After turning right from Longtou Rd onto Longtou Rd (**after** the bookstore), Longtou Rd will, without warning or due process of law, become Guxin Rd, which leads you past grand old villas and the Xiamen Museum, and then dumps you at Sanming Rd near the Hong Kong Bank Residence and the former U.S. Consulate, which I suspect Americans abandoned because they could never find it!

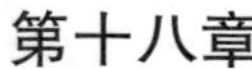

第十八章

鼓新路和三明路

“大量涌向海外的中国移民主要来自华南的福建及广东省。凡有阳光照耀之处总能看到中国人。别的民族不能居住的地方，他们安营扎寨，开矿挖井，兴修道路，变沙漠为沃土良田、繁华城镇……海外华侨总人数多达 1000 万，主要来自两个省份……每年平均有 65000 人离开厦门。”

选自毕腓力 1912 年著《厦门方志》第 159～160 页

走进鼓新路　鼓新路到底在中国的什么地方？想到鼓新路上的厦门博物馆和杨家园，最简单的办法就是在轮渡龙头路与位于书店后的龙头路的交汇处右拐（注意：此龙头路非书店前的龙头，而是书店后第三龙头路）

有点懵？跟着大伙走吧！

鼓浪屿上有许多同名的路，纵横交错得让你晕头转向。我想这是中国人对外国人的报复，抗议他们从自己手中抢走这座美丽的岛屿，还把它沦为国际殖民地。正如孔夫子言，如果他是个美国人，他会“以其人之道还治其人之身”。中国人以牙还牙的方式之一，就是设下许多名字相同的路，让这群野蛮的入侵者在研究了一整天如何贩卖鸦片和苦力之后，一筹莫展找不着回家的路。不过不用担心，鼓浪屿是个小岛，即使转错了路说不定还会是个意想不到的新乐趣。

从龙头路向右拐到龙头路（书店后的），没有任何告示，或是应有的法律程序，龙头路就变成了鼓新路。沿着这条路走，会经过许多老别墅和厦门博物馆，走到汇丰公馆和前美国领事馆附近，鼓新路又换成了三明路。我怀疑美国人当初弃领事馆不用，很可能是因为他们老是迷路。

Guxin Rd. & Sanming Rd. at a Glance

#18 Guxin Rd. Xu (许) Family Residence (Philippine Chinese).

#24 Guxin Rd Little White House (one of my favorites)

#40 Guxin Rd Former "Taili" company building，1903 (原泰利公司—船头行).

#42 Guxin Rd Huang Yizhu Villa (Huang Yizhu Huayuan 黄奕住花园), originally an Englishman's home but bought and renovated in 1919 by Indonesian Overseas Chinese Mr. Huang Yizhu.

#43 Guxin Rd 8 Diagrams Bldg./Xiamen Museum (Bagua Lou, 八卦楼). Designed by missionary doctor/architect John Otte; built in 1907.

#48 Guxin Rd Huang Mansion ("Ship House"); supposedly designed by American John Otte.

#54 Guxin Rd Philippine Overseas Chinese former residence, early 20th century.

#60 Guxin Rd Maritime Affairs Residence (理船厅公所)

#67 Guxin Rd Lin Zumi's Former home (林祖密) Lin was from Zhanghua, Taiwan（台湾，彰化）

#82 Guxin Rd Former Hope Hospital

#26 Sanming Rd Former U.S. Consulate (Meiguo Lingshiguan 美国领事馆). It is now a hotel.

#24 Guxin Rd Little White House Chinese guidebooks skip this home but I like it because it reminds me of a small White House, with its curved central balconies, tall, graceful columns, and rooftop balustrades (I can almost imagine the secret service patrolling the roof). I also like the scraggly but lush garden, awash in such tropical fruit as loquats, mangoes and papayas. For the best photo, stand on the ledge by the electrical transformer across the street—and take a few photos of the locals who stare at you and ask what on earth you're doing up there.

鼓新路和三明路一览

鼓新路 18 号——许宅（菲律宾华侨）
鼓新路 24 号——小白宫（我的最爱之一）
鼓新路 40 号——原泰利公司船头行，建于 1903 年
鼓新路 42 号——黄奕住花园，原为英国人住宅，1919 年印尼华人黄奕住买下并翻修
鼓新路 43 号——八卦楼/厦门博物馆，由传教士、设计师郁约翰设计，始建于 1907 年
鼓新路 48 号——黄宅（“船屋”），据说由美国人郁约翰设计
鼓新路 54 号——民居，菲律宾华侨 20 世纪初建造
鼓新路 60 号——理船厅公所
鼓新路 67 号——台湾彰化人**林祖密故居**
鼓新路 82 号——前救世医院
三明路 26 号——原美国领事馆，在这过夜吧，因为现在这里已经是宾馆了！

鼓新路 24 号 小白宫 所有导游手册上都没有介绍，但我喜欢这儿，因为它有弯曲的中央露台，高大气派的廊柱及屋顶的扶栏（我甚至可以想像顶层有内仆在走动），让我觉得像座微型白宫。我还喜欢它那高低有致、枝繁叶茂的花园，就好像淹没在枇杷、芒果和木瓜等水果中。街对面的变电站边是拍照的最佳位置，顺便给好奇的行人来几张，他们会纳闷儿地追问你到底在倒腾些什么。

#42 Guxin Rd Huang Yizhu Villa (黄奕住花园), originally an Englishman's home, was bought and renovated in 1919 by Indonesian Overseas Chinese Mr. Huang Yizhu (黄奕住).

#43 Guxin Rd Eight Diagrams Building (Bagua Lou, 八卦楼). This red-domed building at the foot of Brushholder Hill (Bijia Shan, 笔架山) is now the Xiamen Museum and Organ Museum and gets its name from the eight sectioned dome and octagonal foundation.

Bagua Lou was built in the 33rd year of Guangxu in the Qing Dynasty (the Chinese' barbarian-befuddling way of saying 1907). Credit (or blame) for the fanciful but fatally expensive design goes to John Otte (郁约翰), dean of Hope Hospital (which he also designed). Lin Heshou donated 1,000 silver Yuan to Hope, and the versatile Dr. Otte, who also had a degree in civil engineering, volunteered his architectural skills—and promptly impoverished his benefactor!

The Prince or the Pauper

The imposing Bagua Building was not a Western power's consulate but the fanciful creation of Mr. Lin Heshou (林鹤寿), a wealthy Taiwanese cousin of Lin Erjia who had less sense than cents—and in the end lacked cents as well.

After Taiwan was handed over to the Japanese, Lin Heshou fled to Gulangyu and founded the Jianxiang Private Bank. Heshou was not exactly a model of modesty, and he set out to build a villa with a view—and one befitting Gulangyu royalty. But the exotic ten-year project required such expensive materials that Heshou had to continually sell off properties to finance the construction. Eventually, the bankrupted Heshou hightailed it back to Taiwan as pauper, not prince, and never returned. The grounds became overgrown, swallows nested in the eaves, and the building was rumored to be haunted by a worker who had fallen to his death during the building's construction.

鼓新路 42 号黄奕住花园 最初是个英国人的住宅，1919 年被印尼华侨黄奕住买下并翻修。

鼓新路 43 号八卦楼 笔架山下的这座红顶建筑现为厦门博物馆和管风琴博物馆，因底部及屋顶的八角形状而得名。

八卦楼始建于清光绪 33 年（这是中国人的说法，蛮夷之辈听了就蒙，其实就是 1907 年）。救世医院院长郁约翰担纲设计（救世医院也是他设计的），对于这座构思奇特，但造价不菲的建筑，后人褒贬不一。林鹤寿捐资了 1000 银圆给救世医院，多才多艺、拥有土木工程学位的郁约翰博士，便志愿贡献其建筑才华，很快也让恩人钱财散尽。

王子还是贫民

这座气势雄伟的八卦楼并不是西方列强的领事馆，而是林鹤寿先生的奇思妙想之作。林是个台湾富商，是林尔嘉的堂弟。他的钱财比脑子多——最终也是钱财散尽。

台湾被日本占领后，林鹤寿逃亡到鼓浪屿并开设了“建祥钱庄”。鹤寿并非谦逊之辈，他决定建造一座与鼓浪屿的皇家气质相称的景观别墅。但这个设计奇特，耗时十年的大工程所需的建材都十分昂贵，他不得不变卖家产来保证施工运转。最后，破产的鹤寿只得撤回台湾再没有回来。那时的他已成贫民，不再是王子了。之后，他终生未回鼓浪屿。从此，工地上杂草丛生，燕子在檐下作窝，一片荒芜。又有谣传说，大楼在施工时摔死了一个工人，冤魂不散，经常闹鬼。

Otte incorporated many ancient middle Eastern, Roman, Greek and Chinese styles and techniques into this unusual building. The red octagonal dome, for instance, was inspired by a Palestinian mosque's dome. The crosspieces resembled those in a temple in Athens. The 82 round pillars were reminiscent of the great stone pillars of a 5th century A.D. structure. The ornamented Greek columns and the design inside the four entrances were of an ancient style that had been adopted by the Vatican.

Alas, this grand edifice eventually fell into the very hands of those that Lin Heshou had fled to Gulangyu to escape. The Japanese viewed Gulangyu as their private estate, and in 1924 hung upon the gate a Japanese sign, Xuying Study 旭瀛书院. During the war with Japan, the house was again abandoned and became a refugee asylum.

After the war, the government confiscated Bagua Lou as an "enemy possession", and until Liberation used it as Xiamen University's department of freshman literature.

By 1949, the magnificent palace-cum-haunted house was in shambles, the victim of age, neglect, and vandalism (the floor boards and precious sandalwood had been hauled off). The government rebuilt Bagua Lou and used it as the Luchao Art School 鹭潮美术学校 (today, the Provincial Crafts School). In 1958, Bagua Lou was taken over by the city's Science Committee and was used as the base for a Chinese Medicine School. The building then became a factory for producing capacitors, and towards the end of the 1960s the government remodeled Bagua Lou and in March 1983, it became the Xiamen Museum. The 2,000m^2, 26.6 meter high three-storey villa is now the Organ Museum.

#48 Guxin Rd Ship House A Gulangyu guidebook says Hope Hospital's Doctor Huang Dapi (黄大辟) asked John Otte to design this home, but since Otte died in 1910 I don't see how he could have—unless he designed it long before his death.

Otte was admired for his aesthetic designs and the Huang Mansion was no exception, combining both Chinese and American features in a manner that harmonized with its environs.

郁约翰在设计这座非同一般的建筑时融合了古中东、罗马、希腊和中国的风格和建筑技巧。比如，红色的八角屋顶就是受巴勒斯坦清真寺圆顶建筑的启发，横档则是仿造雅典神庙。82 根圆柱秉承了公元 5 世纪建筑结构中的大石柱风格，希腊饰柱及四进内设计则是梵蒂冈古建筑样式的再现。

可惜的是，这座豪宅最终还是落到了日本人手里。想当初林鹤寿就是为了躲避日本人才逃到鼓浪屿的。日本人把鼓浪屿视为他们的私人地盘，1924 年的时候，他们在门口挂上了“旭瀛书院”的牌子。抗战期间，房子又被遗弃，成了难民所。

战争结束后八卦楼作为“敌产”被政府没收，解放前一直作为厦门大学文学院的新生院。1949 年时，由于年代久远、疏于管理以及人为的破坏，这座宏伟的宫殿兼鬼屋已摇摇欲坠（许多地板和珍贵檀香木都已损毁）。之后，政府重修八卦楼，创办鹭潮美术学校（即现在的省工艺美术学校）。1958 年，厦门市科委迁入，并办了中医学校。之后，八卦楼成为电容厂。60 年代末政府翻建楼体，1983 年拨作厦门博物馆。这座三层别墅现高 26.6 米，底层占地 2000 平方米，内设管风琴博物馆。

鼓新路 48 号 船屋 据鼓浪屿导游手册介绍，船屋是救世医院医生黄大辟请郁约翰设计的，但郁约翰逝于 1910 年，我不知道他怎么能够设计呢——除非他在生前早就设计好了。

郁约翰建筑审美观独特，黄宅的设计也不例外，中、美建筑风格和谐统一，浑然天成。

The 400m^2 4-storey brick and concrete mansion stands upon a triangular foundation and is nicknamed "Ship House" because it resembles a ship headed out to sea. To heighten the ship-effect and improve light and ventilation, the walls are joined at a 135 degree angle and two rows of windows resemble those of a navigation tower. Window blinds and wide front corridors tastefully complement the red bricks, and both house and furniture are of fine woods. The wide floor planks are of nanmu (楠木), a giant evergreen from West China's Yunnan and Sichuan), and much of the furniture is of Thai Rosewood (酸枝, Dalbergia cochinchinensis).

Gulangyu Foreigners Sink a Well

Water supply was a perennial problem on Gulangyu, so the Ship House's fourth floor reservoir stored rain water. Nowadays, Gulangyu's water is piped in from Xiamen and the Ship House reservoir is a backup. The Huang house is also unusual in its modern and complete bathroom facilities. Because of water shortages, many of even the finest Gulangyu homes used only chamber pots, or outhouses.[1] Below is an account of the International Settlement's 1910 attempt to sink an Artesian well.

> "At a special meeting of the ratepayers of the International Settlement held on the 22nd of November, 1910, it was unanimously decided to construct an Artesian well... The primitive method of sinking this well was most interesting. A scaffold, some fifteen or twenty feet high with a long sweep made of a dozen or more bamboo poles and securely bound at one end to the scaffolding, and nicely tapered at the other so as to afford great elasticity (forming a most powerful spring); and a wheel about ten feet in diameter, which was used to wind up the drilling apparatus when necessary, formed the mechanical arrangement by which the work was done.
>
> "A drill, composed of long strips of split bamboo, strongly bound together at the joints with iron bands, and having a three pronged heavy steel punch at the end, was attached to the long sweep and then manipulated in a twisting grinding fashion by hand. The process was exceedingly slow. On account of rock, some days only three inches were bored. Dynamite was used to some extent, but from the time of starting on December 19th 1910 to June 15th 1911 only 130 feet and 3 inches had been bored. More than 50 feet of this was right down thro solid flint-like rock....on June 15th all work on the well was finally abandoned...the problem of a water supply for this island settlement still remains unsolved."

Pitcher, *In and about Amoy*, 1912, p. 260

黄宅占地 400 平方米，为四层砖混结构，坐落在三角形的地基上，因形似一艘待发的大船，故得名“船屋”。为强化船形效果和增加光透性，郁约翰把墙壁夹角建成 135 度，增开了两排窗，看起来更像一座领航塔。百叶窗和宽大的前廊与清水红砖相映成趣，房屋主体和屋内家居均选用上好木材。宽宽的地板条是用中国云南、四川产的常绿树楠木打造而成的，家具大多采用泰国酸枝木。

鼓浪屿老外挖井

供水是长期困扰鼓浪屿的一个问题，所以船屋在第四层设了个可储存雨水的池子。现在岛上供水主要来自厦门，水池便留做备用。黄宅现代化一应俱全的卫生间设施也令人赞叹。由于缺水，鼓浪屿上许多上好的人家也只能使用罐子盛水或户外厕所。下面马上要讲的便是 1910 年的国际居民怎样试图挖一口自流井。

“1910 年 11 月 22 日召开了一次国际移民纳税人特别会议，大家一致同意打一口自流井……最初的办法很有意思：一个高约 15～20 英尺的支架，一根用一打多竹棍紧扎成的长长的笤帚，一头牢牢系在支架上，另一头削尖，这样就可以产生巨大的弹力（形成一个有力的弹簧）。还有一个直径约 10 英尺的轮子，必要时可卷起挖井工具。这些就是挖井用的全部家当了。

“把一捆劈开了的细竹条，用铁丝牢牢地捆住，一头用重钢钉凿出三叉，这便是钻头，把钻头绑在扫把上，用手来回扭动，工程进度非常缓慢。碰上岩石时，好几天也只能挖 3 英寸，有些时候还得用炸药碎石。从 1910 年 12 月 19 日动工到 1911 年 6 月 15 日只掘了 130 英尺 3 英寸，另外还有 50 多英尺在青石板似的岩石下……6 月 15 日人们最终放弃了继续挖掘的计划，岛上缺水的问题还是没有解决。”

——毕腓力 1912 年著《厦门方志》第 260 页

The Huang Family's Medical and Musical Legacy Huang Dapi's son, Huang Zhende (黄祯德), was also a doctor and a former head of Hope Hospital, and his grandson, Huang Yunxi (黄孕西) is a thoracic surgeon. The Huangs are also a family of music lovers. Three generations have received excellent music training and perfected their skills in the well-lighted drawing room that serves as the recital hall for both family and guest musicians and singers.

The family frequently holds weekend recitals, and in 1988, when the American Chinese embassy's cultural counselor visited Gulangyu, the Ship House's drawing room was chosen to hold a formal family recital. Since then, the Huang family has held many recitals for visiting foreign dignitaries, and for several domestic and foreign TV channels.

#60 Guxin Rd Maritime Affairs Residence (理船厅公所). Xiamen established its Custom's Office in 1683 and by 1725 was Fujian's #1 port. In 1883, Xiamen Customs bought an old seaside house on Gulangyu in Sanqiutian（三丘田）for work and residence, and renovated it in 1914. The 4087m^2 grounds were bordered by a cemetery to the west, a wireless station to the north, and Lin's Home to the South.

This striking 3-story red brick and white granite building, with its three long corridors, numerous arches, and parapet, was designed by an Englishmen and consists of the main structure and an attached annex.

#67 Guxin Rd Lin Zumi (林祖密) from Zhanghua, Taiwan （台湾，彰化), moved to Gulangyu in 1904 and was the first Chinese to regain Chinese nationality after the Republican Revolution of 1911. Lin joined the Chinese Revolutionary Party and conducted revolutionary activities in S. Fujian. Dr. Sun Yatsen promoted him to Major General but he was assassinated by a local warlord's gunmen in 1925.

黄家的医学、音乐遗产　黄大辟之子黄祯德也是位医生，曾任救世医院院长；孙子黄孕西是胸外科医生。黄氏也是音乐世家，三代人都接受过严格的音乐训练并常在灯火通明的画室与前来做客的音乐家、歌唱家一起举办演奏会，技艺日臻娴熟。

黄家周末常举办演奏会。1988 年，美国驻华文化参赞访问鼓浪屿，船屋画室被选中，用于举办一场正式的家庭演奏会。打那儿以后，黄家为来访的外国政要以及国内外电视台举办、录制了多场演奏会。

鼓新路 60 号　理船厅公所。厦门 1683 年设海关署，1725 年成为“闽海关第一口岸”。1883 年，厦门海关在鼓浪屿三丘田购置了一座海边旧屋作办公和宿舍之用，并于 1914 年进行了翻修。4087 平方米的占地西拥墓地，北临无线电台，南靠林宅。

这座抢眼的红砖白玉三层建筑有三个长廊及许多拱门、栏杆，包含了主体及附楼，设计者是个英国人。

鼓新路 67 号　　台湾彰化人林祖密故居。他 1904 年搬来鼓浪屿，是 1911 年辛亥革命后第一位重获中国国籍的中国人。林加入中国革命党并在闽南从事革命活动。孙中山先生提升他为大将军，但 1925 年他不幸被当地军阀的手下暗杀。

Mr. Lin Zumi (Hong Buren)

Sanming Rd 三明路

"T. Hart Hyatt, the very able first American consul at Amoy, shows by his reports to Washington that at one time he was more than $4,600 out of pocket because of funds advanced for consular maintenance expenses, jail rent, and feeding of prisoners. He reported that his rental expenses and maintenance for himself and his family exceeded by about $2,000 every year his total income from salary and authorized consular fees collected.

"...Thomas G. Peachy, a Virginian, was named consul at Amoy in 1844 but never occupied the post. There was no provision of any kind for a salary or for consular expenses, so for nearly five years the United States had no consul at Amoy." Abend, "Treaty Ports," 1944

#26 Sanming Rd Former U.S. Consulate (Meiguo Lingshiguan 美国领事馆) Brits barged into Amoy in 1841 and we Americans were right on their tail, setting up an office for consular affairs in 1844. The first U.S. consulate was built in 1865 but destroyed by a fire in 1905. A 6,300 m^2 consulate was built in 1930 with red bricks from the U.S.

The Japanese closed the consulate on December 8th, 1941. It was reopened after the war but in 1948 U.S. affairs were transferred to the Shanghai consulate and the building was rented out as the Philippine consulate. After liberation, the former U.S. consulate was used as a sanatorium, and in October 1979 it became the Fujian Provincial Oceanographic Research Institute. The Chinese Ministry of Foreign Affairs took over the building in 1992, and today it is Jinquan Villa—so spend the night in style.

Note: the former Hope Hospital is just up the coastal Yanping Rd

Pitcher, 1912
U.S. Consulate

三明路

“哈特·海亚特是美国首任驻华领事，他非常能干，在给华盛顿的报告中，他曾提到自掏腰包 4600 美元用于支付领事馆的各项费用，如维修费用、监狱租金、供养犯人的开销等，他报告说，他的工资加上领事馆的官方收入还不足以维持他和家人的生活起居，每年他都要超支 2000 美元。”

“维吉尼亚人汤姆斯· 皮切 1844 年被任命为继任领事，但从未真正上任。因为没有配给薪金或其他领事费用到任，所以之后将近五年的时间，美国在厦门没有领事。”

——Abend 1944 年著《港口条约》

三明路 26 号　前美国领事馆。1841 年英国人闯上鼓浪屿，我们美国人紧随其后，在 1844 年设立领事处，第一座美国领事馆建于 1865 年，但毁于 1905 年的一场大火。1930 年用来自美国本土的红砖重修了一座面积为 6300 平方米的领事馆。

1941 年 12 月 8 号日本关闭了该领事馆，战后重新开放。但 1948 年后，所有美国事务均移交上海领事馆，原址出租给菲律宾领事馆。解放后，前美国领事馆辟为疗养院，1979 年 10 月成为福建省海洋研究所。1992 年，中国外交部接管。如今，它已经变成金泉宾馆——那就在这住一晚，摆摆排场吧！

注：沿海边的道路往上就是前救世医院。

Former U.S. Consulate

Chapter 19
Anhai Rd

#4 Anhai Rd

Anhai Road, on the slope of Brush Stand Hill (Bijia Shan, 笔架山), has some of Gulangyu's more delightful architecture, including Trinity Church (one of the best in China) and the Foreign Mother-in-law mansion. But Anhai Road itself is an absolute maze!

At half a dozen intersections Anhai Lu goes off in every direction but up, because the name Anhai Rd. is given to several large and small streets and alleys. Fortunately, most major intersections have bilingual (Chinese/English) signs pointing tourists in the general direction of major sites.

#56 Anhai Rd.

Anhai Rd at a Glance

#4 Anhai Rd Yang Villa (Yangjia Yuan, 杨家园).

#71 Anhai Rd Trinity Church (Sanyi Tang, 三一堂)

#34 Anhai Rd West European Bldg., circa 1897

#36 Anhai Rd Foreign Lady Villa (Fanpo Lou, 番婆楼); one of islet's three best estate gates.

#55 Anhai Rd Pleasant Garden (Yiyuan, 宜园 1930s).

#56 Anhai Rd Delightful triangular yellow home

Getting to Anhai From the ferry turn right and follow the coast on Yanping Road, past Xiamen Undersea World. Make a left on Fuzhou Road, jog left on Guxin Road, and Anhai Road is the first right, just past Yang Villa. And this Anhai will of course lead you to the half dozen other Anhai Roads!

第十九章

安 海 路

安海路位于笔架山的斜坡上，拥有鼓浪屿上最令人赏心悦目的建筑。这些建筑包括三一堂（被认为是国内最好的教堂之一）和番婆楼。但是安海路又是一条错综复杂的路。因为安海路是一系列大街小巷的统称，所以安海路上有五六个交叉路口，这些路口可以通往岛上任何地方。庆幸的是大多数的交叉路口都有中英双语的路标，这些路标可以把游客指引到岛上的主要景点。

安海路一览

安海路 4 号　杨家园
安海路 71 号　三一堂
安海路 34 号　西欧小筑，大约建于 1897 年
安海路 36 号　番婆楼，鼓浪屿三大门楼之一
安海路 55 号　宜园，建于 20 世纪 30 年代
安海路 56 号　漂亮的三角形黄色房子

前往安海路　出了码头，沿着海岸往右一直走到延平路，经过海底世界，上福州路后往左转，到鼓新路后往左走，过了杨家园后右边的第一条路就是安海路。从这条安海路可以进入另外的五六条安海路。

#4 Anhai Rd Yang Villa (Yangjia Yuan, 杨家园), the sprawling 4 building complex at the corner of Anhai Rd. and Guxin Rd. (安海路和鼓新路), was built around 1913 by two Philippine overseas Chinese, Yang Zhongquan of Longxi (龙溪) and Yang Qitai.

At age 14, Yang went to the Philippines with his uncle to help start the Iron Works Company (Tieye Gongsi, 铁业公司).

In July 1913, Yang bought an old residence on Brush Stand Hill from the London Missionary Society and renovated it under the guidance of a Chinese designer. Yang Zhongquan died in 1932, and in 1989 his descendants returned from overseas, reclaimed the villas, and renamed them Zhongquan Building in honor of their ancestor.

I was embarrassed when my friend, the photographer Mr. Bai Hua, waltzed right into the house, where folks were eating, washing their hair, sleeping, watching TV. But no one minded. It turned out this was Bai Hua's childhood home before he left to seek his fortune in HK.

Yang Villa Servants' Alleys

Bai Hua showed me around the 4 houses, which used to be interconnected with narrow walled alleys used by the army of invisible servants toting provisions or nightsoil (many Gulangyu homes lacked toilets, so the "nightsoil man" emptied chamber pots daily).

The Yang family, more than most, were careful to keep masters and servants separate. Servants and "little wives" (all but the 1st wife) used small "servants' doors" and under no conditions used the main entrance. (An upstairs room has photos of the owner flanked by his four wives).

Mr. Yang and his 4 wives

安海路 4 号：杨家园，位于安海路和鼓新路交汇处的连在一起的 4 栋房子就是杨家园，它是菲律宾华侨、祖籍龙溪的杨忠权和杨启泰于 1913 年修建。

杨忠权 14 岁即随伯父去菲律宾创办铁业公司。

1913 年 7 月，杨忠权从伦敦差会手中买下笔架山麓的一栋老房子，并请了一名中国设计师指导翻新。杨忠权死于 1932 年，1989 年他的子孙从海外回来办理了房产继承手续，并把别墅命名为“忠权楼”，以示对先人的纪念。

我的朋友白桦先生，他是一位摄影师。我和他进入别墅时，居住在里面的乡亲们有的在吃饭，有的在洗头，有的在睡觉，有的在看电视。我觉得有点唐突，但是他们都不介意。原来白桦的童年就在这里度过的，在去香港发展之前他一直住在这里。白桦带我参观了这 4 栋房子，过去它们之间由狭窄的小巷连在一起。仆人们通过这些小巷搬运粮食（或者粪便，鼓浪屿的许多房子都没有厕所，每天掏粪工人都会把夜壶清空）。

比起其他家庭来说，杨家的主仆分得很清。仆人、小老婆（大老婆以外的妻子都叫小老婆）只能走“下人专用的小门”，不允许从正门进出。（楼上其中一个房间挂了一幅房屋建立者的照片，他的四个老婆的照片分列左右）。

Anhai #4 Yang Family Villa

Yang Villa is also known for its columns, unique windows, and interior teak floors. The complex's smaller auxiliary cooking and storage facilities and servants' quarters were all built of coarser materials to make sure the servants remembered their place.

Yang Villa Reservoir System

Bai Hua grew up in these houses, but still showed endless delight in pointing out their intricately carved windows. "I've photographed hundreds of windows," he enthused. But he complained about the massive trees he played upon as a child, "They should trim them so we can see Sunlight Rock! It's becoming a jungle!"

With water a scarce commodity, in spite of Koxinga's legendary well, Gulangyu folk captured every drop of rain. Flat roofs' funneled precious rainwater down each level to massive reservoirs under spacious porches, assuring a plentiful year-round supply of water for residents and gardens. Most villas had wells or rain collecting systems (or both), But the Yang water system was one of the island's best. The villa was also unique in that it had a bomb-proof underground bunker. It did little to fend off Japanese invaders but it may well have given Mr. Yang some respite from his four feuding wives.

#34 Anhai Rd Former Trinity Council Building This small building, built in 1897, was originally a residence for the Trinity Council (三工会), which was established by three different denominations working together. This council established the Sino-British School (Yinghua Shuyuan, 英华书院). In 1909, Wang Ziheng (王子恒), from Longhai's Zhuoqi Village (卓岐村,港尾,龙海), bought this building from Zheng Bonian (郑柏年) and it has been a residence ever since.

Wang Ziheng is a rags-to-riches story if there ever was one! An uneducated ferryman in Zhuoqi Village, in his youth he moved to Vietnam and saved his pennies to go into the rice business. After making a bundle he returned home and built the largest and most beautiful house in Zhuoqi Village. But even though he tried to help develop his impoverished home by helping to build roads and bridges and giving to charitable causes, some locals begrudged his success, so he moved to the wealthy international enclave on Gulangyu Island, which had a uniquely democratic outlook on money. Gulangyu welcomed and protected all peoples, regardless of race—provided you were rich!

这几栋别墅最显著的特征是它们的柱子、独特的窗子、室内的柚木地板。除了这 4 栋别墅外，杨家园还有几栋矮小的附属建筑，如厨房、储物间和佣人的住所。这些小房子用料比较粗糙，像是提醒仆人们不要忘记他们的身份。

虽然白桦是在这些房子里长大的，指着那些雕刻精细的窗子，他还是显出无尽的喜悦。他充满激情地说："我已经拍了数百张窗户的照片了！"他指着那片小时候玩耍过的树丛，抱怨说他们应该把树木修剪成原来的样子，那样就可以看到日光岩，现在简直成了一片森林！

#44 Anhai Rd. (1932)

尽管有极富传奇的国姓井，水依然是鼓浪屿上的稀缺品。鼓浪屿上的居民发明了各种方法，试图不漏掉一滴雨水。水平屋顶上的水槽把珍贵的雨水积蓄起来，一层一层，把水引到宽阔的门廊下巨大的蓄水池里，常年如此，就有了充足的水资源储备，保证居民和花园用水。尽管绝大多数别墅要不有井，要不有收集雨水的装置，甚至是二者兼有，杨家园的供水系统被认为是岛上最好的。最后一点与众不同的是，杨家园楼房底层建有避弹室。然而日本人入侵鼓浪屿后，这个防空掩体似乎不能提供任何保护（之前对于长期不和的妻妾也许起了相当程度的缓解作用）。

安海路 34 号　原三公会所。这栋小房子建于 1897 年，最初是给三公会办公用的。三公会是由三个不同派别的布道团体创立的。这个公会还创办了英华书院。1909 年，龙海卓岐村人王子恒从郑柏年手中买下这栋楼，此后就成了民居。

如果真有其人的话，王子恒演绎了一个从乞丐到富翁的传奇梦。他没有上过学，原为卓岐村的渡工，年轻时去了越南。他攒下辛苦赚来的每一分钱，后来转做大米生意，终于发家致富。回家后，他在卓岐建造了当地最大最漂亮的房子。即使他通过修路、建桥和热心参与慈善事业来帮助家乡发展，王子恒的财富还是招来不少乡亲的嫉妒。于是，他搬到富裕的公共租界——鼓浪屿。鼓浪屿对金钱表现出特殊的民主，它欢迎并保护所有的有钱人，不管他的种族。

Five generations of Wangs have come and gone in this home, and Wang Ziheng's 100+ descendants are now scattered around China and abroad, and largely engaged in education and science.

The former Trinity Council Building is a modest two-floor western-style building, with wooden floors of fir, and shuttered doors and windows. Each of the three 20m^2 rooms had a fireplace, but the most distinctive feature was the pinkish exterior, and the doors' and windows' slanting wicker grills, which shielded the interior from wind, rain and sun, but allowed ventilation. Locals boast that this is the only house in China with this unique grillwork.

#36 Anhai Rd Foreign Lady Villa (Fanpo Lou, 番婆楼) This two-story red-brick French villa was built in 1927 by Xu Jingquan (许经权), a Philippine Chinese from Jinjiang (just up the coast from Xiamen).

#36 Anhai Rd. Fan Po Villa

The Foreign Lady Villa has been the setting for several movies, including "Earthen House Family" (土楼人家) and "Liao Zhongkai" (廖仲恺).

Why the name? Xu Jingquan's mother accompanied him to the Philippines but she could not get used to life overseas, so Xu built her a villa on Gulangyu rather than in their ancestral home of Jinjiang. In addition to the villa and servants quarters, he built a drama stage in the front yard and invited opera troupes to perform for his mother.

Xu's brothers and sisters also doted on their mother, buying her so many fine clothes and so much jewelry that she looked more like a rich woman from South Asia than a South Fujianese—hence the neighbors' nickname for her, "Foreign Grandmother," and name for the villa.

As befitting the "Foreign Lady", the villa has the largest gate on the island. The carved canaries with coins in their mouth depict the family's wealth, and the characters for good fortune on the iron doors represent the family's wish to have good fortune whether going in or coming out. The fine calligraphy on the wall was destroyed during the Cultural Revolution.

No expense was spared, inside or out. The doorframes and window frames are of white marble; the walls have numerous paintings of flowers and angels. The bas-reliefs below the eaves depict such Chinese tales as "Golden Monkey Presents the Peach" and "Four Chinese Beauties."

如今，王家五代人在此出生，又走出了这栋房子。王子恒的子孙已逾百人，分散在海内外，大多从事科教事业。

原三公会所是一栋不大的两层楼的西洋风格建筑，室内铺杉木地板，门窗均装百页。这栋房子有三间 20 平方米大的房间，室内均有壁炉。这栋房子最与众不同的是，外墙刷有红粉，前门和窗户上全部使用柳条木斜格装饰。这些柳条木可以避风、挡雨和遮阳，且能通风。当地人说这是中国唯一一栋柳条木斜格装饰的房子。

安海路 36 号　番婆楼。这栋两层结构红砖法式风格别墅是许经权于 1927 年建造的。许经权是晋江籍菲律宾华侨（晋江与厦门邻近）。

包括《土楼人家》和《廖仲恺》在内的好几部电影都选用了番婆楼作为外景。

为什么取这样的名字呢？许经权的母亲随他一起去菲律宾，但是她不习惯海外生活。许经权选择在鼓浪屿，而不是他的祖居地晋江为母亲建了一栋别墅。除了这栋别墅和仆人的住所外，他还在前院搭建一座戏台，经常请来戏班，为其母唱戏。

许经权的兄弟姐妹也都十分孝敬母亲，给母亲买了非常多高档服装和各式首饰。这样一来，许母与其说是闽南人，更像是一位南洋富婆。街坊邻居都称她“番婆”，别墅的名字就是这样得来的。

为了适合老太太居住，番婆楼的门是岛上最大的。嘴里衔着铜钱的金丝鸟雕塑显示房屋主人的富有，刻上好运等字的铁门表明这个家庭希望进出家门都能好运相随。但是墙上非常优美的书法在“文革”期间被毁了。

番婆楼里里外外的装饰，主人都毫不吝啬。门框和窗架是用白色大理石做的，墙上满是各种花和天使的漆画。屋檐下的浮雕描绘了“金猴献桃”和“四大美女”等中国传统故事。

#38 Anhai Rd.

All doorframes and window frames are made of white marble. The villa also had a well, Dragon Hole Well (Longkeng Jing, 龙坑井) which has since been plugged. The "Foreign Lady's" descendants still live in this villa, which has also been borrowed by various departments for offices.

#55 Anhai Rd Bell Mansion (时钟楼), aka Pleasant Garden (Yiyuan, 宜园). The Bell Mansion was built during the 20s or 30s, supposedly by a rich businessman named Chen with a surplus of wives—hence the large number of rooms. The mansion's western style is said to resemble the former American Consulate, and is noted for its unique pillars, its use of colored granite, and the ornate bas-reliefs, particularly on the third floor. The dwelling also has a small garden with various fruit and shade trees.

In 1933, an overseas Chinese, Yang Peihe (杨丕河), purchased the building but never stayed there himself, letting his relatives use it instead. Yang Peihe died soon after liberation and the government took over. It was used first as a private residence for several families, and later as a health office and police station. After the police built an office on Bishan Mountain, the home was returned to Yang's four sons, who today are businessmen in the Philippines.

#71 Anhai Rd Trinity Church (三一堂) Please read the Gulangyu Churches chapter for more about Trinity, one of China's most beautiful churches.

所有的门框和窗台都是用白色大理石做的。这栋别墅也有一口井，叫作龙坑井，不知何时井被填了。

番婆的子孙们现在还住在那里，其中有几间作为办公室租了出去。

安海路 55 号　时钟楼，也叫宜园。时钟楼建于 20 世纪二三十年代，是由陈姓富商出资兴建的。他拥有众多小妾，所以时钟楼的房间特别多。时钟楼模仿原美国领事馆，是一栋西洋风格的别墅。它以奇特的柱子、彩色花岗岩、装饰华丽的浮雕而著称。三楼的浮雕尤其有名。这栋别墅也有一个小庭院，院子里种有各种果树和遮阳树。

1933 年，华侨杨丕河买下时钟楼，供他的亲戚居住（他本人从来没有住过）。解放后不久，杨丕河就去世了，政府接管了他的别墅。起初时钟楼被用作好几户人家的住所，接着又改作卫生院，后来又成了公安局。公安局在笔架山建了新的办公楼后，时钟楼归还给杨丕河的四个儿子，如今他们都在菲律宾经商。

安海路 71 号　三一堂。是中国最漂亮的教堂之一。在《鼓浪屿教堂》那一章有详细的介绍。

Anhai #55　Bell Mansion

Chapter 20
Quanzhou & Jishan Rds

"And I assure you that for one shipload of pepper that goes to Alexandria or elsewhere, destined for Christendom, there come a hundred such, aye and more too, to this haven of Zaitun [the Arab's name for Quanzhou], for it is one of the greatest havens in the world for commerce." Marco Polo

Quanzhou Rd 泉州路 Arab legends claim Sinbad sought the legendary wealth of Quanzhou, the ancient commercial and cultural crossroads 70 miles up the coast from Xiamen. Columbus, too, sought not a new world but a shorter route to an ancient world—Quanzhou. Gulangyu's Quanzhou Rd., like the city, was a crossroads—the home of patriots, Chinese and foreign merchants, missionaries, scholars, and heroines like Qiu Jin.

Quanzhou & Jishan (Hen Hill) Rds at a Glance

#73 Quanzhou Rd Former Residence of Heroine Qiu Jin (秋瑾故居)

#82 Quanzhou Rd Lin House (林屋) circa 1930. Elegant N. European steeply-sloped roofs; magnificent white eucalyptus ("ghost gums").

#99 Quanzhou Rd Golden Melon Building (金瓜楼) Two golden domes, and one of Gulangyu's best three estate gates.

#105 Quanzhou Rd Inquest Law Court (会审公堂) Later moved to #1-3 Bishan Rd.

Jishan Rd

#1 Jishan Rd Pastor's Home (牧师楼)

#2 Jishan Rd Originally a London Missionary Society missionary home, now "Xiamen Christian Training and Retreat Center."

#3 Jishan Rd American missionary's home, built between 1915-1925

#12 Jishan Rd Chen Shijing's Tomb (陈士京墓照)

#16 Jishan Rd The Yin Family Home (殷承宗宅)

#18 Jishan Rd Anxian Hall (安献堂) 7th Day Adventist

Chinese Christian Cemetery—across from Anxian Hall. Also note the unusual "punctuation" memorial on the granite steps leading to the beach! Read the "Education" chapter for more information.

第二十章

泉州路和鸡山路

“我可以肯定地告诉你，每有一船胡椒运到亚历山大或其他地方，但一定是基督教国家时，就有一百船胡椒，是的可能更多，运到刺桐［泉州的阿拉伯名］，因为它是世界上最大的港口之一。”

——马可·波罗

泉州路　泉州是古时商业和文化中心，与厦门海岸线相距 70 里，阿拉伯神话中说辛巴达在泉州（刺桐）找到了传说中的宝藏。还有，哥伦布发现的并不是新大陆，而是通往古国，更确切地说是泉州的捷径。正如它的名字一样，鼓浪屿的泉州路也是个中枢点——许多爱国英雄如秋瑾，以及中外商人、传教士和学者都曾在此居住。

泉州路和鸡山路一览

泉州路 73 号　**秋瑾故居**
泉州路 82 号　**林屋**，建于 1930 年前。雅致的 N 型欧式大坡折屋面，宏伟的白桉树（“鬼胶”）。
泉州路 99 号　**金瓜楼** 两座金色塔顶，鼓浪屿三大门楼之一。
泉州路 105 号　**会审公堂** 后迁到笔山路 1-3 号。
鸡山路 1 号　牧师楼。
鸡山路 3 号　美传教士居所，建于 1915-1925 年之间。
鸡山路 12 号　陈士京墓。
鸡山路 16 号　殷承宗宅。
鸡山路 18 号　安献堂 安息日会。
中国基督教徒墓——安献堂对面（著名的墓园）——找出台阶里为纪念卢戆章的奇特的“标点”！（参见教育先驱一章结尾部分）

Getting to Quanzhou Rd Walk straight ahead from the ferry onto Longtou Rd.; turn right at bookstore. Quanzhou Rd. veers off to the left just beyond the triangular plaza.

Note the old dwellings at #64, 66, 68 and 70.

#73 Quanzhou Rd Former residence of revolutionary heroine Qiu Jin (秋瑾故居). This red-brick and granite three-storey Western style home was built around the turn of the 20th century by Ye Dingguo (叶定国) and Ye Jintai (叶金泰) from Tong'an (同安). Given its age, it is probable that Qiu Jin lived in the building before the present one. After Liberation the house was used by the local government as a police station and a dormitory for customs workers, and today it is a residence.

Revolutionary Heroine Qiu Jin

One of many martyrs who set the stage for Sun Yat-sen's revolution, Qiu Jin was born on Gulangyu into a well off family in the third year of the Guangxu period (光绪) of the Qing Dynasty (for us benighted barbarians, that was 1875 A.D.). Qiu Jin's family moved to Hunan when she was only ten but she always looked back upon Gulangyu as her 2nd home—and Gulangyu has, of course, claimed her as its own.

As a child Qiu Jin loved reading, writing poetry, horseback riding, and playing with swords. She was an unconventional child, to say the least, and an even more unconventional adult. She married an older man at age 21, but after 7 years left him to study in Japan, where she became an ardent supporter of women's rights and education.

Qiu Jin returned to China in 1906 and founded a magazine to encourage women to resist oppression by families (she fought foot-binding) and society, and to seek financial independence and freedom through professional education and training. Qiu Jin eventually decided that women's salvation required a wholesale change in government, and she and her male cousin Xu Xilin worked to unite the scattered revolutionary societies in overthrowing the corrupt Qing Dynasty's Manchu rulers.

Xu Xilin was captured on July 6, 1907, and after interrogation and torture he confessed and was executed. Six days later Qiu Jin was arrested at the Zhejiang girls' school, where she was the principal. Although she refused to confess, the government found documents proving her complicity, and beheaded her. But she may have accomplished more in death than life because her martyrdom became a rallying point for advocates of women's independence, and she and her cousin's work and deaths helped set the stage for the successful revolution that followed.

前往泉州路 上码头后沿龙头路直走，到书店后右拐。泉州路就在这三角形广场的左边。留意 64、66、68 和 70 号的老房子。

泉州路 73 号　革命女杰秋瑾故居。这座三层的砖夹石西洋建筑建于 20 世纪初，由同安的叶定国和叶金泰修建。按年代推算，秋瑾当时居住的很可能不是现在的这座房子。解放后，房子由当地政府接管，作为公安局及海关员工宿舍，现为民宅。

革命英雄秋瑾

秋瑾，帮助孙中山开创革命事业的烈士之一，清光绪三年时（按我们愚昧的蛮夷历法，应该是公元 1877 年）出生于鼓浪屿一户富人家。秋瑾十岁时，举家迁往湖南，但秋瑾一直视鼓浪屿为其第二故乡——当然鼓浪屿也承认她是自己人。

幼年的秋瑾喜欢看书、写诗、骑马、舞剑。至少可以这样说，她是一个反传统的孩子，甚至也是个反传统的青年。她 21 岁时嫁给了一个比她年长的人，但 7 年后又离开他去日本求学。在日本，她成为一名女权和妇女教育问题的热心拥护者。

1906 年，秋瑾回到中国，创办了一份杂志，鼓励妇女反抗家庭（她反对裹脚）和社会压迫，通过职业学习和培训寻求经济独立和自由。最终秋瑾意识到要拯救妇女就需要将政府彻底改头换面，因此她和堂兄徐锡麟一起将零散的革命社团组织起来，以共同推翻腐朽的满清统治者。

1907 年 7 月 6 日，徐锡麟被捕，严刑拷问之下，他认罪并被处决了。六天后，秋瑾在浙江女子学校也被捕了，当时她是该校校长。虽然她拒不认罪，但当局还是找来证据证明她也参与其中，将她处决。但是她的英勇献身的贡献可能比她生前更多，因为她的烈士精神大大鼓舞了维护女权的人士。她和堂兄为之所作的努力和牺牲也为日后的革命胜利奠定了基础。

#82 Quanzhou Rd Lin House (林屋) Xiamen ABB's Scott Ballantyne wants this villa for an upscale bed 'n breakfast but I doubt they'll sell. When the builder, Lin Zhenxun, passed away in Hong Kong in 1955 at the age of 90, his last words were that the house should never be sold but left to the service of the country. (I think a good bed 'n breakfast might render great service!).

#82 Quanzhou Rd.

Xiamen-born Lin Zhenxun returned to Gulangyu after a stint in Singapore, married, and had five sons, all whom were successful in various careers. His 2nd son, an engineer, designed Shangli (上李) and Gulangyu reservoirs, worked in Shanghai and Hong Kong, and in 1948 moved to the U.S., where he died in 1980. Some of Lin's other sons are in the Chinese Academy of Science.

Lin House was built on the site of the British Presbyterian's memorial for missionary linguist Douglas Carstairs (See Pioneer Educators chapter). After termites destroyed the presbytery, it was relocated, and Lin Zhenxun bought the lot about 1923. Lin's 2nd son designed the 3-story house, and master craftsman from Shanghai finished it about 1927. A unique 80 cm. deep foundation was designed to foil termites, but they're still taking their toll on the elegant old villa.

Unlike many Gulangyu mansions, Lin House is large but unpretentious, graceful but practical, devoid of the ostentatious colonial-era corridors and pillars. The windows were designed to be practical, maximizing light and ventilation. The interior has elegant but practical and durable wooden floors and teak stairs. And like most Gulangyu residents, Lin was a music lover, and designed a French-style hall for the family's frequent music recitals.

The mansion's most distinctive feature is its Northern European style sloped red roof, which contrasts aesthetically with the surrounding greenery, and the pale trunks of the towering "ghost gums" (eucalyptus).

#99 Quanzhou Rd Golden Melon Building (金瓜楼), one of Gulangyu's most unusual buildings, is named after its two golden domes. The house was built in 1922 and bought for 40,000 silver dollars in 1924 by Mr. Huang Ciming, a native of Longhai, Zhangzhou.

泉州路 82 号　林屋 厦门 ABB 公司有个英国人斯科蒂·巴兰坦（Scott Ballantyne）想买下这座别墅做高级私宅，但我怀疑他们不肯卖。林屋的设计师林振勋，1955 年在香港去世，终年 90 岁，他临终遗言：林屋不能卖，留给子孙为祖国服务。（我想一个能提供过夜和次日早餐的私人住家服务一定不错！）

#99 Quanzhou Rd.

出生于厦门的林振勋在新加坡发迹后回到鼓浪屿，结婚生子，他的五个孩子都十分出色，在不同的领域都事业有成。次子是工程师，设计了上李水库和鼓浪屿蓄水池，曾在上海和香港工作过，1948 年去了美国，1980 年在美国逝世。另有几个儿子在中国科学院工作。

林屋的原址是英国长老会为传教士、语言学家杜嘉德（参见教育先驱一章）设立的纪念堂。因遭到白蚁蛀蚀，纪念堂选址新建。1923 年，林振勋买下这块地皮，次子设计成三层别墅，由上海师傅施工，1927 年完工。虽然为防白蚁蛀蚀，林屋的地下室采用了独特的 80 厘米厚的设计，但是这座优雅的老别墅还是留下了白蚁蛀蚀的斑斑痕迹。

和鼓浪屿上的许多建筑不同，林屋虽大但不张扬，优雅却很实用，摒弃了浮华的英式回廊和罗马柱。窗户的设计非常实用，采光通风都很好。厅房设计也是优雅而实用，拼木地板和柚木楼梯结实耐用。和许多鼓浪屿居民一样，林也是个音乐爱好者，因此他还设计了一个法式客厅，经常在这里举行家庭音乐会。

林屋最突出的特点就是北欧风格的坡折红屋面，在周围的绿阴及参天“鬼胶”（桉树）的白色树干的映衬下，十分突出秀美。

泉州路 99 号　金瓜楼 是鼓浪屿最不寻常的建筑之一，因其两座金色塔顶而得名。金瓜楼建于 1922 年。1924 年的时候，漳州龙海人黄赐敏先生以 4 万银元买下。

Huang Ciming and his 8 sons and 2 daughters moved to the Philippines in 1947, and after the Cultural Revolution the Golden Melon was home to four or five families. In 1980, Huang Ciming's third daughter-in-law, Xie, negotiated the villa's return to the family, and now the estate is cared for by Huang Ciming's descendants, who are scattered abroad in 20 countries.

The Golden Melon building is said to be a mix of Chinese and Western architecture—Chinese carvings and designs, with western-style windows and Persian blinds, Chinese style wing-rooms and halls, and Western fireplace and corridors. This estate also has one of the three grandest gates, rivaled only by the flamboyant entrance of Haitian Tanggou Building (海天堂构) at #38 Fujian Rd. or the "Foreign Lady Building" (番婆楼) at #36 Anhai Rd.

> **The Backdoor!** Chinese are always going on about using the "back door" (guanxi, connections), and I've finally found out where the backdoor is! A small, brown metal door in the white wall along Quanzhou Rd., near the Golden Melon building, has red characters on a brass sign that read, "#35 Wudai Rd. (乌埭路)
>
> ***Zou Houmen!* *走后门!***

乌埭路
35号后门

"Back Door"

Chicken Hill estates (1930s)

Jishan (Hen Hill) Rd (鸡山路) is named after a bald granite cliff said to resemble a chicken's head (it looks like a turtle head to me). Take the Sunlight Rock Cable Car for the best view of this unusual formation.

#12 Jishan Rd Chen Shijing's Tomb (陈士京墓) is just outside the doorway of #12 Jishan Rd. Chen was an officer at the end of the Ming Dynasty who sailed to Xiamen with the King of Lu (鲁王) and died on Gulangyu.

1947 年，黄赐敏携 8 子 2 女移居菲律宾。“文化大革命”后，金瓜楼住进了四五户人家。1980 年，黄赐敏的三媳谢女士成功回收了房子的主权，现在金瓜楼由黄赐敏的后代管理。黄的儿孙遍布 20 多个国家。

金瓜楼被认为是中西合璧的典范——既有中式雕刻和设计，又有西式窗户和百叶窗；既有中式厢房和大厅，也有西式壁炉和走廊。金瓜楼的门楼也是岛上最大气的三大门楼之一，唯有福建路 38 号的海天堂构与安海路 36 号的番婆楼能与之抗衡。

后门！

中国人常常讲走“后门”（关系），现在我终于发现后门的位置了！泉州路金瓜楼附近有一堵白墙，墙上有一个小铜门，门上的铜牌用红字写着“乌埭路 35 号后门”。 **走后门！**

鸡山路 因一块形似母鸡头的花岗石而得名，但是我认为它更像乌龟的头。从日光岩缆车上可以最好地观赏到这块奇石。

鸡山路 12 号 陈士京墓就在门口。陈是明末的官员，随鲁王乘船来到厦门，最后逝于鼓浪屿。

#16 Jishan Rd The Yin Family Home (殷承宗宅) is just to the west of Hen Rock (Jimu Shi, 鸡母石). The elder son, Yin Zuze (殷祖泽), studied civil engineering in Philadelphia, U.S.A, and after graduation returned to China to teach in Tsinghua University.

In 1924, he designed a 1700 square meter western-style garden home which boasted, among many other things, four toilets (toilets were rare on water-deprived Gulangyu). Sadly, Yin Zuze died in Beijing during the 30s, but in 1942 the home of his dreams was the birthplace of the famous pianist Yin Chengzong (殷承宗), and today the place is home to Yin Chengzong's brother, Yin Chengdian (殷承典), a founder of the Xiamen Music School. Read more about the Yin Family in the Sounds of Music chapter.

#16 Jishan Rd.

#18 Jishan Rd Anxian Hall (安献堂) Gulangyu's only 3-storey solid granite building, Anxian Hall was designed by a Chinese architect and built by SDA missionaries Mr. and Mrs. B.L. Anderson, who for decades pinched pennies and saved funds from their farms and dairies.

Anxian Hall became a model for many buildings around South Fujian, which boasted far more stone than lumber (S. Fujian has had stone carvers for over 1700 years). Anxian Hall is now the Xiamen Sino-American (Meihua) Adventist Sanitarium and Retirement Center (基督教厦门美华老人院).

Note: Please check the Pioneering Education chapter for more history on the SDA in Amoy—and an explanation for the punctuation marks and Pinyin letters engraved in the granite steps on the path to the beach!

鸡山路 16 号　殷宅就在鸡母石的西面。长子殷祖泽在美国费城学习土木工程，毕业后回国，执教于清华大学。

1924 年，他设计了一座占地 1700 平方米的西式花园洋房，房子有许多闪光点，其中之一就是拥有 4 个卫生间（在缺水的鼓浪屿，卫生间是比较罕见的）。可惜，殷祖泽 30 年代就病逝于北京。1942 年，这座充满他梦想的别墅成了著名音乐家殷承宗的出生地。现在住在这房子里的是殷承宗的哥哥殷承典，他是厦门音乐学校的创始人之一。更多关于殷氏家族的资料参见音乐之声一章。

鸡山路 18 号　安献堂是鼓浪屿唯一的三层花岗岩方块建筑，由中国建筑师设计、安息日会传教士韩谨思·安礼逊（B.L. Anderson）夫妇建造。几十年来，韩谨思·安礼逊夫妇总是节衣缩食，从自己的农场和牧场齐集了不少基金。

安献堂的石材用量远远多于木材，成为闽南地区的建筑典范（闽南地区的石雕已有 1700 多年历史）。安献堂现为基督教厦门美华老人院。

注：请翻到教育先驱一章，参见更多关于安息日会在厦的历史，以及对遍布山海之间的花岗岩台阶上的标点符号的解读。

Chapter 21
Huangyan & Haitan Rds

Gulangyu foreign tombstones

Hong Buren

"I visited the grave of Mrs. Boone. It is in a beautiful quiet garden, a little tree stands at the foot, and an immense banyan spreads its shade over the whole. She died August 30, 1842." (Lowry, 1843, p.210. Lowrie was drowned by pirates August 18th, 1847).

"The only local records of these early [foreign] traders are the tombstones on Kolongsu which mark their last resting place. Recently [1905] they were taken up and placed in the Foreign Cemetery. On their tombstones are these dates 1698, 1700, and 1710." Pitcher, "In and about Amoy," 1912, p.43

"From the beginning, the new arrivals [in Amoy] suffered the loss of loved ones. A few weeks after setting foot in China, the Doty's only son, a boy of six, died. A short time later, the Pohlmans lost two children. On September 30, 1845, Theodosia Pohlman died at age thirty five, and she was followed in death about a week later on October 5 by Eleanor Doty, age thirty-nine. The grief-stricken husbands decided that their motherless children (there were two in each family) should return to America." De Jong, 1992, p.20-21

Burying the Foreigners' Cemetery (番仔墓) Huangyan Road's Foreign Cemetery, resting place of extinguished foreigners (excluding Japanese), was an eloquent reminder that our idyllic islet had a dark side as well. For over two centuries, foreigners on this "white man's graveyard" buried their loved ones in the Foreign Cemetery—and then the Chinese buried the Foreign Cemetery because of Egypt!

When Britain and France bombed Egypt in 1956, Nasser sunk all 40 ships in the canal and closed it until early 1957. Chinese were sympathetic with Egypt because it had suffered repercussions from the West after giving Communist China diplomatic recognition. So in July，1958, Gulangyu folk voiced their support for the downtrodden desert dwellers by destroying the Gulangyu Cemetery.

第二十一章

晃岩路和海坛路

“我参观了布恩太太的墓，在一座漂亮而安静的花园中，墓前有一棵小榕树，浓密的树阴洒满整个墓。她逝于 1842 年 8 月 30 日。”（娄理华（Lowry），1843 年，P.210。娄理华于 1847 年 8 月 18 日被海盗淹死）。

#25 Huangyan Rd.

“当地关于这些早期外商的唯一记录就是鼓浪屿上的墓碑，这是他们的安息之地。最近[1905 年]，他们被迁到了番仔墓。在他们的墓碑上记载着 1698、1700 和 1710 年。”毕腓力，《厦门方志》，1912 年，p.43。

“起初，新到[厦门]来的人都经历了丧亲之痛。踏上中国没几周，Doty 唯一的儿子，一个六岁的小男孩就死了。不久之后，Pohlmans 一家也痛失两个孩子。1845 年 9 月 30 日，Theodosia Pohlman 死了，年仅 35 岁。大约一周之后，10 月 5 日，39 岁的 Eleanor Doty 也死了。悲伤欲绝的丈夫们决定将失去妈妈的孩子们送回美国（每家都有两个小孩）。” De Jong，1992 年，p. 20-21。

埋葬番仔墓　位于海坛路的番仔墓是许多杰出的老外（倭寇除外）的安息之地，它提醒我们这个田园般的小岛也有阴暗的一面。二百多年来，老外在番仔墓，这块白人的墓园里埋葬了他们的至亲至爱——但之后因为埃及的缘故，中国人把番仔墓也埋葬了！

1956 年英法炮轰埃及的时候，纳塞尔将 40 艘船统统潜入运河底，然后关闭运河，直到 1957 年初才重新开放。中国人对埃及充满同情，因为自从埃及外交上承认中华人民共和国以来，就一直遭受西方的压迫抵制。因此，1958 年 7 月，鼓浪屿人民捣毁番仔墓，声援这群倍受蹂躏的沙漠居民。

Alas, many beautifully carved tombstones and statues, some dating back 300 years, were destroyed[1], and only Christian tombstones on Gulangyu today are in the Chinese cemetery near the former Sino-American school on Jishan Rd. (though in 2004 someone discovered a tombstone of a man from Bombay).

Huangyan & Haitan Rds at a Glance

Gulangyu Music Hall, on site of Foreigner's Cemetery (destroyed in 1958 in protest of Britain's invasion of Egypt)

Shops & Restaurants (buy Fujian handicrafts; sample local seafood)

#5 Huangyan Rd Sunlight Rock Temple (Riguangyan Si, 日光岩寺) — "back door" to Sunlight Rock.

#25 Huangyan Rd Huang Family Gardens (Gulangyu Guesthouse, 黄家花园). Nixon stayed here!

#38 Huangyan Rd Chen Wenlong Villa (陈文龙宅), built in 1918 by Philippine Overseas Chinese Mr. Chen Wenlong.

#40 Huangyan Rd Gospel Hall, Fuyin Tang (福音堂), first built in 1880, rebuilt in 1905

#45 Huangyan Rd Shuzhuang Gardens (菽庄花园) & Piano Museum

#47 Huangyan Rd Eight Corner Mansion, Dr. Lin Qiaozhi's childhood home, (林巧稚故居)

Haitan Rd

#33, 37 Haitan Rd Mix of Chinese and Western architecture; early 20th century.

#58 Haitan Rd Dafudi Mansion—built between 1796-1820

#64 Haitan Rd This house was rebuilt from scratch in the original style.

#70 Huangyan Rd Li Wufang Villa（李武芳别墅)

Subtropical Botanical Garden—at foot of Sunlight Rock

[1] As noted earlier, during the Cultural Revolution Chinese destroyed their own heritage as well, so they have more to regret than we do.

唉，许多刻得非常漂亮的墓碑和雕像，有的甚至有 300 年历史，就这样毁了[1]。现在，鼓浪屿上的基督教徒墓碑就只有在鸡山路美华学校附近的华人公墓里才能看到了（不过在 2004 年，有人发现了一孟买人的墓碑）。

#25 Huangyan Rd

晃岩路和海坛路一览

鼓浪屿音乐厅，原为番仔墓（1958 年被毁，以抗议英军入侵埃及）。
商店＆餐厅（可购买福建手工艺品，品尝当地海味）。
晃岩路 5 号　日光岩寺——通往日光岩的“后门”。
晃岩路 25 号　**黄家花园**，尼克松曾在此下榻。
晃岩路 38 号　**陈文龙宅**，菲律宾华人陈文龙建于 1918 年。
晃岩路 40 号　**福音堂**，始建于 1880 年，1905 年重修。
晃岩路 45 号　菽庄花园＆钢琴博物馆。
晃岩路 47 号　**八角楼**，林巧稚故居。
海坛路 33、37 号　融合中西风格的建筑，20 世纪初。
海坛路 58 号　**大夫第**——建于 1796-1820 年。
海坛路 64 号　这些房子是按原有风格重建而成的。
晃岩路 70 号　**李武芳别墅。**
亚热带植物园　**日光岩脚下。**

[1] 前面的注解也介绍过，在“文化大革命”期间，中国人也摧毁了自己的文化遗产，所以他们该后悔的事情比我们多。

Gulangyu Music Hall

Gulangyu Music Hall 鼓浪屿音乐厅 In 1978, the government decided to build a music hall on the former cemetery's site, and after reviewing plans and models for 12 designs, chose a model for a concert hall in the round. But though it looked good on paper, no one could build it. Perhaps they could have consulted conductor Zheng Xiaoying's Hakka relatives, who build roundhouses, but instead they modified the design, and in 1984 opened the 3 million Yuan 900-seat oval concert hall.

Guides claim the hall's front door is like a fish's open mouth, with corridor columns for teeth and tiles for fish scales. Sounds fishy to me, but musicians and conductors have nothing but praise for the fishy hall's fine (or *fin*) acoustics. And today, as a Chinese writer puts it, "the place once haunted by foreign ghosts is now a palace of music." (Read more about Gulangyu's musical heritage in "The Sounds of Music" chapter).

#3 and #11 Huangyan Rd This area just west of the Music Hall has several beautifully renovated Western-style buildings, though I could learn nothing about their background.

A 3rd generation Gulangyu resident, Mr. Zhu Yuanpeng (朱远鹏), whom I met while exploring nearby Zhonghua Rd. claimed an Englishman built the home at #11 and rented it to a teacher named Mr. Wang.

John Ma Memorial Bust, at the People's Stadium, commemorates this Gulangyu-born sports pioneer. Visit Ma's former residence at #58 Zhangzhou Rd., and read more about him in the Pioneer Educators chapter.

鼓浪屿音乐厅　　1978 年，政府决定在番仔墓原址上修建一座音乐厅，经过对 12 个设计方案的反复审核，最后从中挑选出一个圆形方案。虽然设计图的效果很不错，但是当时没人能建。其实他们可以咨询一下指挥家郑小瑛的客家亲戚的，因为他们擅长建土楼。最后政府只好修改设计方案，斥资 300 万建成一座可容纳 900 人的椭圆形音乐厅，并于 1984 年对外开放。

#5 Huangyan Rd

导游介绍说，音乐厅的前门就像鱼张开的嘴，而走廊上的柱子就是牙齿，墙上的瓷砖就是鱼鳞。我听起来觉得很有鱼味，但是音乐家和指挥家们却只对这座鱼形音乐厅完美的音响效果赞不绝口。正如一位中国作家写道的，“这个过去闹洋鬼的地方，现在却成了音乐的殿堂。”（更多关于鼓浪屿的音乐传统，参见“音乐之声”一章）

晃岩路 3、11 号　　这个地方就在音乐厅西面，矗立着好几座经过翻修的漂亮的西式建筑，但我找不到任何背景资料。

#38 Huangyan

就在走访附近的中华路时，我碰到了一位鼓浪屿的第三代居民，朱远鹏先生。他说，11 号的这座房子是一位英国人建的，之后租给一位王老师。

马约翰雕像　　位于人民体育场，以纪念这位在鼓浪屿出生的体育先锋。他的故居位于漳州路 58 号，关于马约翰的更多资料参见教育先驱一章。

#25 Huangyan Rd Huang Family Gardens (Huangjia Huayuan, 黄家花园), which hosted Nixon, is one of China's finest villas. Foreign-designed and built by Shanghai masons in 1923, it belonged to Mr. Huang Yizhu (黄奕住), an

The Celestial's Barber

"Among the everyday sights is… the shaving of the head of the Celestial… The barber is generally both a peripatetic and a philosopher. He carries his whole stock-in-trade upon his shoulder-pole, goes round to see his regular customers, and tells the news of the town as the fraternity of the razor commonly do in England. His apparatus consists of two sets of boxes or drawers, one which serves as till for cash, place for razors, and seat for the person to be shaved; the other of a stand that encloses a pan of lighted charcoal, over which is a basin of warm water. With these various articles hanging from the pole he makes his rounds, taking as much interest in the heads of the people as a shoeblack does in their feet.

(Dukes, 1885)
Street Barber

"Very commonly he is paid in kind, instead of in cash—the purveyors in perishables handing him a few handfuls of rice or potatoes or oil for his trouble in making their heads to shine." Dukes, 1885, p.32

Indonesian Overseas Chinese who began his life, surprisingly enough, as a farmer and barber (in old China, barbers and fortune-tellers were the absolute bottom rung of the social ladder).

In 1888, the 20-year-old Yizhu left Nan'an's Jintao (金淘, 南安) to seek his fortune abroad. He relied at first on his barber skills but eventually expanded into selling local products and candles, and in the end earned some really sweet profits as one of Indonesia's top four sugar merchants.

Yizhu returned to China in 1918, settle down on Gulangyu, and invested broadly in banks and infrastructure. In 1921, he founded "Rixing Yinhao"（日兴银号）on Zhenbang Road (镇邦路), the "Central Southern Bank" in Shanghai, and invested in the "Zhongxing Bank" (中兴银行) in the Philippines. Yizhu invested in Gulangyu's water supply, and founded the Xiamen telephone company and Zhangzhou's Tongmin（通敏） Telephone Company.

In 1930, Yizhu founded the Huang Jude (黄聚德) Real Estate Company, which developed Gulangyu's Rixing Road (日兴路) and was responsible for the construction of over 160 buildings, covering 40000 square meters.

晃岩路 25 号　黄家花园。曾接待过尼克松总统，是中国最棒的别墅之一。1923 年由西方人设计，上海建筑师完成。主人黄奕住是印尼华侨，令人难以置信的是，早年他只是一介农夫和剃头匠（在旧中国，剃头匠和算命先生毫无疑问是社会最底层的职业）。

中国剃头匠

“每日可见的是……中国人在剃头……剃头匠通常是巡行者兼哲人，和英国同行一样，他把所有的家当挑在扁担上，遍访熟客，传播着城里的新闻。他的行头包括两套匣子或箱子，一套用来装钱、剃刀，同时作为客人剃头时的座椅，另一套装着点有炭火的盆子，上面放一盆温水。剃头匠就这样挑着行头，走街串巷留意着人们的头顶，就像擦鞋的盯着行人的脚一样。

“通常人们付给剃头匠的是实物而非现金，比如，有些商贩会给他一些米、土豆或是油之类的东西，以犒劳他这么卖力，把他们的头剃得光亮光亮的。”——Duke1885 年著 第 32 页

1888 年，20 岁的奕住离开南安金淘到海外淘金。开始时他靠理发为生，后来发展为售卖当地特产和蜡烛，最终攒够了创业资金，成为印尼四大糖商之一。

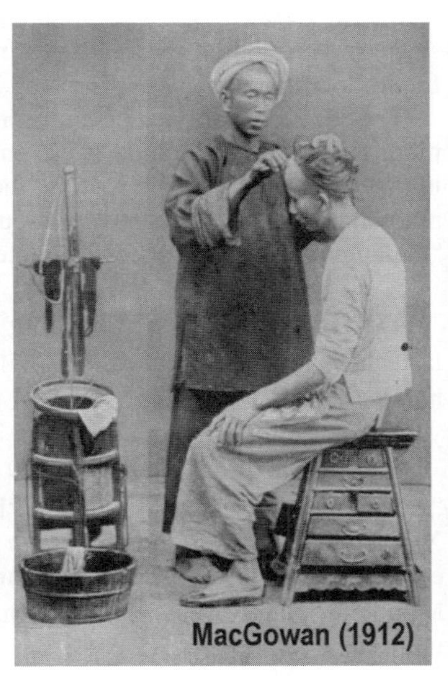

MacGowan (1912)

1918 年奕住回国，定居鼓浪屿并大规模投资银行业和基础建设。1921 年在镇邦路设立了“日兴银号”，在上海设立合资的“中南银行”，并在菲律宾投资“中兴银行”。奕住还投资组建厦门自来水公司，同时还创办了厦门电话公司和漳州通敏电话公司。

1930 年奕住成立了黄聚德房地产公司，兴修了鼓浪屿日兴路，并开发了 160 多处房产，占地面积达 40000 平方米。

Yizhu chaired the Xiamen General Chamber of Commerce from 1928 to 1931, and helped further modern education until his death at age 77 in Shanghai.

Yizhu's most magnificent estate, Huangjia Garden, is considered the finest Western-style building in Fujian province. With its elegant steps and handrails sculpted of white Italian marble, this elegant home has been the setting for many movies (it was here that I played Coyett, the last Dutch Governor of Taiwan).

#40 Huangyan Rd The Gospel Hall (Fuyin Tang, 福音堂), originally the Carstairs Douglas Memorial Hall, was first built by the London Mission Society in 1880. Read more about Gulangyu churches and Carstairs Douglas in the "Gulangyu Churches" chapter.

Lin Qiaozhi's Home (under renovation)

#47 Huangyan Rd Dr. Lin Qiaozhi's Childhood Home. This 2-story brick and wood European home, nicknamed "Small Eight Diagrams Building" (小八卦楼) or "Octagon Building" (八角楼) because of its octagonal shape, was sold after the death of Lin's father, Lin Liangying (林良英), and after Liberation managed by the Housing Bureau.

The second floor became a nursery, and five families moved in. As it became more crowded, the verandas were enclosed as rooms, and other rooms were built in the garden. As of this writing, the house is apparently undergoing a complete renovation and will become a museum. Read more about Dr. Lin Qiaozhi in the "Gulangyu Medical Pioneers" chapter.

#70 Huangyan Rd Li Wufang Villa（李武芳别墅）The English-style villa facing Doctor Lin Qiaozhi's （林巧稚）former residence was originally the home of Guo Chunyang（郭春秧), a native of Nan'an（南安）who in his youth moved to Indonesia and went into business.

Guo returned to Xiamen in 1919 and set up his "Datong（大通）Shop," the "Jinxiang（锦祥）Tea Shop", and began exporting tea, as well as investing in Xiamen real estate. Guo's villa, on the south face of Sunlight Rock, supposedly enjoyed the islet's best view of Xiamen bay and of the Great Southern Warrior Mountain (Nantai Wu, 南太武). But the villa fell into disrepair during the war with Japan.

1928-1931 年间，奕住任厦门总商会会长，一直致力于发展现代教育，直至 77 岁在上海去世。

黄家花园是奕住最气派的房产，被视为福建最精美的西式建筑。华丽的台阶和扶栏均用意大利白色大理石琢成，因而许多影片都选中这座豪宅作为背景拍摄基地（我就是在这里扮演了揆一一角，揆一是末代荷兰驻台总督）。

晃岩路 40 号福音堂，原为杜嘉德纪念馆，最早是由伦敦事务社于 1880 年建立。在“鼓浪屿教堂”一章中有更多关于鼓浪屿教堂和杜嘉德的详细叙述。

基督教徒在鼓浪屿的中华基督教会福 音堂举行婚礼。
Chinese Christian Wedding in the Gospel Hall

晃岩路 47 号林巧稚故居。这座欧式两层砖木建筑因其八角外形，故被称作“小八卦楼”或“八角楼”，林巧稚父亲林良英去世后房子被变卖，解放后由房产局管理。

二楼成了托儿所，有五户人家搬了进来。后来居住的人越来越多，凉台被扩为居室，花园里也盖了房间。撰写此书时，整栋楼正全面翻修成博物馆。详情请参阅“鼓浪屿医学先驱”一章。

晃岩路 70 号　　李武芳别墅。这座英式别墅与林巧稚故居临街而立，原是南安人郭春秧的家宅。郭年轻时移居印尼从商去了，后于 1919 年回到厦门，开办了“大通商店”、“锦祥茶店”，并开始出口茶叶，同时投资于厦门房地产业。郭宅北面日光岩，应该是岛上观赏鹭江和南太武山风光的最佳位置。但抗日战争时期，这座房子就荒废了。

#72 Huangyan Rd.
(Photo by Lily Wang)

Many Overseas Chinese returned to Xiamen in the 1980s, and a Taiwanese named Li Wufang (李武芳) bought this villa and rebuilt it in the identical style as the original, providing a model that has since been followed by others who have undertaken restoration of Gulangyu's historic architecture.

#72 Huangyan Rd I was told a Taiwanese businessman owns this beautifully restored home, and the government uses the building to its left.

Haitan Rd

#33, 37 and 58 Haitan Rd These delightful old Chinese-style buildings remind us that Gulangyu was the home of wealthy and influential Chinese long before the rest of the world showed up. Note the typical southern Fujian architecture, with its mix of red tile, brick, and granite, the rounded eaves, and the various carving styles in wood, stone and brick.(Also see #23 Zhonghua Rd.)

These classic Chinese dwellings' Western-style add-ons reflect the architectural schizophrenia that afflicted Chinese and foreigners alike as they attempted to embrace the modern world while preserving the fiction that colonial-era Gulangyu was still China.

20 世纪 80 年代，许多海外华侨纷纷回到厦门。其中一位叫李武芳的台湾人买下了这座别墅，并按原有风格对房子进行了翻修。之后许多人在保护鼓浪屿岛上的历史古建筑时都遵循了这一修旧如旧的模式。

晃岩路 72 号 听说这座漂亮的度假屋是一位台湾商人的，它左边的建筑就是区政府所在地。

海坛路

海坛路 33、37 和 58 号 这些漂亮的中式古宅提醒人们，早在世界其他地方发达之前，鼓浪屿就聚集了许多有钱有势的中国人。注意看这些典型的闽南建筑，红瓦、红砖和花岗岩混合砌筑，圆形屋檐，还有各式各样的装饰艺术（木雕、石雕和砖雕）。（还可去看看中华路 23 号）

这些典型的中式建筑还融合了西洋风格，反映出当时困扰中国人和外国人的建筑风格分化的问题，因为他们既想拥抱当代世界，又坚信殖民时代的鼓浪屿仍是中国的一部分。

#58 Haitan Rd

Chapter 22
Zhonghua Rd

"Rich Chinese lived in some [Gulangyu mansions], like the family opposite us, but they were mostly those who had had long contact with European merchants or who had made money in the South Seas and, therefore, were not rigidly bound by tradition. Not that they preferred to live among foreigners, but in an International Concession they were better able to safeguard their hard-earned fortunes. Most of them were of humble origin, but the Tan family, whose flowery terrace overlooked our garden, preserved great dignity and a rigid conservatism through their grandfather, who had been a magistrate before the 1911 revolution. In the fine months he was always to be seen sitting among the pots of pink camellias, brush jar and ink slab before him, smoking a long pipe with a minute copper bowl. Occasionally we would meet him, in his long grey silk coat, taking his caged song-bird down to the sea for an airing. He was constantly served by the whole family; filial piety being one of the two basic Confucian principles. But the service was also a genuinely felt tribute to wisdom and experience."

Anne Averil McKenzie, *Gulangyu*, 1920s

Zhonghua Rd. takes in the former Dutch Consulate, the "Weird World" museum (a "Ripley's Believe it or Not" style place), the People's Stadium (with bust of sports pioneer John Ma), the Dafudi residence (read about the pirate king!), and a handful of unidentifiable but fascinating Western-style buildings.

Getting There Take Longtou Rd. from the ferry to the Gulangyu Concert Hall on Huangyan Rd and turn right. Zhonghua Rd intersects Huangyan at the People's Stadium. To the left are the former Masonic Lodge, the "Weird World" museum, and Shuzhuang Gardens; everything else is to the right.

#2 Zhonghua Rd Former Goods Inspection Building (原厦门海关验货员住宅) and residence for British customs workers. This English-style two-storey red brick building with elegantly contrasting white trim was built opposite the former Freemason Lodge in 1923, and completely renovated in 2004.

第二十二章

中 华 路

“富有的中国人住在一些［鼓浪屿别墅］，就像我们对面的那一家人，但他们大多是长期和欧洲商人打交道或是在南洋地区发迹的，因此不是十分拘泥于传统。并不是因为他们比较喜欢和外国人生活在一起，而是在国际地界里他们能更好地保护来之不易的财富。他们当中许多人出生卑微，但是谭氏一家（站在他们家那花团锦簇的阳台上就可以看到我们的花园），却从祖父那里传承并保留了高贵和守旧，他祖父在辛亥革命前曾是个地方官。天气好的季节里，常常可以看到他坐在粉色山茶花丛中，面前摆着笔筒和砚台，还一边用带有小铜碗的长长的烟斗抽着烟。有时，还可以看到他穿一身灰色绸缎长袍，提着鸟笼去海边遛他的燕雀。他一直受到全家人的悉心照料和服侍，孝道是儒教两大精髓之一。但这也归功于他的智慧和阅历。

——安妮·阿维利尔·麦肯基《鼓浪屿》20 世纪 20 年代

中华路上有原荷兰领事馆、珍奇世界博物馆（就像利普莱的信不信由你奇趣馆那样的地方）、人民体育场（这儿有体育先驱马约翰的雕像）、大夫第（了解了解这位海盗王！），还有许多无法鉴定却充满魅力的西洋建筑。

前往中华路　上了码头，沿龙头路走到位于晃岩路的鼓浪屿音乐厅后右拐。人民体育场就在中华路和晃岩路的交汇路口。左边是原荷兰领事馆、“珍奇世界”博物馆和菽庄花园，其他的都在右边。

中华路 2 号　原验货楼和英国海关验货员住宅。这座英式两层红砖建筑，就在原荷兰领事馆对面，建于 1923 年，其红墙面与白装饰形成鲜明对比，于 2004 年完成全面翻修。

One of the building's many nicknames was Dagong Hou (大宫后) because the area was known as Dagong (大宫). It was also called "white rat building".

Zhonghua Road at a Glance

#2 Zhonghua Rd "Weird World Museum" (珍奇世界，以前是大宫后验货楼). The former Dagonghou inspection building is now a Chinese version of a "Ripley's Believe it or Not" museum.

People's Stadium and bust of Sports Pioneer John Ma.

#5 Zhonghua Rd Former Masonic Lodge of Amoy, rebuilt in the 1990s.

#15 Zhonghua Rd Du Family Mansion; best viewed from nearby rooftops.

#19 Zhonghua Rd Interesting but anonymous historic home.

#21 Zhonghua Rd Large residence with beautiful Gothic arched windows that look like they should be on a church. They are said to resemble an iron anchor and an owl's eyes.

#23 and 25 Zhonghua Rd Dafudi and Siluodacuo (大夫第与四落大厝): a fascinating story behind these 200-year-old Chinese residences!

#43 Zhonghua Rd Private residence, early 20th century.

#85 Zhonghua Rd Nothing is visible but the grown over gate, and the jungle behind. One can only imagine…

#2 Zhonghua Rd "Weird World Museum" (珍奇世界). This amazing little museum has it all: a room with the emperor's clothing and writs, rooms devoted to rare creatures like two headed dogs and albino reptiles (supposedly even a mummified mermaid!), colonial-era antiques, swords used to behead prisoners, a mock opium den, and more.

Albino Boa Meets Blonde!

The firm also produces exquisite Chinese hand puppets and gives private puppet shows on an ornate old stage. Open 9 AM to 6 PM. Phone: 206-9933.

这座楼有许多小名，其中一个是大宫后，因为这地方有个供奉吴真人（大道公）的寺庙被称作大宫。另外一个名字是“老鼠楼”，因为老鼠擅长钻洞，而验货员很会钻旅客的空子，受贿肥私，所以他们住的房子被叫做“老鼠楼”。

中华路一览

中华路 2 号　“珍奇世界博物馆”。这座原大宫后验货楼现在成了中国版的“利普莱信不信由你”博物馆。

人民体育场和体育先驱马约翰的雕像。

中华路 5 号　原荷兰领事馆，建于 1937 年，1990 年重建。

中华路 15 号　杜家园，最佳观赏地点是附近的屋顶。

中华路 19 号　另一处很有意思的历史古宅。

中华路 21 号　大型住宅楼，有着漂亮的拱形窗户，这些窗户好像应该装在教堂里才对。他们看起来像铁锚和猫头鹰的眼睛。

中华路 23、25 号　大夫第和四落大厝：拥有 200 年历史的中国古宅背后的传奇故事！

中华路 43 号　私宅，20 世纪初。

中华路 85 号　除了爬满树藤的大门和门后的植物，什么都看不到，只能想像……

中华路 2 号　“珍奇世界博物馆”。这座神奇的小博物馆展品琳琅满目：帝服和圣旨；稀有动物，如两个头的狗和白化体爬行动物（按此推测，甚至还可能有木乃伊美人鱼！）；殖民时期古董；处斩铡刀；模拟鸦片间；等等。

这里还制作独特的中国布袋木偶，并且有私人木偶表演，舞台虽旧却装饰得很漂亮。营业时间：9：00—18：00。电话：206-9933

Amoy Masonic Hall (based on sketch in Illustrated London News)

#5 Zhonghua Rd Former Masonic Hall The Dutch were some of the first Europeans to trade in Xiamen but relatively late setting up their consulate. While one source claims 1857, another states June, 1890, and that the consulate shared a building with the Netherlands-India Commercial Bank. Yet another book claims the consulate was built in the 1920s at #40 Tianwei Rd. As for the so-called Consulate on #5 Zhonghua Rd. …

Historians claim #5 Zhonghua Rd was a Dutch Consulate, but it was built for the Freemasons (Masun Jiao, 麻笋教). According to Chinese, hooded members of the Corinthian Lodge of Amoy (# 1806, formed in 1878; now in Hong Kong), held secret convocations and communicated via signs so that not even family members would recognize each other.

Mr. Ashley Brewin, a freemason in Hong Kong, says records show it was never a consulate, but passed off as one to gain it diplomatic protection from the Japanese. It was razed and rebuilt in the 1990s.

#15 Zhonghua Rd Du Family Garden (杜家园）is a large Western-style villa with a large walled-in garden. The high walls prevented me taking a decent photo, but a 3rd generation Gulangyu resident, Mr. Zhu Yuanpeng (朱远鹏)—his child is 4th generation, he said proudly—led me tc the roof of a house across the street, where I had a bird's eye view of the entire estate.

Masonic Hall of Amoy (about 1900?)
100-year-old postcard; courtesy of Ashley Brewin

中华路 5 号　原麻笋教会所。荷兰人是最早在厦门经商的欧洲人之一，但他们在厦门建立领事馆却是比较晚的了。有书上说建于 1857 年，也有的说是 1890 年 6 月，并且与荷印商业银行同在一幢大楼里。另有一本书上说荷兰领事馆建于 20 世纪 20 年代，位置在田尾路 40 号。至于位于中华路 5 号的这幢所谓的领事馆，历史学家认为它是荷兰领事馆，但实际上它是为麻笋教徒而建的。中国人说这一厦门科林斯式会所（1878 年成立）的成员总是戴着面具，召开秘密集会，用一些暗号进行交流，这样即使是家人也不会互相认出来。

亚士利・布鲁文（Ashley Brewin）先生是香港的一位麻笋教徒，他说历史记录表明这个地方根本不是什么领事馆，当时是为了从日本人那里获得外交保护才把它说成领事馆的。上世纪 90 年代，这里被夷为平地后进行了重建。

中华路 15 号　杜家园是一座很大的西洋别墅，别墅内有一个大花园。高高的围墙害得我没办法拍到好照片，不过第三代鼓浪屿人，朱远鹏先生——他自豪地说，他的孩子是第四代。并带我上了对街一座房子的屋顶，在那里我可以俯瞰整个杜家园。

#19 Zhonghua Rd This old Western-style building with a rounded porch and columns is down a side road facing the gate at #12 Zhonghua Rd. The present occupant saw me standing amongst the bushes taking photos, grinned, and invited me in for tea.

#21 Zhonghua Rd.

#21 Zhonghua Rd Just before the Chinese-style Daifudi building is an old European style building. I could find no info about it, but the arched windows are unique—like something out of an old church.

#23 and 25 Zhonghua Rd Dafudi and Siluodacuo (大夫第与四落大厝), Rev. David Abeel's Former Home. In 1796, this section of Gulangyu was a grassy clearing called Caopu Cheng (草埔埕), but ex-seaman Huang Xuzhai (黄旭斋) changed that.

Huang Xuzhai moved to Gulangyu from Shixun, Tong'an (石浔,同安), and in the small grassy area near Haitan and Zhonghua Rd., built a classic Southern Fujian two-building swallow-tail home (二落燕尾式四合院) at what is now #58 Haitan Rd. The story of how Xuzhai obtained his wealth (and titles) is a story right out of the fairy tale books!

The young seaman Huang Xuzhai was eating in the Narcissus Palace (水仙宫) when he overhead the proprietor quarreling with a customer who could not pay his bill. Xuzhai paid the bill, and even loaned the fellow some money. As the saying goes, "You never know when you might entertain angels unawares", though in this case Xuzhai was aiding not an angel but a devil—the notorious pirate chief, Mr. Cai Qian. But the pirate became Xuzhai's angel when he presented the seaman with an almost magical yellow flag that, when flown from his ships, protected Huang from attacks by the pirates who had ravaged coastal Fujian and Canton for centuries. This immunity enabled Huang to make a fortune, settle down on Gulangyu, build houses, purchase titles, and become the famous "Caopu Huang" (草埔黄).

#23 Zhonghua Rd. (to left)

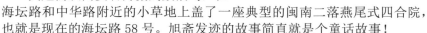

中华路 19 号　这座古老的西洋建筑，有着圆形的门廊和柱子，就在中华路 12 号大门对面的小巷里。房子现在的主人看到我站在灌木丛中照相，就笑着邀请我进去泡茶。

Zhonghua #19

中华路 21 号　就在中式大夫第前有一座古旧的欧式建筑。我找不到任何背景资料，但是它的拱形窗户很特别——像古教堂里的东西。

中华路 23-25 号　大夫第和四落大厝。1796 年的时候，这个地方是一片草地叫做草埔埕，但当过渔民的黄旭斋改变了这一切。

黄旭斋从同安石浔搬到鼓浪屿，在海坛路和中华路附近的小草地上盖了一座典型的闽南二落燕尾式四合院，也就是现在的海坛路 58 号。旭斋发迹的故事简直就是个童话故事！

黄旭斋年轻时是个渔民，一天他在水仙宫吃饭，无意间听到店家和顾客吵架，因为这个客人没钱付账。旭斋就替他付了钱，还借给他一些钱。就像谚语说的，“你也不知道啥时福从天降”，旭斋帮的虽不是天使，却是恶名远播的清朝海盗集团首领蔡牵。就是这个海盗成了旭斋的天使，因为他送给这个渔民一面神奇的黄旗。黄把旗子插在船上后，那些几百年来在福建和广东沿海作威作福的海盗们都不敢碰他了。这一特权使得黄赚了许多钱，于是他在鼓浪屿定居下来，盖房子，买官衔，成了有名的“草埔黄”。

Zhongua #12

Xuzhai's son, Huang Kunshi (黄昆石), accumulated even more titles, such as Vice President of Treasury Department, Supervisor of Salt Transportation, etc., (户部监印, 盐运使). And because Kunshi had such a large family (7 sons, including 2 adopted sons), he built another Southern Fujian red-brick style home (燕尾双曲屋面住宅) at what is now #23 & #25 Zhonghua Rd (just around the corner from his father's home).

The oldest buildings left on Gulangyu today, these homes are quite a contrast from the rest of the islet's Western buildings, and a reminder that Gulangyu was home to renowned Chinese long before the British soldiers commandeered these homes during the first Opium War. Huang's descendants, by the way, fought bitterly, but in the end were forced to retreat to Guankou, Tong'an (灌口同安). It is said that one can still see the British army's flag carved in the stones of Daifudi, but I could not verify that because the couple selling snacks at the entranceway refused to let me in, even though they recognized me. "We love your book Amoy Magic—Guide to Xiamen!" they exclaimed, but they still wouldn't let me in, even though I said I was writing about the place. But I can't blame them. They couldn't keep the British army out so but they can put the brakes on one lone camera-toting American!

Ironically, while the British flag carving is supposedly still visible, the 8 generations of Huang's ancestral tablets, and the ancestral pictures, were destroyed during the Cultural Revolution. It's a pity there wasn't a resolute couple hawking mineral water and roasted melon seeds to keep the Red Guards out.

Where to from Zhonghua Rd?

For a shortcut to Sunlight Rock, turn left just past Daifudi and follow Haitan Rd up the hill to Sunlight Rock Temple.

To visit the nearby Gold Melon Building, turn left onto Quanzhou Rd, and a little further down Quanzhou Rd you'll come to the Lin Mansion.

To see the Foreign Lady Building, turn left from Zhonghua Rd. onto Quanzhou Rd and make an immediate right on Anhai Rd (which will also take you to Trinity Church).

#97 Zhonghua

旭斋的儿子黄昆石拥有更多头衔，比如户部监印、盐运使等等。因为昆石有个大家庭（7 个儿子，其中 2 个是收养的），所以他又建了一座闽南燕尾双曲屋面住宅，就在现在的中华路 23 和 25 号（就在他父亲家的拐角处）。

这些房子是鼓浪屿上保存下来的最古老的建筑，与岛上的其他西洋建筑形成鲜明对比，也提醒人们在英军于第一次鸦片战争期间霸占这些地方之前，鼓浪屿曾是许多中国名人的家。顺便说一下，黄的后代在第一次鸦片战争中进行了艰苦的抗战，但最后还是被迫退回到同安灌口。据说现在还可以在大夫第的石头里看到刻有英国国旗，但是我没有办法去核实，因为门口卖快餐的夫妇不让我进去，虽然他们认得我是谁。“我们很喜欢你的书《魅力厦门——厦门指南》！”他们激动地对我说，可还是不肯让我进去，就算我告诉他们我正在写关于这个地方的书也没用。但我不怪他们。虽然他们没能阻止英军侵略，但他们可以把单枪匹马、手拿照相机的美国人挡在门外！

可笑的是，英国国旗很可能还看得见，但是黄家 8 代祖先的牌匾和画像在“文化大革命”时统统被毁了。真可惜，当时没有一对意志坚决的卖西瓜籽的夫妇把红卫兵挡在门外。

从中华路可以到……

到日光岩有条近路，过了大夫第左拐，沿海坛路往山上走，一直走到日光岩寺。

想去参观附近的金瓜楼，就左拐进泉州路；沿泉州路再往前走一点，就可以到林屋了。

想去参观番婆楼，从中华路左拐进泉州路后马上右拐到安海路。（你还可以到三一堂）

Rev. David Abeel and Dr. Cumming's House

Chapter 23
Bishan Rd

HSBC Residence

Brush Stand Mountain Rd boasts such delightful dwellings as Chuncao Palace (春草堂), Seaview Villa, the magnificent cliff-side Hong Kong Shanghai Bank residence, the Guancai Bldg. (a grey estate that from a distance looks haunted), Yizu Mountain Villa, the former residence of Xiamen University president Lin Wenqing, and more. Traipse through the dense undergrowth of Bishan Park and you'll get a taste of how Gulangyu's early settlers felt (tigers roamed Gulangyu as late as the early 20s!).

Getting There Brush Stand Mountain is easily accessible from Guxin Rd, Neicuowo Rd, Anhai Rd (near Trinity Church), or by parachute.

Brush Mountain Road at a Glance

#1-3 Bishan Rd Inquest Law Court (会审公堂) Formerly at #105 Quanzhou Rd.

#5 Bishan Rd Lin Wenqing's Former Residence, (林文庆故居) Lin lived here from 1921-1937 while President of Xiamen Univ.

#6 Bishan Rd Scenic View Building (Guancai Lou, 观彩楼). Delightful Dutch architecture with Disneyesque windows

Bishan Park – Delightfully undeveloped little wilderness!

#9 Bi Shan Rd Yizu Villa Built between 1910 and 1920 by Vietnamese Overseas Chinese Xuhan (许汉)

#17 Bishan Rd Chuncao Palace (春草堂)Beautifully renovated.

#19 Bishan Rd Xu Feiping's Former Residence

HSBC Residence on the Cliff (悬崖上的汇丰公馆) One of Gulangyu's most striking buildings.

第二十三章

笔 山 路

笔山路有诸如春草堂、观海别墅、悬崖上宏伟的汇丰公馆、观彩楼（一栋灰色的宅院，从远处看像是一栋鬼屋）、亦足山庄、已故厦大校长林文庆故居等令人神往的住宅。

徜徉在笔山公园茂盛的灌木丛中，你将体验到早期鼓浪屿居民曾有过的感受（直到20世纪20年代初曾有老虎在鼓浪屿出没）。

前往笔架山　　经过鼓新路、内厝澳路或安海路（三一教堂附近）可以很轻易地进入笔架山，或许坐降落伞前往。

笔山路掠影一览

笔山路1—3号　会审公堂（原位于泉州路105号）。

笔山路5号　林文庆故居，林文庆于1921年至1937年间在此居住，当时他是厦门大学校长。

笔山路6号　观彩楼，非常精美的荷兰风格建筑，它的窗户和迪斯尼动画片中的一样。

笔山公园，尚待开发，略显荒凉。

笔山路9号　亦足山庄，越籍华侨许汉于1910—1920年间建成。

笔山路17号　春草堂，已经修葺一新。

笔山路19号　许斐平故居。

悬崖上的汇丰公馆：鼓浪屿最引人注目的建筑之一。

#1-3 Bishan Rd Inquest Law Court 会审公堂 (Formerly #105 Quanzhou Rd) Through the gate and past the snack shop are two European style villas that were the former Inquest Law Court.

After the Opium War, the Western powers set up 13 consulates on Gulangyu, but though the island became an international enclave, Chinese still accounted for most of the population. To solve the inevitable disputes between foreigners and Chinese (usually in the foreigner's favor), in 1903 the foreigners allowed Chinese to establish an inquest law court on Jinxiang Rd (锦祥路) near the Huang Family Ferry Dock (黄家渡). In 1920 it was relocated to #105 Quanzhou Rd., and in 1930 moved again to the two 1920s era buildings atop Brush Stand Mountain.

The Inquest Law Court galled Chinese because any case involving a foreigner, from petty misdemeanor to murder, was decided entirely by the foreign consuls. When the #19 Army rebelled in November, 1933, and founded the Fujian People's Revolutionary Government, it ordered the abolishment of the Gulangyu Inquest Law Court, but the foreign consuls ignored the new government, just as they had ignored the old. The Westerners were ousted only in December, 1941—but by the invading Japanese, which did not improve matters. The Inquest Law Court was finally abolished after the Pacific War, and after Liberation all unequal treaties were abolished.

The Inquest Law Court's two buildings were used as the Fujian Cadres Rest Home in the 60s, and then as private residences.

While you're in the area, continue up the hill behind the former Law Court and wander about the derelict old mansion on the peak. At one time it must have been magnificent, but when I visited the crumbling ruins the only living soul I came across was a wary old yellow cat who yawned disdainfully. The place feels haunted—and may well be haunted by the hundreds of thousands of souls destroyed by the piggies 'n poison trade from which Gulangyu's foreign residents derived so much of their wealth (and to think they built a law court to administer "justice").

> "Where there are too many policemen, there is no liberty. Where there are too many soldiers, there is no peace. Where there are too many lawyers, there is no justice." Lin Yutang

#5 Bishan (Brush Mountain) Rd This mountaintop estate built in 1905 was a perfect getaway for Dr. Lin Wenqing, the "Sage of Singapore" and Xiamen University's 2nd president. This multi-talented pioneer of many fields delighted in the garden setting, the rooftop garden, and the panoramic view of Tiger Head Hill (Hutou Shan, 虎头山) and Swan Mountain (Hong Shan, 鸿山). Read more about Dr. Lin in the Pioneer Educators' chapter.

笔山路 1—3 号　会审公堂（原位于泉州路 105 号）。从门口进入，再经过一家小吃店，可以看到两栋欧式风格的别墅，那就是以前的会审公堂。

鸦片战争后，西方列强在鼓浪屿设立了 13 个领事馆。尽管这个小岛已经成为公共租界，但是岛上住的绝大多数依然是中国人。外国人和中国人之间不可避免会发生冲突，为了解决他们之间的冲突（通常是维护外国人的利益），外国人同意中国政府于 1903 年在黄家渡附近的锦祥路设立了会审公堂。1920 年会审公堂被移到泉州路 105 号，1930 年它又被移至笔架山顶上两栋上世纪 20 年代的建筑。

会审公堂总会让中国人蒙受羞辱、冤屈。因为所有涉及外国人的案件，小到不良行为，大到谋杀，全部都由外国的领事来判决。1933 年 11 月，19 路军起义，成立福建人民革命政府。该政府要求废除鼓浪屿会审公堂，但是正如对旧政府一样，对于新政府的要求，外国领事们不予理睬。直到 1941 年 12 月日本人入侵，西方人才被赶出鼓浪屿，但这并没有使当地居民的生活得到改善。在太平洋战争结束后，会审公堂才被彻底废除。解放后，所有的不平等条约都被废除。

20 世纪 60 年代会审公堂的两栋建筑被用作福建干部疗养院，后来又转为私人住宅。

到达这里之后，沿着会审公堂后面的山向上爬，可以在山顶那座被废弃的旧大厦附近漫步。这里曾经是多么宏伟、华丽，但是当我参观这座倒塌的废墟时，看到唯一活着的东西就是一只老黄猫，它正轻蔑地打着哈欠。这像一个鬼魂出没的地方，而且数百上千死于吸食鸦片的鬼魂或许还真的经常在此出现。因为在贪婪的鸦片贸易中，鼓浪屿上的外国人聚敛了巨额的财富（再想想他们还建立公堂来掌管“司法”）。

“警察越多的地方，就越没有自由。士兵越多的地方，就越没有和平。律师越多的地方，就越没有正义。”——林语堂

笔山路 5 号　这栋建于 1905 年的山顶别墅是林文庆博士极好的度假胜地。林文庆被称为新加坡贤哲，是厦门大学第二任校长。这位在许多领域都卓有建树的先贤对花园的布局颇为满意，在屋顶花园他可以欣赏虎头山和鸿山全景。在教育先驱章节可以了解到更多有关林文庆的内容。

#6 Bishan Rd Scenic View Building (Guancai Lou, 观彩楼), circa 1931. Chinese call this Dutch-designed villa the "Bride's Palanquin" because of its resemblance to a traditional bridal sedan. I think it looks more like a somber gray tombstone, at least from a distance (even some Chinese say it looks haunted), but up close the villa is delightful with its whimsically curved dormer windows like a Disney cartoon house.

The corners, window frames, and gate appear to be solid granite, and granite posts flanking the front door are carved to resemble twisted rope (Spanish influence, I'm told). Teak windows, though, are in a sad state of disrepair.

The Dutch owners returned to Holland before the war with Japan in 1937 and left the building in the care of Chinese. Chen Simin bought the villa about 1944. Chen had a degree in chemistry from Cambridge, and started Shanghai's Guchiling toothpaste factory to help China sink its teeth into the foreign firms' market share. He then bought Guancai Lou as a vacation home, and left it to his son. The villa's in fairly bad shape today, but judging from the music blaring through the boarded up side windows, if it isn't inhabited it's haunted—by extinguished Cantonese pop stars.

#9 Brush Stand Mountain Rd Yizu Mountain Villa (亦足山庄) , built between 1910 and 1920 by Vietnamese Overseas Chinese Xuhan (许汉), neighbored the courthouse and Lin Wenqing's (林文庆) villa.

Xu inscribed "Yizu Shanzhuang" (亦足山庄,) on a huge stone to show his happiness with his villa. Chen Peikun (陈培焜) added, "Ziqi Donglai" (紫气东来), or "Purple gas comes from the East"—whatever that means! (Indigestion from the purple taro ice cream locals are so fond of?)

Yizu Villa boasted one of Gulangyu's best European gates and finest traditional Chinese courtyards, but Xuhan did not get to enjoy his creation, dying shortly after its completion. Now, almost a century later, the villa is in very poor condition.

笔山路 6 号　观彩楼，大约建于 1931 年。由于它外形酷似花轿，中国人把这栋荷兰风格的别墅叫做“新娘轿子”。我觉得它更像一座灰色的坟墓，至少从远处看是这样的（甚至有些中国人也说这像鬼屋）。但是走近看，这栋别墅非常别致，它雕刻奇异的窗楣像是来自迪斯尼卡通屋。

它的墙角、窗架以及门都像是用坚固的花岗岩做的，大门两侧的花岗岩门柱被雕刻成纹绳状（有人告诉我这是受西班牙的影响）。高级柚木做的窗子现在却已经破旧不堪了。在 1937 年日本侵华战争爆发之前，房屋的荷兰主人就回国去了。他把这栋房屋交给中国人照看。大约在 1944 年，这栋别墅被卖给陈四民。陈四民曾在剑桥大学获得过化学学士学位。

陈四民是上海固齿龄牙膏厂的老板，因为他的努力，使得中国在外国公司垄断的牙膏市场上占有了一席之地。陈四民用牙膏厂挣来的钱买下观彩楼，用来消夏避暑。他把别墅传给他儿子。现在，这栋别墅已经年久失修。但从被木板封住的窗子传出来的音乐声，可以推测这房子有人居住，要不就是已故广东流行音乐歌手的灵魂在此显灵。

笔山路 9 号　亦足山庄，该别墅由越南籍华侨许汉于 1910 年至 1920 年间建成，毗邻于会审公堂和林文庆故居。

许汉在一块巨石上刻下“亦足山庄”这四个字，以示拥有这栋别墅的愉悦之情。陈培焜添上“紫气东来”，或“来自东方的紫色之气”，不管到底是什么意思！（是不是当地人吃了太多的红芋冰淇淋而消化不良呢？）

亦足山庄拥有鼓浪屿上最漂亮的欧式大门和最传统的中式庭院，但是许汉并没有享受到自己的杰作。山庄落成后不久他便去世了。近一个世纪后的今天，亦足山庄已经破得不成样子了。

#17 Bishan Rd Spring Grass Palace (Chuncao Tang, 春草堂) The pristinely restored Chuncao Tang, which neighbors Guancai Lou, was designed and built in 1933 by Xu Chuncao (许春草), but since he was the first chairman of the Architect's Union it's no surprise he knew what he was doing. The idyllic site offers a panoramic view of the Nine Dragon River (Jiulong Jiang, 九龙江), Dayu Island (大屿), Fire Island (Huoshao Yu 火烧屿), and Haicang (海沧).

#17 Bishan Rd.

The courtyard entrance is flanked by stone creatures resembling the ancient Manichaean statues in neighboring Quanzhou (which has the planet's last temple to this ancient Persian religion). The square corners and carved round pillars of Southern Fujian granite are nicely complimented by the red brick and white mortar.

Xu Chuncao was born into a family impoverished after the father was tricked into working overseas and never returned. Xu became a cement worker at age 12 and he and other workers united as "brothers" to defend themselves from employer's exploitation. In 1918, Xu was elected chairman of a new construction labor union which had as its motto, "Only communal issues, no personal vendettas" (有公愤而无私仇).

After Sun Yat-sen (Sun Zhongshan, 孙中山) founded the "Chinese Revolutionary Party" in 1914, Xu Chuncao became its director of affairs for S. Fujian. Sun Yat-sen asked Chuncao to help prepare for the Northern Expedition, and Xu later led 20,000 troops in revolutionary activities, but after 1923 he changed his focus to business and social endeavors. After 1926 he became the Chinese Director of the Gulangyu Engineering Department, and continued to initiate social welfare projects such as an "Abused Servant Girl Rescue Association" (中国婢女救援团)—an unusual move during an era when servant girls and "little wives" were often little more than chattel.

Xu died in 1960 at age 86, and in 1986 his villa was beautifully restored and half of a third floor added.

A similar villa to the left of Chuncao Villa has a beautiful enclosed garden and some rather unusual statuary (such as a modernistic black stone nude).

笔山路 17 号　春草堂，这栋按原样修复的春草堂，是许春草于 1933 年自己设计并修建的，就在观彩楼旁边。许春草身为建筑工会第一任会长，很清楚自己在做什么。站在这所田园般的住所里，九龙江、大屿、火烧屿和海沧的美景可以尽收眼底。

庭院门口两侧的石雕像是古代泉州摩尼教的雕刻（泉州拥有这种古老的波斯宗教在这个星球上的最后一座寺庙）。闽南花岗岩雕刻的方形墙基和圆柱配上红砖白浆，非常和谐。

许春草自幼家境贫寒，父亲被骗到海外做苦工后再也没有回来。12 岁时，许春草就成了一名泥水工。为了防止资本家过度剥削，他和其他小工结成兄弟。1918 年，许春草被选为新成立的建筑工会会长，正如其座右铭，在建筑工会“有公愤而无私仇”。

1914 年，孙中山创建中华革命党后，委许为“闽南党务主任”。孙中山要许春草协助他进行北伐，许后来率领一支 2 万人的武装力量参与革命活动。但 1923 年后，他把精力转到商业和社会活动方面。1926 年以后，许一度成为鼓浪屿工部局“华董”，他继续发起社会福利活动，如倡议组织“中国婢女救援团”。在一个婢女和妾的地位几乎等同于私有财产的年代，这可算惊人之举。

许死于 1960 年，终年 86 岁。1986 年，春草堂被修复完好，而且加盖了三楼上的半楼。

春草堂左边有一栋类似的别墅，它有一个封闭型的漂亮庭院和一些非同寻常的雕塑（如现代派的黑石裸体雕像）。

Chuncao's Neighbor

Hong Kong-Shanghai Banking Corp. Residence (悬崖上的汇丰公馆) a 400 m^2 villa built atop Brush Mountain in 1876, is one of Gulangyu's 3 most distinctive sights—and what a view! The residence for the bank's president was designed by a British architect and built by Xiamen craftsman with local materials upon a megalithic foundation that will probably outlast the island itself. After 1949, the residence became a dormitory, and then a residence for ship workers. It's still grand from a distance but rather depressing at close quarters.

The Birth of HSBC

HSBC was established by Thomas Sutherland, a Scotsman who was Hong Kong Superintendent of the Peninsular and Oriental Steam Navigation Company.

Most Asian trade was handled by English and Indian banks, but the 30-year-old Sutherland learned that Bombay speculators were planning to start a "Bank of China" based in Hong Kong to finance regional trade between China and Japan.

At first, Sutherland's felt HK merchants "deserved whatever fate might befall them" because they should have started their own bank long before—but fate intervened. Sutherland was on a ship at sea when he came across an article on "Scottish banking principles" in a 20-year-old copy of "Blackwood's" magazine. He decided to "checkmate" the Bombay speculators, and pushed his idea for a local bank through so quickly that, according to HSBC legend, those who met at a dinner on the subject had no idea they were actually founding a bank!

The prospectus was signed by the British merchant house Messrs Dent and Co., and the charter was given in December, 1864. The Hong Kong office opened on March 3, 1865, at 1 Queen's Rd. (and is still there today). The Shanghai office opened 1 month later, on April 3, 1865—and HSBC opened its Gulangyu branch in 1873 with a registered capital of 50 million.

Changee Money?

"The currency question in Amoy is almost sufficient to turn one's hair grey....There are at least six or seven different kinds of the dollar coin in circulation at this port, viz, the Yen, Mexican, Hong Kong, French, Straits, and Hupeh dollar and some Manila pesos....None of these enumerated here pass for the *standard* dollar at this port. The Spanish dollar remains the standard tho it is not in circulation." Rev. Pitcher, "In and About Amoy," 1920, p.221

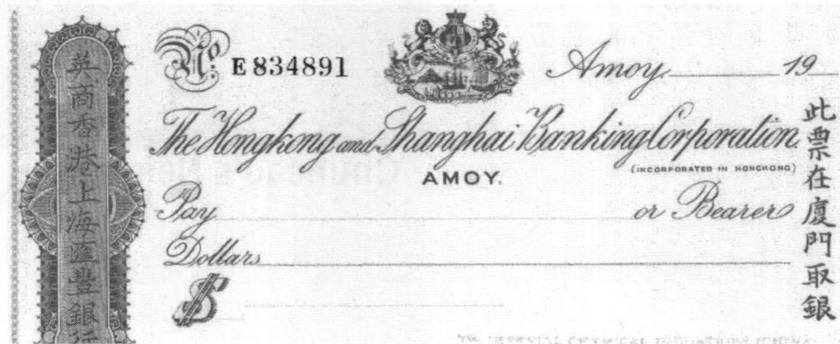

悬崖上的汇丰公馆　这栋占地 400 平方米的别墅于 1876 年建在笔架山顶上。它是鼓浪屿最具特色的三大景点之一，同时也是纵览鼓浪屿壮丽美景的最佳去处之一。

汇丰银行董事长的公馆由一位英国建筑师设计，并且由厦门工匠用当地的材料建成。别墅的基桩打入岩石，异常牢固，堪与鼓浪屿共存亡。

解放后，公馆被改成宿舍，后来成为船工的住所。从远处看，它依然宏伟；但从近处看，它却非常颓废。

汇丰银行的诞生

汇丰银行由苏格兰人托马斯·修打兰创办，他当时是半岛东方轮船公司的香港总监。

那时，大多数亚洲的贸易都通过英国和印度的银行来处理业务。当 30 岁的修打兰了解到孟买的投机商正打算在香港成立中国银行来为中国和日本之间的贸易提供资金。

他的最初反应是香港商人命该如此，因为他们本来早就应该创办自己的银行。但是他们的命运有了转机。有一次在邮轮上，修打兰无意间在一本 20 年前的 Blackwood’s 杂志上看到一篇关于苏格兰银行准则的文章。他突发奇想，决定要成立一家当地银行来挫败孟买的投机商。从汇丰银行志上可以看到，修打兰的这个主意确实来得迅速，以至于那些在餐桌上商讨这一问题的先生们还不清楚他们是要创办一家银行。

和英国商会的甸德洋行签署了招股说明书后，1864 年 12 月就领到了营业执照。1865 年 3 月 3 日，香港总部创立，办公地点设在皇后大道 1 号（至今未变）。一月后，即 1865 年 4 月 3 号，上海分行开业。1873 年，鼓浪屿分行开业，注册资金为 5000 万元。

兑换钱？

厦门的流通货币问题足以烦到让一个人头发变白。那时，这个港口至少有 6 到 7 种不同的货币同时流通，如日圆、墨西哥币、港币、法郎、海峡锡、湖北银元，以及马尼拉比索等。这里列举的所有货币，没有一种成为这个港口的标准货币。尽管没有流通，西班牙币却是这里的标准货币。见毕腓力《厦门方志》，1920 年版 第 221 页。

Chapter 24
Yongchun Rd

"There are several caves or caverns on the Island to be found along its Western shores, more or less interesting, about which the natives are prepared to tell most thrilling stories. However it might be just as well to receive their yarns with some mental reservation. The largest one of these caves may be found on the 'long round' over the hill beyond the Kolongsu Dairy, near the first stone seat. It is some thirty or forty feet long and about ten feet high. What it was in former days it would be difficult to say…But there are those who will inform you that this cave once formed the entrance to an underground passage whose exit was below the London Mission's new house, and directly opposite the gate of the German Consul's residence.

"…Nevertheless the story is that such a subterranean passage did exist, and was the rendezvous of the bold buccaneers and pirates who made this island their camping ground some three or four hundred years ago and which also afforded a means of escape on many an occasion when they were pursued by the authorities who were seeking their capture. Tradition says it was called the "Cave of Rescue." In any case it makes a good story, and lends scope for some speculation about the affairs of the early days of this place, glimpses of which we have already had in the opening chapters of this book."

Pitcher, "In and about Amoy," 1912, p.257

The Koxinga Memorial is the most popular site on Yongchun (Eternal Spring), but I also enjoy the shaded old lane's distinctive architecture—especially the unusual turreted home I've dubbed "The Castle" on the corner of Yongchun Rd. and Wudai Rd.. Yongchun's old garden gates, some of which have been walled up, have unusual carvings, such as the cherubs on the gate to the left of #67. The cherubs' faces were hacked off by hacked off[1] Red Guards during the Cultural Revolution but at least they were democratic in their destruction, for they tried to destroy all vestiges of the old society, whether Chinese or foreign.

On Yongchun Rd

[1] Hacked off: (形容词) discontented; angry. Hack off: (动词) to cut off, or scrape off.

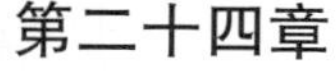

第二十四章 永春路

“鼓浪屿的西岸有一些洞穴或洞窟，有趣的是，当地人有一些关于这些洞穴的令人毛骨悚然的传说。然而，对于那些奇谈，我们自不必全信。最大的一个洞穴位于鼓浪屿牛奶厂前山的坡边上，就在第一个石凳旁边。这个洞穴大约有三四十英尺长，10 英尺高。最初这个洞穴到底用来做什么我们很难猜测。但是有人会告诉你这个洞是一条地道的入口，它的出口处位于伦敦差会新址底下，正好在德国领事馆对面。

“……不过当地人传说中提到的地道确实存在。三四百年前，海盗们在这个岛建立大本营，地道就是他们的集合地点。当遇到当局追捕时（当局想要得到他们的赃物），地道成为他们的逃生之路。传说中这个洞叫做‘逃生洞’。不管怎么说这都是一段动人的故事，而且给我们留下了对于曾经发生在这里的事情遐想的空间。本书的开头的章节已经对这个地方进行过介绍。”

——毕腓力《厦门方志》，1912 年版，第 257 页。

郑成功纪念馆是永春路上最受欢迎的景点，除此之外，我也很喜欢这条树木荫翳的古巷上独具特色的建筑，尤其是位于永春路和乌埭路交汇的那座非同寻常的塔楼（我把它称为城堡）。永春路上一些老院落的大门往往有罕见的雕刻，如位于 67 号左边的一扇大门上雕刻的一群小天使。在“文革”期间，小天使的脸被愤怒的红卫兵刮掉[1]了。至少我认为红卫兵在破坏过程中还是很民主的，他们把旧社会的残余通通毁掉，不管它是中国的，还是外国的。

[1] hacked off：愤怒；hack off：刮去

Getting to Yongchun Rd Take Longtou Rd. from the ferry, turn left at the bookstore to Huangyan Rd., make a right, and turn right at the Gulangyu Hotel onto Yongchun Rd.

Yongchun Road at a Glance

#14 Yongchun Rd **A Castle-like residence** (one of my favorites).

#15 Yongchun Rd **Private residence**, early 20th century, (民居)

#16 Yongchun Rd **Private residence**, early 20th century, (民居).

#71 Yongchun Rd **Kanqing Villa** (瞰青别墅) built in 1918 by Vietnamese Overseas Chinese Zhongxun Huang (黄仲训). It is now the Koxinga Memorial Hall Information Center

#73 Yongchun Rd **Xi Lin Villa** (西林别墅), now Koxinga Memorial Hall, built in 1928 by Overseas Chinese Huang Zhongxun 黄仲训).

#14 Yongchun Rd "The Castle" This imposing white stone and red brick building on the corner of Wudai Rd. and Yongchun Rd. rather resembles a small castle, with its round turret on one corner. Mr. Caiji Cheng (蔡基成), who lived here 40 years and now lives just up the road, said the Castle was built by overseas Chinese Mr. Chen Shuiyan (陈水眼), from Indonesia, and is now cared for by his descendants. One grandson lives on Gulangyu, and another lives in the U.S.

The Wudai Rd. gate is surmounted by two "Long-live Britannia" sort of lions, and scrawled below are the faded characters "Long Live Chairman Mao" (Mao Zhuxi Wansui, 毛主席万岁).

#14 Yongchun
Former resident, Mr. Cai Jicheng

#67 Yongchun Rd The current residents said this home was built by Mr. Huang Zhongxun (黄仲训) as a dowry for his daughter. (See #71 Yongchun Rd)

#69 Yongchun Rd With its high walls and shady lanes, this is one of the more picturesque areas of Gulangyu, evoking images of opium-era wealth, but I've no idea of the histories behind the homes at #63 and 69, or of why nothing was built in the large empty lot across the way.

前往永春路　　出轮渡码头，走龙头路，到达书店后往左拐到晃岩路，再往右拐，到达鼓浪屿宾馆后再往右就到永春路了。

永春路掠影

永春路 14 号　**一栋像城堡的住宅**（我最喜欢的住宅之一）。

永春路 15 号　20 世纪早期的民居。

永春路 16 号　20 世纪早期的民居。

永春路 71 号　瞰青别墅，越南籍华侨黄仲训建于 1918 年。现为郑成功纪念馆的藏书楼。

永春路 73 号　西林别墅，华侨黄仲训建于 1928 年。现为郑成功纪念馆。

永春路 14 号　“城堡”，永春路和乌埭路交汇处矗立着一栋气势宏伟的白石红砖建筑，一座圆形的塔楼竖立在它的一旁，看起来非常像一座小城堡。在这房子里生活了 40 年、而今还住在这条路另一头的蔡基成先生告诉我，这栋城堡是由印尼华侨陈水眼修建的，现在房子由他的后代来照看。他的一个孙子住在鼓浪屿，另外一个居住在美国。

乌埭路的大门上有两只英式石狮，似乎在高呼“英国万岁”，下面散乱地写着“毛主席万岁”这几个字，字迹已经有点模糊了。

永春路 67 号　当地居民说这栋房子是黄仲训修建的，作为他女儿的嫁妆。（见永春路 71 号）

永春路 69 号　高高的墙，绿树成荫的小巷，这是鼓浪屿风景如画的地方之一。这让我们想起鸦片贸易时代的情景，但我不了解 63 号和 69 号房屋后面的故事，或者说不明白为什么这条路上留着这么一大片空地没盖房子。

#71 Yongchun Rd Kanqing Villa (瞰青别墅), a brick and wood villa of French-influenced architecture, is now the Koxinga Memorial Hall Information Center. Kanqing was the ill-fated project started in 1918 by Vietnamese Overseas Chinese Zhongxun Huang (黄仲训), a colorful character whom some honored and others vilified (especially when he tried to steal Sunlight Rock!).

#71 Yongchun Rd.

The Scholar (Xiucai) Who Stole Sunlight Rock Zhongxun Huang, aka Tieyi Huang (黄铁夷), was a native of Leqiu Pingshan in Nan'an (乐邱屏山, 南安). His father, Huang Wenhua (黄文华), was born in Nan'An in 1855 and immigrated to Vietnam, where he made his fortune. Zhongxun Huang also made a fortune in Vietnam and in1918 returned to Xiamen and started the real estate firm "Rongyun Huang Ltd." (黄荣远堂). He built over 60 houses on Gulangyu, including ten Western-style buildings in Tianwei that he rented out to foreigners (one was the Consulate of France). But evidently this real estate tycoon considered the entire islet his private domain!

Zhongxun built a wall completely around Sunlight Rock, turning it into his own private garden, and then proceeded to carve inscriptions on the historic rock. The public protested, and current residents of Yongchun Rd. told me that even children chanted songs condemning him! So Zhongxun shrewdly turned Sunlight Rock into a public garden, then advertised his magnanimous deed in the "*River Song Newspaper*" (江声日报), and invited Gulangyu's elite to discuss the future of Sunlight Rock. But his troubles were only beginning.

In 1918, Zhongxun Huang built the grand Kanqing Villa in "Yanzijiao", beneath Sunlight Rock—and was promptly sued for building on someone else's land! The lawsuit dragged on so long that Zhongxun never did live in Kanqing, and was forced to reside in an old house on Quanzhou Rd. instead.

永春路 71 号　瞰青别墅，这是一栋具有法兰西风韵的砖木结构建筑，现在成了郑成功纪念馆的藏书楼。这栋命运多乖的别墅是越南籍华侨黄仲训于 1918 年开始修建的。黄仲训是个非常复杂的人物，有人尊重他，有人蔑视他（尤其当他试图偷占日光岩时）。

秀才偷日光岩　黄仲训，又名黄铁夷，南安乐邱屏山人。他的父亲叫黄文华，1855 年生于南安，后来移民到越南，在那里发家致富。黄仲训也在越南发了财，1918 年他挟资回厦门，创办“黄荣远堂”，经营房地产。他在鼓浪屿上总共修建了 60 多栋房子，其中田尾路上 10 栋西式建筑是用来租给外国人的（有一栋是法国领事馆）。很显然，这个房地产巨头想把整个鼓浪屿占为己有。

黄仲训在日光岩四周筑长城式围墙，俨然把日光岩变成他的私家花园，后来还在日光岩的巨石上镌刻诗文。他的做法引起了公愤。永春路的居民告诉我甚至是小孩子也通过儿歌来声讨他。不得已，黄仲训又把日光岩变为公园，并在当年的报纸上刊登启事以示他的善意。而且邀请鼓浪屿名流一起商讨日光岩的前景。但是他的麻烦才刚刚开始。

1918 年，黄仲训在岩仔脚日光岩下修建了宏伟的瞰青别墅。别墅刚建好就和他人发生界址争执。官司持续时间很长，以至于黄仲训从来没有在瞰青别墅住过，他不得不住在泉州路上的一座老房子里。

The lawsuits distressed Zhongxun, who felt locals did not appreciate his magnanimous contributions to society, and he responded with a couplet on the left side of Kanqing Villa's front door, which read "出没波涛三万里，笑谈古今几千年" (chumo botao sanwanli, xiaotan gu jin jiqian nian), meaning roughly "I traveled 30,000 miles of rough seas, and can optimistically discuss thousands of years of history." But on the other side of the door he wrote, "此地有人常寄傲，问天假我几多年" (cidi youren chang ji'ao, wen tian jia wo jiduo nian)—"Here is a proud man, asking Heaven for more years of life."

Heaven must not have heard his prayer, because he returned to Vietnam, was tortured by the Japanese, and died in despair. But in spite of his rascally dealings he is remembered today with honor, and often described as a Qing Dynasty Overseas Chinese Xiucai ("Scholar"). And over the years his Kanqing Villa played a significant role in local history.

Chiang Kai Shek (Jiang Jieshi, 蒋介石) selected Kanqing Villa as his home in January, 1949, and assigned a hometown crony, Jiang Hengde (蒋恒德) as director general of Gulangyu's police station. Kanqing Villa was refurbished for the Generalissimo but he never stayed there (He did spend one night, July 23, in the nearly Huang Masion, and fled when the winds of fortune changed).

While at Kanqing Villa in 1962 the famous poet Guo Moruo (郭沫若) wrote his epic drama "Koxinga" (Zheng Chenggong, 郑成功).

The brick and wooden Kanqing Villa is said be French on the outside and Chinese on the inside, with imposing granite doors and an octagonal front hall. The second floor was divided by folding Chinese screens with elegant traditional Chinese paintings, some of which are still in fairly good shape. Locals especially appreciate the villa's garden, which provided neighbors with plenty of flowers and fruits. The villa is now the "Koxinga Memorial" info center, and Houfanglan (厚芳兰) Hall, just beside Kanqing, was built to commemorate the hard work of Zhongxun's father in Vietnam's Houfanglan Wasteland.

官司使他心力交瘁，黄仲训感慨当地人不感激他为社会做出的巨大贡献。在瞰青楼前门留下一幅这样的对联：左边是“出没波涛三万里，笑看古今几千年”，右边写道“此地有人常寄傲，问天假我几多年”。

上苍一定没有注意到他的祈祷，因为他回到越南后遭受日本人的折磨，并在绝望中死去。尽管他曾经要过流氓，人们还是记住了黄仲训的荣耀，他经常被称为清朝秀才华侨。而且这些年来，他的瞰青别墅在当地历史中扮演了重要角色。

1949 年 1 月，蒋介石选定瞰青别墅为他的“临时行辕”，并委派他的同乡蒋恒德担任鼓浪屿警察分局局长。为此，瞰青别墅还装修一新，但是蒋介石因局势变化太快，只在他座舰停泊附近的“黄家花园”住了一个晚上，不得不逃走了。

1962 年，著名诗人郭沫若在此撰写了《郑成功》剧本。

砖木结构的瞰青别墅外面看起来是法兰西风格，而里面却是中式的。它的门是用富丽堂皇的花岗岩做的，前庭呈八角形。第二层用中式隔板隔开，屏风上是雅致的传统中国画，其中一些保存依然完好。当地人特别喜欢别墅的花园，因为它为街坊邻居提供了各种各样的鲜花和水果。瞰青别墅现在成了郑成功纪念馆的藏书资料室。它旁边就是厚芳兰馆，厚芳兰馆是为了纪念黄仲训父亲在越南“厚兰芳”荒地的艰苦创业而修建的。

73 Yongchun Rd Koxinga Museum (Xilin Bieshu, 西林别墅, 现为郑成功纪念馆), a four-storey red-brick building at the base of Sunlight Rock, was completed about 1932 by Huang Zhongxun (黄仲训). This 4-storey 2,100 square meter primarily Western-style villa has a colonnaded front porch with ornamented classic columns.

The ornate stairs and handrails reflect Chinese styles, while the exquisite rosewood doors, windows and blinds are of Western style. The Japanese seized this beautiful building and used it as a "Rat Epidemic Disease Research Hospital" (鼠疫医院), and then Chiang Kai Shek's KMT army (Guomintang, 国民党) turned it into a soldiers' hospital (伤兵营). After Chiang Kai Shek fled to Taiwan, Xilin Villa became a kindergarten for the "Overseas Research Information Center" (海疆学术资料馆) and the local military.

In February, 1962, the villa opened as the Koxinga Museum in celebration of the 300th anniversary of the scholar-cum-warrior's liberation of Taiwan. The entrance's horizontal characters are by the famous historian and poet Guo Moruo.

The museum has over 300 historical relics, models, carvings, and photos arranged in seven rooms, each room devoted to a different stage of Koxinga's career. The first hall depicts the youthful warrior's fight against the Qing, and two halls make the case for Taiwan as an age-old inalienable part of China. Yet another hall explains how Koxinga's son developed Taiwan, and the final hall displays famous Chinese' writings about Koxinga.

永春路 73 号 西林别墅，现为**郑成功纪念馆**。这栋四层楼结构的红砖建筑建在日光岩的底部，由黄仲训在 1932 年修建完工。该别墅占地面积 2100 平方米，以西洋风格为主。别墅前面有一个柱廊，柱廊上有装饰精致的圆柱。装饰华丽的台阶和扶栏折射出中式风格，而精致的红木门窗及窗帘则是西洋风格的。日本人曾占领这栋漂亮别墅，并把它用作“鼠疫医院”。蒋介石的国民党军队曾经把它用做伤兵营。蒋介石逃往台湾之后，西林别墅一度成为“海疆学术资料馆”和驻军的托儿所。1962 年 2 月，在民族英雄郑成功收复台湾 300 周年时，西林别墅改作“郑成功纪念馆”。入口处的横匾是著名诗人、历史学家郭沫若题写的。

郑成功纪念馆拥有 300 多件纪念物、模型、雕刻和照片，这些物品被安放在七个房间，每个房间展示郑成功一生中的一个阶段。第一展厅描述了他青年时期反清的经历，有两个展厅用于介绍台湾，台湾自古以来就是中国领土不可分割的一部分。还有一个展厅介绍了郑成功的儿子治理台湾，最后一个展厅展示了中国历代名人歌颂郑成功的文字资料。

Exhibits include Koxinga's apparel, such as jade belts and fragments of his robe and shoes, and one of the silver coins cast by Koxinga, "Zhangzhou Soldier's Pay" (漳州军饷, Zhangzhou Junxiang). The museum also boasts documents and poems written in Koxinga's own hand. The thought of a great warrior penning poetry is odd, but Chinese leaders over the ages, from the legendary Yellow Emperor to Mao Ze Dong, were known for their literary, calligraphic and academic accomplishments as well as for their military and political prowess. So I can well imagine the patriot taking a break from the heat of battle to pen a poem like, "I miss you so much I can't sleep..."

Koxinga's Genealogy Nan'an's Shijing Town was home to 17 generations of Koxinga's ancestors, dating back to the Song Dynasty. The museum has duplicates of "Zheng's Genealogy" 《郑氏家谱》 and "Zheng's Ancestral Roots" 《郑氏宗谱》, as well as a replica of Koxinga's ancestral tablet.

The Last Dutch Governor's Last Stand One hall exhibits reproductions of Coyett's "Neglected Taiwan" (Verwaerloosde Formosa), a fascinating and sometimes humorous account of Koxinga's conquest of Taiwan. I include a few choice excerpts at the end of the Koxinga chapter.

Where to from Here Golden Melon Building and Lin Mansion on Quanzhou Rd and Anhai Rd's Trinity Church are close to Yongchun Rd.

Overseas Chinese Return to Gulangyu

I lunched in the International Club with Yang Wanghe, a Philippine Chinese whose father bought the Bell Mansion after it was rented out as the Bank of Agriculture. He was with Patrick Hsu, President of Magellan Commodities in Manila, whose family was also from Gulangyu.

His grandfather on his mother's side, Chen Yinghong (陈荣芳), was mayor of Xiamen in 1948, and had homes at Gangzihou # F81（港仔后 F81 号) and Huangyan Rd #55（晃岩路 55 号).

His wife's grandfather, from Gulangyu, constructed the first building in Cebu, and was father of a Philippine president, Sergio Osmena. His descendants also included Manuel Go Tianuy, a Chinese consul for 15 years, and a Grandson Augusto To Tian Nuy, a Consul to Korea.

展出的物品包括郑成功的服饰和着装，如他用过的玉带，鞋或长袍的碎片，以及郑成功铸造的一种叫做“漳州军饷”的银币，纪念馆还有郑成功亲自写的诗句及相关文件。一介武夫写诗听起来令人吃惊，但是多少年来中国的领袖人物，从传说中的黄帝到毛泽东，他们的文学、书法及其他学术成就堪与他们的军事、政治才华相媲美。因而，我能想象得到这位爱国者在硝烟弥漫的战场，抽空写下诸如“思君寝不寐”的诗句。

郑成功家谱 郑成功祖宗十七代都居住在福建南安石井镇，可以一直追溯到宋朝。纪念馆有《郑氏家谱》和《郑氏宗谱》的影印本，以及郑氏祖先牌的复制品。

末任荷兰总督的最后抵抗 有个展厅展出了揆一写的《被忽略的台湾》（又叫《被忽略的福摩萨》）一书的复印件。该书对郑成功收复台湾做了精彩而又不失幽默的描述。在《郑成功》一章的结尾，我摘录了其中一些。

从这里可以到哪里 从永春路到泉州路的金瓜楼和林屋，安海路的三一堂，都只有很短的距离。

华侨归故里

我和杨旺和（音译）一起吃过午餐，他是菲律宾华侨。他的父亲买下了时钟楼，租给农业银行。杨旺和与 Patrick Hsu 一块来的。Patrick Hsu 的祖籍也是鼓浪屿，他现在是马尼拉麦哲伦日用品公司的总裁。

他的外祖父陈荣芳 1948 年时曾任厦门的市长，在港仔后 F81 号和晃岩路 55 号都有房子。

他妻子的祖父，同样来自鼓浪屿，在宿务建起了第一栋楼，并且是菲律宾总统奥斯曼纳的父亲。他的后代还包括曾担任中国领事 15 年的 Manuel Go Tianuy，他的一个孙子 Augusto To Tian Nuy 担任过驻韩国领事。

Mr. Yang and Patrick Hsu

Chapter 25
Gusheng Rd

Gusheng Rd, which winds along the back of Gulangyu past Hero Hill and Gulangyu Villa Ferry Pier, was named after Drumbeat Rock (gushing shi, 鼓声石). Chinese say scientific records date the rock at 108 million years. Only Chinese would keep records for 108 million years.

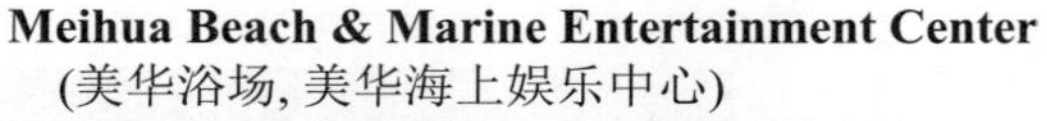

Gusheng Rd. at a Glance

Meihua Beach & Marine Entertainment Center (美华浴场, 美华海上娱乐中心)
Drum Sound Cave (Gusheng Dong, 鼓声洞)
Hero Hill (Yingxiong Shan, 英雄山) Hero Garden (Yingxiong Yuan, 英雄园)
Wave Listening Bluff (Tingtao Ya, 听涛崖); Gulangyu's best sunsets
Xiamen Overseas Chinese Subtropical Plant Introduction Garden (Xiamen Huaqiao Ya're Daiyin Zhongyuan, 厦门华侨亚热带引种园）
Gulangyu Aviary & Cable Car to Sunlight Rock（Bainiao Yuan, Lanche, 百鸟园和缆车). Bird shows and large screen movie theater
#1 Gusheng Rd Liao Xian Villa (了闲别墅) on Hero Mountain (英雄山)
#2 Gusheng Rd Former London Missionary Society home; now a Xiamen Christian Council music training center
#4 Gusheng Rd Former foreigner's residence, early 20th century
#8 Gusheng Rd Chen Jinfang Villa (陈金方宅), circa 1921, was designed by the owner, Chen Jinfang, a member of the Chinese Alliance (中国同盟会会员陈金方)
#10 Gusheng Rd Foreign missionary's home, built between 1915-1925. (原传教士住宅).
#28 Gusheng Rd Lee Kuan Yew's home.
Pinyin Path! (See page 60)

第二十五章

鼓 声 路

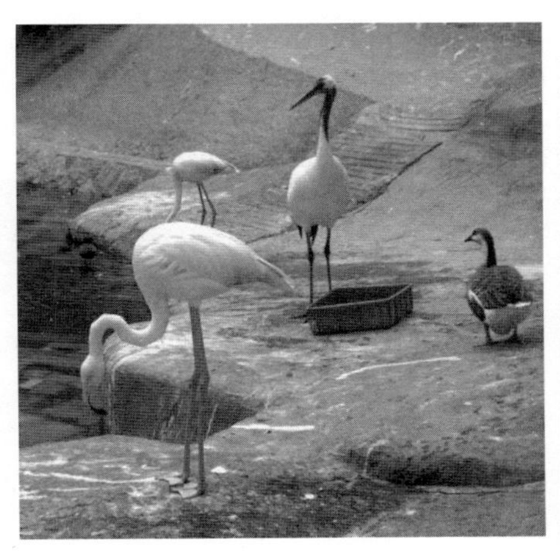

鼓声路，它的名字因鼓声石而来。鼓声路蜿蜒在鼓浪屿的背面，从英雄山一直到鼓浪别墅的轮渡码头。有中国人说关于这块石头的科学记载有一亿零八百万年的历史。也只有中国才可能拥有这么悠久的历史记载。

鼓声路掠影一览

美华浴场　美华海上娱乐中心。

鼓声洞

英雄山　英雄园。

听涛崖　鼓浪屿最佳赏日落处。

厦门华侨亚热带引种园

百鸟园和缆车　鸟类表演和宽屏幕电影院。

鼓声路 1 号　了闲别墅，位于英雄山。

鼓声路 2 号　原伦敦差会；现为厦门基督教派音乐培训中心。

鼓声路 4 号　原外国人住宅，建于 20 世纪初。

鼓声路 8 号　陈金方宅，中国同盟会会员陈金方自行设计，建于 1921 年。

鼓声路 10 号　原外国传教士住宅，建于 1915－1925 年间。

鼓声路 28 号　李光耀先生的住宅。

Getting to Gusheng. Take Longtou Rd from the ferry to the bookstore, go right, and veer to the left onto Quanzhou Rd, which will become Gusheng Rd at Lin Mansion (林屋). Or follow Huangyan Rd （晃岩路） past Gulangyu Hotel (鼓浪屿宾馆) and Lin Qiaozhi's home （林巧稚故居), veer right at the Navy Sanatorium, and Gusheng will branch off to the left.

Hero Hill (Yingxiong Shan, 英雄山) and Hero Garden (Yingxiong Yuan, 英雄园). This 2,000 m^2 memorial garden for martyrs who liberated Xiamen and Gulangyu consists of statues, a memorial square and a memorial hall.

Wave Listening Bluff (Tingtao Ya, 听涛崖). Called Anson Bluff (安逊峭壁) on a 1904 foreigner's map, it is about 500 meters from Drumbeat Rock. Enjoy a picnic as you savor the most spectacular sunsets on the islet.

#1 Gusheng Rd Liao Xian Villa (了闲别墅, 鼓声 1 号) is on the north side of Hero Hill (英雄山). Originally intended to be a Taoist Temple, it was built about 1925 by Xiamen Customs Chief Wang Junxiu (王君秀), Xiamen City Planning officer Zhou Xingnan (周醒南), Lu Guichun (卢桂纯), Lin Jifan (林寄凡) and Wu Youshan (吴友山). Taoist altars were set up for worship, and a small building in back facilitated Guanyin worship.

Liao Xian Villa combines modern Chinese and Western architecture, with shuttered windows and a tall sliding iron door in front. The good-sized garden has many fruit trees, including oranges, lychees, persimmons, and mangos.

In August 1936, the seriously ill Hong Yi, famous "Master of the Law," recuperated at Sunlight Rock Temple (日光岩寺), and after his recovery returned to the temple often to lecture. On March 22, 1938, Yan Xiaotang (严笑棠) invited Hong Yi to lecture in Liao Xian Villa, but just at that time Japanese soldiers moved in upon Xiamen. Monk Chuanguan (传贯法师) warned Hong Yi to stay away, but Hong Yi made it clear that he did not fear the Japanese, and spoke anyway.

According to local historians, Xiamen's Communists preparing for Liberation held secret training sessions in Liao Xian Villa, during which they studied Mao Zedong's "The Present Situation and our Mission". Religious activities ceased after liberation, and after the Cultural Revolution the Housing Bureau took over control of the villa, which now houses three families.

前往鼓声路 在轮渡码头上岸后走龙头路，到了书店之后往右拐，然后在泉州路上向左转……过了林屋就是鼓声路了。或者也可以走晃岩路，经过鼓浪屿宾馆和林巧稚故居，到海军疗养院后向右转，左边的叉路就是鼓声路。

英雄山和英雄园 这个占地 2000 平方米的纪念园是为了纪念解放厦门和鼓浪屿的烈士，由群雕、一个纪念广场和一个纪念厅组成。

听涛崖 在 1904 年由外国人编制的地图上，听涛崖被称为安逊峭壁，距鼓声石大约有 500 米。一边欣赏岛上最壮观的日落，一边野餐真是人生一大美事。

鼓声路 1 号　了闲别墅，它位于英雄山北麓。1925 年由厦门海关监督王君秀和厦门市政公署会办周醒南、卢桂纯、林寄凡和吴友山等人筹建，最初是打算建成一个道观。祭坛用来举办道教仪式，后面一栋小房子是用来供奉观音菩萨的。

了闲别墅是一栋融合了现代中式和西洋风格的建筑。别墅安置了百叶窗，前面是一扇可以滑动的高大铁门。宽敞的院子种满了果树，有桔树、荔枝树、柿子树和芒果树等。

1936 年 8 月，患重病的弘一法师在日光岩寺休养。康复后，弘一法师常回寺里讲经。1938 年 3 月 22 日，应严笑棠之邀，弘一法师来到了闲别墅讲经。日本鬼子进入厦门之前，传贯法师劝弘一法师暂避，弘一法师当众表示他不怕日本人，在任何场合他都不避讳这点。

当地的历史学家介绍，厦门共产党在准备解放厦门时曾在了闲别墅秘密举办过培训班，在那里学员们学习了毛泽东的著作《目前形势和我们的任务》。解放后，了闲别墅的佛道活动停止了，“文革”后房产局接管了闲别墅，现有住户三家。

#8 Gusheng Rd Chen Jinfang Villa (陈金方宅), circa 1921, was designed by the owner, Chen Jinfang, a member of the Chinese Alliance (中国同盟会会员陈金方自行设计).

鼓声路8号 陈金方宅，大约修建于1921年，由房屋主人，中国同盟会会员陈金方自行设计。

#28 Gusheng Rd. Lee Kuan Yew's Home According to Trinity's Pastor, Timothy Hao, this beachfront home is owned by Lee Kuan Yew, the first Prime Minister of Singapore. Rev. Hao said Lee has visited twice).

鼓声路 28 号 按三一堂牧师蒿志强的说法，这幢前门靠海的别墅为新加坡第一任总理李光耀所有。蒿牧师告诉我们，李先生已来过两次。

Pinyin Path! See Education chapter.

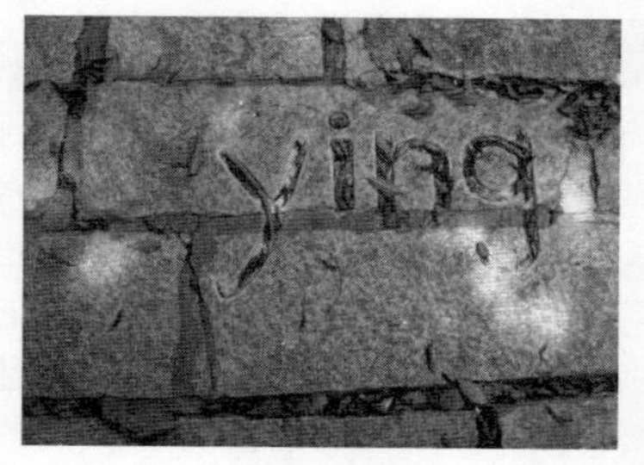

拼音道 为什么从沙滩边的卢戆章雕塑沿鼓声路到安献堂对面他的坟墓整条人行道的花岗岩地砖上都刻着拼音？请翻回第 60 页，自有分晓。

Yet Another Gulangyu Pioneer!

According to Mr. He Bingzhong, assistant curator of Koxinga Memorial, the Gulangyu-born Linzhen was the first modern Chinese to visit the U.S.A... After his 1847 trip he wrote what He said is a "very objective introduction to the U.S.," Xihai Jiyou Cao" (西海记游草)

又一位鼓浪屿先驱！

依据郑成功纪念馆副馆长何丙仲的介绍，鼓浪屿人林鍼是近代第一个到美国的中国人。他 1847 年游历美国，之后著有《西海记游草》向国人客观介绍美国。

Bibliography

Abend, Hallett, *Treaty Ports*, Doubleday, Doran and Company, Inc, New York, 1944

Beach, Harlan P., *Dawn on the Hills of T'ang, or, Missions in China*, Student Volunteer Movement for Foreign Missions, New York, 1905

Cody, Jeffrey W. *Building in China, Henry K. Murphy's "Adaptive Architecture," 1914-1935*, The Chinese University of Hong Kong, 2001

Darley, Mary, *The Light of the Morning*, Church of England Zenana Missionary Society, Missionary Society, 27 Chancery Lane, London, 1903

De Jong, Gerald F., *The Reformed Church in China 1842-1951*, Wm. B. Eerdmans Publishing Co., Michigan, 1992

Dukes, Edwin Joshua, *Everyday Life in China; or, Scenes Along River and Road in Fuh-Kien*, London Missionary Society's Edition, The Religious Tract Society, 56, Paternoster Row; 65, St. Paul's Churchyard; and 164, Piccadilly, 1885

Fisher, Lena Leonard, *The River Dragon's Bride*, Abingdon Press, New York, 1922

Franck, Harry A., *Roving Through Southern China*, The Century Co., New York, 1925.

Fullerton, W.Y., and Wilson, C.E., *New China—A Story of Modern Travel*, Morgan and Scott, Ltd., (Office of the Christian), *12 Paternoster Buildings,*London, 1910.

Gutzlaff, Karl F. A., *Journal of Three Voyages Along the Coast of China in 1831, 1832, and 1833*, Frederick Westley and A.H. Davis, London, 1834.

Haffner, Christopher, *Amoy, the Port and the Lodge*, The Corinthian Lodge of Amoy, No. 1806, Hong Kong, 1997

Hewlett, Sir Meyrick, *Forty Years in China*, Macmillan & Co., Ltd., 1943.

Hollister, Mary Brewster, *Lady Fourth Daughter of China*, The Central Committee on the United Study of Foreign Missions, Cambridge, Massachusetts, 1932

Johnston, Meta and Lena, Jin Ko-Niu,*A Brief Sketch of the Life of Jessie M. Johnston For Eighteen Years W.M.A. Missionary in Amoy, China*, T. French Downie 21 Warwick Lane, London, E.C. 1907

Lin, Yutang, *My Country and My People,* Foreign Language and Teaching Press, Beijing, 1998.

Lowrie, Rev. Walter M., *Memoirs*, Board of Foreign Missions of the Presbyterian Church, New York, 1850.

Macgowan, James, *How England Saved China*, T. Fisher Unwin, London, 1913.

Macgowan, John, *Beside the Bamboo,* London Missionary Society, 16 New Bridge Street, London, 1914.

Macgowan, Rev. John, *Christ or Confucius, Which? or, The Story of the Amoy Mission*, London Missionary Society, 14 Blomfield Street, E.C.; John Snow & Co., 2 Ivy Lane, Paternoster Row, E.C. 1895

Macgowan, Rev. John, *Men and Manners of Modern China*, T. Fisher Unwin, London, 1912. use, 43 Gerrard Street, W. 1907

Macgowan, Rev. John, *Sidelights on Chinese Life*, Kegan Paul, Trench, Trubner & Co., Limited, Dryden H

Manson-Bahr, Sir Philip, *Patrick Manson, The Father of Tropical Medicine,* Thomas Nelson and Sons, Ltd., Edinburgh, 1962

Neill, Desmond, *Elegant Flower—First Steps in China*, John Murray, Albemarle St., London, 1956

Rosengarten, A., *A Handbook of Architectural Styles*, translated from the German by W. Collett-Sandars, Chatto & Windus, Piccadilly, London, 1891.

Thomson, John, *Illustrations of China and its People*, Sampson, Low, London, 1873.

Werner, E.T.C., *Myths & Legends of China,* George G. Harrap & Co. Ltd., London, 1922.

Williamson, Rev. G.R., *Memoir of the Rev. David Abeel, D.D.* Robert Carter, New York, 1848

Gulangyu (Macgowan, 1895)

图书在版编目(CIP)数据

魅力鼓浪屿/(美)潘维廉著;厦门日报双语周刊译. —厦门 :厦门大学出版社,2005.10(2019.2 重印)
(魅力·老潘)
ISBN 978-7-5615-2460-2

Ⅰ.①魅… Ⅱ.①潘…②厦… Ⅲ.①厦门市—概况—汉、英
Ⅳ.①K925.73

中国版本图书馆 CIP 数据核字(2005)第 100584 号

出 版 人 郑文礼
责任编辑 施高翔

出版发行 厦门大学出版社
社　　址 厦门市软件园二期望海路 39 号
邮政编码 361008
总 编 办 0592-2182177 0592-2181406(传真)
营销中心 0592-2184458 0592-2181365
网　　址 http://www.xmupress.com
邮　　箱 xmup@xmupress.com
印　　刷 厦门集大印刷厂

开本 880 mm×1 230 mm 1/32
印张 11.75
插页 6
字数 350 千字
版次 2005 年 10 月第 1 版
印次 2019 年 2 月第 3 次印刷
定价 32.00 元

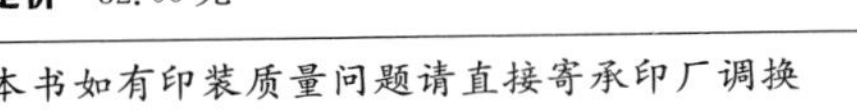
本书如有印装质量问题请直接寄承印厂调换

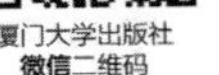
厦门大学出版社
微信二维码

厦门大学出版社
微博二维码